CANADA'S INDIGENOUS CONSTITUTION

Canada's Indigenous Constitution reflects on the nature and sources of law in Canada, beginning with the conviction that the Canadian legal system has helped to engender the high level of wealth and security enjoyed by people across the country. However, long-standing disputes about the origins, legitimacy, and applicability of certain aspects of the legal system have led John Borrows to argue that Canada's constitution is incomplete without a broader acceptance of Indigenous legal traditions.

With characteristic richness and eloquence, Borrows explores legal traditions, the role of governments and courts, and the prospect of a multi-juridical legal culture, all with a view to understanding and improving legal processes in Canada. He discusses the place of individuals, families, and communities in recovering and extending the role of Indigenous law within both Indigenous communities and Canadian society more broadly.

This is a major work by one of Canada's leading legal scholars.

JOHN BORROWS is a professor and Law Foundation Chair in Aboriginal Justice in the Faculty of Law at the University of Victoria and Robina Professor in Law and Public Policy at the University of Minnesota Law School.

JOHN BORROWS

Canada's Indigenous Constitution

UNIVERSITY OF TORONTO PRESS
Toronto   Buffalo   London

© University of Toronto Press Incorporated 2010
Toronto Buffalo London
www.utppublishing.com
Printed in Canada

ISBN 978-1-4426-4103-7 (cloth)
ISBN 978-1-4426-1038-5 (paper)

Library and Archives Canada Cataloguing in Publication

Borrows, John, 1963–
Canada's indigenous constitution / John Borrows.

Includes bibliographical references and index.
ISBN 978-1-4426-4103-7. – ISBN 978-1-4426-1038-5

1. Native peoples – Legal status, laws, etc. – Canada.   2. Customary law –
Canada.   3. Native peoples – Canada – Government relations.   I. Title.

KE7709.B673 2010   342.7108'72   C2009-906295-X
KF8204.5.B673 2010

This book has been published with the help of a grant from the Canadian
Federation for the Humanities and Social Sciences, through the Aid to
Scholarly Publications Program, using funds provided by the Social
Sciences and Humanities Research Council of Canada.

University of Toronto Press acknowledges the financial assistance to its
publishing program of the Canada Council for the Arts and the Ontario
Arts Council.

 Canada Council
for the Arts
 Conseil des Arts
du Canada
 ONTARIO ARTS COUNCIL
CONSEIL DES ARTS DE L'ONTARIO

University of Toronto Press acknowledges the financial support for its
publishing activities of the Government of Canada through the
Book Publishing Industry Development Program (BPIDP).

Contents

Acknowledgments: Ningii-Wiidookaagoo Ongow Emaadizijig   ix

Retroduction   3

1 Living Legal Traditions   6
  A. Law as Tradition   7
  B. Law as Hierarchy   12

2 Sources and Scope of Indigenous Legal Traditions   23
  A. Sacred Law   24
  B. Natural Law   28
  C. Deliberative Law   35
  D. Positivistic Law   46
  E. Customary Law   51
  F. Conclusion   55

3 Indigenous Law Examples   59
  A. Mi'kmaq Legal Traditions   61
  B. Haudenosaunee Legal Traditions   72
  C. Anishinabek Legal Traditions   77
  D. Cree Legal Traditions   84
  E. Métis Legal Traditions   86
  F. Carrier Legal Traditions   91
  G. Nisga'a Legal Traditions   96
  H. Inuit Legal Traditions   101
  I. Conclusion   104

4 Learning from Bijuridicalism   107
  A. Civil Law Legal Traditions   109
  B. Common Law Legal Traditions   111

C. Relationships between Canada's Legal Traditions   113
    i.   Interactions between Civil Law and Common
         Law: Lessons for Indigenous Law?   114
    ii. Interactions: Recognizing Connections across
         Legal Traditions   118

5 Recognizing a Multi-Juridical Legal Culture   125
    A. The Recognition of Law in Historical Context   129
        i.   Aboriginal Land and Resources:
             Aboriginal-to-Aboriginal Relations   129
        ii. The Arrival of Non-Aboriginal Peoples   132

6 Challenges and Opportunities in Recognizing Indigenous
  Legal Traditions   137
    A. Intelligibility   138
    B. Accessibility   142
    C. Equality   150
    D. Applicability   155
    E. Legitimacy   165
    F. Conclusion   174

7 The Role of Governments and Courts in Entrenching
  Indigenous Legal Traditions   177
    A. Indigenous Governments and Recognition Acts   181
    B. Canadian Governments and Recognition Legislation   185
        i.   The Relevance of International Law to
              Recognizing Indigenous Legal Traditions   191
        ii.   The Royal Commission, Section 35(1) Jurisprudence,
              and Canadian Government Recognition   195
        iii. A Caution about Section 35(1):
              Remembering Federalism   198
        iv.   Indigenous Law Harmonization Acts   201
    C. The Role of Courts   206
        i.   Indigenous Bodies and Dispute Resolution   207
        ii. Canadian Courts   215

8 Indigenous Legal Institution Development   219
    A. Law Societies and Associations   221
    B. Indigenous Legal Education   228
    C. Conclusion   237

9 Living Law on a Living Earth:
 Religion, Law, and the Constitution   239
 A. Introduction   239
 B. Sacred Relationships: The Earth and Anishinabek
     Spiritual Beliefs   241
 C. Anishinabek Law and the Earth   244
 D. Section 2(a) of the *Charter*:
     Anishinabek Beliefs and Freedom of Religion   248
 E. Section 35(1):
     Aboriginal Rights, Lands, and Religious Belief   260
 F. Conclusion   269

10 The Work Ahead:
 Cultivating Indigenous Legal Traditions   271
 A. Mandamin and the Law   274
 B. Conclusion   282

Reproduction   284

Notes   287

Index   417

Acknowledgments:
Ningii-Wiidookaagoo Ongow Emaadizijig

Law is a very social activity, though writing about it can be a solitary endeavour. I had both experiences composing this book. I was inspired by the ideas and work of numerous Elders, law professors, lawyers, law students, and friends. I enjoyed their companionship, gentle criticism, and strong encouragement as we discussed matters that lie at the heart of this work. At the same time I also spent long hours by myself researching and writing about what I was learning. I was able to take the time to engage in both of these activities as a result of support from several sources. I want to acknowledge the many people and organizations that made it possible for me to have these varied experiences. In particular, the former Law Commission of Canada and the Social Sciences and Humanities Research Council made my initial work possible by funding me as a Virtual Scholar in Residence. This led to the production of a Report for the Commission entitled 'Justice Within: Indigenous Legal Traditions,' released the week the Commission closed. Since the Commission could not do much to distribute the work in the circumstances, I re-acquired the publication rights and spent the next two years substantially adding to what I had written. I want to thank the Trudeau Foundation for their financial support during this period. As a Fellow of the Foundation I received resources that made it possible for me to travel to Utah and Minnesota for the final push to get these ideas in greater circulation. I also received tremendous support from my home faculty at the Law School of the University of Victoria. They gave me the time and the flexibility to write and visit many people whose perspectives greatly shaped this work. Dean Andrew Petter was particularly helpful in this respect. I also spent teaching semesters at J. Rueben Clark Law School of Brigham Young University and the University of Minnesota Law

School while creating this book. I greatly benefited from the strong intellectual environments in both settings.

As my writing neared completion, the Social Sciences and Humanities Research Council once again assisted by providing aid to the University of Toronto Press for the publication of this work. This book has been published with the help of a grant from the Canadian Federation for the Humanities and Social Sciences, through the Aid to Scholarly Publications Program, using funds provided by the Social Sciences and Humanities Research Council of Canada. I would also like to acknowledge that portions of chapters 1, 4, and 7, while substantially reworked in this book, were previously published as 'Indigenous Legal Traditions in Canada' (2005) 19 *Washington University Journal of Law and Policy* 167. Most of chapter 9 was previously published as 'Living Law on a Living Earth: Aboriginal Religion, Law and the Constitution' in *Law and Religious Pluralism in Canada* (Vancouver: UBC Press, 2008). I gratefully acknowledge UBC Press for their permission to reproduce this work.

I also want to acknowledge individuals from organizations who provided valuable insights in commenting on earlier drafts of this work. I met with members of the Indigenous Bar Association who were incredibly generous with their time. I also taught intensive courses at the University of Toronto Law School and the University of Victoria Law School based on the final draft of this book and want to thank the students in those classes for their help. The students at my alma mater never fail to impress me with their brilliance, and the class I taught was no exception. I also had many colleagues read early drafts of this book. In particular, I want to thank the following individuals for their influence on and comments about the ideas contained herein: Ben Berger, Bruno Bonneville, Frank Calder, Paul Chartrand, Gordon Christie, Dianne Corbiere, Lorena Fontaine, Sakej Henderson, Jeff Hewitt, Basil Johnston, Darlene Johnston, Dawnis Kennedy, Kelly LaRocca, Johnny Mack, June McCue, Richard Moon, Val Napoleon, David Nahwagahboh, Mark Stevenson, Lucien Ukaliannuk, and Wendy Whitecloud. I also gratefully acknowledge the helpful comments of anonymous reviewers for this manuscript who were contacted by the University of Toronto Press. Special thanks go to Kerry Sloan and Josef Rosenthal for their excellent work as research assistants in the final stages of this manuscript's preparation.

Most of all I would like to thank my wife Kim, who travelled with me across North America and into New Zealand and Australia as this work unfolded. I recognize it is not easy living with someone who doesn't live in any one place for very long. Her love and support underlies everything written in the pages that follow.

CANADA'S INDIGENOUS CONSTITUTION

Retroduction

Three otters and an eagle. They are all fishing. They hug the kelp-strewn shoreline, searching for their next meal. The tide is out, revealing the land's generous gifts, and opening new possibilities for life. Salt winds cleanse the air. The sun is warm, and stray clouds smudge the brilliant blue sky.

Pulling at a strand of green, a seagull is surrounded by curious friends. Nearby, a crow snatches a clam from the sand then smashes its shell on a rock. A fight breaks out. Gangs of black-jacketed brothers all try to claim the prize. Flesh is pulled from the shell and passed through two or three beaks before finally being choked down the first bird's gullet. When the frenzy subsides, they all spot the eagle overhead. Seagulls and crows take up a chorus of protest. Swirls of black and white fury whirl wildly over the beach. The crows give chase to the eagle and another fight breaks out. The eagle screams and the crows shriek. They become entangled in mid-air. The crows soon get the better of the large bird. The eagle's wings, breast and white tail feathers are mercilessly ravaged. Three or four crows chase the eagle down the shore and away from the coast, tailed by some seagulls. Their calls carry and eventually subside in the distance.

The otters cautiously watch the fray from the water's safety before resuming their activity. They form a triangle and begin swimming with purpose, diving and surfacing like a multi-headed serpent. They eventually close in on one another, driving a small school of fish before them, into the waiting grasp of the otter at the triad's apex. Success. The hunt's beneficiary drags its catch to the shore and nearly swallows its prey whole. When she is finished she rubs her neck over the kelp, squirming and writhing over the slippery shore. She pauses to see her companions and dives into salt waters once more. The group reestablishes formation. They herd the fish until a different otter catches something in its jaws. The shore to sea cycle repeats itself once more.

Nanabush sits with his laptop computer, taking it all in, disgorging the scene's pieces onto his screen. He is a long way from home, but some things feel familiar. He has seen these fights before, in another place, another time. He remembers the escarpments of his Ontario home. Crows, eagles, and otters also inhabit Georgian Bay's shore. Indians live there too, just like on this so-called reserve. He marvels at the Olympic Mountains across the strait. They rise out of the clouds. Not like the ancient limestone escarpments at home, but solidly witnessing the life of the land in a similar way. He feels the happy sorrow of too much beauty in the world. His wishes he could be in both places at once. He longs for Cape Croker – the reserve. He loves Vancouver Island. It is a good place to live, for now.

He welcomes death as it surrounds him, and is happy in the destruction of the fish, clams, and kelp at the mercy of the birds. The violence of the morning blends with its beauty and peace. He feels a part of this violence and regeneration. In fact, he practises it every day, gorging on and regurgitating life and the words of power as they destroy and regenerate the world around him.

The words of power he is most familiar with are found in the law. He hates them. He loves them. They are just like him: conflicted, cross-cutting, double-edged, and inconsistent. They hold the ability to heal and they have the potential to destroy. And much has been destroyed, and that is so delicious. Law can be like the frail, empty-souled creatures washed up on the tideline, now dead. The law is a vicious, delightful thing. Yet he also knows the law can be like the diamond-crested waters beyond the shore, teeming with life and purifying in its potential. The law is a nurturing, hopeful being too. Yes, he thinks to himself, the law is just like him – a trickster – simultaneously full of charm and cunning, good and evil, kindness and mean tricks.

He writes to destroy and he writes to create, though he can never be quite sure if he is destroying or creating the things he cares about. He often wonders if, in the end, his words will help or hurt what he most deeply cares for and treasures. Sometimes he even forgets to be concerned. He takes so much pleasure in being a transformer that he occasionally forgets what he really loves.

A gust of wind passes over him and Nanabush looks up from his screen. The eagle has returned with his entourage of black crows; a few seagulls leisurely circle behind. Nanabush sets aside his computer to watch the commotion above. He wonders if he should join the battle today. He can feel the shape of their wings in his muscles. He understands the contours of their conflict. He wants to fight – as an eagle or crow. He yearns to join some petty squabble. His longing to leave his work stretches out from him, while his feeling for the words he has written keeps him down. In a moment of decision, as he stands to leave, one crow turns and digs his beak into the eagle's neck. A long white feather dislodges and is caught in the breeze. It drifts and dives. The feather comes to rest on the grass in front of Nanabush. He stoops to pick it up and then turns it over in his hands. He marvels at the intricacy of its form, the slender tendrils rise so perfectly from its spine. He raises the feather to the wind and hears its quiet voice as it rushes through the plume. It whispers of peace. The message sinks deep into his heart. He changes course, once again. He thinks to himself, I don't want to be an eagle or a crow today. I'll be my truer self. I'll be an otter. That is my 'dodem': nigig. *They have taught me better than anything else today. I will write about power from their perspective, that of my clan, kin, and people, working together, for sustenance, in harmony. Four otters and the law ...*

1 Living Legal Traditions

[T]he world is filled with law. Every human behavior is subject to a legal norm ... Wherever there are living human beings, law is there. There are no areas in life which are outside of law.

Aharon Barak, 'Judicial Philosophy and Judicial Activism'[1]

This book examines the standards that we consider authoritative in making judgments about the law in Canada. It asks questions about the criteria we use in measuring the regulation of activities and in guiding the resolution of disputes. In understanding these issues, it is clear that Canadians have much to be thankful for as a result of our legal system. It has contributed to a level of wealth that, for many people, is nearly unrivalled in the world. The peace and prosperity it has generated should be preserved, extended, and strengthened. While Canadians have much to celebrate because of our law, we simultaneously continue to suffer from conflicts rooted in long-standing disputes about the legitimacy of its origins and the justice of its contemporary application. The circumstances of Indigenous peoples illustrate one such tension. Put simply, the continent's original inhabitants have never been convinced that the rule of law lies at the heart of their experiences with others in this land. In this respect, Canada's legal system is incomplete. Many Indigenous peoples believe their laws provide significant context and detail for judging our relationships with the land, and with one another. Yet Indigenous laws are often ignored, diminished, or denied as being relevant or authoritative in answering these questions. This has led to important queries about the sources of Canada's law, as well as its cultural commitments, institutional receptiveness, and interpretive competency.

The posing of such fundamental questions can be troubling for a country if they lead to a rejection of law as persuasively guiding our relationships. I believe we should not be forced to live with such reservations about the law's potential.[2] Law's aspiration for certainty, order, persuasion, reason, and justice should be considered one of our society's essential strengths. It is much better than the alternative, which would build our relationships on a base of doubt, disorder, coercion, confusion, and crass manipulation, by appeals to unmediated power of personal or institutional force. Thus, while it may be challenging to ask deep questions about the underpinnings of Canada's legal system, we should not regard these inquiries as being without value. In fact, such searching questions can be crucial to our societies if they reveal ways of organizing ourselves that draw us even closer to our collective aspirations. This book suggests that we can do a better job of building our country upon our highest ideals. We can respect and fortify the rule of law, even as we identify areas in which we can improve. This work seeks to take such a path.[3] It argues that Canada needs to be constructed on a broader base, recognizing Indigenous legal traditions as giving rise to jurisdictional rights and obligations in our land.

A. Law as Tradition

Law is an important organizing force within Canadian society. However, there are many definitions and disagreements about what constitutes law.[4] Its meaning can be the subject of great conflict. Its effect can simultaneously produce peace and chaos, depending in whose name it is administered and from whose perspective it is processed. Law includes both formal and informal elements.[5] It pivots around deeply complex explicit and implicit ideas and practices related to respect, order, and authority.[6] Laws arise whenever interpersonal interactions create expectations and obligations about proper conduct.[7] We often analyse different legal systems by placing them within broader groupings or traditions to better understand them.[8] It has been said, 'A legal tradition ... is a set of deeply rooted, historically conditioned attitudes about the nature of law, about the role of law in the society and the polity, about the proper organization and operation of a legal system, and about the ways law is or should be made, applied, studied, perfected, and taught.'[9] A legal tradition is an aspect of general culture; it can be distinguished from a state's legal system if a national system does not explicitly recognize its force.[10] Legal traditions are cultural phenomena; they provide categories into which the 'untidy business of life' may be organized and where disputes may be resolved.[11] Sometimes different traditions can operate within a single state or overlap between states.[12] This is known as legal pluralism: 'the simultaneous existence within a single legal order of different rules applying to identical situations.'[13]

In applying these insights to our country, it could be said that Canada is a legally pluralistic state: civil law, common law, and Indigenous legal traditions organize dispute resolution in our country in different ways. Although there are similarities between traditions, each has its own distinctive methods for development and application. The vitality of each legal tradition does not rest solely on its historic acceptance or how it is received by other traditions.[14] 'The strength of a tradition does not depend upon how closely it adheres to its original form but on how well it develops and remains relevant under changing circumstances.'[15] When recognized, provided with resources, and given jurisdictional space, each legal tradition is applicable in a modern context. A mark of authentic and living tradition is that it points us beyond itself.[16] Each of Canada's three major legal traditions is relevant in this respect, and each continues to grow amidst changing circumstances.

On the one hand, traditions can be positive forces in our communities if they exist as living, contemporary systems that are revised as we learn more about how we should live with one another.[17] On the other, traditions can be destructive if they become static and frozen in their orientation, interpretation, and application.[18] They become negative forces if they are overly romanticized, essentialized, and fossilized in an inflexible framework. To avoid these pitfalls, tradition must not only be seen as helping to set the parameters of our lives, but it should also 'provide us with the means of questioning and developing those parameters' for it to be effective.[19] The keepers of Canada's legal traditions must guard against rigidly fundamentalist and oppressive ideas and practices.[20] An overly static interpretation of the common law, civil law, or Indigenous peoples' law could crush cherished rights and freedoms. For example, if common law practitioners develop a closed or inappropriately narrow interpretation of their tradition, this could diminish its healthy development and growth. Furthermore, if the common law cultivated a dogmatic intolerance of the civil law or Indigenous legal traditions, this could damage these traditions too. The same could be said about the civil law or Indigenous peoples' laws. We often tend to regard other traditions as potentially threatening, despotic, or severe, if our own ethnocentrism prevents us from seeing problems arising in our own systems. We must ensure that we turn a critical eye on each legal tradition, including our own, to ensure it promotes respect and dignity for those who depend upon it.

Empirical research on the impact of legal traditions can be an important tool in analysing their effectiveness in people's lives.[21] The social sciences can test the influence of different legal traditions on our cultures, economies, educational attainments, ethical awareness, environmental use, gender relations, histories, political systems, psychological and physical health, racial relations, sociological development, and technological state. These semi-external measures of law in relation to society can be significant determinants of whether our legal traditions are serving us well. Over the past several decades, an increasing number of scholars in various disciplines have devoted substantial attention to the systematic study of law and legal institutions.[22] While there have been many studies of civil law and common law traditions from a social science perspective, including studies of the effects of these traditions on Indigenous peoples,[23] outside of anthropology there have been relatively few studies of Canadian Indigenous legal traditions themselves.[24] This, in part, reveals imbalances between legal traditions in Canadian public life. It also exposes scholars' historic lack of regard for, interest in, knowledge of, and predisposition towards the contemporary nature of Indigenous law throughout the last century. It may also reflect the distrust some Indigenous communities have towards research and engagement with broader society, in the wake of centuries of colonialism.[25] Some Indigenous peoples have turned researchers away from their communities because of their past negative experiences with university-trained personnel. Misrepresentation and misappropriation are commonly cited as reasons for the closing of these doors. The relative dearth of social science treatment of contemporary Indigenous legal traditions means more extended and respectful quantitative and qualitative research is required to evaluate their positive and negative effects and potential. This analysis is necessary to ensure that each of our traditions does not slip into archaic, oppressive fundamentalism.

Another important way to ensure that our legal traditions remain open to new and healthy influences is to regard them as being situated within interpretive communities in which those who are affected by them are able to participate in their continued construction.[26] In contrast with the social science research on Indigenous legal traditions, there is a nascent law review literature beginning to explore them from a normative perspective.[27] This book flows in this tide. It explores the potential scope of Canada's interpretive communities in relation to its varied legal traditions. It builds upon previous work I have done in the area.[28] It responds to invitations received from Indigenous communities and the former Law Commission of Canada to more fully understand the place of Indigenous law in our country.[29] It is my hope that this work represents a further invitation for those interested in this topic to join with me and other willing scholars, practitioners, politicians, policy analysts, Elders, chiefs, and leaders in the identification, recognition, questioning, and further development of our legal traditions.[30] Law is, among other things, a social experience that requires us to associate with one another and communicate about how we should best conduct our affairs. We should always remember that law is a practice, not just an idea.[31] Our constitutional arrangements are best worked out through 'a continuous process of discussion ... compromise, negotiation and delibration,' as the Supreme Court counselled.[32] As more people participate in understanding and applying Indigenous norms, the potential exists for the widening of our interpretive legal communities and the improvement of each legal tradition.[33]

In keeping with this approach, this book suggests that Indigenous peoples' laws hold modern relevance for themselves and for others, and can be developed through contemporary practices. While Indigenous legal traditions have ancient roots, they can also speak to the present and future needs of all Canadians.[34] They should not be just about, or even primarily about, the past. They contain guidance about how to live peacefully in the present world. They can be continually reformulated to show us how to create stronger order. They can be constantly recast to teach us how to appropriately channel and cope with conflict.[35] At the same time, while Indigenous legal traditions hold great potential for Canada's future, they have their limitations too. Like all legal traditions, they remain imperfect. Indigenous laws developed because conflict has always been present in Indigenous cultures.[36] Indigenous peoples are just as susceptible to petty squabbles and large-scale controversies as other societies in the world.[37] There is no romantic time of pre-contact which was an idyllic existence for Indigenous societies, at least over extended periods. Violence, tension, creation, destruction, harmony, and tenuous peace have always been with us in varying degrees. Colonialism has compounded the challenges Indigenous peoples have always faced.[38] Thus, Indigenous laws incorporate certain deficiencies related to their societies' imperfections, as is the case with the civil law and common law in their contexts. Therefore, we should not idealize Indigenous laws in our attempts to constructively apply their precepts. Indigenous law remains relevant as long as there is discord and dissension in the world and the desire to address its consequences. Indigenous peoples participate in this discord. They also participate in the search for harmony. Thus, in dealing with disharmony, Indigenous laws may contain some guidance in curtailing our worst excesses. Such laws are especially relevant when Indigenous peoples are involved. Disputes within Indigenous communities and with other societies could potentially be reduced if their laws were more widely applied.

The Supreme Court of Canada has recognized that Indigenous peoples possessed legal traditions and continue to possess them. While the implications of this recognition have been largely ignored, a nascent framework is in place for extending their reach. In *R. v. Van der Peet*, the Court held that 'traditional laws or customs are those things passed down, and arising from the pre-existing culture and customs of Aboriginal peoples.'[39] It held that Aboriginal rights are based in Indigenous legal customs and traditions,[40] and are concerned with the protection of customary laws.[41] In *R. v. Mitchell*, the Supreme Court affirmed the survival of Indigenous law and wrote that 'European settlement did not terminate the interests of Aboriginal peoples arising from their historical occupation and use of the land. To the contrary, Aboriginal interests and customary laws were presumed to survive the assertion of sovereignty ...'[42] This book contends that Indigenous legal traditions continue to exist. While they have been changed and constrained, they have not been widely extinguished.[43] Though negatively affected by past Canadian actions, Indigenous peoples continue to experience the operation of their legal traditions in such diverse fields as, inter alia, family life, land ownership, resource relationships, trade and commerce, and political organization.[44] Indigenous legal traditions are inextricably intertwined with the present-day Aboriginal customs, practices, and traditions that are now recognized and affirmed in section 35(1) of the *Constitution Act, 1982*.[45] In this respect, they are also a part of Canadian law.

B. Law as Hierarchy

Despite their potential to answer pressing questions, Indigenous laws have an uncertain status in Canada's formal legal system. There is a debate about what constitutes 'law' and whether Indigenous peoples in Canada practised law prior to European arrival. Some contemporary commentators have said that Indigenous peoples in North America were pre-legal.[46] Those who take this view believe that societies only possess laws if they are declared by some recognized power that is capable of enforcing such a proclamation. They may argue that Indigenous tradition is only customary, and therefore not clothed with legality. Philosopher John Austin expressed the idea that custom was not law when he wrote:

> At its origin, a custom is a rule of conduct which the governed observe spontaneously, or not in pursuance of a law set by a political superior. The custom is transmuted into positive law, when it is adopted by the courts of justice, and when judicial decisions fashioned upon it are enforced by the power of the state. But before it is adopted by the courts and clothed with the legal sanction, it is merely a rule of positive morality: a rule generally observed by the citizens or subjects but deriving the only force, which it can be said to possess, from the general disapprobation falling on those who transgress it.[47]

For legal positivists who side with Austin, centralized authority and explicit command are necessary for a legal system to exist. Those who take issue with this conclusion argue that Austin's view rests on inaccurate assumptions about law,[48] and that not all law flows from a sovereign authority or explicit command.[49] When Austin's views about customary law are applied to Indigenous peoples, they potentially replicate troubling stereotypes about these societies.[50] While some Indigenous law is customary, it can also be positivistic, deliberative, or based on theories of divine or natural law (as will be explained in the next chapter). Furthermore, even if an Indigenous society practised customary law exclusively, it is misleading to regard customary laws as holding only moral force.[51] Sometimes customs are belittled by scholars like Austin because the societies who follow them have been inappropriately labelled as inferior or even 'savage.'[52] Indigenous peoples have been described as 'living without 'subjection' because of their 'ignorance' and 'stupidity' in not submitting to hierarchical political government.[53]

Viewpoints such as these have caused me deep concern throughout my career. I first encountered them when I was a law student at the University of Toronto. Assumptions were made about Indigenous peoples and the law that seemed to remove or subordinate their authoritative force. At the time, I did not know how to effectively question what I was learning, because I lacked the confidence and conceptual language to introduce my perspective on the materials that we studied. One idea I wanted to more thoroughly interrogate concerned the hierarchy of laws said to exist in Canada. Most law students are taught that some legal sources are above others, and those lower on the scale of authority must give way to those at higher levels. I remember my property law professor telling me that all laws had to be consistent with the Constitution Acts to be valid. Then we were told that below the Constitution were parliamentary or legislative enactments, which were greater in authority than common law pronouncements made by judges. Underneath these sources came law's subsidiary origins, such as parliamentary privilege, the royal prerogative, particularly persuasive published commentaries, followed finally by customs and conventions.[54] This pattern for organizing the sources of Canadian law is evident in many of today's legal textbooks.[55] I could not help but notice that custom was at the bottom of Canada's legal structure, and that custom was the kind of law Indigenous peoples were presumed to have, if they were regarded as having any law at all.

The formal hierarchy of law's sources is buttressed by theories about the so-called reception of law in Canada. In the legal literature, Canada is largely regarded as a settled territory, meaning that it is considered legally vacant at its foundation.[56] While Indigenous peoples lived in the territory prior to its colonization, it has been said that 'their laws and customs were either too unfamiliar or too primitive to justify compelling British subjects to obey them.'[57] These labels are offensive to me and many others because they presume the legal inferiority of Indigenous peoples.[58] Yet most parliamentarians, lawyers, and judges have not adequately questioned this presumption. Everywhere but in Quebec they have largely acted as if only English law applied in the country when English settlers or governors created colonies in the so-called New World.[59] The reception of English law formed fictional hierarchies that made some laws more binding than others.

Professor Peter Hogg, a former colleague of mine at Osgoode Hall Law School, wrote about the rules of reception and asked: 'How did Canada acquire its legal systems?' In response, he proclaimed: 'The answer is that they were received in Canada from the former Imperial power, the United Kingdom, and, to a much lesser extent, France, during the colonial period.'[60] He further stated, 'In the absence of any competing legal system, English law followed British subjects and filled the legal void in the new territory.'[61] Professor McCallum of the University of New Brunswick Law School expressed a similar sentiment, as a critique, when she wrote, 'A colony government by the law of England begins life endowed with the wisdom and learning experienced in judicial decisions and in the legislation of England, or at least as much of the legislation as was suited to the circumstances of the colony.'[62] The doctrine of reception holds that 'we look to the English common law of colonization for the basic rules' for the sources of law in Canada.[63] In this respect the doctrine of reception does not incorporate Indigenous peoples' wisdom and learning to formulate the basic rules of our legal system.

Unfortunately, the doctrine of reception came through clearly in my legal training. We focused almost exclusively on England for the root sources of Canadian law. Colonialism's advent was presented as the foundational fact of the law's development in this country. Yet I knew there was more to the reception of law in Canada than the distant assertions of an Imperial Crown. I believed 'reception' also requires some form of interaction with Indigenous peoples to be a peaceful process.[64] I understood from my own family's history that the Crown often sought Indigenous agreement before it settled and started governing its own people in our traditional territories.[65] In areas of the country where agreements were not secured, I viewed reception as being incomplete, thus requiring future action. Despite the complex nature of the common law's reception in Canada, most legal texts proceed as if law only arrived in the country with the first colonial legislatures or governors. This myth presents practical and theoretical problems. Colonization is not a strong place to rest the foundation of Canada's laws. It creates a fiction that continues to erase Indigenous legal systems as a source of law in Canada.

This fiction lies at the root of conflict between Indigenous peoples and the Crown. Under the law's current formulation, the doctrine of reception is indefensibly Eurocentric.[66] It ignores the prior presence and laws of Indigenous peoples in Canada and disregards them as a potential source of law in the country today. Professor Hogg has also been critical of this view. He has written that so-called received laws 'were often applied in disregard of the existence of Aboriginal peoples, who were in possession of much of North America before the arrival of Europeans ... It is clear that all Aboriginal customary law did not disappear at the time of European settlement, as the rule of reception for a settled British colony might imply.'[67] Indeed, as Justice McLachlin (as she then was) said in dissent in the *Van der Peet* case:

> The history of the interface of Europeans and the common law with aboriginal peoples is a long one. As might be expected of such a long history, the principles by which the interface has been governed have not always been consistently applied. Yet running through this history, from its earliest beginnings to the present time is a golden thread – the recognition by the common law of the ancestral laws and customs of the aboriginal peoples who occupied the land prior to European settlement.[68]

The predominant descriptions of law's sources have not followed Chief Justice McLachlin's wise observations regarding Indigenous law. Such non-recognition has created a legal hierarchy which has generated an incorrect and impoverished view of Canadian law. As noted, this book attempts to address this deficiency. My thesis is that Canada cannot presently, historically, legally, or morally claim to be built upon European-derived law alone. In this work I attempt to develop conceptual language to strengthen the law's foundation and contemporary status in this country. I take this approach because insufficient attention has been given to this project. In fact, even Professor Hogg, who acknowledges the problems underlying the law's ethnocentrism relative to Aboriginal peoples, begins his influential text *Constitutional Law of Canada* as if Indigenous legal traditions can be ignored. In this otherwise fine manuscript, Professor Hogg constructs a legal hierarchy that replaces Indigenous law with the reception of European laws. He writes: 'The account which follows will not pursue the complex issue of the survival of Aboriginal customary law but will simply attempt to trace the reception of English and French law in British North America.'[69] It is a mistake to write about Canada's constitutional foundations without taking account of Indigenous law. You cannot create an accurate description of the law's foundation in Canada by only dealing with one side of its colonial legal history. When you build a structure on an unstable base, you risk harming all who depend upon it for security and protection.[70] This book is about attempting to put Canadian law on a stronger footing. Acknowledging the traditional and contemporary place of Indigenous law in this country – alongside the common law and civil law – is a necessary step in this process. It is crucial to creating a healthier and more accurate conception of Canada's broader constitutional order.

If Indigenous laws are not recognized, we potentially construct Canadian law on a faulty premise that places Indigenous peoples lower on the 'scale of civilization' because of their non-European organization. Judicial opinions based on the supposed 'cultural inferiority' of Indigenous peoples have not withstood scrutiny. In the last century, the Judicial Committee of the Privy Council advised that 'much caution is essential' when interpreting 'the various systems of native jurisprudence throughout the Empire.'[71] They noted that such caution is essential because judges are susceptible to the danger of only recognizing law within Indigenous societies if they find analogies to concepts within English law. The court said 'this tendency has to be held in check' because it would prevent the recognition of beneficial rights that developed under Indigenous systems.[72] Legal scholars have also rejected the placement of Indigenous forms of law on a lower level.[73] For example, noted legal theorist Lon Fuller summarized the mischaracterizations of customary law as follows:

> If, in an effort to understand what customary law is and what lends moral force to it, we consult treatises on jurisprudence, we are apt to encounter some such explanation as the following … Customary law expresses the force of habit that prevails so strongly in the early history of the race. One man treads across an area previously unexplored, following a pattern set by accident or some momentary purpose of his own, others then follow the path until a path is worn. [This] presents, I believe, a grotesque caricature of what customary law really means in the lives of those who govern themselves by it.[74]

In *Calder v. A.G.B.C.*, the Supreme Court of Canada has also condemned an approach that discounts Indigenous customs. It commented:

> The assessment and interpretation of the historical documents and enactments tendered in evidence must be approached in the light of present day research and knowledge disregarding ancient concepts formulated when understanding of the customs and culture of our original people was rudimentary and incomplete and when they were thought to be wholly without cohesion, laws or cultures, in effect subhuman species.[75]

Notwithstanding philosophical and judicial statements rejecting ideologies of Indigenous peoples' inferiority, the so-called European discovery of Canada continues to provide a troubling justification for the diminishment of Indigenous legal traditions.[76] It perpetuates the myth of inferiority. The Supreme Court of Canada applied this troubling doctrine in *R. v. Guerin* and wrote: 'The principle of discovery which justified these [Canada's] claims gave the ultimate title in the land in a particular area to the nation which had discovered and claimed it. In that respect at least the [Court ruled that] Indians' rights in the land were obviously diminished.'[77] The Court's insult to the pre-contact nature of Indigenous societies was further entrenched in the leading case on Aboriginal rights, *R. v. Sparrow*, in which the Court wrote, '… there was from the outset never any doubt that sovereignty and legislative power, and indeed the underlying title, to such lands vested in the Crown.'[78] This conclusion was drawn despite substantial doubts about the Crown's claims relative to Indigenous peoples' lands and governments at the 'outset' of their relationship.[79]

Despite these rulings, it is factually apparent that at Canada's formation there was no first *discovery* on the part of the Crown that would justify displacing Indigenous law.[80] Indigenous peoples had already discovered most land within their territories and exercised jurisdiction over it prior to the arrival of Europeans.[81] If any legal consequences flow from 'discovery' these should vest in favour of Indigenous peoples, not the Crown, if this doctrine was applied without discrimination.[82] The doctrine of discovery should only give the Crown the ability to claim exclusive or pre-eminent legal authority in areas that were *terra nullius*, literally 'barren and deserted.'[83] Of course, when the Crown arrived in North America Indigenous peoples' territories were not barren and deserted.[84] The Supreme Court of Canada has written: 'At the time of the assertion of British sovereignty, North America was not treated by the Crown as *res nullius*.'[85] Canada's Royal Commission on Aboriginal Peoples recommended governmental recognition that the doctrine of discovery is 'legally, morally and factually wrong.'[86] Discovery should not be accepted as a basis for diminishing Indigenous law.

A related justification for removing or discounting Indigenous legal traditions which should be rejected is linked to ideas about occupation. Occupation by a political grouping on a territorial basis is one reason for recognizing broad legal rights over a territory.[87] Yet, if the doctrine of occupation were applied without bias, most people would likely conclude that at Canada's formation the Crown had not effectively *occupied* Indigenous lands in this manner such as to justify displacing their laws.[88] In fact, the Supreme Court of Canada recognized as much when it wrote: 'When the settlers came, the Indians were there, organized in societies and occupying the land as their forefathers had done for centuries.'[89] Regrettably, the concept of occupation is often applied in an ethnocentric manner to read Indigenous people out of occupation.[90] This seems to be the situation in the Supreme Court of Canada's case of *R. v. Marshall; R. v. Bernard,* where the Mi'kmaq people were regarded as too nomadic to establish effective organization sufficient to achieve occupation at the time British sovereignty was asserted.[91] This finding was made despite Mi'kmaq trade with Acadians and other Europeans for over 150 years, and wars with the British over their incursions on their lands for well over half a century.[92] In failing to give sufficient weight to these facts, the Court neglected the tie between the jurisdictional and territorial aspects of Mi'kmaq occupation. The judges in this case did not adequately follow the Privy Council's earlier caution because they failed to recognize Indigenous beneficial interests when analogies between the common law and Indigenous legal system were lacking.

The *Marshall/Bernard* decision follows a long European tradition of prejudicial displacement of peoples, ethnocentrically viewing them as being lower on the so-called scale of civilization because of their differing social organization.[93] For example, John Locke wrote that land is only effectively occupied and therefore capable of legal possession when a person 'hath mixed his *Labour* with, and joyned to it something that is his own, and thereby makes it his *Property*.'[94] Some believe Indigenous people did not mix their labour with the soil sufficient to secure occupation,[95] which as a generalization is patently false.[96] Additionally, some have interpreted Blackstone as the authority for the proposition that Indigenous peoples were insufficiently organized to claim sovereignty flowing from group occupation.[97] Other theorists, politicians, lawyers, and courts have fallen into the same trap and regarded Indigenous occupation as insufficient to vest these groups with law-making powers.[98] Ethnocentric standards concerning occupation that are discriminatory at their roots should be discarded as a basis for diminishing Indigenous law.

Despite this injunction, some may attempt to justify the demotion of Indigenous legal traditions by reference to the passage of time and the growth of the common law and civil law in relation to them. They may even claim the strengthening of transplanted European traditions eclipsed or extinguished Indigenous laws. In some ways this argument is analogous to the property law doctrine of prescription.[99] This doctrine permits a subsequent claimant to acquire rights if they openly occupy an area over a period of time and the original owner acquiesces to the subsequent presence. In a private law setting, this doctrine is sometimes labelled adverse possession.[100] It requires a *de facto* exercise of sovereignty which is peaceful and unchallenged.[101] While this doctrine may be attractive on one level because it justifies displacement in a seemingly peaceful way, on another level one would encounter problems in applying this concept to discount Indigenous legal traditions. Indigenous peoples have not generally acquiesced to the common law's purported replacement of their laws. Historically, the relationship of the common law and civil law to Indigenous legal traditions has not been peaceful and unchallenged. Indigenous peoples have frequently objected to the common law's presumptions of complete displacement. In contemporary terms, the application of prescription-like doctrines generates hostility, and not peace, amongst Indigenous peoples to whom it is said to apply. These facts make it difficult to construct prescription-like arguments for placing Indigenous legal traditions lower in the country's legal hierarchy. Indigenous activism and opinions have been resolutely turned against the displacement of their cultures, laws, and traditions.[102]

Closely related to the idea that Indigenous legal traditions were minimized through adverse common law and civil law application is the notion of conquest. Once again, the idea is that Indigenous laws gave way in the face of overwhelming force and power. Most people in Canada likely believe Indigenous laws were displaced through conquest. This belief would be contrary to law. Despite conflict between Aboriginal peoples and the Crown in Canada, the country's legal framework does not treat Indigenous peoples as conquered peoples. The Supreme Court of Canada has written: 'Put simply, Canada's Aboriginal peoples were here when Europeans came, and were never conquered.'[103] Furthermore, Canada would have had difficulty declaring rights by conquest because conquest is only justified for a 'just cause,' as when a nation's security or rights are threatened.[104] Additionally, the doctrine of conquest usually only has force if the conquered terri- tory is annexed, formally possessed by the conqueror, and if subse- quent rights are described in a peace treaty that ends a war.[105] These criteria were generally not met in this country. Moreover, even if the conditions for conquest had been met, Indigenous laws would have remained in effect until clearly and plainly extinguished by a colonial legislature.[106] The Supreme Court of Canada has written: 'The "clear and plain" hurdle for extinguishment is … quite high.'[107] Given these many complications, the doctrine of conquest cannot persuasively be relied upon to argue that Indigenous legal traditions are without force in Canada.

Aside from these legal challenges, the doctrine of conquest is not a morally sound concept upon which to build our legal system. If con- quest were the operable framework for Canada's creation, this could potentially set Indigenous peoples in perpetual opposition to the state. Some, made to feel vanquished under this paradigm, could cul- tivate bitter feelings of resentment towards the country. Indigenous people's wealth, privilege, success, and honour in the wider society might not eradicate these feelings of dispossession. Furthermore, poverty, subordination, failure, and prejudice within the state could continually rekindle a hostile view of the state. These feelings of enmity might then be passed on by friends and family through the generations. They might simmer until circumstances arose to turn the tables on their 'oppressors' and until they could seek to reconquer the state regarded as the 'enemy.' It is easy to nurture these views in coun- tries where conquest is the operative framework. The application of the doctrine of conquest to Crown – Indigenous relations would be the framework that would most likely create continued conflict and future confrontation.

Thus, there are problems with theories of discovery, occupation, pre- scription, and conquest when considering the place of Indigenous legal traditions in Canada's legal hierarchy. Fortunately, there is an alternative. We do not have to abandon *law* to overcome past injus- tices. In placing our country on firmer footing, we only have to relin- quish those *interpretations of law* that are discriminatory. A repudiation of these damaging doctrines could be found by further developing at least one strand of Canadian law. Working out the fuller implications of treaties between Indigenous peoples and the Crown is a way out of the impasse created by the rejection of other legal theories. Treaties have the potential to build Canada on more solid ground.[108] Since First

Nations legal traditions were the first laws of our countries and were not extinguished through discovery, occupation, prescription, or conquest, they could be viewed as retaining their force. Furthermore, when treaties are made they can be seen as creating an inter-societal framework in which first laws intermingle with Imperial laws to foster peace and order across communities.

Where treaties have been agreed upon, they could allow for the peaceful reception of common law and civil law traditions within Canada.[109] Treaties at this level make it possible to say: The *Constitution Acts* and other Imperial legislation partially created Canada, but First Nations laws also created the country. The *Constitution Acts* transplanted British institutions onto northern North American soil, while First Nations laws significantly modified their operation and force through treaties. The *Constitution Acts* and First Nations laws continue to construct our countries as they develop through time; but treaties also continue to construct them as new agreements are signed and historic treaties interpreted. Without treaties, the so-called reception of the common law remains an act of forced dispossession. The doctrine of reception alone, without Indigenous participation, is antagonistic to peace, friendship, and respect. Imperialism wanes when the *Constitution Acts* are seen as consistent with the preservation of Indigenous legal traditions and the creation of inter-societal norms in their relationship with the common law and civil law.[110] While some First Nations would regard their treaties as separating them from common law and civil law traditions, others see treaties as a means of recognizing their traditions alongside others. When constitutional instruments are regarded as resting upon treaties, then Canadian law is firmly on the path to becoming truly Indigenous – home-grown in its place of application.[111]

As noted earlier, this book will argue that there is a strong case for recognizing Indigenous legal traditions in Canada. This requires the ongoing cultivation of solidarity within, between, and across legal cultures throughout the land. As such, the common law, civil law, and Indigenous legal traditions must grow beyond their tribal roots, even as these roots continue to nourish our country's ongoing constitution. We must come to see that we are free to modify ourselves and how we are constituted.[112] Our society is not insular, one-dimensional, monocultural, or complete. Relationships can be strengthened as we affirm the overlapping, interacting, and negotiated nature of our traditions through time.[113] One dimension of effective constitutionalism involves cultivating and refining laws that implement Indigenous peoples own aspirations and perspectives, alongside the common law and civil law, and in harmony with international human rights standards. Affirming Indigenous legal traditions in this way would expand and improve Canada's legal system and benefit Aboriginal peoples along with our society as a whole.

2 Sources and Scope of
Indigenous Legal Traditions

When nation states can learn from and embrace the best traditions of its peoples, they can be strengthened and become more unified. If this process occurs in a fair, orderly, transparent, non-discriminatory yet authoritative way the rule of law is reinforced in the process. The blending and/or coexistence of legal traditions is possible. Many countries successfully incorporate diverse legal traditions that respect different ethnic, cultural, and national groupings.[1] Some of these countries are bijuridical and include both civil law and common law systems.[2] Others are multi-juridical and include customary law regimes alongside civil or common law.[3] Canada should be counted among these multi-juridical countries: it embraces common law, civil law, and Indigenous legal traditions. Canada could be characterized as a juridically pluralistic state because it draws on many sources of law to sustain order.[4] While civil and common law traditions are generally recognized across the country, this is not always the case with Indigenous legal traditions. Yet Indigenous legal traditions can have great force in people's lives despite their lack of prominence in broader circles.[5] Indigenous legal traditions are a reality in Canada and should be more effectively recognized.

There are many negative stereotypes in circulation regarding Indigenous law. Recognition can be enhanced if Indigenous laws are understood in greater detail, free from misleading characterizations. For example, Indigenous peoples are diverse and their laws flow from many sources.[6] Understanding their communities' legal foundations can lead to a better appreciation of their contemporary potential, including how they might be recognized, interpreted, enforced, and implemented. The underpinnings of Indigenous law are entwined with the social, historical, political, biological, economic, and spiritual circumstances of each group.[7] They are based on many sources, including sacred teachings, naturalistic observations, positivistic proclamations, deliberative practices, and local and national customs. Note that I am specifically making the point that not all Indigenous laws are customary at their root or in their expression, as people often assume.

There are many sources of law within Indigenous communities. Indigenous peoples hold many different views about the character and practice of law, as is the case in Western legal theory. Indigenous peoples hold diverse theories about what gives law its binding force. Disagreement can be an important part of the law, as long as there are sufficient convergences to produce continuous interim settlements.[8] The civil and common law traditions are not disregarded because of deep philosophical disagreements about their nature and sources. Differences of opinion are a part of the vibrancy and strength of Western law because they provide for shifting appeals to legitimacy through time, or even within a single case.[9] When working with Indigenous legal traditions one must take care not to oversimplify their character. Indigenous legal traditions can be just as varied and diverse as Canada's other legal traditions, although they are often expressed in their own unique ways. This chapter will explore Indigenous legal traditions by focusing on their varied sources. It is hoped that by categorizing Indigenous laws in this way readers will be better able to grasp their complexity and understand the choices available to Indigenous peoples when they exercise their laws. It is also hoped that this approach will allow other people to see the choices they have in relation to Indigenous law in Canada.

A. Sacred Law

As in other legal traditions, some Indigenous laws have sacred sources. Laws can be regarded as sacred if they stem from the Creator, creation stories or revered ancient teachings that have withstood the test of time. When laws exist within these categories they are often given the highest respect. Legal traditions based on spiritual principles form an important part of most every culture's legal inheritance.[10] While Canada's legal traditions are becoming increasingly secularized, one cannot deny the role of the metaphysical in our law's formation.[11] For example, the civil law and the common law have been significantly influenced by ideas about religion.[12] The receipt of evidence and the test for truth often rests on appeals to the divine.[13] Our Constitution's preamble states that Canada is 'founded on principles that recognize the supremacy of God.'[14]

Within Indigenous legal traditions, creation stories are often one source of sacred law. These accounts contain rules and norms that give guidance about how to live with the world and overcome conflict. Their reach can be quite expansive because they contain instructions about how all beings should relate to specific territories. They are often meant to apply over an entire region, and in some cases are universal in their range. Due to their broad reach and revered nature, laws that have sacred aspects at their source may be less flexible than laws flowing from other sources. Similarly, their recognition, enforcement, and implementation can often be regarded as foundational to the operation of other laws. Sometimes creation stories involve the formation of the world; at other times they reference the founding of other significant habitations. One notable 'creation story' for some Indigenous people describes how parts of Canada were formed through the application of Indigenous legal traditions. This is particularly apparent in those areas where First Nations used their own laws in negotiating treaties.

I encountered this view when working with Elders in Saskatchewan. They spoke of their treaties as being sacred because they brought Canada into existence within their territories. I encountered this viewpoint when I was asked to prepare a report on the meaning of the 'peace and order' clauses in the numbered treaties in the Canadian West.[15] This work was done through the Office of the Treaty Commissioner, and examined the nature of law within Cree, Anishinabek, and Dene societies.[16] The report also examined the peace and order promises within the treaties which spoke of the need to respect and apply Indigenous law throughout the territories covered by these agreements. From a government perspective, the clauses said the Indians would 'maintain peace and order between each other and also between themselves and other tribes of Indians or whites.'[17] They also said the Indians would 'aid and assist the officers of Her Majesty in bringing to justice and punishment any Indian offending against the stipulations of this treaty or infringing the laws in force in the country so ceded.'

In listening to the Elders speak about the meaning of these legally binding promises, it was clear that they regarded the treaty as flowing from a sacred source. They did not rely on the written text of the treaty to arrive at this conclusion. Because First Nations followed their own legal traditions in creating treaties, their interpretation was that treaties were made with the Creator as well as with the Crown. First Nations felt encouraged in their view by the presence of Christian missionaries during the negotiations, and the Crown's invocation of God throughout their meetings.[18] Elder Norman Sunchild of Treaty 6 said: 'When [Treaty 6 First Nations] finally agreed to the treaty, the Commissioner took the promises in his hand and raised them to the skies, placed the treaties in the hands of the Great Spirit.'[19] Elder Jacob Bill also of Treaty 6 commented: 'It was the will of the Creator that the White man would come to live with us, among us, to share our lives together with him, and also both of us collectively to benefit from the bounty of Mother Earth for all time to come.' He further said: 'Just like the treaty, that's what that is, one law was given, Indian and white, we both gave something special, something to keep, something to reverence, just like the treaty, both Indian and white beneficiaries, we were given a gift from the Creator. The Creator owns us, he is still the boss, nothing is hidden … just like that little flicker [of fire], that little flame's going out, that's the way the treaty looks, but now that we are sitting here it seems like we need a big flame so we can revive our lives and our relationship, just like we're trying to revive this life so that our young people will have a good life for a long time, for many generations to come. That's why we are here, that's what the Elders seen a long time ago, if the white man listens he too will benefit, a long life for his children and his future generations because he, too, won't sin [*pastahowin*], he will not feel the brunt of that whip that the Creator has. Nothing will be hurt if both sides start talking to each other as beneficiaries of the treaty.'[20] Some Indigenous laws have sacred sources and the numbered treaties are an example of this type of law.

The laws surrounding Canada's formation in many treaty territories are profound because they are meant to encourage the spiritual, moral and legal capacities of all the people who would come to live here. The sacred nature of the treaties is one reason why many First Nations would not consider abandoning them despite generations of government neglect. It would be a violation of the Creator's law, sacred law, to turn away from their promises to him and others in maintaining peace and order throughout the lands on which they lived.

This view of Canada's creation potentially challenges the approach of some critics who may regard Canada's existence in treaty areas as a transgression of rather than an application of Indigenous law. However, the fact that treaties helped to bring Canada into existence within certain areas should not for that reason alone be regarded as contrary to Indigenous law. Many things, including treaties, can be considered sacred even if they are not given the respect they deserve. However, to appropriately clarify this issue it should be acknowledged that there are some people who regard Canada's creation as profane and understand their history very differently from that taught by some Elders in Saskatchewan. For example, many Haudenosaunee of the eastern Great Lakes do not regard themselves as participating in the creation of Canada. Instead, they regard their treaties as bringing their Confederacy into an alliance with the Crown.[21] As such, many Haudenosaunee people would resist being labelled as Canadian citizens because of their distinct status. For this reason they would not likely regard Canada's creation as a sacred event. Another prominent exception to Canada's creation being regarded as sacred is found within British Columbia – where historic treaties were rare. First Nations in this region would have a hard time accepting claims that Canada was formed through promises to the Creator by reference to their laws. In their case, other people moved into their territories and established governments without their formalized participation and legal consent. In this light, the harsh injustice of British Columbia's resettlement can hardly be[22] regarded as a sacred event. There are other places in Canada where First Nations have suffered a similar fate and thus would look skeptically upon claims that Canada's creation flows from a sacred source. Finally, a sacred view of the treaties might also be somewhat problematic from a certain government perspective, as demonstrated by arguments often made by government lawyers who give treaties the narrowest possible technical interpretation in order to increase the Crown's authority relative to the Indians. Some might even view treaties as filled with fraud, duress, and manipulation – or as expedient temporary bargains, designed by the Crown to separate Indians from their lands and resources for the lowest possible price. However, despite these very real challenges there are large areas of the country where treaties between Indigenous peoples and the Crown referenced Indigenous traditions. The fact that Canada's creation is not universally regarded as flowing from a sacred source does not undermine the laws of those First Nations who see things differently. For people in these spaces, treaties can be regarded as sacred creation stories about Canada's formation if placed in their best light.

Professor Noel Lyon, who taught for thirty years at Queen's Law School, summed up his interpretation of the sacred nature of Saskatchewan's First Nations' Elders views on Canada's law in the following fashion: 'As I've listened to the Elders, I have begun to understand that what I've learned about Aboriginal peoples and their situation in Canada has largely come from written sources, from books, and there are a lot of things that were embedded in me in my legal education that I haven't overcome. The most important one, I think, is that law school indoctrinated me with the belief that the Crown is all-powerful, and I think that's a real problem, because I think legal education, it may not be that bad today, but I think there is a tendency to regard the Crown almost in the way that the First Nations people regard the Creator, as being the source of all things. And from that flows the proposition that the treaties are seen by the non-Aboriginal community as just another body of laws that define the status and rights of Aboriginal peoples, rather than seeing the treaties as a nation-to-nation partnership, inter-societal law … It had never occurred to me until Elder Crowe said this yesterday or the day before: that the right of the white people to be on this land is founded in the treaty.'[23] From this explanation one can see how treaties can be regarded as a sacred creation story. As such, they join other Indigenous laws that flow from sources that are revered or most highly respected.

B. Natural Law

Aside from sacred sources, Indigenous peoples also find and develop law from observations of the physical world around them.[24] When considering laws from this source, it is often necessary to understand how the earth maintains functions that benefit us and all other beings.[25] This approach to legal interpretation attempts to develop rules for regulation and conflict resolution from a study of the world's behaviour. Law in this vein can be seen to flow from the consequences of creation or the 'natural' world or environment. Indigenous peoples who practise this form of law might watch how a plant interacts with an insect, and draw legal principles from that experience. Others may study how an insect interrelates with a bird, and take legal guidance from that encounter. Some might examine how a certain bird relates to an animal or another bird and see standards for judgment in this relationship. There might also be analogies drawn from the behaviours of watersheds, rivers, mountains, valleys, meadows or shorelines to guide legal actions. As such, these laws may be regarded as literally being written on the earth.[26]

Note how Indigenous definitions of natural law may at times have a somewhat different emphasis than what is found in many leading natural law theories within Western jurisprudence. The separation of man from nature may not be as stark as in Aristotle's philosophy, where man 'alone has any sense of good and evil, of just and unjust, and the like.'[27] There may also be less emphasis on 'right reason' as universal, and the measure of law's commands and prohibitions, as in the Roman jurist Cicero's works.[28] Furthermore, while Indigenous legal theories about natural law can be diverse and certainly overlap with Western legal theory, there may be less of a belief that living within nature is impossible for human beings without some profound human political intervention, a belief reflected in the works of Thomas Hobbes, Jean-Jacques Rousseau, or John Locke.[29] In contrast with many Western theorists many Indigenous societies do not act in the same way to restrain nature, because they find more to embrace within it. Finally, perhaps many Indigenous peoples might de-emphasize particular Western natural law theories (if they were conscious of them) because these theories so often provided the justification for Indigenous peoples' dispossession.[30] For many Indigenous people, the casebook for learning natural law requires an intimate knowledge of how to read the world;[31] understanding natural law from this point of view does not require an intimate knowledge of how to read legal philosophy.

I have experienced this form of legal reasoning in my own life. My mother is an Elder on our reserve and possesses a sound knowledge of the world immediately surrounding her. She is a person who studies and interprets nature's laws for her family's benefit. Not all legal traditions within Indigenous societies are immediately state-focused. Authority can be based upon kinship and family networks. My mother does not have an education beyond grade eight because she ran away from home at an early age due to family challenges and the threat of removal to a residential school. Despite this lack of formal education, perhaps even because of it, she is one of the wisest people I know. She has an unquenchable thirst for learning. Her knowledge of the earth around her is profound. She frequently talks of her experiences on the land and relates how her perceptions could guide our actions as a family. When we do not follow her judgments we find that we are often in breach of important environmental laws.

For example, in the summer my mother watches for the return of the monarch butterflies and notes how they seem to be scarce when the milkweed plants are fewer in number. Of course she understands that their decline may be attributed to other factors; she is very respectful of scientific explanations and understands the profound complexity of natural forces. However, if no other explanations are forthcoming, and if there are fewer milkweeds on hand, she will inevitably urge us to protect and increase the number of milkweeds around our house. If we do not, she says we will see fewer monarch butterflies. We will also be less likely to enjoy the beauty and variety of other plants that the existence of these butterflies will eventually help to flourish. For her, recognizing and protecting the relationship between butterflies and milkweeds is a principle of natural law. She is our family's prime jurist in such matters because she helps us understand the specific obligations we have in the territories surrounding our home on the reserve. She talks about many other plants besides the milkweeds and will tell us stories about what they teach us.[32] Then she usually takes the principle up one notch and observes that if we have a smaller plant population this usually means we will have fewer bees and other insects in the area. Their absence might affect the availability of fruits and berries in the fall and thus negatively diminish the variety in our diet during that season. My mother also says that fewer insects can lead to fewer birds, and thus we would find less harmony and song in the trees around us. She believes that, for our family, their diminishment affects our emotional outlook in a negative way. She says that we need to hear the birds to know more about ourselves and our environment. When she has been gravely ill, and barely able to leave her home, the songs of the birds have been a source of healing for her. It is thus no surprise that she believes that birdsong is vital to her family's well-being, and thus she watches to ensure we do not do things that will weaken the so-called weeds in the fields and roadsides surrounding our home on the reserve. She has always lamented the use of pesticides and the creation of monocultures in our territories because she feels they negatively affect the plants, insects, birds, and humans on their own terms, and in their relationships with one another. This form of environmentally based family law can be a significant source of legal regulation.

I have heard and read similar teachings and stories from other people around my reserve at Cape Croker. I can remember the time when I more fully realized that the environmental stories I had been hearing for most of my life were one of the sources of law at home. I was just about to begin teaching at Osgoode Hall Law School when I was invited to a discussion about Anishinabek constitutional and environmental law after our annual late summer pow-wow on the reserve. It was a hot August weekend and we had assembled in the Maadookii Senior's Centre to discuss how we might regulate our fisheries and overcome conflict with our peninsula neighbours, who were suspicious or angry about how we would practise conservation. About twenty people were in attendance, including Elders, band councillors, schoolteachers, fishermen, and some youth who were home from university for the season. We had recently won a significant case that recognized our treaty right to fish for commercial purposes around the Bruce Peninsula in Georgian Bay.[33] While this was an important victory for our people, non-native fishers were concerned that we would deplete the stocks and disregard provincial conservation laws. We even experienced some violent backlash from a small number of them in the surrounding towns and communities, as our boats were burned and our fishermen were publicly threatened. Everyone assembled wanted to find ways to regulate our own people's use of the resource and assure the broader public that we would not be overfishing because we had laws that penalized this kind of abuse.

As the meeting began, Elder Basil Johnston took the floor for most of the morning and spoke of the world's creation in our territory. He spoke of how the sun, moon, and earth came into being. He related how the first plants, animals, and humans lived peacefully together on the earth. Each being that came to life had a story attached to its genesis, and these stories taught about how each was to be respected and how we were to best relate to them. As I listened to him, I understood he was speaking about the natural sources of our laws and how they could teach us about what was required of us to regulate our behaviour. After some time, he came to the matter at hand: the right to fish. He spoke about how whitefish had been central to our society for generations. He referred to these fish by their Anishinabek name, *adigmeg*, which translated means 'caribou of the sea.' He then told us a story about them. He said the fish would roam where they wanted, and would fail to live in the adjoining waters if they were offended by our overuse or if we desecrated their underwater homes. At this point a fisherman joined the conversation and said that he had witnessed just such an offence when lake trout had been crossed with brook trout and introduced as 'splake' into the waters of Lake Huron at the behest of so-called sports fishermen. The splake did not have the same strong natural enemies and thus they more successfully competed for the same resources as the whitefish, with the result that most whitefish left the area for a time.

At that point, someone else entered the conversation to indicate a way in which our own fishers might offend the fish. There was some concern that certain of our own First Nations citizens would abuse the whitefish. An Elder, Winona Ariaga, told of her remembrance of how her grandparents only took fish from the waters in selected seasons, and at limited times. She said that she was told that if we troubled *adigmeg* by taking them all year long, it would lead to their disappearance. She said this was one reason the old people diversified their economic pursuits and engaged in sugar maple extraction in the spring, hunting in the fall, farming in the summer, and fishing in the remaining intervals. She said no one should take fish all the time, during every season. Her observations were rooted in the long experience of our community's interactions with the natural world, from which she drew principles to guide our discussion. Her teachings were also intermingled with personal observations of the lake, land, fish, and people.

After all these viewpoints had been expressed, it was suggested that the band council should approach the provincial government to determine whether they would be willing to enter into an agreement that respected our laws but also satisfied the provincial authorities that we would not overfish the lake. Many Elders and fishermen put forward their views about what would best protect the fish and still ensure a prosperous livelihood for members of the community. The band also insisted on hiring their own professionally trained ichthyologist to ensure that the latest science would be incorporated into their laws. In 1999, an agreement was concluded that allowed some space for our laws in the regulation of our traditional territories' fisheries.[34] While I am not completely sure if or how our August meeting had an effect on these subsequent developments, I do feel that the broader issues we canvassed reinforced the determination to act in accordance with the laws as we interpreted them from the world around us. The legal traditions we reviewed certainly helped to regulate the behaviour of the fishermen I knew.

Perhaps a more public example of law being derived from the environment can be found in the trial of the *Delgamuukw v. Attorney General (British Columbia)* which took place in British Columbia in the early 1990s.[35] In this case, Justice McEachern of the British Columbia

Supreme Court heard evidence about the Gitksan peoples' historic use of land in the upper Skeena River area, around Seeley Lake. Over one hundred years prior to the *Delgamuukw* case, Gitksan Chiefs from Git-wangak described their relationship to the land in natural law terms. They said: 'We would liken this district to an animal, and our village, which is situated on it, to its heart. Lorne Creek, which is almost at the end of it, may be likened to one of the animal's feet. We feel that the whiteman by occupying the creek, are, as it were, cutting off a foot. We know that an animal may live without one foot, even without both feet; but we also know that every such loss renders him more help-less.'[36] This statement reveals how the Gitksan drew upon environ-mental observations to form legal principles to guide their relation-ships. Their concern about the implications of a fragmented approach to watershed management led them to predict its crippling effects upon the land and people. The analogy of territories to animals and the lessons that are drawn from their use acts as a guide to legally reg-ulate behaviour and minimize disputes.

One hundred years later, during the *Delgamuukw* case, the Gitksan followed a similar pattern, referring to animals' and peoples' activities relative to land to provide criteria for judgment. Elders gave evidence of their laws through their *adaawk*, which are verbal records of their group's origins and experiences with others and the land.[37] For example, Elder Mary Johnson related an *adaawk* about an ancient grizzly bear, a landslide, and the people's transgression of natural law.[38] Her account contains principles about how people should appropriately relate to the fish and contains an interpretation of what would happen to them if they did not respect these beings. Her testi-mony was recorded by the court as follows:

After all the fishing is finished and all the hunting for – for mountain goats and groundhogs and the mountain and all the berry picking is fin-ished, then they got nothing to do, so the maidens would go and make the camp at the lake, at the foot of Stekyooden, and they caught some grouse ... [A]fter they were caught many trouts, they cut out the back bone of the skin, and tails are still on the back bone. And as they was staying there, they learned the dances of the people and all the songs, and the way they were – they move when they were dancing. So one time, one young lady cut one of these back bone and put it on her head as a deco ration while dancing. And she would happen to be near the – near the lake, and she look at herself at the edge of the lake, and she saw it was the bone looks really, really beautiful and why she dances gracefully. So she ran and told the others what she have found, and show them. Then they all got back bones and decorated their heads with it and some of the people used to come over and watch them and they didn't put a stop to it, and they smiled at what's going on. So after they all went home when it's time to go home, the people of T'am Lax amit heard a terrible noise, and they [...] left the lake and the people watched where the noise comes from, and they've seen some great big trees were throwing about the top of the rest of the tall trees, and they just stood there wondering what happened, until it comes – there is a little stream that runs from the lake and goes into the Skeena River, and that's – and this thing followed the little stream, tramping down the trees. And finally they see this great huge bear, grizzly bear that they have never seen before. And the chiefs sent messengers through the village to – after warriors, to have the warriors ready, which they did. And not long after the messenger went out, all the warriors came out with their spears and arrows and bow and arrow, and hammers that are made with stone, all those from weapons that strong young men use, they all come out bravely to meet this great grizzly bear. And he gets to the water and swam across and – and they went in front, they all went in front of him, but he is – he is a supernatural grizzly bear, they call him Mediik, and whenever they are shot him with an arrow, the arrow flies way up high instead and fall back down again and it hit the warriors, and they were wounded. And this grizzly bear tramped them until they were crushed to the ground, and goes through the village and kills a lot of people. And after that he – he came – he turned and go into the water again, follow the stream where he came from the first place. So the brave warriors went to – to see where he went, and it goes into the lake, disappeared into the lake. That's why the wise elders told the young people not to play around with fish or meat or anything, because the – because the Sun God gave them food to eat and those who – just they should just take enough to eat and not to play with it, that's why this tragedy happens to them.

Q.   Did any of the people go back up the trail that this grizzly bear followed down the mountain afterwards?

A.   Yeah. They went – they went to follow the trail and that's when they see that he disappeared, his track disappeared into the lake. So they believed that it's the revenge of those trouts, because they played around with their bones.

Q. And is that lake – do you know what that lake is known to the non-Indian today, the name of that lake?

A. They call it see Seeley Lake.[39]

Mary Johnson's *adaawk* reveals how Gitksan Elders might use their laws to communicate important principles about how fish should be treated when they are harvested. Past environmental events can be interpreted to provide future guidance to regulate people's conduct. For the Gitksan, as with many Indigenous peoples, the law is read from the land. In Gitksan territory this occurs when one encounters Seely Lake and sees the landslide created by the Giant Grizzly Bear who rushed down the mountain to punish people for their wrongful behaviour with the fish. Standards for judgment are recorded on the earth. While Justice McEachern did not rely upon these accounts to formulate his opinion in the *Delgamuukw* case,[40] the Gitksan continue to reference their *adaawk* and their other legal traditions to regulate and guide their relationships.[41]

C. Deliberative Law

An especially broad source of Indigenous legal tradition is formed through processes of persuasion, deliberation, council, and discussion. While sacred and natural law might sometimes form the backdrop against which debate occurs, the proximate source of most Indigenous law is developed through people talking with one another. The human dimension of these laws means that recognition, enforcement, and implementation make them subject to re-examination and revision through the generations. Indigenous law is not static and can move with the times. The deliberative nature of many Indigenous laws means they can be continuously updated and remain relevant in the contemporary world. When Indigenous people have to persuade one another within their traditions, they must also do so by reference to the entire body of knowledge to which they have access, which includes ancient and modern understandings of human rights, due process, gender equality, and economic considerations. While contemporary concepts will modify and be modified by very old principles and processes, they will also remain distinct by virtue of their particular cultural-legal contexts. Thus, since deliberative Indigenous laws draw upon historical and current legal ideas, they can also more explicitly take account of (and even incorporate where appropriate) legal standards from other legal systems. They can be harmonized with or distinguished from the laws around them based on what counts as persuasive to the group involved in the debate. Since no Indigenous person or community is completely detached from the world, many influences will be brought to bear on Indigenous legal developments. Deliberation aimed at making Indigenous law can occur in formal and informal meetings and gatherings; in these settings laws can be constructed through highly structured or ad hoc means.

The deliberative nature of the Indigenous legal tradition is also a key to resisting fundamentalist and dogmatic legal practices and ideas. When I have discussed Indigenous legal traditions, some people unfamiliar with them have raised concerns about available safeguards and protections for those who are most vulnerable within Indigenous societies. Often these concerns are based on how 'backwards' some Indigenous communities appear in their social relationships,[42] particularly given colonialism's crushing weight.[43] It must be admitted that Indigenous communities experience many pathologies flowing from the dysfunctions of substance abuse, sexual abuse, residential schools, economic dislocation, and non-Aboriginal political interference.[44] Indigenous individuals can also make poor life decisions, like people from any other group. These negative choices are often compounded and made more destructive because of substandard government infrastructure and support within their communities. Such challenges can make it difficult for certain communities to administer their legal traditions in healthy ways. The remedy for this problem lies in helping these communities to heal themselves so that they are in a better position to develop and follow constructive and dynamic laws.[45] Persuasion is most effective when people have confidence in one another's personal and social integrity; thus, healthier relationships can create stronger legal systems because of the increased social capital upon which they can rely.[46] Social capital is the resource generated in group relationships;[47] it can provide important nourishment for Indigenous law because it can foster trust and goodwill, and can engender mutual obligations necessary for effective group action.[48] Thus, as is the case with all societies, Indigenous peoples need to attend to their socio-economic health to strengthen the effectiveness of deliberation within their communities. Healthy participatory legal processes are an important bulwark against oppressive leadership and overbearingly inflexible laws.

At the same time, while it is important to acknowledge the significant struggles some Indigenous communities face in revitalizing their legal traditions, we must also inoculate ourselves against drawing inaccurate and stereotypical conclusions about how Indigenous people will apply their laws in a contemporary context. Indigenous peoples are not 'backwards.'[49] Sometimes, when people say they are concerned about Indigenous legal traditions, their worry is not as much with the community's social state but with the ancient nature and connection Indigenous peoples have to their laws. I have been asked: 'Won't the application of Indigenous law lead to injustice?' When pressed further as to what they mean, people often think Indigenous law will inevitably demean women, deny due process, and be inconsistent with democracy and cherished ideas about the rule of law.

While it is true that the application of Indigenous law may violate individual rights, all legal systems face potential challenges in this regard. Nevertheless, we must guard against stereotypes which might cause us to see such problems as inevitable within Indigenous societies.[50] Of course, as with any system, Indigenous legal traditions must be attentive to foundational questions of human dignity to have any chance of continued growth and acceptance. Fortunately, Indigenous peoples are very aware of foundational principles of civil, political, social and economic rights and responsibilities upon which legal systems rest. In fact, they call on these ideas all the time in their fight against colonial state domination. The development and application of Indigenous law is unlikely to thrive unless Indigenous peoples themselves also express these core precepts within their own distinctive systems. In fact, a large number of Indigenous people would likely not accept the double standard of expecting colonial governments to respect international human rights while their own governments failed to recognize similar principles. I know I would not accept this result in my own First Nation.

For Indigenous peoples to be persuasive in declaring and developing law they must incorporate human rights principles in some form within their legal systems. These systems of human rights protection may be found in their own historic laws and experience, as well as in current human rights documents and declarations. The problem with the *Indian Act* for many years has been its failure to incorporate human rights standards.[51] While the application of the Canadian *Human Rights Act* may help to partially remedy this deficiency, a fuller solution would allow Indigenous peoples to develop their own legal traditions consistent with international human rights standards.[52] While obligations vary according to the international instrument in question, Indigenous incorporation of these laws would include providing remedies for breaches of human rights, along with educative initiatives, independent monitoring and complaints procedures. The self-governing adoption of international human rights instruments would likely be more persuasive and generate greater loyalty within Indigenous communities than the forced application of another parliamentary enactment which further props up a discredited *Indian Act*. It is just not acceptable to have a racist and sexist document such as the *Indian Act* control peoples' lives. The Canadian *Human Rights Act* does not contain the level of detail necessary to overturn the *Indian Act*'s central assimilatory premises.

Indigenous legal traditions will more likely facilitate dignity and freedom if people inside and outside of our communities drop stereotypes about the timeless, past-tense nature of First Nations life and laws. Of course, many time-revered practices thankfully remain and will positively affect how our laws continue to develop. There is room for ancient precedent in most legal cultures, including those based on Indigenous traditions. At the same time, Indigenous peoples are situated within and increasingly participate in a global context, and many of our laws reflect these diverse influences. Some traditions will eventually be dropped if they are not widely accepted within a contemporary Indigenous community. Indigenous traditions are syncretic, and fused with ideas and practices from many sources. They adapt to changing circumstances in accordance with the needs and priorities of their members and in response to external pressures. Tradition is not abandoned as new ways are introduced. In fact, it is renewed as it combines with vibrant healthy influences from other worthy sources. Indigenous law must continue to engage in conversations with other legal traditions to stand any chance of continually being embraced by a sufficient number people within our communities.

Fortunately, the fact that many Indigenous laws are based on deliberative processes means that non-aligned or dissenting viewpoints can be taken into account in the law's formulation. When any society identifies, proclaims, and enforces its laws, there is bound to be disagreement. Most legal systems that respect individual freedoms and dignity must find peaceful ways to deal with opposition in their midst. This requires that conflicting viewpoints be processed in a manner that is conducive to orderly and respectful listening, discussion, and resolution. In this spirit, Indigenous peoples often use circles to invite participation in developing legal standards. Circles are considered sacred and represent the bringing together of people in an atmosphere of equality, as they do not raise one person above another.[53] In a circle discussion, everyone is permitted to speak, although only one person speaks at a time. Each must listen and wait his or her turn to respond to others, in an orderly fashion from right to left. Circles are meant to remind people of Mother Earth and their journey through life: from the earth, to infant, to child, through adulthood to old age and back to the earth. As such, circles incorporate environmental patterns in human terms in many ways. Of course, circles can also be conducted in a coercive manner if they become dominated by an unhealthy group or individual, who may unduly pressure participants to give deference to the viewpoints of the dominators. Relationships of power and hierarchy do not necessarily disappear when people make decisions using a circle format. Those who make decisions in a circle setting must be attuned to their potential for duress and must implement proper procedures for their conduct.[54] Nevertheless, much deliberative Indigenous law development can be conducted through circles – such as talking circles, healing circles, and reconciliation circles – if protective procedures are present. Band council deliberations and Peacemaker Tribal Courts can also use circles to create rules and regulations or to process disputes.

I have participated in circles in which important legal decisions were made and later enforced. Some of these circles have occurred in the criminal law context and demonstrate how Indigenous legal traditions can become a part of and influence the law's development in broader Canadian society. Perhaps the most prominent example of Indigenous legal traditions being used in an urban context is found in the experiences of Aboriginal Legal Services of Toronto (ALST).[55] ALST was established on 21 February 1990, following years of deliberation, debate, and discussion within Toronto's Indigenous communities. A number of exceptionally knowledgeable and supportive non-Aboriginal people such as Jonathon Rudin also contributed to the development of ALST. The Native Canadian Centre of Toronto compiled the results of community consultations in the mid-1980s through a Needs Assessment Report. Later in the process, prominent yet humble Indigenous Elders gave ALST's founders an important set of traditional teachings and principles to guide their work.[56] As a result, ALST was established to strengthen the capacity of the Aboriginal communities and their citizens to deal with justice issues and provide Aboriginal-controlled and culturally-based justice alternatives.[57] It is instructive to note that ALST's existence flows from an inspiring combination of Indigenous and Western legal concerns and knowledge that developed through persuasion, counselling together, and consensus-building.

The deliberative aspects of ALST are also present in the program's daily operation. For example, ALST runs a Community Council Pogram which draws heavily on dialogical sources of Indigenous law.[58] The Community Council is a criminal diversion program for Indigenous people who live in Toronto and are accused of criminal behaviour. The project provides justice alternatives and brings these individuals before men and women who are trained to deal with criminal law issues from an Indigenous legal perspective and who represent a cross-section of Toronto's Indigenous population. In performing their work, the Community Council focuses on consensually developing a plan to allow the accused person to take responsibility for his or her actions. The council also develops plans to address the root causes of the individual's problem and to facilitate reintegration into the community in a positive way. The people at ALST believe the Community Council concept builds upon the way justice was delivered in Indigenous communities in Central and Eastern Canada for centuries before the arrival of Europeans to North America. As such, the initiative is a current example of Indigenous legal traditions in the present context. ALST also does impressive work in attempting to introduce Indigenous perspectives in test case litigation, law reform advocacy, and for individuals before the courts in the Toronto area.[59]

While some Indigenous peoples use circles to conduct their legal affairs, others prefer gatherings such as feasts and other large public assemblies to encourage discussion and resolution of issues. Feast structures are particularly prominent amongst societies in the Pacific Northwest region, including the Haida, Tsimshian, Salish, Heiltsuk, Tlingit, Nuu-chah-nulth, Nisga'a, Gitksan, Wetsuwet'en, and Kwakwaka'wakw. [60] They contain elaborate protocols to engage communities in important celebrations and decision-making issues.[61] Some of these feasts are best known as potlatches. While the Canadian government unsuccessfully tried to abolish them in the late nineteenth and early twentieth centuries, they have remained an important legal tradition within most West Coast Indigenous societies.[62] Some of these feasts deal with property law disputes and build upon debate and discussion to sort out boundary issues. Gitksan Elder Johnny David explained that such disputes could arise from 'one person crossing the boundary of another person's and when that happened, they usually talked about it and that was the end of the problem.'[63] If informal discussions were unsuccessful, a potlatch process could be initiated as follows: 'They [c]ould invite each other to a feast and gifts would be distributed, and the person who crossed over a boundary would be spoken to by the chiefs and after than happened, the problem was solved and it never occurred again.'[64] Hereditary chiefs direct the proceedings with guidance from the Elders, and the disputants build consensus under this structure by talking to one another through narrative, dance, music, and gift-giving. These deliberations help to create a legal resolution that aims for reconciliation between the parties so that they walk away as friends.[65] Other feasts can deal with family law issues,[66] commercial disputes, or criminal law matters.[67] There is tremendous potential for the continued operation and development of feasting structures and other large gatherings to develop law through the exercise of Indigenous deliberative practices.

One particularly poignant example of feasting as an exercise of law was brought to my attention by former graduate student Perry Shawna. Perry worked with the Carrier Sekani Family Services Agency (CSFS) for over sixteen years until his untimely death by heart attack. Before teaching at the University of Northern British Columbia and pursuing his LL.M. with me at the University of Victoria, Perry worked with CSFS to offer community-based, professional, and culturally appropriate child and family services to the eleven First Nations communities located to the north-east of Prince George in British Columbia.[68] While Perry was at CSFS, he worked with others to ensure that Carrier Sekani laws and values were followed in reuniting Carrier Sekani children with their communities. During his tenure, the Society implemented the procedures and principles underlying the feast or *bahlats* structure to welcome back children and adults previously removed from their communities. In developing these feasts, there was much discussion, debate, and consultation. Wide-ranging dialogue was needed to ensure that the appropriate people were being recognized for their efforts in helping the children of the community. There was also a great deal of attention paid to learning and following proper legal process at the feasting event. While the welcome home feast was not a *bahlats* in the strict way of gathering community members, *bahlats* values provided the main inspiration for the event.

CSFS is now researching and developing a framework to deal with family conflict through the use of Carrier Sekani legal traditions.[69] This process also involves deliberation and discussion through feasting and other large community gatherings.

Of course, besides circles and feasting, there are also other ways in which Indigenous peoples might gather together to develop their laws through persuasion, council, and debate. For example, the Haudenosaunee of the eastern Great Lakes build and maintain their Great Law of Peace on the consensus and agreement of six different nations. While this legal tradition will be discussed in greater detail in the next chapter, it is sufficient at this point to note that structured deliberation is central to making binding legal decisions. For example, past and future generations are considered and consulted as a formal part of their society's deliberations. A council of fifty chiefs chosen by clan mothers takes account of the community's concerns. They administer confederacy business through a deliberative process by repeatedly passing ideas across a longhouse fire to explore and analyse them before taking action. This system also allows any Iroquois nation of the Haudenosaunee Confederacy to request a meeting of the council.[70] Clan mothers, youth, and others can also greatly influence decisions through their involvement in bringing matters to council for discussion and resolution.[71] Unanimity is most often necessary for the adoption of council decisions within the longhouse system of government, which demonstrates the importance of debate and persuasion for making law within Haudenosaunee legal traditions. The reinvigoration of Haudenosaunee law is one of the reasons the Canadian and Ontario governments have had to work differently with the Six Nations community near Brantford, Ontario in recent years, and their laws' influence was especially evident in the disputes concerning subdivision land in the Caledonia dispute in 2006–9.[72]

Today, perhaps the most visible example of Indigenous legal tradition developed through deliberation and persuasive debate occurs in band council settings. Although the full expression of their laws is constrained by the harsh overlay of non-Indigenous rules under the *Indian Act*, bands often, though sometimes inconsistently, use traditional legal teachings to conduct their business and regulate their communities. The strictures created by the federal *Indian Act* do create problems because they unnecessarily restrict and occupy jurisdictional space and thus hinder healthier law-making procedures and patterns. Indigenous law-making power through deliberation under the *Indian*

Act is thus a poor reflection of what would be possible if this restrictive legislation were repealed. The *Indian Act*'s constraints could lead to concerns that band councils cannot properly claim to administer Indigenous legal traditions in the contemporary context because they are a creation of the Canadian government and therefore only function as a non-Indigenous law-making body. While it is true that band councils may owe some of their life to the federal government, it must also be acknowledged that many continue to be recreated through community participation.

I have known many *Indian Act* elected chiefs and councillors who reference their own First Nation's legal values in debating and making decisions under its structures. Furthermore, many so-called Indian bands pre-existed the *Indian Act* and find their inherent governmental power in their pre-Confederation authority. In that respect, they are not a product of the *Indian Act*. In fact, in my own family, my great-grandfather was both a hereditary chief and an elected chief under the *Indian Act*.[73] Thus, some band councils are well situated to apply Indigenous legal traditions and have a long history of implementing their own community's procedures and principles in their decision-making, despite the *Indian Act*'s strictures. Other band councils, such as those found on the Six Nations reserve in Ontario, have very little legitimacy in administering Indigenous legal traditions because the government's imposition of the band council has never been broadly accepted by their community.

Indian bands can also operate on a customary basis. Section 2(1) of the *Indian Act* defines an Indian 'band' as a 'body of Indians.'[74] Regulations under the *Indian Act* set out procedures for conducting band council meetings,[75] although section 2(1) of the *Indian Act* also states that an Indian band council can be 'chosen according to the custom of the band.' One in three Indian bands in Canada has chosen to organize their political affairs in accordance with their own customs. The fact that Indian bands continue to function under a degree of their own inherent authority demonstrates that, rather than extinguishing Indian governance, the *Indian Act* could be interpreted as explicitly recognizing and affirming pre-existing law-making powers. Despite the potential for the *Indian Act*'s band council structure to allow for the exercise of Indigenous customs, further steps should be taken to remove First Nations from the *Indian Act*'s suffocating embrace. Operating as a custom band under the *Indian Act* does not adequately facilitate the growth and development of Indigenous law because the surrounding legislative framework largely assumes a relatively low level of decision-making ability and authority. More First Nations must escape from the *Indian Act* to increase their law-making powers in accordance with their own priorities. Nevertheless, in studying Indigenous legal traditions in Canada, one cannot overlook the fact that band councils are a rich source of Indigenous law, despite the problems that exist.

These examples demonstrate that many Indigenous legal traditions develop in a deliberative fashion, through councils, circles, feasts, and other informal and formal meetings and gatherings. Some of the great civilizations in early northern North America were built on a very generous notion of participation in the law-making functions of society. Many Indigenous societies today continue to encourage very broad participation across their citizenry and might be regarded as being radically egalitarian. Some societies are so generous and liberal in extending personal liberties to their members that every being has a legal right and practical opportunity to assist in the development of their laws. At the same time, it should be noted that other Indigenous communities may, at points, severely restrict participation as a result of rules related to status, heredity, special accomplishment, or Canadian legal impediment.

Rules related to the scope of disclosure and participation must be understood in order to effectively understand deliberation within Indigenous legal traditions. Just as cabinet discussions in a parliamentary democracy may be privileged, some Indigenous legal procedures can be analogously limited. Some of these limits exist because selected Indigenous laws require special position, ceremonial recognition, and hard work to receive them.[76] Others may have limited application or reception because of their hereditary nature. These limits may lead a few to devalue Indigenous law as being secretive, non-transparent, or undemocratic within its deliberative processes. However, before jumping to such conclusions, one must remember the pragmatic limits that also surround other Canadian legal traditions. Sometimes, restrictions on participation are important in preserving the orderly and peaceful flow of our law's development. At other times, a high degree of specialization is necessary in order to understand, produce, or practise law. In this regard, Canadian legal process may be considered somewhat analogous to the special positions, ceremonies, and hard work required by some Indigenous legal traditions. On a more sobering note, the substantial resources, societal position, or family connections required for Canadians to receive legal education, practise law, or become a judge may not be far removed from the hereditary privileges in some Indigenous societies. Indigenous legal traditions are not alone in requiring special ceremonies, hard work, and family connections. Fortunately, even most hereditary positions within Indigenous law also require more of the individual recipient of power than simply being born into the right family. When one balances the radically egalitarian nature of many Indigenous communities with the more limited hereditary roles currently found within them, most observers would quickly understand that heredity alone does not mean much without that person's own hard work and good reputation. Thus, family status may not in itself be either a help or hindrance to participating in the creation of law within Indigenous communities, and thus should not be a reason to defeat fuller deliberation.

The points made in the past few paragraphs demonstrate that many criticisms related to the scope of disclosure and participation within Indigenous societies can be successfully addressed if widespread deliberation remains the heart and focus of a community's legal system. In such cases, the form of deliberation (hereditary office, etc.) would have to give way to the substance (persuasion, choice, etc.) of what a community's tradition protected in order for them to act consistently with their laws. However, to fairly and even-handedly evaluate questions of participation within Indigenous legal traditions, it is also crucial to observe that certain Indigenous legal traditions were, and continue to be, decidedly undemocratic and thereby restrictive of deliberation. Such traditions are far from encouraging an individual's free, uncoerced, and unfettered involvement in the life of the community. When this is the case, these traditions should be renounced and discarded. Fortunately, this has generally taken place. For example, in the past some Indigenous societies practised slavery, and placed numerous limitations on personal rights and freedoms.[77] As in other countries, Indigenous peoples have forsaken slavery and it is clear that this practice has no relevance to their contemporary legal traditions. While the past existence of slavery demonstrates a high degree of social and legal organization, it no longer restricts any Indigenous person in Canada from participating in the formulation and application of their laws. Any remnants of such odious and abhorrent past traditions have long since been repudiated and abandoned, because they are inconsistent with contemporary norms and legal procedures of Indigenous, Canadian, and international legal communities. Where restrictions on deliberation do occur, slavery is rarely, if ever, at the root of such injustice within contemporary Indigenous communities.

Where participation in the creation of Indigenous law is restricted in inappropriate ways, it is usually because some powerful individual or group has used positivistic law to usurp authority from a community. This issue will be discussed in the next section and is hopefully implicit throughout this text because my intolerance for such behaviour is one of the most important reasons for writing this book. In all that is contained herein, I am attempting to show that legitimate and orderly ways can be drawn upon to restrain such people from inappropriately using laws found within our own traditions. At the same time, I am also writing this book because, unfortunately, one of the most profound sources of restrictions on broader participation within Indigenous legal regimes today is Canadian law itself.[78] The attitude of most lawyers, judges, and parliamentarians towards Indigenous law prevents its growth. That is, Indigenous law is regarded as second-rate or incomplete, if it is given any regard at all. For example, one Chief Justice of a provincial Court of Appeal said to me in a personal conversation: 'You say Indigenous law exists; I don't believe it for a moment.' Jurispathic attitudes can 'kill diverse legal traditions' if they are falsely regarded as competing with the state.[79] Furthermore, Canada's legislatures have not been very responsive or supportive of Indigenous legal orders. The *Indian Act*, passed in 1876 to assimilate and manipulate Indigenous legal traditions, severely restricts rules on participation.[80] It has also caused some First Nations to abandon specific legal traditions; others have subverted its precepts or incorporated them within their legal orders.[81] Additionally, Canadian governments have restricted the general franchise for many Aboriginal people, thus affecting the deliberative aspect of their legal traditions.[82] When Canadian interferences with Indigenous legal traditions are curbed, Indigenous laws can better facilitate Indigenous participation in their own legal systems, as well as ensuring broader participation within Canadian and international legal debates. Indigenous peoples themselves can also take significant steps to cast aside traditions that interfere with deliberation, persuasion and wide-ranging participation in the creation of their laws.

D. Positivistic Law

Another source of Indigenous law can be found in the proclamations, rules, regulations, codes, teachings, and axioms that are regarded as binding or regulating people's behaviour.[83] The laws to which I refer are somewhat distinct from those above because they do not necessarily depend on appeals to the Creator, the environment, or deliberative processes to possess their force. Legal traditions in this mode have weight because proclamations are made by a person or group regarded by a sufficient number of people within a community as authoritative. Individuals who are seen to possess such power may be hereditary chiefs, clan mothers, headmen, sachems, or band leaders. Their laws may be regarded as positivistic because they rely more on the authority and intelligence of those who issue them than on the notion of creation, nature, or community deliberation. Philosopher John Austin referred to legal positivism as being based upon command. He said that those who have binding legal authority are those who are 'determinate rational being[s] or bod[ies] that the other rational beings are in the habit of obeying.'[84] Rationality is, of course, present in every community and laws flowing from trusted individuals and groups are given due regard as a result. In an Indigenous context, positivistic laws may be formally proclaimed in feast halls, council houses, wampum readings, band council chambers, and other such public settings. In announcing these laws, ancient and contemporary legal ideas can mingle together and become the basis for bylaws, statutes, conventions, and protocols.

Some positivistic Indigenous legal traditions may once have been explicitly connected to a larger normative system, but the reasons underlying their original adoption might have been deliberately abandoned or forgotten as circumstances changed. Thus, laws that once drew their authority from deliberation or creation may now be followed for different reasons – because some group or individual has garnered enough power (through respect or fear) that others will now follow their pronouncements without considering the reasons behind the law's development. I have met a few of these First Nations leaders and groups in my travels throughout Canada, and they have managed to effectively regulate their communities by drawing law from this source. In these experiences, I have seen some wonderful people lead with excellent results because of their kindness, knowledge, and care for their communities. Unfortunately, I have also witnessed some leaders who 'command' almost exclusively from their own narrow material interests, without proper motive or beneficial effect.

I must confess that positivistic law as a source of authority (without a broader justification for its use) prompts greater concern for me than the other sources we have been discussing. My concern about statutes and commands not only relates to Indigenous legal traditions; I see problems with the over-reliance on this source within common law and civil law traditions too. My worry is that if a prominent leader or group rules through this form of law for too long, without the restraining influences found in the other sources identified to this point, this could lead to great corruption. The exercise of positivistic law potentially places too much authority in the hands of powerful individuals or popular majorities without other checks, balances, or measurement against a broader normative base. In time, the exercise of legal traditions through positivistic law could lead to abusive domination if the person or group in authority does not submit to other normative legal considerations. Thus, while positivistic law is a legal tradition with force in Indigenous, common law, and civil law communities, my hope is that it will constantly be tempered by other factors to ensure that those who proclaim law do not become a source of oppression to those who follow them. If Indigenous peoples who are governed through positivistic law recognize that they can place their traditions on a broader footing, they may be more inclined to choose those traditions which further facilitate freedom and dignity, while still maintaining crucial connections to their past. Fortunately, in my view, it is rare to see positivistic law existing within Indigenous communities without other sources of law being studied and followed. In fact, Indigenous legal traditions are most often criticized for not having a so-called recognizable sovereign who can pronounce laws and command obedience to them. This, while not strictly true, does demonstrate their decentralized operation.[85]

When positivistic laws operate without being couched in persuasion, deliberation, or a sound understanding of nature and what is sacred, Indigenous peoples may be left with legal traditions that sound like a chronicle of 'dos and don'ts.' Such laws are somewhat like commandments or codes from which much of the context for their development is no longer remembered or considered irrelevant. Examples of these types of laws might be: 'don't swim in that part of the stream,' 'don't walk on that part of the glacier,' 'when you take something from that place, you must leave something there from another place,' 'make sure you walk around the perimeter of an area four times before you leave.' These laws are called positivistic in my formulation because they may be followed by people with little understanding of why they are binding, beyond their trust in or fear of the individual or group who gave them the rules.[86]

Along with traditions fashioned through deliberation, Indigenous laws formulated in a positivistic manner might be most recognizable to people schooled in other legal traditions. Most would probably recognize a leader or party's commands or rules as a type of law, and many can relate to the idea that sometimes such rules do not seem to have much relationship to reason or morality. Many societies often obey such laws because they are regarded as necessary to the proper maintenance of order within their jurisdictions.[87] When someone breaks a law, our concern is not usually whether the law-breaker was persuaded at some point to support the law but that they had failed to obey it. When we know someone is flaunting the law, we may not immediately care whether that person sees the law as being in harmony with some broader sacred, natural, or deliberative source. Rather, when a person acts contrary to the law, most people who witness the disobedience are more concerned about their own safety and self-interest, and with that of their neighbours.

Thus, when people feel threatened by illegal activity, they may not immediately be concerned about larger questions of legitimacy surrounding the law. Therefore, in understanding positivistic law's legitimacy, it is important to remind ourselves that such power flows from a leader or group's claim or endowment of reason and responsibility. If there are disquieting concerns with a person's use of tradition, that person could be removed without offending other legal traditions that may flow from deliberation, nature, or the community's sense of the sacred. The narrow base for legitimacy on which positivistic power rests provides some measure of protection to Indigenous peoples who may be in the grip of an autocratic leader. If the law in question is merely a product of a powerful person or group's misdirected preferences, then that law can be changed, or the person can be removed, without any perceived natural or divine consequences. Such removal will also hopefully strengthen the deliberative capacities and processes within a community. This is not to underestimate the political upheaval that could occur if a community, whose laws rest on proclamation alone, sought to remove their leader. It is, however, to acknowledge that bigger underlying normative changes would not necessarily be required if power largely rested on personality or preference alone. Thus, since the major consequence of disobedience in regard to positivistic laws would usually be a change in the political alignment of the group, going against positivistic rules would not typically be seen as a breach of sacred or natural law, and therefore would not directly challenge the deliberative consensus of the larger group. Thus, if an Elder named chief or clan mother suffers from a loss of reputation, people could cease to follow their rules without dire consequences. A respected person or group's fall from community favour does not necessarily create a crisis in the theory of law as would be the case if someone violated the other forms of law developed in this chapter. The person who loses credibility is often merely replaced by someone else who can fill the leadership vacuum. Alternatively, if no one immediately arises to fill the role left by the formerly powerful person, other sources of law, such as deliberation or custom, could fill the void.

On occasion, however, the consequences of a leader's loss of reputation may be more complex and the subject of much greater conflict. This could be the case if the formerly respected person or group were to make claims that they were the only ones able to understand, interpret, or proclaim sacred or natural law, or were somehow indispensable to the process of law developed through deliberative sources. No one person should be granted this degree of authority, but most legal systems struggle to contain powerful groups and individuals who proclaim the infallibility, necessity, or inevitability of their rules. In such cases, there could be a struggle to separate the leader's personality from their expression of the other legal sources followed by the community. It might be difficult to disentangle a powerful group's claims to authority from laws flowing from the Creator, nature, or from the functioning of a deliberative council. The challenge of separating political power from legal sources should not be underestimated, because the sources of law identified in this chapter are not as discrete as they might appear. For instance, leaders will sometimes attempt to align their positivistic proclamations with a normative system, such as has been described in the preceding sections. In categorizing discrete sources of Indigenous law, I hope to show that appeals to authority can be based on ideas much broader than those often attributed to Indigenous legal traditions. However, just as critical legal scholars have appropriately attacked claims that purport to separate law from politics,[88] Indigenous legal traditions themselves are also enmeshed with political considerations, as is the case in other legal systems.[89] While this chapter only attempts to identify sources of law that are more distinct from the community's norms because they more firmly rest on the force of an individual personality or group, on the ground, application tends to be messier in mingling the practice of politics and law. Thus, there is always the danger that changes in leadership or group dynamics may make it more difficult to abandon rules that seem, at first glance, to be tied to a person's or group's will-to-power through their proclamations.

Therefore, while we must be attentive to the relationship between law and politics within Indigenous legal traditions, these dynamics should also not lead us to overestimate the problem of leadership conflict or change within Indigenous legal systems where positivistic law is in force. Indigenous people affected by the waning of a certain set of rules closely associated with one powerful person or group would still have many other options to which they could turn in ensuring their affairs remained ordered through the law. The availability of appeals to the Creator, the environment, and reasoned consensus or custom greatly assists communities when an individual or group's proclaimed rules or formerly binding teachings become less compelling for reasons related to their reputations.

E. Customary Law

The final source of law discussed in this chapter relates to the variety of Indigenous legal traditions often referred to as custom.[90] Custom is the label that most people would likely give Indigenous law if they were unfamiliar with the complexity of these societies' social organization.[91] Of course, customary law is not peculiar to Indigenous societies.[92] The common law, civil law, and international law also rely on custom as a source of binding obligation for those subject to their operation.[93] Customary law can be defined as those practices developed through repetitive patterns of social interaction that are accepted as binding on those who participate in them.[94] Customary laws are often inductive, meaning that observations of specific behaviour often lead to general conclusions about how to act; as a result, the obligations they produce are regularly implied from a society's surrounding context.[95] An effective way of learning custom would involve examining or living specific routines and procedures associated with conduct within a community and talking to people about why they felt obliged to act in a particular manner. Such an investigation might lead one to conclude that customary law rests heavily on an individual's unspoken agreement about how rights and obligations will be regulated between community members. The communally layered and individually intuitive nature of this legal form means that disputes are often regulated through social pressures that distribute incentives and dis-

incentives to act or refrain from acting in certain ways. Since customary laws are not always as explicit as other forms of law, their recognition, interpretation, and enforcement is often initially more difficult to
achieve when other sources of law intervene. However, this does not
mean that customary law should give way to other sources of Indigenous legal tradition. Customary law can be a creative source of law in
its own right, and in its proper context can be very effective in producing strong and healthy community relationships.

Indigenous customary law in Canada has been most strongly recognized in the context of marriage and family relationships. In *Casimel v.
I.C.B.C.*, the British Columbia Court of Appeal held that a seventy-
seven-year-old woman and a ninety-nine-year-old man had legally
adopted their daughter's thirty-year-old son according to Carrier law
and, thus, when he died, were entitled to death benefits as dependent
parents under the province's *Insurance Act*.[96] This case rested upon the
finding that Carrier law allowed grandparents to be considered as full
parents in their customary regime, and that natural parents were no
longer considered to possess the rights or obligations of a parent under
this system.[97] Furthermore, the court held that neither Canadian common law, nor federal or provincial statute, nor constitutional law abrogated Carrier customary law. In summarizing the reasons for upholding Carrier legal tradition, Justice Lambert wrote: 'I conclude that there
is a well-established body of authority in Canada for the proposition
that the status conferred by aboriginal customary adoption will be recognized by the courts for the purposes of application of the principles
of the common law and the provisions of statute law to the persons
whose status is established by customary adoption.'[98] There are
numerous other examples of Canadian courts and legislatures recognizing Indigenous peoples' family law customs.[99] Customary law can
also be found in matters related to Indigenous governance,[100] land,[101]
and resource use.[102]

Another example of the recognition of Indigenous customary law is
found in recent land claim agreements signed throughout the country.
These agreements are significant because they implement an extensive
array of Indigenous customs across Canada. For example, the *Labrador
Inuit Land Claims Agreement* (LILCA), which applies to a large area of
coastal Labrador, acknowledges that Inuit law will be a significant
source of authority in the region.[103] The extension of custom is possible because LILCA creates a central government that is controlled by
the Inuit and enables this government to pass binding laws that are

constitutionally protected under section 35(1) of the *Constitution Act, 1982.*[104] The central Inuit government, called Nunatsiavut, works with local Inuit governments and individuals, and operates in accordance with the *Labrador Inuit Constitution* (LIC). The LIC, which was approved by Inuit electors in an April 2002 referendum, proclaims that 'Labrador Inuit customary law is the underlying law of the Labrador Inuit and of Nunatsiavut for all matters within the jurisdiction or authority of the Nunatsiavut Assembly.'[105] Furthermore, LILCA also accepts that Inuit customary law will have force throughout the region and that 'Inuit Law' means a law of the Inuit Central Government, which includes an Inuit customary law proclaimed, published, and registered in accordance with part 17.5.[106] To supplement this explanation of LILCA's grant of law-making authority, the *Labrador Inuit Constitution* defines customary law in the following terms: 'The customs, traditions, observances, practices and beliefs of the Inuit of Labrador which, despite changes over time, continue to be accepted by Labrador Inuit as establishing standards or procedures that are to be respected by Labrador Inuit are the customary laws of the Labrador Inuit and are referred to as Labrador Inuit customary law.'[107] The continued development of custom alongside Inuit positivistic law demonstrates its importance as a source of law to the Indigenous peoples of this area.

To help keep each source of law vibrant and strong, there are detailed provisions within the *Labrador Inuit Constitution* and *Labrador Inuit Land Claims Agreement* dealing with the interaction of customary law and positivistic Inuit and Canadian law. For example, the LIC includes a *Charter of Rights and Responsibilities*, which contains provisions relating to equality, dignity, security of the person, personal integrity, religious observance, freedom of expression, elections, freedom of movement, private land rights, freedom of trade, fair labour practices, collective bargaining, environment, rights of children, water, health care, social services, education, language, culture, housing, access to information, right to administrative actions, and access to court.[108] This extensive list of protections illustrates the scope of Inuit law's potential impact on the people to whom the LILCA will apply. It is also noteworthy that the *Inuit Charter* shows that Inuit people regard rights and freedoms as an important part of their legal regime and do not consider such rights as being necessarily contrary to their own customary laws. In fact, the *Labrador Inuit Constitution* goes so far as to proclaim, 'The Labrador Inuit Charter of Rights and

Responsibilities does not deny the existence of any other rights or freedoms of Labrador Inuit, including those that are recognized or confirmed by Labrador Inuit customary law to the extent that those rights and freedoms are consistent with the Labrador Inuit Charter of Rights and Responsibilities.'[109] The idea here is that Inuit customary law might help to facilitate rights and freedoms within Nunatsiavut communities and should not be regarded as preventing their protection and extension. Nevertheless, while there is a lively confidence about the general harmonization of customary law with Charter rights and responsibilities, there is also an acknowledgment that sometimes the application of both legal sources might conflict. Therefore, the LIC contains provisions relating to the relationship between customary laws and *Inuit Charter* rights in the event of an inconsistency; section 9.1.3 of the LIC states that the *Inuit Charter* prevails in such circumstances. In addition, the LIC also provides rules for the application of Inuit customary law alongside other Inuit laws passed by the central and local governments. In fact, Inuit customary law is given paramountcy over laws passed by the Nunasiavut government, unless that law is expressly extinguished by them or contrary to their Charter.[110]

Other interesting provisions dealing with customary law within the *Labrador Inuit Constitution* include provisions for the Nunatsiavut Assembly to make laws for the codification and recognition of Inuit customary law.[111] This provision complements section 17.5 of the *Labrador Inuit Land Claims Agreement*, which states that the Nunasiavut Government shall 'maintain a public registry of the Labrador Inuit Constitution, Inuit Laws, including Inuit customary laws in respect of matters within the jurisdiction of the Nunasiavut Government and Bylaws.'[112] Furthermore, LILCA also provides guidance about how Inuit customary law can be recognized and proved if it has not been codified by the assembly. Thus, LILCA gives power to any judicial or administrative authority to establish customary law as a question of fact in any proceeding where the existence and content of such law may be relevant.[113] In time, this provision is bound to inspire a host of new interpretations concerning custom through Labrador as the Inuit court and various tribunals set up under LILCA more fully detail their ancient law's contemporary scope and content.

Section 9.1.7 of the *Labrador Inuit Constitution* even provides procedures to assist decision-makers with the task of proving custom. It reads:

9.1.7 A person alleging the existence or content of Labrador Inuit customary law under subsection 9.1.6(b) must prove the existence and the content of the Inuit customary law on the balance of probabilities and for that purpose may introduce:

(a) the oral and written traditions, observances and practices of the Labrador Inuit, an Inuit Community or a relevant group of Labrador Inuit;

(b) the opinions of Labrador Inuit elders or other persons who have special knowledge or experience of Inuit customary law in relation to the matter or would be likely to have such knowledge or experience if such law existed;

(c) evidence of the consensus of the Labrador Inuit or community or group of Labrador Inuit, as appropriate; and

(d) any other evidence that is relevant.

This procedure, which allows decision-makers to come to conclusions about the proof of Inuit customary law, will likely prove to be an important source for identifying binding legal traditions that have not been previously committed to writing within the territory covered by the *Labrador Inuit Land Claims Agreement*.

F. Conclusion

It should be noted that the distinctions between the different sources of law outlined in this chapter can be defined too formally and separate from one another. In the real world, Indigenous legal traditions usually involve the interaction of two or more of the sources described above. In fact, in practice it would be hard to separate them from one another. Furthermore, even in the somewhat artificial way they are presented in this chapter, it is easy to see how the sources of law would change as Indigenous communities worked with them. For example, some aspects of customary law could become positivistic if codification is undertaken. Positivistic law could take on a deliberative source if debate occurs about the appropriateness of rules derived from custom. Similarly, sacred law might influence natural law, if people relate to the Creator through natural processes. Once again, my point in making the distinctions using these classifications (sacred, natural, deliberative, positivistic, and customary) is to illustrate the complex nature of Indigenous law. I am attempting to highlight the fact that

Indigenous peoples have choices when they turn to their laws for answers. While complexity and choice might make working with the law appear more complicated, it should also provide greater opportunities for those interested in recognizing, interpreting, enforcing, and implementing these laws. Understanding that a source of law is natural, deliberative, positivistic, or customary might help those people who think of Indigenous legal traditions as static to see a much greater space for their application and development in modern Canada. If Indigenous legal traditions are going to expand and be a creative source of authority in Canada, we must reject the view that Indigenous law lies at the bottom of the legal hierarchy, labelled as simply customary. While it is true that many Indigenous laws are customary, this chapter has illustrated that they are much more as well. If understood in this broader light, Indigenous legal traditions can be regarded as living systems of law, open to human choice and agency, within the context of the communities who will use them.

One of the ways Indigenous societies can best keep their legal traditions alive and connected to broader normative bases is by continuing to emphasize the oral transmission of their laws. While Indigenous peoples have been no strangers to recording their laws on paper throughout the past century, many Indigenous societies prefer to express their legal principles through oral tradition to maintain flexibility and relevance amidst changing circumstances. For many Indigenous societies, the spoken word ensures the law's vitality because it sustains connections to their community's underlying cultural foundations. It also ensures that laws remain connected to a living community. This is in contrast with views of the written word, which causes some Indigenous people to fear that law will become disconnected from their lived experiences and ordinary understandings if it is reduced to paper. While most contemporary legal systems rely upon the printed word to communicate important rules, oral tradition is also an accepted part of the common law and civil law,[114] and has a long and distinguished history within Indigenous legal traditions.[115] There is no reason why oral traditions cannot remain strong even as Indigenous peoples write them down, as long as such writing is regarded as supplementary to its existence in the hearts, minds, actions, and voices of the people to whom such laws apply.

For many Indigenous people, the oral transmission of law is an important protection against narrowing influences because it allows for a stronger weaving of the past and the present. The spoken word is given pride of place because the transmission of law in orally-based legal systems is bound up with face-to-face persuasion, reason, the configuration of language, political structures, kinship, clan, economic systems, social relations, intellectual methodologies, morality, ideology, and the physical world. These factors assist powerful individuals and groups in knitting legal memories more tightly in their adherents' minds, keeping the laws living in places other than dusty old books full of overly technical rules. Rather than by being hoarded by a professionalized legal elite, laws can be transmitted through memorized speech, historical gossip, personal reminiscences, formalized group accounts, representations of origins and genesis, genealogies, epics, tales, proverbs, and sayings.[116]

Furthermore, oral recitation is also an important legal principle within Indigenous communities because it allows issues from non-Indigenous systems to be incorporated with flexibility. As noted above, one must take care not to assume that oral proclamations of law will contain no references to ideas from other cultures and legal systems. Since oral communications necessarily take place in a contemporary context, Indigenous proclamations will be intermixed with ideas from other sources. They may be lodged in commentaries relating to stories, songs, ceremonies, feasts, dances, scrolls, totems, button blankets, wampum belts, et cetera. Clues to their historic existence and to the way in which they are applied may be found in missionaries' journals, government reports, settlers' correspondence, the research of anthropologists or other academics, newspaper articles, or fur trade records. These sources can be valuable, though extreme care must be used in drawing implications from them: their creators may have an incomplete understanding of the cultures they observed, as well as potential self-interest or bias.

Nevertheless, all of these strands of oral law, whether ancient or more recently incorporated, can be woven together and reinforced by mnemonic devices or other cultural practices, which also encourage broader participation and normative links. Memory aids which may record legal ideas can include wampum belts, masks, totem poles, medicine bundles, culturally modified trees, birch bark scrolls, petroglyphs, button blankets, land forms, and crests. These mnemonic devices can be supplemented by practices which include such complex customs as pre-hearing preparations, ceremonial repetition, the appointment of witnesses, dances, feasts, songs, poems, the use of testing, and the use and importance of place and geographic space.

The existence of these formalities and processes can help to ensure that certain legal traditions are accredited within a community. It is very rare to see oral tradition standing alone to communicate significant legal obligations; oral tradition is often best given its meaning through the larger cultural experiences that surround such proclamations. Thus, oral tradition often blends the sources of law discussed in this chapter – sacred, natural, deliberative, positivistic, and customary – and keeps Indigenous legal traditions alive and growing.

3 Indigenous Law Examples

The previous chapter introduced Indigenous legal traditions by focusing on their various sources. This categorization attempted to highlight the many reasons Indigenous laws are part of living, contemporary systems. However, there are additional ways to examine Indigenous legal traditions. While the foregoing philosophical and doctrinal delineations may have helped to illuminate the main contours of these traditions, an understanding of how they are positioned within a community or historical context will offer further insights.[1] Therefore, to help increase understanding of Indigenous legal traditions, this chapter will examine them within their Indigenous societal frameworks.

At the same time, there are dangers in focusing on discrete groups when trying to gain an understanding of Indigenous law. Care must be taken not to oversimplify Indigenous societies by presenting each group's laws as completely isolated and self-contained. Law, like culture, is not frozen. Legal traditions are permeable and subject to cross-cutting influences.[2] When making laws, Indigenous peoples often draw upon the best legal ideas from their own culture, and then combine them with others. They compare, contrast, accept, and reject legal standards from many sources, including their own. As we saw in the last chapter, this is an important aspect in making Indigenous law a living system of social order. Some might label the contemporary and comparative nature of Indigenous law as revisionist, and thereby seek to undermine Indigenous governance and law by regarding these developments as inauthentic or potentially even non-Aboriginal. This criticism would be unfortunate and inaccurate. Legal systems are at their healthiest when they are at least somewhat revisionist. Legal traditions must continually be reinterpreted and reapplied in order to remain relevant amidst changing conditions. Law can become unjust and irrelevant if it is not continually reviewed and revised. Indigenous law is no different, and should not be held to unrealistic standards.

It is for these reasons that I have argued that we must jettison stereotypes that imply the ancient legal traditions of Indigenous peoples are static. Such views confine Indigenous peoples to a past-tense legal world where outsiders alternately regard them as being unremittingly savage or romantically existing in a state of continual harmony and peace – and thus not contemplating or requiring law. Furthermore, it is not helpful or true to suggest that Indigenous peoples lose their Indigeneity if they adopt contemporary codes of conduct. Indigenous legal traditions do not cease being Indigenous if they are called upon to deal with matters such as computer technology, stem-cell research, or insider trading in securities law. The authenticity of Indigenous law and governance is not measured by how closely they mirror the perceived past, but by how consistent they are with the current ideas of their communities.[3]

It should also be remembered that all legal traditions are subject to various interpretations. Disagreement is endemic in human affairs. Indigenous peoples are no different, and their societies are likely to contain divergent interpretations of any law that could be examined. In the following examples, I will assume that there are differences of opinion about the matters presented. The complexity of Indigenous laws demands that we see them in their great variety and allow for the existence of significant internal conflicts. Incongruities and differing interpretations should not be taken as a clear sign that the community does not have law. On the contrary, multiple perspectives of a legal tradition could be a signal that the tradition is vibrant and strong. Internal diversity about how law is created, interpreted and enforced can allow those with opposing viewpoints to maintain a relationship within the tradition. As long as there is a way to temporarily resolve inconsistencies for the finite moments when decisions actually require deference, legal systems can live with a great deal of variation. Canada's other legal traditions admit wide disagreements internally and vis-à-vis each other and are still accorded legitimacy and relevance. The dissenting opinions found in case law judgments and the opposing parties formed in legislatures and Parliament illustrate that complete accord is not needed in a functioning legal system. We should give at least the same degree of deference to dissent within

Indigenous legal traditions, and perhaps even more, since these traditions are often less centralized or hierarchical than is the case with the common law or civil law.

Thus, to reiterate, the examples of Indigenous legal traditions in this chapter are intended to develop a further appreciation of how norms, practices, and interpretation coincide to provide authoritative direction within particular societies. At the same time, these examples pay more attention to their historic and cultural roots than was the case in the last chapter. They attempt to develop an understanding of Indigenous law in a more applied context and attempt to show how Indigenous law channels behaviour by regulation, prevention and 'cleaning up social mess.'[4] The traditions that will be examined include the Mi'kmaq, Haudenosaunee, Anishinabek, Cree, Métis, Carrier, Nisga'a, and Inuit.[5] The choices are not in themselves representative of the different categories of Indigenous law, but they do convey a sense of the variety and complexity of Indigenous legal traditions in North America.

A. Mi'kmaq Legal Traditions

The Mi'kmaq people live in what is now called Nova Scotia, eastern New Brunswick, Newfoundland, Prince Edward Island, and southern Gaspé in Quebec. They are known by other Indigenous groups as the People of the Dawn. The Mi'kmaq refer to themselves as *L'nu'k*, which means 'the people.' The title Mi'kmaq derives from their word *nikmak*, or 'my kin-friends,' which illustrates the family-based nature of their associations. In keeping with their kinship connections, members of the Mi'kmaq confederacy, or *Awitkatultik,* see their contemporary territory as being divided into districts or *sakamowati*. While Mi'kmaq people now live in many places throughout Canada, including a significant number within their traditional territories, many continue to regard their relationships to land through their *sakamowati*. These districts exist to acknowledge family rights to certain hunting grounds and fishing waters. The presence of *sakamowati* allows families to remain connected to their territories even if they are living elsewhere in the country.

When decisions are made within each *sakamowati*, they are based on what members have learned from other living beings within their territory. Law is derived from their observations, discussions, and daily routines. Professor Sakej Henderson has expressed this source of their laws in the following terms: 'The ecosystem in which they lived was their classroom; the life forms who shared the land were their teachers.'[6] Building upon the earth's teachings in this manner, the Mi'kmaq people seek to apply natural law to their relationships with others. In order to bring attention to these legal traditions, the leaders of extended families (*saya*) and community spiritual leaders (*kaptins*) are charged with identifying and proclaiming these ecological relationships to guide and sustain order and continuity within their districts.[7] While a certain degree of concentrated authority is important to their legal order, their tradition also aspires to give everyone an opportunity to participate in decision-making (*wikamou*) during certain seasons.[8] To accomplish this objective, the districts are to periodically gather to form a Grand Council, or *Santé Mawíomi*, where they can deliberate and build consensus to enhance their relationships.[9] Grand Councils are designed to be occasions for airing disagreements and developing solutions to help people live together more peaceably. Through these traditions, Mi'kmaq law aims to develop unity by reference to their 'cognitive realm: their language, culture and spirituality,'[10] and to an ecological understanding of their territories.[11]

Professor Sakej Henderson has provided an excellent summary of the Mi'kmaq peoples' legal inheritance. He describes their legal traditions as being based in ecological relationships that find their jurisgenesis in linguistic expressions.[12] He says the Mi'kmaq language was formulated by experiencing and empirically identifying states of being within North Atlantic ecosystems.[13] As such, the language is verb-centred and emphasizes states of being rather than fixed, noun-oriented categorizations of life. This has great significance for the formation of legal obligations because objects are secondary to relationships within their laws. Verbs take precedence over nouns in their laws. Since Mi'kmaq legal thought builds upon this linguistic emphasis, it is shaped by 'ecological considerations mediated through their experiences, knowledge, spiritual understanding or interpretation and relationship to a local ecological order.'[14]

Mi'kmaq legal traditions also enjoy flexibility in their operation, 'where flux was the universal norm and there was no noun-based system of positive law.'[15] When considered as a whole, one can detect within Mi'kmaq legal traditions many of the sources of law described in the last chapter: natural, customary, deliberative, and sacred. Historically, this legal tradition also dealt with issues that would be considered criminal law matters under Canadian law,[16] making distinctions, for example, between murder, manslaughter, and accidental death.[17] Mi'kmaq legal practices constantly change with the times and react to ideas and events within and surrounding their society. The dynamic nature of Mi'kmaq law means that great care should be taken not to freeze the interpretation or application of these laws in an artificial past. Codification in an idealized form could violate the processes the Mi'kmaq have designed to balance the inherent flexibility of their worldview. Since customary and deliberative practices develop solutions based on the experiences and consensual understandings of the people (L'nu'k), it is important that the continued development of Mi'kmaq law not be removed too far from the people in the present day. Mi'kmaq customs must continue to address the realities of Mi'kmaq life to enjoy ongoing relevance. This legal tradition has much to say about individual freedoms, family responsibility, national organization, and trans-national relations,[18] and could be as important to Mi'kmaq living in Halifax as those who reside on reserves at Membertou, Eskasoni, or Eel Ground.

In addition to the Mi'kmaq deriving their laws from nature, deliberation, and custom, many Mi'kmaq legal traditions developed from their views of creation and their explanations about their sacred responsibilities in the world. These views and their implications were described in the following terms by the Royal Commission on Aboriginal Peoples:

> The Mi'kmaq were taught that the spark of life in living things has three parts: a form that decays and disappears after death; a *mntu* or spark that travels after death to the lands of the souls; and the guardian spark or spirits that aid people during their earth walk. While the form is different, all *mntu* and guardian spirits are alike but of different forces. No human being possessed all the forces, nor could human beings control the forces of the stars, sun or moon, wind, water, rocks, plants and animals. Yet they belong to these forces, which are a source of awe and to which entreaties for assistance are often addressed.
>
> Since all objects possess the sparks of life, every life form has to be given respect. Just as a human being has intelligence, so too does a plant, a river or an animal. Therefore, the people were taught that everything they see, touch or are aware of must be respected, and this respect requires a special consciousness that discourages carelessness about things. Thus, when people gather roots or leaves for medicines, they propitiate the soul of each plant by placing a small offering of tobacco at its

base, believing that without the co-operation of the *mntu*, the mere form of the plant cannot work cures.

Mi'kmaq were taught that all form decays, but the *mntu* continues. Just as autumn folds into winter and winter transforms into spring, what was dead returns to life. The tree does not die; it grows up again where it falls. When a plant or animal is killed, its *mntu* goes into the ground with its blood; later it comes back and reincarnates from the ground.

Each person, too, whether male or female, elder or youth, has a unique gift or spark and a place in Mi'kmaq society. Each has a complementary role that enables communities to flourish in solidarity. Like every generation, each person must find his or her gifts, and each person also needs to have the cumulative knowledge and wisdom of previous generations to survive successfully in a changing environment. In this respect, oral accounts such as the creation story served not only to communicate a particular story, but also to give guidance to succeeding generations on the appropriate way to live – how to communicate with other life forms, how to hunt and fish and respect what is taken, and how to take medicines from the earth. Stories that feature visions and dreams help to communicate lessons learned from the past.[19]

The quotation shows the multifaceted relevance of creation for Mi'kmaq legal freedoms and responsibilities. The existence of *mntu* in every being extends legal personality beyond that present in other Canadian legal traditions. Rocks, plants, insects, birds, and animals have a more central role in Mi'kmaq law as a result. The need for respect, demonstrated by an awareness of the natural world's participation in forming Mi'kmaq life, has deep legal implications for these people. It gives higher priority to stories, dreams, and visions than is the case in the common or civil law. This approach more freely accommodates the protection and facilitation of life forces that we do not fully understand or contain. As such, Mi'kmaq law does not shy away from discussions based on experiences that occur outside linear legal argumentation. Of course, there are checks and balances within traditions that do not dismiss judgment on these grounds. Nevertheless, these forms of experience and expression are an important a part of the jurisprudential obligations felt by Mi'kmaq citizens.[20]

At the same time that Mi'kmaq legal tradition can give respect to life's *mntus*, their laws can also embrace ideas based on positivistic processes. For example, the Mi'kmaq often proclaimed their legal relationships through regularized wampum readings, or *lnapskuk*.[21]

Wampum was traditionally made of *quahog* or clam shells that were drilled and threaded into strings or woven into belts.[22] Larger belts could be beaded into a pattern that represented important legal agreements or principles. Different colours on the belts could possess different symbolic meanings and would often relate to deeper normative values.[23] Wampum strings and belts are thus important memory aids to assist people in remembering and reciting their community's laws. As such, their presence validates the authority of persons carrying messages between communities and nations, and can increase the respect people give to a law's declaration.[24] During wampum recitations, information about Mi'kmaq creation, migrations, and relationships with other nations can be recounted and reproduced. The concept of peace, order, and good government within Mi'kmaq society is facilitated by using these legal traditions to interpret the world around them. These 'readings,' which are orally transmitted, can sometimes be accompanied by ceremonies that address other legal issues. Wampum readings also include more recent events to ensure that Mi'kmaq legal traditions remain relevant by speaking to the contemporary community.

Wampum belts and other Indigenous legal records have sometimes been brought before Canadian courts as evidence of Mi'kmaq use and occupation of lands and resources. Unfortunately, this strategy can result in Mi'kmaq law being misunderstood and doubt being cast on its authenticity. When Indigenous legal traditions are measured by historians, the wrong questions are often asked. Law is not simply a matter of history; law uses a normative framework to interpret past events and make contemporary assessments. Historians risk applying inappropriate criteria to Indigenous legal traditions when they read them solely as proof of past events.[25] It is wrong to treat Mi'kmaq law simply as history, just as it would be inappropriate to see the common law only as history in decisions before the Canadian courts. Mi'kmaq history is related to Mi'kmaq law because past events structure contemporary legal options; however, history is not law. Law is more explicitly normative and iterative than history; law develops through time in a more explicitly value-laden context to take account of contemporary circumstances.

Judges who are requested to treat legal traditions (such as wampum belts) as history should be clear about what is being asked of them. They should consider the distinctions between their discipline and that of historians. The historical method and legal analysis are significantly different. In law school, future judges are taught to measure law by its relationship to past cases and to broader policy issues. Lawyers do not evaluate law by measuring how closely it correlates with a historian's explanation of the past. Through time, legal accounts of prior events can diverge from historical accounts. This divergence is necessary to preserve the law's persuasiveness.

The divergence between law and history is also seen in Canadian jurisprudence. During the early decades of the last century, a dispute arose about whether 'persons' in section 24 of the *British North America Act, 1867* included females.[26] This case, known as the Persons Case, developed the distinction between history and law. The historical approach to the issue was to give the word 'persons' the meaning it possessed when the act was passed. This approach was rejected by the Judicial Committee of the Privy Council in favour of one that recognized the law's normative aspects. The Privy Council wrote that while it may be 'legitimate to call history in aid to show what facts existed to bring about a statute, the inferences to be drawn therefrom are extremely slight.'[27] Judges would do well to recall that *history is not law* when they hear about wampum belts and otherwise interpret Indigenous legal traditions. History might be useful to show what facts existed at the time legal traditions like those of the Mi'kmaq developed in the distant past. But major legal inferences should not be drawn solely from these historical facts, because law serves a different purpose.

Canadian jurisprudence has given reasons for the distinction between historical and legal methodologies when interpreting the past. For example, in the Persons Case, the Privy Council wrote that it was 'not right to apply rigidly to Canada of today the decisions or reasons thereof ... to those who had to apply the law in different circumstances, in different centuries, to countries in different stages of development.'[28] The law recognizes that communities and peoples undergo a continuous process of evolution.[29] Great care must be taken not to interpret one community's law by rigid adherence to the customs and traditions of another.[30] Lord Sankey of the Privy Council wrote:

> The British North America Act planted in Canada a living tree capable of growth and expansion within its natural limits. The object of the Act was to grant a Constitution to Canada. Like all written constitutions it has been subject to development through usage and convention.[31]

With this statement, the courts explicitly recognized that formative laws should not be treated as history when drawing inferences about past events. This same insight has significant implications for evaluating Mi'kmaq and other Indigenous legal traditions. Mi'kmaq legal traditions develop through usage and convention. Their present articulation should be judged accordingly; they should not be seen as inauthentic or false because current interpretations are not in accordance with 'facts' at the time they developed.

Historical interpretations should be considered distinctly from legal interpretations, as demonstrated in the Persons Case. The same distinction should be applied when analysing Mi'kmaq or other Indigenous legal traditions. Indigenous people are sometimes judged as being 'in error' when their legal traditions do not corroborate historical facts. No judge or court would appreciate being labelled as 'not credible' because their interpretations of the past are different from those of historians. Yet Indigenous legal officials have often faced similar damaging labels.

Some of the blame can be placed on the framework created for recognizing and affirming Aboriginal rights under section 35(1). Courts are required to evaluate Indigenous traditions as historical relics rather than as contemporary law-making communities. Treating Aboriginal rights as practices that were once upon a time integral to ancient societies does not encourage courts to judge Indigenous peoples' relationship to land in accordance with present Indigenous legal traditions. The case of *R. v. Marshall* from Nova Scotia, testing Aboriginal and treaty rights to log for commercial purposes, is an illustration.[32] At trial, Chief Stephen Augustine presented stories and read wampum related to Mi'kmaq law.[33] The framework of section 35(1) caused his testimony to be judged as though he were presenting pure history as proof of past events.[34] When elements of his testimony did not accord with how the Trial Court found Mi'kmaq law historically developed, Chief Augustine was found to be 'in error.'[35] This unfortunately diminished his credibility within the court and obscured the normative framework of the legal tradition he presented.

In particular, there was a dispute over whether one of the wampum belts he presented was from the 1600s or from a later date. Chief Augustine believed that it came from the 1600s, but an anthropologist was able to persuade the court that it was made much later. The focus on calendar dates required by section 35's focus on the past, rather than on Mi'kmaq jurisprudential norms, misconstrued Chief Augustine's legal knowledge as historical evidence rather than law. As previously noted, the judge was not entirely responsible for this error. The main criticism must lie with the framework of Canada's legal tests related to Indigenous legal traditions.

The inappropriateness of treating Mi'kmaq legal tradition as history rather than law must be addressed. Section 35(1) must be reformulated to allow Indigenous law to become a guiding standard in judging Indigenous claims. If this does not occur, those who practise and proclaim Indigenous law will be discredited when their submissions do not accord with the historical record. The danger created by section 35(1)'s framework is shown in the following portion of the provincial court's decision in *R. v. Marshall*:

59. It is worthy of note that Chief Augustine also testified about a wampum belt at the Vatican Archives. He and others had seen a photograph of the belt in a book. He and others had concluded that the belt was a representation of the linking of the Mi'kmaq Nation with Christianity when Membertou was baptized in the early 1600s. There is no doubt Chief Augustine firmly believed what he said about the belt. His good faith was demonstrated by the months of painstaking work he did to produce a replica of the belt. The replica itself is a beautiful work of art.
60. The crown witness Dr. von Gernet went to the Vatican Archives and studied the belt. He found conclusive evidence it had been made by aboriginals in Quebec as a gift for the Pope more than 200 years after Membertou's baptism. It had nothing to do with Nova Scotia or the Mi'kmaq.
61. When the defence received Dr. von Gernet's report, Mr. Wildsmith first purported to withdraw the portion of Chief Augustine's testimony dealing with the belt and then said the defence would no longer rely on the belt as part of its case. I said that amounted to an acknowledgement that Chief Augustine was wrong about the belt. I said I would consider that error in weighing Chief Augustine's other evidence.
62. Dr. von Gernet testified at length about oral traditions. He said beliefs in themselves must always be respected, but when offered as proof of historical fact, they can't be accepted uncritically. They must be examined for accuracy. He said aboriginal memories are not biologically superior to those of non-aboriginals. He said there were ways of improving the accuracy of oral traditions, such as training and group validation. There was no evidence of those or other methods of improvement being used by Chief Augustine and the Mi'kmaq. He referred to the 'feedback effect' by which ideas generated outside a culture are adopted by the culture. He

pointed out that Mi'kmaq are literate and many have been for generations. He said after exposure to written materials it becomes increasingly
difficult for the individual or the culture to distinguish between ancient
traditions and those more recently arrived from the outside.

63. Chief Augustine knows a great deal about Mi'kmaq culture and
history. He is a man of great dignity. [...] I found him thoroughly truth-
ful, but I was not persuaded by him that the Grand Council or the seven
districts were ancient Mi'kmaq traditions. The written record proves
otherwise.

64. In *R. v. Van der Peet*, [1996] 2 S.C.R. 507 and *Delgamuukw v. British
Columbia*, [1997] 3 S.C.R. 1010, the Supreme Court of Canada said courts
must put oral traditions on the same footing as documentary evidence in
cases involving aboriginals. The court did not say oral tradition was
better than documentary evidence or that the smallest amount of oral tradition was to be accepted over a mountain of documentary evidence.

65. In the present case we have evidence of oral tradition provided by a
single witness. We don't know whether the traditions he relates were
influenced by his own literacy or that of his forebears. We don't know
whether there are other Mi'kmaq tradition bearers or other traditions
about the same topics. On the other hand, we do have a mass of 18th-
century documents, both French and British, containing no evidence of
seven districts or a grand council. The massive written record is far more
convincing than the minimal oral evidence.[36]

It is unfortunate that Chief Augustine's testimony was improperly
presented as 'pure' history, and not law. He should not have been put
on the stand as an historical witness. He should have been seen as a
Mi'kmaq judge who could testify to the normative significance of early
colonial encounters in the Maritimes. By placing him in an improper
context, Chief Augustine's testimony is undermined. This illustrates a
fatal flaw in section 35(1)'s framework. From a Mi'kmaq legal perspective it is simply not the case that the reconstructed belt 'had
nothing to do with Nova Scotia or the Mi'kmaq.' The belt exists as a
present-day legal text and is of great relevance for Nova Scotia and the
Mi'kmaq even if Chief Augustine's history was wrong, and the agreement it signifies was made 200 years later than he believed. By treating Mi'kmaq legal tradition as history, section 35(1)'s framework
caused the judge to draw different inferences than would be the case if
the wampum were viewed as a contemporary legal text and related to
Mi'kmaq constitutionalism. Without this perspective, the written

record is used to crush Mi'kmaq normative judgments about their wampum, districts, and Grand Council. They are simply not to be believed as history, which collaterally casts doubt on their reliability as present-day legal traditions. Chief Augustine is labelled in a derogatory fashion as the 'self-proclaimed interpreter of wampum belts.'[37]

Another unfortunate aspect of the judgment, caused by casting Chief Augustine's testimony solely in an historic light, is that it seems to diminish traditions if they take account of and speak to other traditions. Law is not static in this way. Canadian judges, lawyers, and legal academics would bristle at the suggestion that their legal opinions could not be influenced by their study of factors outside their home culture. Yet Chief Augustine's testimony seemed to have less weight because it was influenced by his 'own literacy' and was subject to the 'feedback effect' of ideas generated outside his culture. Canadian legal frameworks appear to discount Indigenous traditions if they intermingle with those that arrived later. The danger is that this conclusion will be imported into the legal field to discount Indigenous traditions as law if they are influenced by other Canadian legal traditions.

It would be a grave mistake to judge Indigenous legal traditions as inauthentic or inaccurate if they are not historically 'pure.' Law is a deliberative cultural phenomenon that engages the past in the light of subsequent normative interpretations. Indigenous legal traditions should not be measured primarily as expressions of past historical events, but rather as contemporary normative frameworks for peace and order. If Chief Augustine had been considered to be interpreting Mi'kmaq legal tradition, rather than historical evidence, different inferences and a very different methodology would be in play. We would be more interested in why creation stories, wampum, councils, and districts are important in contemporary Mi'kmaq interpretations of their relationships. If we examined Chief Augustine's testimony from this perspective, we might see that peace, order, and continuity is achieved in Mi'kmaq law by highlighting their more recent interpretive opinion. Mi'kmaq legal order is maintained by its ongoing performative re-enactment and reinterpretation. Just as precedent is measured by the most recent cases, rather than by their first formulation, so Mi'kmaq legal tradition must be considered in its most recent light. It is freely accepted that law as a living, interpretive engagement between the past and the present is a necessary part of other legal traditions. The same acceptance should not be denied to Indigenous legal traditions.

Some common law illustrations might help to demonstrate the necessity of judging Indigenous law as distinct from history.[38] Judges and legal commentators have sometimes made statements that are historically inaccurate but are, nonetheless, legally valid. For example, in the case of *Woolmington v. D.P.P.*, Lord Sankey, this time speaking for the English House of Lords, proclaimed that an accused is presumed innocent until proven guilty.[39] This remark was central to the resolution of the issue in the case. In arriving at this conclusion, he wrote: 'Throughout the web of the English Criminal Law one golden thread is always to be seen, that is the duty of the prosecution to prove the prisoner's guilt.'[40] In fact, Lord Sankey is historically inaccurate, even if his conclusion is legally correct. It has not *always* been the case that people were presumed innocent. Bruce Smith has concluded: 'Many English criminal defendants in the late eighteenth and early nineteenth centuries did *not* benefit from a presumption of innocence but, rather, struggled against a statutory presumption of *guilt*.'[41] One can imagine the indignities Lord Sankey might suffer if he were asked to give testimony about the historical presumption of innocence in English criminal law in court and his opinion was valued only for the proof of past treatment of prisoners. He would be in the same position as Chief Augustine, and might not fare too well under cross-examination. Lord Sankey was not acting as a historian when he expressed his opinion about presumptions of innocence in England; he was drawing legal inferences to arrive at his conclusion.

Similarly, William Blackstone's historically inaccurate comments about juries show the need to distinguish between law and history. Prior to 1215, an individual accused of a criminal offence in England would have faced a trial by ordeal.[42] Even after 1215, and well into the eighteenth century, juries were far from the pristine institutions that Blackstone suggests. Judges exerted substantial control over jury decision-making.[43] Despite the historical fact that, in England, juries were not always present, or that their availability in criminal trials was limited until recently, Blackstone wrote that 'the trial by jury ever has been, and I trust ever will be, looked upon as the glory of the English law.'[44] In his famous *Commentaries*, Blackstone cannot be regarded as making an accurate historical claim.[45] Instead, he finds himself in the same company as Chief Augustine sharing his interpretation of Mi'kmaq legal traditions in the *Marshall* case. It is more helpful to consider both Blackstone and Augustine not as historical commentators but as legal ones who are drawing inferences about the past for normative purposes.

This distinction between law and history is important to our consideration of other Indigenous traditions reviewed in this chapter. For legal purposes, their relevance is determined by the contemporary normative congruity between the tradition and the community. If these traditions are tested by historical methods alone, not only will readers miss their relevance for Indigenous peace and order, they will also find themselves mired in an inquiry that may not be capable of resolution. Who is to say that belts such as the one Chief Augustine replicated did not exist among the Mi'kmaq prior to a possible papal regifting to Quebec Indians at a much later period? They may have existed, but we simply may not have found the originals. Chief Augustine's copy could have come from a later representation of an earlier event. More generally, approaching Indigenous legal traditions from a historical perspective will likely never produce agreement on the 'facts' of virgin-born peacemakers, stone canoes, living rocks, talking plants, gossiping animals, transforming humans, and supernatural beings from other worlds. While these characters can be regarded as factual by those who relate them, they can also be viewed as constitutional metaphors, like living trees, that guide practitioner's interpretations of their laws. Indigenous legal traditions must be understood in the context of their own interpretive rules, just as common law and civil law are understood in accordance with their own distinctive cultural traditions.

B. Haudenosaunee Legal Traditions

Haudenosaunee people also have long-standing and powerful legal traditions. The Haudenosaunee are perhaps more widely known as the Iroquois Confederacy, who historically lived in fortified villages in lands now called southern Ontario, southern Quebec, New York, and Wisconsin.[46] Law lies close to the heart of the Haudenosaunee's genesis as a unified people. This is because the Iroquois of the lower Great Lakes and St Lawrence valley learned about their Great Law as they created a confederacy to forge and consolidate peace between themselves and their neighbours. The confederacy was first made up of five nations: the Mohawk, Oneida, Onondaga, Cayuga, and Seneca. They were joined by the Tuscaroras in 1722 when they migrated from Carolina. The confederacy is still organized in this manner and resides in its historical territories. Anyone who has followed the controversies at Oka or Caledonia knows the confederacy has great power in the lives of its members. Although disrupted by U.S. and Canadian attempts to eradicate this tradition,[47] the Great Law of Peace continues to be the most important legal tradition guiding these communities today.

Haudenosaunee legal traditions are complex and sophisticated. As noted, the Great Law of Peace, *Kaianerekowa,* bound the Iroquois nations together into a confederacy of considerable strength.[48] Its narrative and principles brought peace, power, and righteousness to generations of Iroquois people, and continues to be important to Haudenosaunee people today.[49] Its influence has generated debate beyond its longhouses,[50] and has had a profound impact on neighbouring Indigenous peoples.[51] The *Kaianerekowa* is a complex and significant legal code and stands as a testament to the power of human creativity and accomplishment. The Great Law of Peace is one of North America's most recognizable Indigenous constitutions.[52]

There are numerous written descriptions of the Great Law but its primary authority continues to reside in its spoken version.[53] The Great Law begins with the Peacemaker who was born into the Wendat Nation of a virgin mother.[54] His early life was filled with trials until his grandmother was told in a dream that the Creator had a great work for him to perform. When he was old enough, the Peacemaker travelled in a white stone canoe away from his people who rejected his message. He landed in the Mohawk Nation amidst war, chaos, destruction and cannibalism and delivered the Creator's message that war must cease. The Peacemaker was rejected by the Mohawks for this message and he was taken in by Jikonsahseh, a strong woman who changed her life when she accepted his message. As a result of her willingness to hear the Peacemaker's words, Jikonsahseh became the Mother of Nations. The Peacemaker explained to her the principles of peace, power, and righteousness and the concept of the longhouse as a metaphor for the Great Law. In the confederacy that the Peacemaker proposed, women were given the role of clan mothers.

The Great Peace narration continued with the Peacemaker journeying onward, where he eventually met Hayehwatha, after spying on him from the roof of his house and observing his cannibalism. When Hayehwatha spotted the Peacemaker's reflection from the roof in his pot of soup, Hayehwatha was transformed by the experience. The Peacemaker then taught him the evils of cannibalism and taught him to eat deer meat. From this act, deer antlers became an important symbol of authority within the confederacy.

With Hayehwatha, the Peacemaker journeyed back to meet with the Mohawks and once again gave his message. His powers were recognized when he emerged unscathed from a fall into a deep ravine from a tall tree that was chopped down from underneath him. The Mohawk chiefs accepted his message of peace from that point onward. After their acceptance he sought out the Onondaga, but was prevented from meeting them by Tododaho, an evil trickster. Hayehwatha also faced trials with the Onondaga when Osinoh, a witch, transformed himself into an owl and murdered his own daughters. These challenges caused Hayehwatha to battle with depression that he partially overcame with wampum strings.[55] He took these strings to the Mohawks who then received him as an honoured chief. At this meeting, Hayehwatha taught the Mohawks proper protocols for creating peaceful relations, such as announcing the arrival of a peaceful visitor by building a signal fire at the village edge, and making wampum strings to be used to deliver messages. Next, the Peacemaker taught Hayehwatha even deeper principles about wampum when he alleviated his depression by using eight of Hiawatha's thirteen wampum strings. Since this action freed Hayehwatha's mind from pain, the Peacemaker determined that wampum would be used to carry the Creator's message to their meetings and into their relationships with others. In this way, these messages are taught as part of the Great Law.

At this point in the chronicle, the Peacemaker once again went searching for Tododaho, the twisted, evil man of the Onondaga. To accomplish his purpose, the Peacemaker sent him transformed animals and messages to bear his words, but each time the Peacemaker's efforts were rebuffed. While he continued to strive to meet with Tododaho, he carried his message to other nations, with the result that the Cayuga, Oneida, and Seneca eventually joined the confederacy. When these other nations had joined with him, the Peacemaker then led them to Tododaho in an attempt to soothe his wrath. The Onondaga finally received this delegation, joined the confederacy, and accepted the *Kaianerekowa*. As a result of these efforts, Tododaho himself finally accepted the message of peace. At the same time, he received a promise that his position in the confederacy would be central and that the Onondaga would be the firekeepers at the centre of the league.

Out of that meeting and agreement, the Peacemaker and Hayehwatha created chieftainships to protect the peace. The chiefs were given instructions about how to live their lives and run their councils through roll calls and protocols. The clans' central role in the confederacy structure was described and future warnings were given. The chiefs were to be adorned with deer antlers as a sign of their authority. The path to communication was then cleared. Wing fans and poles were used to sweep dirt and keep unwanted beings away from the council fire. Laws were taught in greater depth through the development of analogies and metaphors. They deal with many things: the five fireplaces of the longhouse, wampum, the tree of peace, the circle of chiefs, the eagle, the white roots of peace, the burying of weapons under the tree, a feast of beaver tail, the binding of five arrows, and the council fire's smoke which pierces the sky. It is not my purpose to relate the meaning of these metaphors in this brief account but to note that each of these symbols communicates important aspects of Haudenosaunee law. Like most legal traditions, they are subject to wide interpretation and reinterpretation because their framing encourages listeners to broadly apply their messages. The Great Law also communicates laws relating to adoption, emigration, individual rights, and international relations. When a chief dies, a condolence ceremony is prescribed to help maintain the stability and health of the confederacy's other chiefs. Once these principles were taught, the Peacemaker departed, leaving a promise of his return and a warning not to use his name except in special cases.

The Great Law is built on the agreement and creativity of many Haudenosaunee people. Future generations are considered in deliberations under the law, and their anticipated needs were to be a significant part of any resolution. Unanimity is necessary for council decisions to be adopted.[56] Each of the nations of the confederacy retains their independence and individuality within a centralized decision-making structure.[57] A council of fifty chief administrators is responsible for transacting confederacy business, repeatedly passing ideas across a fire to explore and analyse them before actions are taken. Any Iroquois Nation of the Haudenosaunee can request a meeting of the council by sending runners with wampum belts to indicate the time, place, and agenda of the meeting.[58] The Onondaga Nation, as the fire-keepers of the council, are entitled to decide whether an issue will come before the confederacy for full debate.

The Haudenosaunee developed intricate diplomatic traditions in their relations with other nations.[59] Agreements flowing from these activities continue to resonate with many Indigenous people today. One of the most prominent accords relates to the *Gus Wen Tah*, or Two

Row Wampum. The fundamental principles of the Two Row Wampum became the basis for the agreements made between the Haudenosaunee and the Dutch in 1645, with the French in 1701, and with the English in 1763–4. The belt consists of two rows of purple wampum beads on a white background. Three rows of white beads symbolizing peace, friendship, and respect separate the two purple rows. The two purple rows symbolize two paths or two vessels travelling down the same river. One row symbolizes the Haudenosaunee people with their law and customs, while the other row symbolizes European laws and customs. As nations move together side by side on the river of life, they are to avoid overlapping or interfering with one another. These legal precepts are said to be embedded in subsequent agreements. Another symbol related to the *Gus Wen Tah* that communicates Haudenosaunee independence is the Silver Covenant Chain. It is to be pure, strong, and untarnished, and bind nations together without causing them to lose their individual characteristics or their independence. Those holding the Covenant Chain are responsible for keeping their relationships bright and preventing them from breaking. Haudenosaunee law seems to maintain an independence from other legal traditions that prevents its assimilation or integration.[60]

As a result of this stance towards other nations, the Haudenosaunee are the least likely of any Indigenous group to support or embrace the application of their laws as part of the Canadian legal system.[61] However, many Haudenosaunee would welcome seeing their legal traditions given greater recognition. The Haudenosaunee generally see themselves as more independent in an international sense than many other First Nations. They tend to regard themselves as allies of Canada, rather than citizens of the Canadian nation state.[62] They do not generally consider band councils elected under the *Indian Act* or other Canadian-derived laws as authoritative within their communities.[63] These views are rooted deeply in their legal history and resettlement along the Grand River and north shore of Lake Ontario after the American War of Independence.[64] The Haudenosaunee who live south of the Great Lakes have similar views about their political detachment and separateness. Many do not think of themselves as United States citizens because of their allegiance to the confederacy and the Great Law of Peace.[65] As a result, this book's conclusions about the nature of Canadian multi-juridicalism will likely be rejected by many people of the longhouse. They would not want to see their legal traditions as part of Canada's Constitution, unless they consented to such an arrangement through a treaty with their confederacy, which is unlikely in the present circumstances. At the same time, many Haudenosaunee would likely accept renewal of the *Gus Wen Tah* and the Silver Covenant Chain, both of which symbolize their ancient treaty relationship with the Crown and affirm their decision-making powers and distinctiveness.[66] Many would be happy to see their legal traditions recognized by Great Britain (an earlier Covenant Chain treaty partner) and affirmed by Canada. Thus, while the Haudenosaunee might invite others into a political and legal alliance through their 'great white roots of peace,'[67] they are less likely to accept invitations to participate in the Canadian federation because of their strongly felt independence. Despite these sentiments, it is important to recognize the effect that their legal traditions have on other Canadians. Haudenosaunee law has a continuing and significant influence on how Canadians organize their affairs.

C. Anishinabek Legal Traditions

The Anishinabek are Algonkian-speaking and more recently English-speaking people who live around the upper Great Lakes and on the prairies to the north-east of the lakes.[68] Historically, the Anishinabek lived in communities as clans organized in a loose confederacy, which more recently was called the Council of the Three Fires.[69] They collectively refer to themselves as the Anishinabek, meaning 'people' or 'good people.' Others have labelled them as the Odawa,[70] Potawatomi,[71] and Ojibway or Saulteaux.[72] Many still live in mixed 'Three Fires' communities in their ancient homelands.[73]

The Anishinabek often manage their resources through kinship allocations,[74] agreed upon through discussion and consensus.[75] In some locations, these kin-based allocations have been confirmed, overlain or displaced by band council-sanctioned certificates of possessions under the *Indian Act*. The Odawa, Potawatomi, and Ojibway have well-developed totemic or clan systems that can assist in regulating behaviour and resolving disputes. Each family is classified by a *dodem* (totem), designated by taking a symbol from nature, which descends along the male line, or along the female line if the father is not an Ojibway.[76] Persons who are not Anishinabek by birth may be granted citizenship and legal standing to participate in community life through an adopted clan. Marriage is usually not permitted in the same *dodem*.[77] This system is the early foundation of Anishinabek law and facilitates the allocation of resources,[78] although this has been influenced recently by the *Indian Act*. A person's *dodem* creates reciprocal obligations among fellow clan members, thereby establishing a horizontal relationship with different communities and creating allegiances that extend beyond the confines of the home village. For example, persons of one *dodem*, travelling throughout their Three Fires territory, can expect social and material obligations with clan members situated hundreds of miles away.

Totemic obligations have helped the Anishinabek allocate resources to their hunting grounds, fishing grounds,[79] village sites,[80] and harvesting/gathering sites.[81] A conservation ethic is apparent in resource allocations under Anishinabek practitioners using this system.[82] Historically, this system of resource use combined common stewardship with exclusive rights:

> Among the Ottawas and Chippewas, the band – a group of extended families identified with a specific locale – was the centre of the allocation system ... [The band] owned the common goods on which their members subsisted [...] they owned the right to harvest wild animals, fruits of the land and fish. The band apportioned this general right among its members by assigning to families and groups of families 'territory' in which they harvested common goods. The right to take the scarcest and most crucial goods – animals for winter hunting – was assigned to small groups as an exclusive right to harvest game within a specified territory. Rights to more abundant goods, maple sugar and fish for example, were assigned to larger groups on a less exclusive basis ... Family hunting territories grew out of scarcity as a way to increase efficiency and decrease competition for food.[83]

These allocation measures are meant to help reduce conflict and to ensure there is a relatively equal supply of food for all members of the community. The practices are best facilitated by the use of conservation procedures that leave hunting areas 'fallow' from year to year. Where this tradition is continued, some areas are hunted only every third year, while other areas are hunted every second year.[84] Other conservation practices involve leaving a certain number of animals in a region to repopulate the land.[85] These historical precedents have current relevance for the Anishinabek. I have seen them followed by my uncles and other close kin.

The Anishinabek people have a number of legal principles that guide their relationship with other living beings in a conservationist mode. For example, humans and others have rights relative to the earth, and they also have duties. Duties or obligations are central to relationships under Anishinabek law. This is demonstrated in formalized patterns of speech. For example, when Anishinabek people historically met, they would first ask one another: '*Weanaesh k'dodem?*' ('What is your totem?').[86] Once clan and family were determined, people would be asked: '*Ahniish aen-anookeeyin?*' ('What do you do for a living?'). Both of these questions are related to a person's responsibility within the community. A person's *dodem* indicates more than their lineage: obligations are attached to their clan affiliations. Like a *dodem*, a person's *anookeewin* also connotes ideas of duty and right (*daebinaewiziwin*). Anishinabek peoples have obligations (*daebizitawaugaewin*) to their families and community: to support them, to help them prosper, and to exercise their rights to live and work.[87] In an Anishinabek legal context, rights and responsibilities are intertwined.[88] Some common law theorists recognize the same point in their system. [89] W.N. Hohfeld observed: '[A] duty is the invariable correlative of that legal relation which is most properly called a right or claim.'[90] An 1894 legal citation reads: 'A duty or a legal obligation is that which one ought or ought not to do. "Duty" and "right" are correlative terms. When a right is invaded, a duty is violated.'[91] This is the case within Anishinabek law. Wherever a potential right exists, a correlative obligation can usually be found, based on individual's relationship with the other orders of the world.

The Anishinabek have strong legal traditions that convey their duties relative to the world. These are stewardship-like concepts (*bimeekumaugaewin*) and apply to their use of land, plants, and others. Principles of acknowledgment, accomplishment, accountability, and approbation are embedded in the Anishinabek creation epic and associated stories. Ojibway legal traditions concerning *bimeekumaugaewin* speak of how the world was created and how beings came to live on the earth.[92] They tell of how they depended on the earth, plants, and animals for their sustenance and survival once they arrived.[93] The Ojibway's acknowledgment (*gaamiinigooyang*) of a Creator and an appreciation of their reliance on their relationship to the world comprise the first principle of *bimeekumaugaewin* within Ojibway society.[94] As these traditions progress, the second principle of *bimeekumaugaewin* emerges: how to accomplish (*gikinoo'amaadiwin*) the Creator's vision in setting life in motion.[95] The stories convey the manner in which plants, animals, and humans should relate to and respect one another.[96] They contain important teachings about the preparation necessary for living a good life. They talk of principles that must be followed so that all the orders of creation can live together in peace and friendship. The tradition goes on to explore the third principle of *bimeekumaugaewin*: accountability (*gwayakochigewin*). As with the pipe, ceremonies are often performed in conjunction with these stories to communicate to the Creator, and to acknowledge before others how one's duties and responsibilities have been performed.[97] Dancing, feasting, and singing sometimes accompany these rituals as a way to ratify legal relationships. Finally, the traditions talk about the consequences of living in accordance with, or contrary to, these principles.[98] Stories about Mandamin,[99] Gowkopshee,[100] Animoosh,[101] Pauguk,[102] Pitchee,[103] Nanabush,[104] and a hundred other characters communicate the notion that every being will face the consequences of his or her actions.[105] The idea of approbation received for proper performance of duty, or disapprobation (*tubuhumahgawin*) flowing from failure to fulfil a responsibility, complete the Ojibway circle of *bimeekumaugaewin*. These are the enforcement mechanisms of Anishinabek law.

An interesting Anishinabek story teaches the principle of *bimeekumaugaewin* in the context of approbation. As the Ojibway creation epic spoken of earlier comes to an end, a character named Odaemin is introduced into the narrative.[106] After the first woman returned to her own realm, the world was plagued by disease, and Odaemin was among the many who died from this affliction. As he left this world, he travelled four days along the path of souls to the land of the dead. He reached a great gorge that separated the two spheres, pleaded for his people, and was shown the way to bridge the gap between the world of the living and the dead. With great sacrifice, he placed a fallen tree across the chasm that divided the two worlds. His deed is said to be of benefit to all Anishinabek peoples because it allows them to proceed on further journeys once they leave this life.

In recognition and appreciation of his selfless acts, Odaemin was restored to life. He was then given a further responsibility to teach people what they must do to live a good life and to find safe passage to the next world. He was also told that a great teacher would come to provide further information that would build on his message. Odaemin is honoured for his acts by identifying his life with that of the wild strawberry. These small red berries are in the shape of a heart and are found in abundance in rocky places surrounding the Great Lakes.

They are called Odaemin (heart berry) as a symbol of *approbation* for his accomplishments.[107] Every time a person sees this fruit, the name is intended to help them remember Odaemin's acts and to remind them of their own preparation for their future journey to the land of the dead. Anishinabek people often encode legal principles on the land by identifying some living thing with a particular right or responsibility. In this way, they teach important principles of approbation that could have application for *bimeekumaugaewin* today. Like Odaemin, if people live by principles that respect and facilitate stewardship, such as loyalty, patience, and bravery, they should receive the approbation of their community. In Anishinabek law, legal remedies are not usually punitive. However, examples can be found in which drastic action had to be taken against individuals to preserve community safety.

A case from the French River in Ontario where a man was put to death using Anishinabek law illustrates this approach. The individual was known as Mayamaking; the case was recorded by William Jarvis, Superintendent of Indian Affairs in 1838. The circumstances unfolded as follows:

> He came among us at the very beginning of last winter, having in most severe weather walked six days, without either kindling a fire, or eating any food.
>
> During the most part of this winter he was quiet enough, but as the sugar season approached got noisy and restless. He went off to a lodge, and there remained ten days, frequently eating a whole deer at two meals. After that he went to another [lodge] WHEN a great change was visible in his person. His form seemed to have dilated and his face was the color of death. At this lodge he first exhibited the most decided professions of madness; and we all considered that he had become a Windigo (giant). He did not sleep but kept on walking round the lodge saying 'I shall have a fine feast.' Soon this (caused) plenty of fears in this lodge, among both the old and growing. He then tore open the veins at his wrist with his teeth, and drank his blood. The next night was the same, he went out from the lodge and without an axe broke off many saplings about 9 inches in circumference. [He] never slept but worked all that night, and in the morning brought in the poles he had broken off, and at two TRIPS filled a large sugar camp. He continued to drink his blood. The Indians then all became alarmed and we all started off to join our friends. The snow was deep and soft and we sank deeply into it with our snow shoes, but he without shoes or stockings barely left the indent of his toes on the

surface. He was stark naked, tearing all his clothes given to him off as fast as they were put on. He still continued drinking blood and refused all food eating nothing but ice and snow. We then formed a council to determine how to act as we feared he would eat our children.

It was unanimously agreed that he must die. His most intimate friend undertook to shoot him not wishing any other hand to do it.

After his death we burned the body, and all was consumed but the chest which we examined and found to contain an immense lump of ice which completely filled the cavity.

The LAD, who carried into effect the determination of the council, has given himself to the father of him who is no more: to hunt for him, plant and fill all the duties of a son. We also have all made the old man presents and he is now perfectly satisfied.

This deed was not done under the influence of whiskey. There was none there, it was the deliberate act of this tribe in council.[108]

This real life historical case is an interesting example of Anishinabek law. The community dealt with the issue in accordance with their own legal traditions. The community had no other resources for their protection but themselves, their extended family and friends. They used their law to deal with a pressing issue. The onset of their problems with the man was slow and gradual and developed over most of the winter. They tried to help him. His health and mental state worsened as time went by to the point that he began uttering threats. The group did not take action right away but waited for two or three weeks, despite the threat to the community and the harm the man was causing to himself. When it became clear that he was not getting any better and that his threats were becoming a matter of life and death, they went to council together rather than take action individually. This is an important Anishinabek legal principle. Their method of making judgments was a collective, not an individualized one. They relied upon one another's viewpoints. They were deliberative. They clearly felt that this method of deciding was very important because they travelled through heavy snow to meet together.

When the group finally deliberated, the legal principles that led to the man's death were noteworthy. The matter was not about retribution or anger, but rather defence and compassion (another legal principle related to intent): the man's closest friend was charged with the duty of carrying out the task. The action also had restorative aspects. The father received gifts from the community, and the man who killed the son stepped into his role, also performing restitution. Even the man who lost his son seemed to be satisfied with the council's decision. This example shows how Anishinabek law can be very different from non-Indigenous law. Imagine what our legal systems would be like if judges or lawyers had to take the place of those they prosecute or send to jail.

It is important to focus on the process and principles that guided the actions, rather than on the specific outcome. Some might read this case as an example of ad hoc, 'uncivilized' practices. But a vast literature shows this pattern of dealing over long periods of time, and in different geographic regions where the Anishinabek lived. Furthermore, psychological illness (from which the man was probably suffering) would now be handled very differently. The Anishinabek, like other peoples around the world, have developed a more refined understanding of mental disorders. They would *not* kill the man. However, the underlying principles in this account remain, even if the process does not lead to the same result. Even today people can still:

1 wait, observe and collect information,
2 consult with their friends and neighbours when it is apparent something is wrong,
3 help the person who is threatening or causing imminent harm,
4 if the person does not respond to help and becomes an imminent threat to individuals or the community, he or she can be removed so that he or she does not harm others (though, to re-emphasize, the act does not involve what the common law has labelled capital punishment),
5 help those who rely on that person by restoring what might be taken from them by the treatment,
6 invite both the community and the individual to participate in the restoration.

These legal principles provide the important elements of the case, and they show what can be learned from looking at the past. Anishinabek peoples will likely find familiarity with many of these approaches in their contemporary lives. As the Supreme Court of Canada wrote in the *Rodriguez* case in 1993, when it comes to determining principles of fundamental justice, '[t]he way to resolve these problems is not to avoid historical analysis, but to make sure that one is looking not just at the existence of the practice itself ... but the rationale behind that practice and the principles that underlie it.'[109] For the Anishinabek, *windigos* come in different forms, even today. There are other harmful forms of cannibalistic consumption that destroy lands and people. The principles that underlie the practice in the *Mayakiming* case are important for dealing with these problems.

D. Cree Legal Traditions

The Cree are a people of the boreal forest and prairie. Their homeland stretches from James Bay to the Rocky Mountains; the diverse ecologies of this terrain influence their laws.[110] The Cree are anthropologically divided into two groups known as the Plains Cree and the Woodland or Swampy Cree. Like the Anishinabek and the Mi'kmaq, the Cree are Algonkian-speaking and now English-speaking peoples, with some French speakers in Quebec and Manitoba. The Cree language encodes many Cree legal principles and is a key to understanding their legal perspectives.[111] Those who keep the law are known as *Onisinweuk*. Cree law contains many fundamental principles expressed by the words *wahkohtowin, miyo-wicehtowin, pastahowin, ohcinewin, kwayaskitotamowin*.[112] While these terms are not exclusive as expressions of Cree law, nor placed in any priority, understanding them provides a glimpse into Cree traditions.

Wahkohtowin is viewed as the overarching law governing all relations.[113] This law is said to flow from the Creator who placed all life on earth. Humans are a part of this order and are organized into families. Since humans exist within the overarching natural law, they are counselled to observe other living things for guidance in practising this law. A body of stories describes what people have learned from observing the natural world; the stories are used to facilitate order in Cree law.[114] The sun, moon, winds, clouds, rocks, fish, insects, and animals all provide illustrations of *wahkohtowin*, which the Cree interpret into law. *Wahkohtowin* has implications for individuals, families, governments, and nations. For example, in the family law context, *wahkohtowin* is said to require different levels of conduct: parents are to nurture and care for their child with loyalty and fidelity; brothers and sisters are to live close but separately in an atmosphere of non-interference; cousins and other relatives are to be treated respectfully in a non-coercive manner.[115] Within larger governmental relationships, unrelated people are to apply *wahkohtowin* in accordance with the ideas found in *miyo-wicehtowin, pastahowin, ohcinewin*, and *kwayaskitotamowin*.

Miyo-wicehtowin is said to have originated in the laws and relationships that Cree people have with their Creator.[116] 'It asks, directs, admonishes or requires Cree peoples as individuals and as a nation to conduct themselves in a manner such that they create positive good relations in all relationships.'[117] 'The root of *wicehtowin* is *wiceht*, which means to come alongside or to support.'[118] Like most human societies that have struggled to live by their highest values, the Cree have not always managed to sustain the harmony they desired. There have been periods of conflict. Nevertheless, *miyo-wicehtowin* is an important legal principle because it speaks to maintaining peace between people of different places and perspectives. The maintenance of mutual good relationships, through positive support and assistance (*miyo-wicehtowin*) is often represented by the circle in Cree law.[119] Circles are considered sacred and represent the bringing together of people.[120] They are meant to remind people of Mother Earth and their journey through life: from the earth, to infant, to child, through adulthood to old age and back to the earth. Cree legal traditions can be conducted in circles, such as talking circles, healing circles, and reconciliation circles.

Consequences for failing to abide by Cree law are described as *pastahowin* and *ohcinewin*.[121] *Pastahowin* is used to describe something that goes against natural law. If such an offence occurs, negative consequences will follow, making the concept of *ohcinewin* relevant. *Ohcinewin* is part of the concept of *pastahowin* and means to suffer in retribution for an action against creation. *Pastahowin* and *ohcinewin* can apply to any circumstance in which the law is not followed, either through action or omission. Cree law has many retributive aspects, such as '*meskotsehowin* (redress), *kakweskasowehk* (reproval), *apehowin* (revenge), *naskwawin* (reprisal), *pasastehokowisowin* (retributive justice), *naskwastamasowin apo apehowin* (vengeance), *pasihiwewin* (vindication), *atameyimew* (blame), *sihkiskakewin* (obligation), *masinahikepayowin* (indebtedness), and *tipuhikewin* (recompense).'[122]

Examples of *pastahowin* and *ohcinewin* can be found in Cree-animal relationships. Animals are regarded as persons in their own right; the relationship between the Cree and animal-persons is governed by the same legal considerations that govern human relationships.[123] For the Cree, 'animals are spoken of as possessing their own *itatisiwin* "nature": it is *itatisiwak* that caribou migrate, that beavers build lodges, and so forth. In the shaking lodge and in dreams, animals share human *itatisiwin*: They come to be like humans.'[124] If animals are not treated appropriately, *pastahowin* and *ohcinewin* can result: something bad will happen. Many stories interpret the law relating to animals in these terms.[125]

A contemporary application of Cree linguistic concepts in Canadian law is found in Saskatchewan's Provincial Court. The Cree Court creates an important space for Cree legal traditions to find expression. This initiative might be considered in light of the idea of *Kwayaskitotamowin*: doing things in a right way, treating creation in a good way, a just or legal dealing. In 2001, Cree-speaking Judge Gerald Morin was appointed to the bench and called to preside over a Cree Court in northern Saskatchewan. A majority of the people who appear before the court are Cree. All proceedings of the court are conducted in the Cree language and translators are provided to non-Cree speakers. Canadian law continues to apply in every respect; people receive due process, rights, and substantive freedoms in conformity with the *Canadian Charter of Rights and Freedoms*. At the same time, while Canadian law forms the basis of the court's jurisdiction, its focus can be different from conventional Provincial Court proceedings. When proceedings are conducted in Cree, the dynamics of the legal process are different. Linguistic relationships are possible that are not easily comprehended in English. Concepts like *wahkohtowin*, *pastahowin*, and *ohcinewin* come naturally to life when Cree people participate in their own language. Restorative concepts seem to play a large role in the Cree Court.

But while the Cree Court is an important initiative, it does *not* represent anything close to a fully functioning Cree legal system. The initiative could be extended throughout Cree territory, and among other willing Indigenous-language groups. But it only faintly affirms Cree legal traditions. The substance and procedures of Canadian law continue to contain many cultural incongruities that are considered incompatible with Cree legal traditions. Despite the Cree Court's great success, more work lies ahead to appropriately recognize and affirm the Cree legal system on its own terms.

E. Métis Legal Traditions

The Métis peoples in Canada have unique origins. Their cultures grew out of the interactions between First Nation and European peoples in northern North America. Métis people formed communities throughout Canada, including present-day Labrador, Atlantic Canada, Ontario, Manitoba, Saskatchewan, Alberta, British Columbia, and the North. Children of First Nations and European parents developed distinctive languages, artistic expressions, political identities, and legal traditions.[126]

For example, in 1840, the Métis of the prairies developed buffalo hunting laws to organize their economic and social activities. The buffalo hunt involved hundreds of men, women, and children, together with their Red River carts, horses, and tools for processing and preserving the meat and hides.[127] The complex activity was ordered through laws that identified appropriate behaviour during a potentially difficult and dangerous pursuit. The captain of the hunt could impose penalties if these laws were broken. A codified portion of these laws contained the following provisions:

a. No buffalo to be run on the Sabbath-Day.
b. No party to fork off, lag behind, or go before, without permission.
c. No person or party to run buffalo before the general order.
d. Every captain with his men, in turn, to patrol the camp, and keep guard.
e. For the first trespass against these laws, the offender to have his saddle and bridle cut up.
f. For the second offence, the coat to be taken off the offender's back, and be cut up.
g. For the third offence, the offender to be flogged.
h. Any person convicted of theft, even to the value of a sinew, to be brought to the middle of the camp, and the crier to call out his or her name three times, adding the word 'Thief,' at each time.[128]

The law of the hunt as expressed in these principles was important in asserting Métis control over one of their main socio-economic activities. But it is also important to note that this set of laws was not a complete code for the hunt. There were, in addition, significant customary legal principles involving the respectful killing and use of animals. Métis law also extended to trade, family obligations, political organization, and land use.[129]

Métis legal traditions were evident in Canada's first encounters with the Métis people after Confederation. Their existence and organization in the west prior to Confederation was pivotal to the economic development and expansion of the east. Without the order they created, the fur trade would have floundered, and political and economic development on the St Lawrence River and eastern Great Lakes would have been severely delayed or restricted.[130] The Métis Nation was also crucial in ushering western and northern Canada into Confederation and in increasing the wealth of the Canadian nation by opening up the prairies to agriculture and settlement. These developments could not have occurred without Métis intercession and legal presence.[131]

Métis legal traditions were most prominent when the Dominion Parliament attempted to unilaterally survey the old North-West Territories around the Red River in 1869.[132] The Métis did not want to become a part of the Dominion without participation and consent, so they blocked surveyors from doing their work. This prevented Canada's expansion into the region and compelled the government of Sir John A. Macdonald to negotiate with them. The Red River Métis even developed their legal traditions to form a Provisional Government that was given authority to negotiate the terms of union with Ottawa and bring the area into Confederation. Representatives of this government travelled to Ottawa as delegates of the Métis people to negotiate conditions for entry. They brought with them a locally developed Bill of Rights that expressed their demands. The negotiations were challenging, but an agreement was reached and its terms were embodied in the *Manitoba Act* of 1870.[133] The democratic legitimacy of this process was sealed through the Métis Provisional Government's acceptance of the agreement even before the Dominion and Imperial Parliament's statutory endorsement that made it part of the constitutional law of Canada.[134] The people of the Métis Nation regard the *Manitoba Act* as a treaty that recognizes and affirms their nation-to-nation relationship with Canada, even though they argue that its provisions concerning land and resources have not been fulfilled.[135] Métis law was important to the development of the country in this region.

Métis laws continued in the period following the Provisional Government. In 1873, the laws relating to the buffalo hunt are of particular note. After being pushed from the Red River settlement (when the *Manitoba Act* was violated), a group of Métis established a democratically elected government in St Laurent, near Batoche, Saskatchewan. Gabriel Dumont and eight councillors passed rules, patterned after their ancient buffalo hunt laws, in the following areas:

> [T]he duties of the council, regulating contracts (e.g. agreements made on Sunday were null and void) and authorizing the raising of money by taxing households. They also passed laws related to penalties for crimes such as horse stealing, dishonouring girls and lighting fires on the prairie in midsummer. On January 27, 1875 the council passed laws regulating the buffalo hunt: old laws which specifically forbade anyone from proceeding ahead of the designated departure date for the hunt were

enacted, and new laws prohibiting anyone from leaving behind unused buffalo carcasses were also passed.[136]

The Métis laws at St Laurent contained the following provisions:

Article I. On the First Mondays of the Month, the president and members of his council shall be obliged to assemble in a house indicated before hand by the president, in order to judge the cases that may be submitted to their arbitration.

Article II. Any Counsellor who, unless by reason of illness, or impossibility shall not be present at the indicated place shall pay a fine of five Louis.

Article III. The president who by his own fault shall not meet his Counsellors in the indicated place shall pay a fine of five Louis.

Article IV. Any captain refusing to execute the orders that he shall receive in the name of the Council shall pay a fine of three Louis.

Article V. Any soldier, who shall refuse to execute the orders of his captain shall pay a fine of one Louis and a half.

Article VI. Any person who shall insult the Council or a member of the Council in the public exercise of his functions shall pay a fine of three Louis.

Article VII. Any person who shall be guilty of contempt of any measure of the Council or of one passed in a general Assembly, shall pay a fine of one Louis.

Article VIII. Any person wishing to plead shall inform the president beforehand and shall deposit with him, as security, the sum of five shillings.

Article IX. In every case the plaintiff shall deposit two Louis, five shillings with the president to remunerate him and the members of the Council for their loss of time, but at the termination of the case, the person losing shall pay all the costs and the plaintiff if he gains shall receive back the money deposited.

Article X. Any person shall call the Assembly together, shall pay five shillings to the president and to each member, should he come to a compromise with the other side and abandon the prosecution of the case.

Article XI. Every witness in a case shall receive two and a half shillings a day.

Article XII. Any case once brought before the Council, can no longer be judged by any arbitrators outside the Council.

Article XIII. Any person judged by the Council, shall be allowed ten days to make arrangements with the person with whom the quarrel is; at the expiration of that term the Council shall cause its order to be forcibly executed.

Article XIV. Any person, who only has three animals, shall not be compelled to give up any one of them in payment of his debts: This clause does not apply to unmarried men, who shall be compelled to pay even to the last animal.

Article XV. Any person who shall be known to have taken another person's horse without permission, shall pay a fine of two shillings.

Article XVI. Any contract made without witnesses shall be null and void and its executive cannot be sought for in the Council.

Article XVII. Any bargain made on a Sunday even before witnesses, cannot be prosecuted in Court.

Article XVIII. Any bargain any contract any sale shall be valid, written in French, English or Indian characters even if made without witness, if the plaintiff testified on oath to the correctness of his account or contract.

Article XIX. Any affair decided by the Council of St Laurent shall never be appealed by any of the parties before any other tribunal when the government of Canada shall have placed its regular magistrates in the country, and all persons pleading do it with the knowledge that they promise never to appeal against the decision given by the Council and no one is permitted to enjoy the privileges of this community, except on the express condition of submitting to this law.

Article XX. Any money contribution shall not exceed one Louis and every public tax levied by the Council shall be obligatory for the inhabitants of St Laurent, and those who shall refuse to submit to the levy shall be liable to pay a fine, the amount of which shall be determined by the Council.

Article XXI. Any young man, who, under pretext of marriage, shall dishonour a young girl and afterwards refuses to marry her, shall be liable to pay a fine of fifteen Louis: This law applies equally to the case of married men dishonouring girls.

Article XXII. Any person who shall defame the character of another person shall attack his honour, his virtue or his probity shall be liable to a fine in proportion to the quality and rank of the person attacked or to the degree of injury caused.

Article XXIII. Any person who shall set fire to the prairie from the 1st August and causes damage shall pay a fine of four Louis.

Article XXIV. On Sundays and obligatory festivals the river ferrys shall be free for people riding or driving to church, but any person who shall crop without going to church, shall pay as on ordinary days.

Article XXV. All the horses shall be free, but he whose horse causes injury or annoyance shall be warned and should he not hobble his horse he shall pay a fine of 5 shillings a day from the time he was warned to look after his horse.

Article XXVI. If any dogs kill a little foal, the owner of the dogs shall be held responsible for the damage done.

Article XXVII. Any servant who shall leave his employer before the expiration of the term agreed upon, shall forfeit all right to his wages: in the same way, any employer dismissing his servant without proper cause shall pay him his wages in full.

Article XXVIII. On Sunday no servant shall be obliged to perform any but duties absolutely necessary, however, on urgent occasion, the master can order the servant to look after his horses on Sundays only after the great mass: he shall never prevent him from going to church, at least in the morning.

Métis legal traditions are a strong and important part of Canada's legal inheritance. Their laws have survived in customary form, and still have relevance today.[137]

Métis legal traditions also survive in Canada as positivistic law. In Alberta, Métis people operate a quasi-judicial system to deal with disputes about membership, land dealings, surface rights, and any other matter to which the parties agree. This body, called the Métis Settlement Appeal Tribunal, was set up in 1990 under provincial legislation.[138] The tribunal's jurisdiction covers eight Métis settlements on 1.25 million acres of land in northern Alberta. It has developed an extensive body of jurisprudence as a living legal tradition.[139] Alberta Métis also see their legal traditions reflected through settlement governance involving issues such as membership, hunting, fishing, trapping, timber, and other matters relating to land. The Métis Settlements General Council may enact laws (General Council policies) that are binding on the General Council and every settlement. These laws are equal in status to other provincial laws. The General Council also has an administrative body that includes strategic training initiatives (education and training) and programs and services development. Métis in other parts of the country have also enacted their laws in a contemporary context.

F. Carrier Legal Traditions

The Carrier people live in north-central British Columbia in twenty-two bands, speaking six Athapaskan (Dene) dialects.[140] Their law is organized around a house group with a head chief (*Diniizee* or *Dzaki-izee*), subsidiary wing chiefs, and house members. A group of houses constitutes a clan, within which there is generally no single head chief.[141] Membership in a house and a clan is generally determined through matrilineal descent.[142] Carrier legal traditions contain principles of societal organization.[143] These laws are central to the proper distribution of decision-making power.[144]

An integral part of Carrier legal heritage is their *kungax*, or 'own spirit power.'[145] *Kungax* tell of the land's creation, the people's earliest history, territorial boundaries, major battles, and the origins of house crests, titles, names, and significant past events. *Kungax* are often performative, using song and dance to communicate major themes and specific principles. *Kungax* are first taught to children when they are quite young. As they grow and mature, children are expected to deepen their memory and understanding of the *kungax* until they can recite them accurately.[146] While every attempt is made to ensure that those with proper authority perform the *kungax* in official gatherings, parallel or divergent accounts often circulate.[147]

Kungax teach specific principles for regulating behaviour as well as outlining remedies for breaches of social order. Several fundamental principles intended to govern individual conduct have been identified within Carrier law. These are respect, responsibility, obligation, compassion, balance, wisdom, caring, sharing, and love.[148] It has been said: 'Each of these principles is expected to be followed concurrently and with equal weight. No one principle is understood to have greater significance than any other principle.'[149]

An example of a principle found within the *kungax* concerns animals and the obligation to treat them with respect. If fish, birds, or animals are not well treated, they will leave Carrier territories, and could even exact retribution. To mark respect for fish, the Carrier enact a ceremony each year to honour the salmon's return. Honour continues throughout the salmon's cyclical visits with rules governing its allocation, catch, use, preparation, and disposal.[150] These regulations are present because the Carrier believe that 'the salmon's spirit moves out of its body when you hit it with a stick.[151] They believe that this 'is why the body wiggles – the spirit is leaving.'[152] *Kungax* reinforce the rules governing the proper treatment of salmon by providing commentaries about consequences for mistreatment. Anthropologist Diamond Jenness heard stories that taught this principle. He wrote:

Many years ago the Natives gathered in *Shin* [summer] to set their weirs in the river. They caught and dried large numbers of fish, while the children played happily around the camp. Then a boy named Mek made a girdle of some fish heads and began to dance with them. An old man scolded him saying, 'Don't do that. Sa [the Sun] will see you and by and by you will be hungry!' A year passed, and the people gathered again at the same spot, but this time they caught no fish at all. The men left the women to attend the net and went away to hunt, but the game too had vanished. Before long they were starving and the first to die was Mek. No sooner was he dead than the river seemed to teem with fish and the people had no difficulty in catching all they needed.[153]

This *kungax* not only provides precedent to guide future behaviour, it also creates strong feelings that motivates and encourages listeners to properly meet their obligations to the salmon. Feelings are an important part of the law; reason is not separated from emotion in making decisions and taking action. Reason and emotion operate together to motivate proper conduct. Carrier woman Helen Nikal illustrates this connection in commenting about the *kungax* and the salmon: 'I start to feel strange, I *feel* the salmon all go down the river, leave.'[154]

The *kungax* also teach proper rules of respect, love, and obligation towards others. If people are not well treated, they are said to transform into animals and leave their partners. To stress the importance of taking proper care of one's spouse and animals, Diamond Jenness recounted the following ancient story about the origin of the beaver.

A newly married couple left Fraser Lake to hunt in the mountains to the southward, where they camped all alone near a small stream. The woman grew lonely when her husband was absent from morning until evening, and to pass the time made a small dam across the stream; but her husband, finding that it made the water too deep for him to wade across, broke it down with his foot. She burst into tears and said, 'Why did you break it? I was lonely while you were away and built it to pass the time.' The next day she made another dam, and he broke that also. This happened again and again until she became very angry.

One evening when her husband returned from his hunting he found a very large dam spanning the stream and a beaver house in the middle of the water. His wife was kneeling on the edge of the pond with her breech-cloth in her hand. She tucked it between her legs as soon as she saw her husband coming, leaped into the water and entered the beaver house. The man broke down the dam and let out all the water; but he could not find her. Then he broke down the beaver house. Still he could not find her. So that night he slept alone.

He went hunting again the next morning, and when he returned, his wife had repaired the dam and was working on the lodge. Already she was changing into a beaver. He broke the dam and let the water out again, but she eluded all his attempts to capture her.

... Then a large beaver leaped out of the water and sat on top of its house. It was his wife, whose trailing breech-cloth had become a tail. She called to her people, 'My husband did not kill me, but I have changed into a beaver. Now go back home, for I cannot live with you anymore.'[155]

Jenness concludes his account by noting: 'That is why the beaver's belly and intestines resemble those of a human being.'[156] This case illustrates the consequences of ill treatment of animals and one's spouse. It demonstrates the fluid relationship between people and animals, and shows the importance of remembering these connections.

With the *kungax* providing a principled context, Carrier people regulate their society through the *bah'lats* or Potlatch laws. The *bah'lats* laws are the legal basis for succession and inheritance, territorial laws and resource management, family law (including marriage, divorce and mourning), dispute settlement, village governance, special rules of conduct for women, and principles of justice taught to children.[157] The *bah'lats* are administered through head clan and subclan chiefs who determine questions of Carrier law.[158] Hereditary chiefs receive their authority from matrilineal clan assignments in the *bah'lats*, if they live in a way that merits the honour. Wealth, service, generosity, wisdom, respect, family and community support all qualify people for the authority. Without living in accordance with these principles, a person cannot expect to be effective in interpreting and adjudicating disputes.[159] If they have the respect of the people, head chiefs from each clan are responsible for determining breaches of Carrier law and, in consultation with wing chiefs, adjudicate an appropriate remedy.[160] Once an infraction has been identified, remedies are administered by a clan member known as a 'whip man' from the father clan (the clan of one's father responsible for the rearing and care of that individual).[161] In describing the chiefs' authority and responsibility, anthropologist Antonia Mills has written the following about the Wetsuwet'en, one of the Carrier groups:

The head chiefs have the authority to decide how the law should be applied in individual disputes, both in the feasts, out in the territories, and in the villages. Some disputes involve other peoples, and some are internal to the Witsuwit'en [sic]. In dealing with the latter the chiefs call upon their deep acquaintance, kinship, and understanding of the people; conversely the respect the Witsuwit'en [sic] have for their chiefs makes them effective mediators in internal disputes.

The Witsuwit'en [sic] chiefs are in a position to effectively intervene in the sensitive areas of marital relations and territorial disputes because they have a thorough knowledge of the nature of the participants. This gives them a distinct advantage over outside adjudicators ...[162]

The chiefs exercise dispute resolution powers within their authority and can enforce breaches of their society's laws in formal and informal ways. Their judicial role facilitates peace and order whenever conflict needs to be resolved.

Formal business within the *bah'lats* takes place in the feast hall. The Wetsuwet'en say: 'The feast has forged their law.'[163] The *bah'lats* is also sometimes referred to as the feast, and is guided by a major legal tenet, *dinii biits wa aden*, or 'the way the Feast works.'[164] People must be properly seated in their house groups before the feast begins. There are requirements for the proper welcome and acknowledgment of guests, as well as for the order and content of speeches. The giving of gifts within the *bah'lats* is also guided by detailed rules. Practices and principles must be followed when a hereditary chief's name is being assigned, when law is solidified, when shaming occurs, and when a birth, marriage, or adoption is announced.[165] Precise legal procedures are followed within the feast.

Mechanisms within the *bah'lats* certify the binding nature of the business conducted. The feast structure has built-in procedures to seal and validate rights and obligations. Two important practices ratify the feast's legal procedures and results: the distribution of eagle down and the proper calling of witnesses.

Actions and decisions within the *bah'lats* can be endorsed through the scattering of eagle down. When eagle down is distributed to feast participants after all the decisions have been made and agreed to, 'the peace is binding and retaliation is stopped.'[166] Eagle down has great power for the Carrier people because of the bird's pre-eminence among other animals. Distributing it symbolizes the peace and forbearance that should be maintained between those present and shown towards all creation, including humans and animals, birds, and fish.[167] Antonia Mills has described this relationship as follows:

> The chiefs are responsible for seeing that relations between all these beings are in balance. The power of the chiefs rests on their recognition of, and participation in, the spirit world, where one meets and marries the animals. Contact with the spirit powers is acted out in the feasts through the use of crests and songs.[168]

Carrier law is attentive to all the relationships of living beings on the land, in the air, and under the water. The sanctioning of decisions, plans, and transactions is an integral component of Carrier law and has been called *Chus*, the law of the eagle feather plumes.[169]

The appointment of witnesses is another important mechanism in the *bah'lats* for endorsing and confirming legal transactions. Clan members act as witnesses and memorize the transactions agreed between the parties.[170] These witnesses are important because they may be called upon at a future feast to verify past actions. The recording of the *bah'lats* proceedings ensures that the witnesses are specifically prepared to testify in the event of a potential conflict over what has transpired. In this respect, the Carrier's legal structure is similar to that of other north-west coast nations, such as the Gitksan, Tsimshian, Haida, Kwakwaka'wakw, Coast Salish, and Nisga'a.

G. Nisga'a Legal Traditions

The Nisga'a Nation of north-western British Columbia provides an important example of how Indigenous legal tradition can be applied and practised in a contemporary context. The Nisga'a people divide themselves into four clans or *pdeek: Gisk'ahaast* (Killer Whale), *Laxgibuu* (Wolf), *Ganada* (Raven), *and Laxsgiik* (Eagle). *Pdeek* members may not marry within their clan, even if they are not Nisga'a. Times are changing, but if a couple broke this law in the past, they were k̲'aats or shunned by the community. Nisga'a people also historically organized themselves into *wilp*s or house groups. Each *wilp* had its own chiefs, territories, rights, history, stories, songs, dances, and traditions. These customs are handed down through matrilineal succession.

Wilps are matrilineal and matrilocal. The highest ranking woman in a *wilp* is called the *sigidimnak'*; she makes the final decisions on names and inheritance. On her death, her position would be assumed by her oldest sister or daughter. The highest ranking man in a *wilp* is called the *sim'oogit*. When he dies, his entitlements are usually passed on to his eldest living brother or the oldest son of his eldest sister. *Wilp* chiefs are responsible for passing *adaawks* and associated prerogatives from one generation to the next. This is usually done through a series of feasts to make these prerogatives public and have them validated by other chiefs.[171]

Each *wilp* has an *adaawk* that describes how their ancient territories were acquired; they can take the listener back to the beginning of time. The *adaawk* will also describe the *wilp's* ancient migrations, territorial defence, and 'major events in the life of the house, such as natural disasters, epidemics, war, the arrival of new peoples, the establishment of trade alliances, and major shifts in power.'[172] The *adaawk* records property rights such as fishing sites, hunting territories, and gathering grounds. It also details rights and responsibilities in family law. For example, *adaawk* convey information about how ancestors were given animals to be used as crests by each *wilp* and to show them how to live, eat, and prepare food.[173] They also relate details about how these entitlements and obligations should be passed on to the next generation.

The Nisga'a people remember their *adaawk* by referring to their *ayuukhl*. The *ayuukhl* is an ancient legal code that has guided Nisga'a social, economic, and political relationships from 'time of memory.'[174] Centuries before Canada proclaimed itself a nation 'founded upon the principles that recognize the supremacy of God and the rule of law, the people of the Nass River were living according to *Ayuukhl Nisga'a*, an ancient code of laws that will stand comparison to any modern constitution or declaration of statehood and nationality.'[175] The *ayuukhl*, in conjunction with the *adaawk*, historically governed land ownership, education, succession, citizenship, and the institutions of the chieftain and matriarch. The laws also governed marriage, divorce, war, peace, trading relationships, and restitution,[176] though these have been modified in some degree by a recent treaty. For example, on matters of succession, property is passed on when a *wilp* chief dies and his next older brother or his oldest sister's son assumes the role of custodian for all the property of the house.[177] 'This process occurs through a sophisticated ceremony known as a Settlement Feast. Like a deed in a land registry office, the Settlement Feast is a formal registration of title and ownership.'[178] Some *ayuukhl* are related to the Nisga'a narrative of their origins, such as having been placed in *Ginsk'eexkw* by *K'amligihahlhaahl* who is regarded as the Supreme God.[179] Other *ayuukhl* are founded upon *K'amligihahlhaahl*'s teachings to *Txeemsim*, the trickster, who identified central legal tenets for Nisga'a peace and order.[180] His deeds and misdeeds illustrate consequences that can flow from certain behaviours.

Some *ayuukhl* seem to come from the direct experience and observation of the people. There are many cases of people being rewarded or punished because of the respect or disrespect they showed in following the *ayuukhl*. For example, Chief Joseph Gosnell has spoken about an *ayuukhl* that warns against disrespect for animals. In this *ayuukhl*, young boys were playing with salmon and setting tiny pitch lamps on the backs of the fish so they could watch the lights swim away upriver. Chief Gosnell reported that: 'For this crime, the animals took their vengeance upon the valley, causing the eruption of a dormant volcano known as *Wilksi Baxhl Mihl*. More than 2,000 of our people were entombed in the lava that flowed from the volcano, and the lava beds remain the dominant feature of much of the Nass Valley to this day.'[181] This account demonstrates that Nisga'a legal principles can also be embedded in the very landscape of their nation.

A reading of Nisga'a law makes it apparent that sanctions and restitution are an important part of their legal regime. Nisga'a Elder Bert McKay has described the shaming and cleansing nature of Nisga'a law:

> And the last of our laws were, I guess you would call them, penalties. One is called restitution, or *Ksiiskw*. It's a very, very difficult and important law. When a life is lost over carelessness or over greed the law states very plainly, that before the sun sets if the offending family does not settle the issue with the grieved family, then those people have a right to take double the lives that they lost. So the only way that was resolved was by restitution payment. And then the other part, where certain of the ten laws were broken, not restitution but to make amends, to make a complete break from the shame that you imposed on your family, and that was called public cleansing.[182]

Nisga'a legal traditions, therefore, cover many significant aspects of human behaviour. The *ayuukhl* and *adaawk* are an important part of Nisga'a legal traditions because they connect the people to their territories, families, and past. They teach them how to live in relationship with the earth around them.

Recently, the Nisga'a Nation has modified its legal traditions to a degree by entering into a treaty with the Governments of Canada and British Columbia. After having taken the *Calder* case before the Supreme Court and having their legal position in Canadian law recognized, the Nisga'a entered into a two-decade-long negotiation that culminated in a comprehensive treaty in 1999. The agreement is an ambitious one, providing for collective Nisga'a ownership of approximately 2,000 square kilometres of land in the Nass Valley watershed of north-western British Columbia. The treaty covers issues as diverse as land titles, minerals, water, forests, fisheries, wildlife, governance, the administration of justice, fiscal relations (including taxation), cultural property, and dispute resolution. Many of these provisions provide significant benefits for the Nisga'a people that are far greater than anything contemplated under the current *Indian Act*. Of particular importance is the agreement's reference to the *ayuukhl* as a source of Nisga'a law, and the creation of Nisga'a courts to interpret its meaning under the new treaty. This institution will help Nisga'a stories to rise to the surface and perforate the cover of the Canadian legal fictions that previously denied them rights in their traditional territories.

Nisga'a legal traditions such as the *ayuukhl* now operate in a contemporary Canadian context through the Nisga'a Lisims Government (a modern, forward-thinking administration developing traditional culture and values) because of the *Nisga'a Final Agreement Act*.[183] They will be adapted and find expression in Nisga'a parliamentary procedure. They will be evident in statutory laws governing marriage, divorce, commerce, resource use, education, dispute resolution, wills and estates, citizenship, governance, and land. They will be the background 'common law' principles in Nisga'a courts. In its preamble, the *Nisga'a Final Agreement Act* recognizes the continued importance of Nisga'a legal traditions:

> WHEREAS the Parties acknowledge the ongoing importance to the Nisga'a Nation of the Simgigat and Sigidimhaanak (hereditary chiefs and matriarchs) continuing to tell their Adaawak (oral histories) relating to their Ango'oskw (family hunting, fishing, and gathering territories) in accordance with the Ayuuk (Nisga'a traditional laws and practices).[184]

The 'Ayuukhl Nisga'a' and 'Ayuukl' are defined within the Final Agreement to mean 'the traditional laws and practices of the Nisga'a

Nation.'[185] Through the Final Agreement, Nisga'a legal traditions continue to exist today. Their authority and use provide evidence that there is tolerance and respect of Indigenous legal traditions in contemporary Canada, although the process has not been without critique and challenge.[186]

Since the Nisga'a Final Agreement came into effect, the Wilp Si'ayuukhl Nisga'a, the central Nisga'a governing body, has enacted over thirty acts and other pieces of legislation.[187] Some of these acts are *Nisga'a Effective Day Procedures Act, Nisga'a Lisims Government Act, Nisga'a Interpretation Act, Nisga'a Citizenship Act, Nisga'a Elections Act, Nisga'a Financial Administration Act, Nisga'a Capital Finance Commission Act, Nisga'a Administrative Decisions Review Act, Nisga'a Personnel Administration Act, Nisga'a Land Act, Nisga'a Land Designation Act, Nisga'a Village Entitlement Act, Nisga'a Nation Entitlement Act, Nisga'a Land Title Act, Nisga'a Fisheries and Wildlife Act, Nisga'a Forest Act, Nisga'a Programs and Services Delivery Act,* and the *Nisga'a Offence Act.* The Nisga'a Constitution describes how law-making power is to be exercised by the Wilp Si'ayuukhl Nisga'a and has rules describing the process for enacting laws.[188] Furthermore, a Nisga'a executive[189] has the power to make regulations under laws enacted by the Wilp Si'ayuukhl Nisga'a, and village governments also have jurisdiction in their areas of law-making authority.[190]

Under the Final Agreement, the Nisga'a Lisims Government has no exclusive jurisdiction.[191] Its jurisdiction is always concurrent with federal or provincial jurisdiction; because of this, it is necessary to provide rules that determine which law prevails in the event of inconsistency or conflict. 'Generally, Nisga'a laws prevail in relation to matters that are internal to the Nisga'a Nation, integral to their distinct culture, essential to the operation of their government or the exercise of their other treaty rights.'[192] In some cases, Nisga'a laws must comply with provincial standards in order to be valid. If those standards are met or exceeded, then Nisga'a laws prevail. In other cases, Canada, British Columbia, and the Nisga'a Nation agree that, while the Nisga'a Lisims Government should have the authority to make laws, if there is a conflict, federal or provincial laws should prevail.[193] Finally, there are many subject matters over which the Nisga'a Lisims Government has no jurisdiction.[194]

Edmond Wright has argued that, under the Nisga'a Final Agreement, Nisga'a laws prevail in the following matters: administration, management, and operation of the Nisga'a Lisims Government; creation, continuation, amalgamation, dissolution, naming or renaming of Nisga'a villages on Nisga'a lands, and Nisga'a urban locals; Nisga'a citizenship; preservation, promotion, and development of Nisga'a language and culture; use, management, possession, and disposition of Nisga'a lands owned by the Nisga'a Nation; a Nisga'a village or a Nisga'a corporation and similar matters relating to the property interests of the Nisga'a Nation; Nisga'a villages and Nisga'a corporations; Nisga'a land use, management, planning, zoning, development, and similar matters related to the regulation and administration of Nisga'a lands (including establishment of a land title or land registry system), and designation of Nisga'a lands; use, possession, management, and similar matters relating to the property interests of the Nisga'a Nation; Nisga'a villages and Nisga'a corporations and their assets, other than real property on Nisga'a lands; organization and structure for the delivery of health services on Nisga'a lands; authorization or licensing of Aboriginal healers on Nisga'a lands, including measures in respect of competence, ethics, and quality of practice that are reasonably required to protect the public; child and family services on Nisga'a lands, if Nisga'a laws include standards comparable to provincial standards intended to ensure the safety and well-being of children and families; adoption of Nisga'a children, if Nisga'a laws expressly provide that the best interests of the child is the paramount consideration and that British Columbia and Canada are provided with records of all adoptions occurring under Nisga'a laws; pre-school to Grade 12 education on Nisga'a lands of Nisga'a children, if Nisga'a laws include provisions for curriculum, examination and other standards that permit transfers between school systems, and for appropriate certification of teachers; post-secondary education within Nisga'a lands, if Nisga'a laws include standards comparable to provincial standards in respect of matters such as institutional structure and accountability, admission, and curriculum standards; devolution of cultural property (ceremonial regalia and similar property associated with a Nisga'a clan and other personal property having cultural significance to the Nisga'a Nation) of a Nisga'a citizen who dies intestate.[195]

H. Inuit Legal Traditions

The Inuit are a circumpolar people who live in the Arctic, in parts of Alaska, Greenland, Siberia, and Canada. In Canada, they occupy the western and central part of the Arctic, the Keewatin region of the barren lands, Baffin Island, the High Arctic, the coastal areas of Hudson's Bay, and parts of northern Quebec and Labrador. Like the Nisga'a, the Inuit are implementing their legal traditions in a contemporary context as a result of their land claims agreement and powers of public governance in Canada's newest territory, Nunavut.

Among the most important legal terms in Inuit law are *maligait*, *piqujait*, and *tirigusuusiit*.[196] *Maligait* refers to things that have to be followed.[197] It is a relational term focusing on the result of a request (the obligation to obey).[198] *Piqujait* deals with things that have to be done. The obligation that is the focus of *piqujait* is the wish of an authorized person about something that is to be done. *Tirigusuusiit* refers to things that have to be avoided. If a person transgresses *tirigusuusiit*, he or she will face the consequences of his or her actions.

These legal traditions are of ancient origin but have the potential to be applied to present-day circumstances. Inuit Elder Aupilaarjuk stated: 'Today, the problem is to retain from the old traditions what is valuable to the present. When I think about this, I wonder how we can solve the problem. I would like to look at the Inuit *maligait* that we had in the past and compare them with the laws we have today, so we could develop better laws for the future.'[199] When Aupilaarjuk was asked which *tirigusuusiit* could be applied today, he said:

> I think some of them could be brought back because they are not dangerous. We *tirigusuk* when we refrain from doing something. *Qallunaat* (non-Inuit) also have *tirigusuusiit* such as not working on Sundays. This is a modern day *tirigusungniq*. Following *tirigusungniq* is not bad, it is good because it is part of our tradition ... I think it is important we take back some of the *tirigusuusiit*. They will not cause people to become bad. Just because they are a part of Inuit *ukpirusuusiit*, some people think they are no good and come from Satan. We are wrong to think like that. What we are following today is wrong and people are killing themselves. Inuit weren't like that before. We have to look at where we came from and where we are today. Back then we truly believed in *tirigusuusiit*. You need to think about this when you are preparing for your future.[200]

Tirigusuusiit could be used as an Inuit legal device to highlight inappropriate actions. While not all ancient *tirigusuusiit* would be followed in a contemporary setting, they could be compared and contrasted with other Canadian legal traditions to create a better future, as Aupilaarjuk suggested. For example, *tirigusuusiit* requires that campsites be kept clean out of respect for the land and the animals. Joan Atuat of Qairnirmiut noted: 'We used to have to keep our garbage area in one small place away from children and tents. My grandmother was very strict about people throwing garbage in the lakes. She would not have anything to do with dirty fish … She was so strict about cleanliness that she didn't even want small pieces lying around the tent.'[201] This *tirigusuusiit* principle is an important foundational idea for creating environmental and land use planning regimes. There are *tirigusuusiit* related to visiting peoples in other lands, clothing, hunting, and other life activities.[202]

Inuit Qaujimajatuqangit is a particularly important concept in Inuit law that contains guidance for the future. *Inuit Qaujimajatuqangit* 'includes unwritten traditional knowledge, family and political structures, learning, social development schemes, and even the understanding of local weather patterns.'[203] It has also been described as a living technology for rationalizing thought and action, organizing tasks, managing resources and family, and seeing society as a coherent whole.[204]

Today, the Nunavut territorial government is one of the most important institutions implementing Inuit legal traditions in Canada. The government has taken great guidance from *Inuit Qaujimajatuqangit* to structure its legislative and administrative agenda and actions. For example, the *Nunavut Integrity Act* integrates *Inuit Qaujimajatuqangit* into its process and substance for dealing with conflicts of interest.[205] This was recognized by members of the Nunavut legislature when it was introduced.[206] At the opening of the 2004 session, there were constant references to Inuit legal traditions.[207] Inuit legal procedures are also evident in the functioning of the executive. There are no political parties at the territorial level, and the cabinet operates on the basis of consensus politics.[208] Concepts applied under *Inuit Qaujimajatuqangit* include *Pijitsirniq* (serving), *Aajiiqatigiinniq* (decision-making), *Pilimmatsaniq* (passing on knowledge and skills through observation, action, and practice); *Piliriqatigiinniq* (working together for a common cause); *Avatittinnik Kamattiarnik* (environmental stewardship); *Qanuqtuurniq* (creative, resourceful problem-solving); *Tunnganarniq* (openness, acceptance, and inclusivity), *Ippigusuttiarniq* (caring for others); *Angiqatigiinniq* (proceeding forward with clear understanding); *Ikajuqatigiinniq* (assistance and cooperation without barriers); *Qaujimautittiarniq* (information sharing); *Uppiriqattautiniq* (fair treatment); *Tukisiumaqatigiinniq* (conscious understanding of others as the basis of mutual relationships); *Ilainnasiunnginniq* (sensitivity to difference); *Ila-jjuttigiinniq* (encouragement of others); *Aaqqiumatitsiniq* (keeping order in place); *Iqqaqtuijjiqattariaqannginniq* (restraint on personal judgment); *Piviqaqtittiniq* (opportunity for participation and contribution); *Silatuniq* (wisdom to know how to apply your knowledge); and *Ajuqsatittinginniq piviqarialinnik* (support for growth, development, and success).[209] The Nunavut government has taken many opportunities to apply these and other Inuit legal traditions to their statutes, regulations, and government procedures.[210]

I. Conclusion

This chapter has identified eight different Indigenous legal traditions in their contexts. It has reinforced the lessons learned in the last chapter, that is, that Indigenous law has many roots and sources. This chapter has also provided a broader understanding of the differences among Indigenous legal traditions in their varied settings. The point to take from this discussion is that Indigenous laws are a rich and complex source of guidance for regulating and resolving disputes within their various spheres.

In outlining these diverse traditions it should also be re-emphasized that their details will receive different emphases and interpretations depending on the person relating them and the context in which they are being recounted. Readers should identify the differences of opinion they have about the ideas presented in this chapter and are encouraged to debate them, because such debate could lead to further clarification and more refined applications of the law at issue. Great benefits could accrue by others adding their critical voices or their commendations of the concepts covered here. Further discussion and development of these descriptions are essential to ensure that Indigenous legal traditions do not become withdrawn from critical inquiry or become lost in mythologies of the past.

For these reasons, it is vitally important that Indigenous laws remain relevant through their continual interaction with the contemporary facts of life. If this does not take place, they could become detached from the everyday concerns and experiences of Indigenous peoples today. Practitioners of every legal tradition must be ever watchful that hyperfanciful mythology does not overtake practical guidance about how laws should influence people's lives. Of course, a certain degree of folklore surrounds each legal tradition. Enhancing a law's status by elevating certain of its features can be a healthy activity. Proper esteem and special regard can bolster the reverence and respect that people have for their traditions. However, significant problems can develop if too much deference is given to how traditions (including common law, civil law, and Indigenous law) were practised in past eras. While ancient understandings can give significant guidance to present practitioners, problems develop when traditions are held hostage to historical interpretations that do not take into account the modern contexts. In these circumstances, placing too much weight on the 'hallowed' nature of traditions can become an obstacle to their present-day applications. If an overexalted view of a tradition is applied, it could limit ordinary people from connecting to it when faced with their messy and often mundane circumstances. Legal traditions must have an air of reality about their present-day applications. People will have trouble making their laws work for them if a hard-edged realism is not combined with the necessary idealism that underlies most legal systems.

Thus, traditions should not be frozen in some past-tense state because of misplaced notions of reverence and respect. In fact, it could be exceedingly disrespectful if such an attitude leads one to believe that one's legal tradition cannot intermingle with other ideas to provide guidance in circumstances that differ from the past. Respect should not be equated with non-use. Preservation of one's legal traditions is not accomplished by hermetically sealing them off from present-day application. Removing traditions from people's complicated contemporary lives often promotes and privileges the socio-cultural elite. These people may claim extraordinary knowledge, beyond the reach of 'normal' learning. To perpetuate their special position such people may resist making connections with other traditions. Sealing-off societies through seclusion and segregation can allow specialists to claim distinctive authority over others whose lives are more fully consumed with current events and concerns. The replication of a class of people who interpret traditions without input from those who are buffeted by the so-called impurities of other legal traditions can lead to troubling hierarchies. Resistance to 'non-approved' ideas that come from other sources can allow elites to selectively shield themselves from complicated counter-narratives. This can lead to a narrowing of perspective and can threaten a tradition's relevance in a complicated world.

Legal traditions must be brought out of the past and into the present to increase their scope and vitality. Respect and reverence for traditions can be expanded if people have enough confidence to apply their ancient principles in the here and now. This is as true for the common law and civil law traditions as it is for Indigenous legal traditions. Theorists and practitioners of every legal tradition can benefit from considering how their laws might learn from and interact with other approaches to regulation and decision-making. This is the focus of the remaining chapters in this book.

4 Learning from Bijuridicalism

Now that we have considered the existence of Canada's Indigenous legal traditions in some detail, it is time to once again turn our attention to the country's other legal traditions. This chapter will consider whether any lessons for Indigenous law can be drawn from the coexistence of the common law and civil law within Canada. The concept of Canadian bijuridicalism is an important touchstone in this inquiry. It is also a central fact of Canadian legal life. Bijuridicalism refers to 'the co-existence of two contemporaneous legal systems' and is firmly entrenched within Canadian legal thought and practice.[1] The concept behind bijuridicalism holds significant legal implications for our consideration of Indigenous legal traditions. While bijuridicalism is a fair description of Canada's legal framework, it can also be problematic because it is underinclusive. As has already been noted, numerous Indigenous legal traditions continue to function in ways that are integral to Canada's legal system. Therefore, Canada would better be described as multi-juridical in its actual constitution. Our discussion of Indigenous law in this book allows us to build on bijuridicalism and take a more pluralistic approach to recognizing and affirming our country's rich legal inheritance. In this vein, this chapter will explore how the continued development of Indigenous legal traditions can take guidance from the relationship between the common law and civil law in Canada.

A more thorough understanding of the development of common and civil law will demonstrate the historically fluid, socially constructed, and culturally contingent nature of legal traditions in Canada. It also provides an important reminder not to stereotype or overexaggerate the positivistic nature of non-Indigenous legal tradi-

tions.[2] Without this broader context, common law and civil law traditions are often regarded as 'natural' and 'time-honoured,' while
Indigenous traditions are thought to be 'unusual' and an exception to
what is considered 'normal' within our law. The previous chapters
attempt to demonstrate that the civil and common law traditions are
not the only established legal orders in Canada; they are neither exclusive nor inherently intrinsic to maintaining peace and order. Understanding the conditional development of civil and common law over
time, as they waxed and waned depending on sociocultural factors,
increases awareness of the need for choice and moral agency in the
broader adoption and adaptation of Indigenous legal traditions at this
point in Canada's history. The recognition of Indigenous legal traditions is important to Canada's further improvement as a nation, and
such action will enable us to exercise similar powers of choice and
agency in the development of our laws.

When comparing Indigenous and Western legal traditions, it is
tempting to make broad, nearly irreconcilable distinctions between
them because of their different histories, social organization, and
values. This is why it is important to note that, like Indigenous legal
traditions, Canada's broader legal traditions also rest upon unwritten
cultural assumptions.[3] The Supreme Court has ruled that, while
Canada's Constitution is primarily a written one, there is, behind the
written word, 'an historical lineage stretching back through the ages,
which aids in the consideration of underlying constitutional principles. These unwritten principles inform and sustain the constitutional
text: they are the vital un-stated assumptions upon which the text is
based.'[4] The Court further noted that these unwritten principles are
'not merely descriptive but are also invested with a powerful normative force, and are binding upon both courts and governments.'[5]
Indigenous legal traditions are among Canada's unwritten normative
principles and, with common and civil law, can be said to 'form the
very foundation of the Constitution of Canada.'[6]

If the similarities between our legal traditions are not appreciated,
their differences can give rise to misconceptions and stereotypical
ideas about Indigenous legal systems. The Supreme Court of Canada
may have fallen into this trap when it reflected on the similarities and
differences between Aboriginal and non-Aboriginal traditions. In *R. v.
Delgamuuukw,* Chief Justice Lamer observed: 'In the Aboriginal tradition the purpose of repeating oral accounts from the past is broader
than the written history of western societies. It may be to educate the

listener, to communicate aspects of culture, to socialize people into a cultural tradition, or to validate the claims of a particular family to authority or prestige.'[7]

This description of the social role of Indigenous people's oral histories is striking not because it is inaccurate – the court is, in fact, sensitive to the various roles these traditions can play – but because the court seems to overlook the broader social function of Canadian law. The 'broad social role' of Indigenous tradition, as the 'expression of the values and mores' of culture, is not very different from the broad social role of common and civil law traditions, in expressing 'values and mores.'[8] Yet, by dichotomizing Aboriginal and non-Aboriginal traditions, the Supreme Court did not give sufficient emphasis to the broad social function of common or civil law.

These stereotypical ideas about Indigenous law can be problematic because they neglect the role of civil and common law as cultural mediums that educate, communicate, and socialize. They make Indigenous principles and traditions appear overly subjective and 'non-legal' because of their 'broad social role,' while not assigning these same functions to the civil and common law. It is too easy to detach the civil and common law from their cultural contexts and this must be avoided. We must be especially cautious when the civil and common law's cultural components seem almost invisible precisely because they correspond with the values of a wide portion of society. A fair assessment of the similarities and differences between Indigenous, civil, and common law traditions should pay equal attention to the cultural aspects of each. Canada's two most dominant legal traditions, civil and common law, also have deep cultural roots. They are not removed from society, nor do they exist apart from it. The development of the civil and common law flows from, and is embedded in, the cultures of specific groups of Canadians.

A. Civil Law Legal Traditions

Civil law tradition has its origin in Roman law, and was originally codified in the *Corpus Juris Civilis* of Justinian.[9] It developed subsequently in continental Europe and then spread around the world in codified and uncodified forms. Civil law is a highly structured tradition; it is based on broad declarations of general principles that provide guidance to its adherents. It was first received in North America when New France became a royal province in 1663, more than a century before the

French Revolution of 1789. Canada's civil law originally derived from a decree by King Louis XIV that New France would follow the Custom of Paris: this was the body of laws that governed the Île de France (the region around Paris) at the time. The centralized transplant of customs from one part of the world and their application to people in another part of the world (even if they do not necessarily share the same customs), is a feature of principle-based laws. The laws of New France demonstrate this pattern; they are directed from the top, with royal ordinances, edicts, and decisions from the Conseil Souverain (Sovereign Council) proclaiming the laws by which people would live.[10] Fortunately, there was some early recognition that law is not effective if it does not reflect local values. It was implicitly acknowledged that the 'top' of the social hierarchy has to interact with the 'bottom' for law to be effective.[11] The code therefore went through several changes in 1667, 1678, and 1685, and helped to accommodate the particular cultural circumstances of New France.

In 1763, after the British conquest and the Treaty of Paris, a choice was made to abolish civil law in New France. The British common law system was imposed on the people of New France. In practice, though, civil law continued to exist, and it is interesting to note that positivistic proclamations of formal British law were not sufficient to displace laws that had come to reflect more local values. The culture of local law among the French settlers was not easily erased. As a result, the British reinstated the civil law system (for property and civil rights) in the *Quebec Act, 1774. They recognized that the best way to secure order and a degree of allegiance was to have people live closer to their own customs and values.* Since that date, civil law has survived in Canada.[12]

For example, the *Constitutional Act, 1791* split the province of Quebec into Upper and Lower Canada and did not extinguish civil law.[13] While Upper Canada became a common law jurisdiction, Lower Canada retained its civil law tradition. Close to fifty years later, another change occurred as a result of the *Act of Union of 1840*. This placed Lower and Upper Canada in a political union. It did not modify civil law rights, though it did create unique pressures on the system. This resulted in the development of a bilingual civil code for Canada East (still called Lower Canada) in 1857, intended to reconcile the problems that had developed from mixing British common law and the Custom of Paris. Civil law in Canada had not been codified before this initiative. In 1866, the *Civil Code of Lower Canada* was enacted, which also drew inspiration from the 1804 *Code Napoléon*. The 1866 code had four books: Persons, Property and Its Different Modifications, Acquisition and Exercise of Rights of Property, and Commercial Law.

Confederation also allowed for the continuation of civil law in Canada in private law matters. This explicit choice was made by Canada's founders and was supported by the Imperial Parliament. Section 92(13), gave the provinces exclusive power over 'property and civil rights.' This continued Quebec's legal tradition under this head of power, although the federal government retained jurisdiction over criminal law. From 1866, the *Civil Code of Lower Canada* remained virtually unchanged until 1955. In the late 1980s, it became apparent that a major revision of the code was required. As a result, a new *Civil Code of Quebec* came into force on 1 February 1994. The new code contains ten books and includes some concepts from common law.[14]

The interpretive tradition of civil law emphasizes the primacy of broad principles and embodies deeper societal commitments. Professor Rod Macdonald has written: 'A civil code may be described as a social or civil constitution – a text documenting the compact between people by which fundamental terms of civil society are established.'[15] Civil law remains a powerful legal tradition in Canada because of its historical use and its relationship to the society and culture in which it is applicable.

B. Common Law Legal Traditions

At the same time that civil law grew in Canada, the common law tradition also began to be widely practised. Canada was not designed as a common law country by nature or deity. Those who settled the land outside Quebec brought a cultural preference for this legal tradition and made a conscious choice to adopt this system. The origins of common law are not grounded in any text; the system developed from a tradition 'expressed in action.'[16] Much like some Indigenous legal traditions, common law has a strong customary law component. In fact, customary law is still important in the development of common law reasoning. English common law was the product of a great diversity of cultures in medieval England. It grew out of a society in which a bewildering diversity of courts, from a broad array of cultures, enforced a wide variety of laws.[17] Throughout England, there were courts of all kinds: courts of equity, market courts, manor courts, university courts, county courts, borough courts, ecclesiastical courts, and aristocratic courts.[18] Common law was born when the use of writs expanded at the expense of these other legal jurisdictions.[19] The great English historian F.W. Maitland observed that writs were 'the means whereby justice became centralized, whereby the king's court drew away business from other courts.'[20] Common law in medieval England was a formulary system, developed around a complex of writs that a litigant could obtain from the Chancery to initiate litigation in the Royal Courts.[21] Each writ gave rise to a specific manner of proceeding or 'form of action,' each with its own rules and procedures.[22] These 'forms of action' were the procedural devices used by courts to give expression to the theories of liability recognized by the common law.[23] Through these writs, litigants chose their remedies in advance of trial. They could not subsequently amend their pleadings to conform to the proof needed for the case or to meet the court's choice of another theory of liability.[24] If litigants did not select the proper writ for their action, they could not succeed in their claim.[25] This uniformity allowed for the more centralized control of the entire common law structure,[26] and the sovereignty of the Crown expanded as the jurisdiction of common law became more widespread.[27]

Common law was exported to Canada when English governors arrived on its shores and asserted its application to their new home. They made a choice. The so-called date for the common law's reception varies across the country.[28] Before Confederation, Newfoundland, Prince Edward Island, New Brunswick, and Nova Scotia all followed common law after the Acadian expulsion. Similarly, the colonies of Vancouver Island and British Columbia were said to be common law jurisdictions before union. Establishment of common law in what became Ontario is generally placed at 1763, while the prairies and the old north-west were deemed to have received common law in 1870. It was not until 1949 that decisions and developments in English law ceased to be directly incorporated into Canadian common law. Of course, many Indigenous people wonder how these colonies came to be viewed almost exclusively as common law jurisdictions when Indigenous legal traditions continued to apply in all of them.

Nevertheless, the common law tradition in contemporary Canada operates through *stare decisis* and a hierarchy of courts. *Stare decisis* is the principle by which decisions in previous cases are applied to current cases that are materially similar. In their decisions, judges are expected to provide reasons justifying their selection of applicable cases and principles. As previously noted, the doctrine of precedent was not originally a part of the common law method; this came with the development of industrialization in the seventeenth century and the need to have standardized rules.[79] With precedent, previous cases provide guidance and act as constraints on judges. It provides a measure of uniformity to the law and attempts to avoid arbitrariness in decision-making. Another aspect of common law that is now accepted, but was not originally a part of its operation, is the hierarchy of courts. Lower court decisions can be appealed to higher courts, and the decisions of the higher or superior courts are binding on inferior tribunals. The Supreme Court of Canada is at the top of this hierarchy; below it are provincial Courts of Appeal, followed by trial courts. Hierarchy also promotes uniformity and attempts to remove arbitrariness. The culture of common law is of incremental development on a case-by-case basis.

This brief examination of the civil and common law illustrates the importance of history and culture in the development of legal traditions. Without such understanding, some people might not recognize that the development of civil and common law traditions is based on specific historical and cultural circumstances. Choice and moral agency both played a role in the adoption and adaptation of these traditions. Choice and agency will be as important to the adoption and continued adaptation of Indigenous legal traditions. Since legal traditions are subject to human intervention, they can change, grow, and develop.

C. Relationships between Canada's Legal Traditions

It is important to understand the relationship between Canada's legal traditions in order to appreciate their effect on one another. None is fully autonomous; each influences the other for better or for worse. For most of the country's history, common law has been a dominant force in Canada; at times, this has made it difficult for civil and Indigenous legal traditions to develop and grow. However, in the past three decades, civil law has increasingly emerged from the shadow of common law, and now enjoys greater prominence. The growth of Indigenous legal traditions may follow the same course if appropriate measures are taken.

*i. Interactions between Civil Law and Common Law:
    Lessons for Indigenous Law?*

Legal traditions within Canada interact with one another, and this may hold lessons for Indigenous laws' growth. The civil law has been inordinately influenced by the common law and still maintains its authority; perhaps the same conclusions will apply to Indigenous traditions influenced by the other legal traditions. Indigenous traditions may still maintain their power despite being heavily and inappropriately overshadowed by other legal traditions in the courts, parliament, and provincial legislatures.

For many years, courts, Parliament, and legislatures outside Quebec paid very little attention to civil law. Even within Quebec there was a long period of concern about the creeping of common law principles into the judicial interpretation of the Civil Code.[30] During these years, civil law did not enjoy the same weight as common law in the Supreme Court of Canada. It seemed in danger of being assimilated.[31] The Privy Council and Supreme Court did not appear to understand that the Civil Code was a founding document of Quebec's legal system; as a result, they treated it like an ordinary statute.[32] This lack of reciprocity between the two systems caused many to worry about the continued vitality of civil law tradition.[33] Some scholars even went so far as to wonder whether the civil law would be undermined and assimilated through the influence of common law interpretive principles.[34] The tide seems to have turned in the last few years.[35] The influence of civil law began to grow after 1949 when the Supreme Court of Canada replaced the Privy Council in Great Britain as the country's final appellate body. Since 1975, the growth in the influence of civil law on common law has been most noticeable. Both the Supreme Court of Canada and the Parliament of Canada have taken steps to rebalance the relationship between the two systems.

While common law has historically had the more dominant influence, civil law has at times affected common law.[36] Taking care not to over-emphasize the impact,[37] we can nevertheless point to several examples in which the Supreme Court has referred to civil law in common law decisions. A paper written for the Department of Justice notes some examples:[38]

> [There] was the case in *Rivtow Marine Ltd.* v. *Washington Iron Works*, in which the Court cited *Ross* v. *Dunstall* on manufacturer's liability. It is interesting to note that, in *Ross* v. *Dunstall*, the Supreme Court interpreted

article 1053 of the *Civil Code of Lower Canada* ensuring that its interpretation was not inconsistent with a rule established by English precedent. In *Sorochan* v. *Sorochan*, it cited *Cie Immobilière Viger Ltée* v. *Lauréat Giguère Inc.*, but only for comparison as the basis of unjust enrichment can also find basis in common law. In another case, that of *Arndt* v. *Smith*, McLachlin J. cited *Laferrière* v. *Lawson* in support of her reasons on the balance of probabilities test in evaluating causation. Despite the varying levels of influence of civil law in these examples, they nevertheless illustrate an increased receptivity to comparative analysis of Canadian common law with Quebec civil law.

In family law, and more particularly with regard to child custody, the Court has seen fit to consider common law decisions in its civil law judgments, and vice versa, while recognizing the conceptual differences of the concepts in both traditions. The dialogue established between the two traditions in this field with regard to questions involving children, may be explained by a common thread running between them relating to the basis for every decision concerning children: the concept of the best interest of the child. This shared principle encourages common solutions, even if the reasons expressed based on the concepts specific to each tradition differ. L'Heureux-Dubé J.'s comparison in *Gordon* v. *Goertz* which is based on the distinctions established on the concept of custody in *C. (G.)* v. *V.-F. (T)*, is a good example of this trend, as is the analysis in *W. (V.)* v. *S. (D.)*.

Furthermore, when the issue before the Court concerns universal values, there is a more pronounced tendency to mention the rules and solutions of either tradition. This finds expression in the decisions, for example in matters pertaining to human rights and freedoms, including questions related to the protection of the fetus and the rights of the mother. The use of *Montreal Tramways Co.* v. *Léveillé* or *Tremblay* v. *Daigle* in *Dobson (Litigation Guardian of)* v. *Dobson* and *Winnipeg Child and Family Services (Northwest Area)* v. *D.F.G.* reflect this bridging of the gap between the two traditions. Each of these judgments, regardless of the question to be decided, turned on the same fundamental characterisation: the legal personality of the fetus before birth.[39]

The dialogue between these two legal traditions has proved beneficial. Greater reciprocity has facilitated access to a richer body of laws with which to answer legal questions. While it is possible to overstate the impact of the civil law on the common law, the fact remains that each tradition influences the other in Canada.

Despite the recent growing successes in harmonizing civil law and common law traditions, some civil law trained lawyers worried about the system's integrity, especially during the dark years of assimilation. They feared that civil law had become or would become tainted through its interaction with common law. Those who took this view felt that the best way to preserve the authenticity of civil law was to look inward. They tried to purify its doctrines by removing common law influences.

This approach fails to recognize that the integrity of a legal system is not solely dependent on its relative isolation, internal logic, or doctrinal purity. Integrity also depends upon the system's recognition, from within and by others. Recognition secures a jurisdictional space for its operation that encourages the respect of the public and facilitates access to resources. When legal systems do not have to continually defend and justify their existence or worth, they are less vulnerable to arguments that challenge their authenticity. When they gain recognition, they are much freer to interact with other systems without fear of assimilation.

The survival of civil law was greatly assisted by its broader recognition. To gain this recognition, civil law jurists did not have to concede the autonomy of the system's single source and intellectual approach to dispute resolution. Once the courts and Parliament acknowledged the authority and scope of civil law, it became easier for its influence to grow. Because it has been more firmly recognized by Canada's dominant legal institutions, civil law has been revitalized.

Indigenous legal traditions could benefit from this process. They could grow stronger through greater recognition by the courts and Parliament. The civil law experience should not be lost on those who seek to extend Indigenous legal traditions. Indigenous legal practitioners might consider the civil law experience and identify potential dangers that could develop from an exclusively inward-looking approach to tradition. Excessive introspection may not have always served the civil law well; nor will it always be beneficial to Indigenous legal traditions. At the same time it is important to contemplate the idea that perhaps the formal separation of Quebec as a civil law jurisdiction has been the strongest reason for its growth, more so *than the normative strength it acquired from interacting with the common law.*[40] There might be valid reasons for considering the separation of legal traditions even as we work towards their harmonization.

Greater discussion is needed within Indigenous communities about the benefits and potential problems of trying to purify Indigenous traditions by the removal of the 'contamination' from common law and civil law traditions. Those wishing to live solely by their traditions could usefully ponder whether disproportionately negative effects flow from attempts to completely isolate themselves from surrounding relationships. Many Indigenous peoples have close ties with surrounding Canadian life: through intermarriage (50 per cent of Aboriginal people marry non-Aboriginal people), through commercial relationships, and through other important private or societal relationships. Indigenous peoples may not have to secure the autonomy of the sources and approaches of Indigenous legal traditions to ensure their survival. At the same time, there are many persuasive arguments to be made about the benefits of having separate recognition of legal systems functioning within their own spheres. There are compelling arguments that Indigenous traditions could be strengthened by their separation from *and* interaction with the principles and approaches that are found in Canada's other legal traditions.

Of course, the civil law experience may not provide the best guide. Indigenous traditions are somewhat different from Canada's other legal systems. Indigenous peoples are a much smaller proportion of the population than those living under civil law in the province of Quebec. These smaller numbers might give less political weight to the recognition of Indigenous legal traditions nationally. Furthermore, the Quebec government (which protects property and civil rights through civil law), has specific protections in the Canadian Constitution, whereas Indigenous governance may not have the same status. It may be implicitly protected under section 35(1) of the *Constitution Act, 1982*; but, so far, this recognition has been less than optimal. Additionally, the fact that civil law and common law both stem from European cultures may make their harmonization easier than would be the case with the interface of Indigenous and non-Indigenous legal traditions. I hasten to add, however, that these differences must not be used as a convenient excuse to ignore potential recognition. We must be especially cautious that we do not cast differences between European law and Indigenous law in terms that subordinate Indigenous traditions on disguised grounds that they are somehow less civilized. Another way in which the civil law experience may not provide the best guide for Indigenous traditions is evident when one examines the surrounding transnational context. The international legal systems and most domestic systems seem to favour common and civil law modes of organization. This congruence should be a further caution against too strong an application of civil law history in Canada to Indigenous legal traditions. Finally, civil law is limited to matters of private law, whereas Indigenous legal traditions deal also with aspects of public law. While there are similarities, the differences between civil law and Indigenous law must be acknowledged, and form part of any strategy designed to preserve and develop Indigenous legal traditions.

ii. Interactions: Recognizing Connections across Legal Traditions

In order to have the common law, civil law, and Indigenous law work together in a more harmonious way, we will have to find better words, phrases, and frameworks to acknowledge and facilitate their coexistence. The search for such congruence will take us deeper into the realm of interpretation, dialogue, and argument. Law is 'a culture of argument' that 'provides a place and a set of institutions and methods where this conversational process can go on, as well as a second conversation by which the first is criticized and judged.'[41] Indigenous legal traditions, like all legal traditions, require a translation process to properly understand them,[42] though one must be careful that such translations do not always flow one way, to the benefit of the dominant systems. Canada's other legal traditions are also embedded in a culture of argument. Each contains a degree of ambiguity that requires judgment beyond its initial formulation. This is why every legal system employs different methods of interpretation to help bridge ambiguities. Judges and lawyers interpret civil and common law through case law judgments. Parliament and legislatures promulgate administrative regulations to further implement and clarify statutory grants of power. Indigenous traditions also require further explication beyond bare practice and presentation in order to understand and apply their meaning.

Canadians are by and large familiar with the process of dealing with ambiguities in civil and common law traditions through judicial decision-making and executive regulation-making. They are much less familiar with the ways in which ambiguities are addressed within Indigenous legal traditions. This presents a challenge for Canadian law, especially when ambiguities exist not only within legal traditions but also between them. As we have seen, each of the many Indigenous legal traditions might possess a different method of interpretation. As noted in chapters 2 and 3, the best way to understand and overcome ambiguity within an Indigenous tradition is to become more familiar with their nature and scope. However, greater familiarity with Indigenous legal systems must not be an isolated activity with practitioners unconnected and unmindful of the common law and civil law. While detailed attention should be given to how to resolve ambiguities within each tradition, the most important step we can take in developing a culture of argument in relation to the place of Indigenous legal traditions in Canada is to develop a framework that does not subordinate them to the common law and civil law. When Indigenous peoples and their traditions are given equal status, this will reveal ways to achieve their greater coordination.

Indigenous law will more fully permeate the consciousness of common law and civil law practitioners and theorists when it is regarded as a real source of rights and obligations in our country. The expansion of our conventional conceptions of Canadian law will also require greater participation by Indigenous peoples. While detailed attention will be given to this point in subsequent chapters, this idea can be illustrated by drawing upon principles from Indigenous law. To provide an example, the following account will draw on Cree law to point out general principles that can help to bridge the ambiguities between the civil/common law and Indigenous legal traditions.

IN THE TIME BEFORE *there were human beings on Earth, the Creator called a great meeting of the Animal People.*

During that period of the world's history, the Animal People lived harmoniously with one another and could speak to the Creator with one mind. They were very curious about the reason for the gathering. When they had all assembled together, the Creator spoke.

'I am sending a strange new creature to live among you,' he told the Animal People. 'He is to be called Man and he is to be your brother.'

'But unlike you he will have no fur on his body, will walk on two legs and will not be able to speak with you. Because of this he will need your help in order to survive and become who I am creating him to be. You will need to be more than brothers and sisters, you will need to be his teachers.'

'Man will not be like you. He will not come into the world like you. He will not be born knowing and understanding who and what he is. He will have to search for that. And it is in the search that he will find himself.'

'He will also have a tremendous gift that you do not have. He will have the ability to dream. With this ability he will be able to invent great things and because of this he will move further and further away from you and will need your help even more when this happens.'

'But to help him I am going to send him out into the world with one very special gift. I am going to give him the gift of the knowledge of Truth and Justice. But like his identity it must be a search, because if he finds this knowledge too easily he will take it for granted. So I am going to hide it and I need your help to find a good hiding-place. That is why I have called you here.'

A great murmur ran through the crowd of Animal People. They were excited at the prospect of welcoming a new creature into the world and they were honoured by the Creator's request for their help. This was truly an important day.

One by one the Animal People came forward with suggestions of where the Creator should hide the gift of knowledge of Truth and Justice.

'Give it to me, my Creator,' said the Buffalo, 'and I will carry it on my hump to the very centre of the plains and bury it there.'

'A good idea, my brother,' the Creator said, 'but it is destined that Man should cover most of the world and he would find it there too easily and take it for granted.'

'Then give it to me,' said the Salmon, 'and I will carry it in my mouth to the deepest part of the ocean and I will hide it there.'

'Another excellent idea,' said the Creator, 'but it is destined that with his power to dream, Man will invent a device that will carry him there and he would find it too easily and take it for granted.'

'Then I will take it,' said the Eagle, 'and carry it in my talons and fly to the very face of the Moon and hide it there.'

'No, my brother,' said the Creator, 'even there he would find it too easily because Man will one day travel there as well.'

Animal after animal came forward with marvellous suggestions on where to hide this precious gift, and one by one the Creator turned down their ideas. Finally, just when discouragement was about to invade their circle, a tiny voice spoke from the back of the gathering. The Animal People were all surprised to find that the voice belonged to the Mole.

The Mole was a small creature who spent his life tunnelling through the earth and because of this had lost most of the use of his eyes. Yet because he was always in touch with Mother Earth, the Mole had developed true spiritual insight.

The Animal People listened respectfully when Mole began to speak.

'I know where to hide it, my Creator,' he said. 'I know where to hide the gift of the knowledge of Truth and Justice.'

'Where then, my brother?' asked the Creator. 'Where should I hide this gift?'

'Put it inside them,' said the Mole. 'Put it inside them because then only the wisest and purest of heart will have the courage to look there.'

And that is where the Creator placed the gift of the knowledge of Truth and Justice.[43]

The principles in the foregoing narrative convey the importance of participation and equality in the interpretation of Indigenous legal traditions.[44] In this account, the power of interpretation and judgment is not vested solely in so-called greater beings, such as the Creator or powerful animals. Even the smallest animals have something to contribute to a decision or the resolution of an issue. If we apply these principles to Indigenous traditions, we can conclude that powers of interpretation and judgment should not all be vested in legislators or judges. If we extended them to the coexistence of each of Canada's legal traditions, we would also acknowledge that the common law and civil law should not be the only reference points in the country's legal lexicon. Those with less formal power in society should also have a role in deciding how law should be interpreted and should apply to them. Decision-making within Indigenous communities should not necessarily be done by those who are distant, professionalized, and impersonal; Indigenous dispute resolution has the potential to involve a greater range of people in determining the consequences for actions.[45] Furthermore, decision-making between the common law and civil law (on the one hand) and Indigenous law (on the other) should not presume a hierarchy that places Indigenous legal traditions lower in force or authority. Mutual mechanisms of regulation and dispute resolution could be devised to bring each tradition into contact with the other on a more equal basis.

When equality becomes an important part of Canada's legal framework in this way, Indigenous legal traditions will more thoroughly interact with the common law and civil law in autonomous and interdependent ways. This would help prevent the erosion of Indigenous legal traditions, which must be halted. Their weakening influence has at least two negative effects. First, undermining Indigenous law destabilizes normative order within Indigenous communities. The subversion of values that sustain Indigenous legal traditions generates confusion and disrespect for 'the law' in the broad sense within these communities. When people's respect for law is diminished, this creates a significant challenge for peace, order, and development. The destabilization of any society's sense of obligation generates substantial uncertainty, and Indigenous peoples certainly experience this result when their laws are denied. Some may think that legal certainty is best achieved by having only one legal tradition, such as common law.[46] But this is not necessarily the case. Whenever common law or a legislative rule ignores or overturns an Indigenous law without Indigenous participation, or in a manner hostile to Indigenous law, Indigenous people conclude that the rules governing their lives are arbitrary and unjust. Arbitrariness and injustice are contrary to the rule of law in Canada.[47] Indigenous legal traditions must gain recognition so that they can influence that rule of law.

Second, the undermining of Indigenous legal traditions also diminishes Canada as a nation. The culture of law is weakened in the country as a whole if Indigenous peoples' legal traditions are excluded from its matrix. Not only do we lose the wisdom they could provide about how to organize relationships and reduce disputes, but we also fail to attend to the underlying justice of Canada's creation and development. The recognition of Indigenous legal traditions could connect Aboriginal and other Canadians to land in ways not possible under the current administration of common or civil law. When common or civil law is applied solely to remove Indigenous people from their lands and environments, the highest principles of Canada's legal system are not served. For example, as noted in chapter 1, there are significant problems with the prevailing and conventional explanations concerning the so-called reception of law in Canada. To review, there was no *conquest* of Indigenous peoples that extinguished their jurisdictional rights over their own affairs. There was no *discovery* by the Crown that would justify the extinguishing Indigenous legal jurisdiction. The Crown's claims of *effective occupation* and *adverse possession* over lands where Indigenous peoples still reside are not very persuasive doctrines when they are used to undercut pre-existing and contemporary Indigenous laws.

Legal certainty is strengthened when Canadian law is built on doctrines that acknowledge the flaws of these other justifications. The recognition of Indigenous legal traditions places Canadian law on a firmer foundation because Indigenous law provides ways to allocate or alienate or share land within their communities and with others in ways that are more consistent with the demands of justice. When land and power is transferred in harmony with Indigenous law, all people of Canada can claim a relationship to land and jurisdiction that rests on consent and mutual respect. The Supreme Court of the United States recognized the truth of this statement in the *Winans* case: 'treaty rights are a grant of rights *from* the Indians, not *to* the Indians.'[48] This is known as the 'reserved rights' notion of treaties. This doctrine holds that Indigenous peoples have rights and jurisdictions under their laws until those rights are expressly altered in treaty negotiations. Canadian law has recognized the 'reserved rights' doctrine in connection with Aboriginal title.[49] The doctrine implies that anything not agreed to or expressed in the treaty remains vested in Indigenous populations, and cannot be claimed by the non-Indigenous governments as a general right that flows from the treaty negotiations. The 'reserved rights' doctrine highlights the inherent nature of Aboriginal rights. It builds upon the fact that when the Europeans arrived in North America, the Indians were already here, living in organized societies and occupying their lands as they had done for centuries.[50]

This is why treaties are so important to Canada's legal framework. They can draw the common law, civil law, and Indigenous legal traditions together. Treaties recognize Indigenous peoples' right to make decisions in accordance with their laws to share or give land to others. They recognize non-Indigenous peoples' right to do the same thing, to share and give land in accordance with their legal traditions. Such mutuality should make it obvious that *Indigenous peoples are not the only beneficiaries under the treaties. Non-Indigenous peoples also have treaty rights.* Both groups are recipients of the promises made in the negotiation process. The mutuality of the treaties is often overlooked because Indigenous peoples are those most often striving to assert their rights. Yet there are a number of potential inheritors of treaty rights other than Indigenous nations, bands, and individuals. The British and Canadian Crown certainly received many benefits from the treaties. Their citizens were able to peacefully settle and develop most parts of the country by consent. In those parts of the country where there are no treaties (such as British Columbia, Quebec, Labrador, and parts of the North), Indigenous consent is now being negotiated. Where there are treaties, Canadians can trace many of their rights in this country to the consent that was granted to the Crown by Indigenous peoples in the treaty process.

Yet the notion that non-Indigenous peoples might trace certain rights to land or governance through the treaties is, for many, still an emergent concept. Because people have not been exposed to Indigenous understandings of law or the treaties, they are only now beginning to consider them in this light. Most other nations do not have these same protocols, conventions, history, or traditions of cooperation and communication in dealings among diverse populations. As a result, many nations struggle to create better regimes without the advantage of shared ideological roots of intercultural understanding and association. While some jurisdictions try to start *tabula rasa* and revolutionize how people will relate to one another in society,[51] most simply do not have wide enough support from across the political spectrum to undertake so radical a change. They are left with the arduous task of reforming their systems without ideologies or institutions that have a shared resonance for the members of disparate groups.

Canada is different. In many places it was created through multi-juridical meetings that mediated differences throughout most of the land. Canada is still being created in this way in vast parts of the North, Quebec, British Columbia, and Labrador. Treaties between Indigenous peoples and the Crown promote peace and order across cultures and are the basis of the country's formation and continued reformation. The use of treaties provides a living example of multi-juridicalism. Canadians are fortunate to have agreements that provide mutually recognized conventions for the resolution of disputes between peoples that draw on different legal traditions. New policies or norms to solve our challenges need not be invented. Treaties and other such recognitions of Indigenous traditions already provide a common starting point of poly-juridical connectivity. Much of the world is not founded on such high principles.[52]

The continued existence of Indigenous legal traditions could be of great benefit to Indigenous peoples and the wider public if they were given space to grow and develop. Canada has distinguished itself as a country that effectively operates with a bijuridical tradition. There is much that can be learned and analogized from this experience. Recognizing and affirming Canada's legal structures within a framework of multi-juridical diversity is one more step in this learning.

5 Recognizing a Multi-Juridical Legal Culture

The operation of multiple legal systems is a Canadian tradition, though its full diversity has been largely hidden from the country's common law and civil law communities. Despite these and other challenges, Canada has strong aspirations towards tolerance and respect for difference.[1] Our national laws aim to allow individuals the freedom to practise their customs and traditions as long as they do not inappropriately infringe on the legal interests of others.[2] Our legal system endeavours to facilitate group organization and association to improve the lives of the participants and those around them.[3] A vibrant constitutional framework supports this respect for individual and community belief, conscience, expression, assembly, and association.[4] The federal structure is designed to facilitate laws, customs, and traditions particular to its various provinces and regions.[5] The *Charter of Rights and Freedoms* guarantees individual rights to democratic participation, mobility, due process, and equality.[6] This instrument enshrines French and English linguistic equality.[7] Laws are to be interpreted in a manner consistent with the preservation and enhancement of Canadians' multicultural heritage.[8] *Charter* rights are designed to empower people to practise their cultures and traditions and to pursue their goals and aspirations subject only to such reasonable limits prescribed by law as can be demonstrably justified in a free and democratic society.[9]

Canada's founders rejected the idea of forced cultural coercion, at least as it related to the most critical challenges they encountered: French and English, juridical, cultural, religious, and linguistic differences.[10] Although this framework was not broadly extended to Indigenous peoples, it is not too late to do so. Important analogies can be drawn from constitutional history to accomplish this objective. The *British North America Act, 1867* was designed to unify along federal lines to protect their differences.[11] It enabled French and English speakers to continue their unique political, religious, cultural, linguistic, and legal traditions within provincial frameworks.[12] Minority educational rights were constitutionally enshrined in section 93 to ensure that groups could practise their traditions, even in provinces where the dominant culture was not their own.[13] This was the constitutional bargain that made the foundation of the country possible. The *British North America Act* (now the *Constitution Act, 1867*), while an incomplete governance instrument, was nevertheless sufficient to unite disparate peoples. Georges-Étienne Cartier, one of its architects, observed:

> It was lamented by some that we had this diversity of races, and hopes were expressed that this distinctive feature would cease. The idea of unity of races [is] utopian – it [is] impossible. Distinctions of this kind always exist. Dissimilarity, in fact, appear[s] to be the order of the physical world and of the moral world, as well as in the political world. But with regard to the objection based on this fact, to the effect that a great nation [can]not be formed because Lower Canada [is] in great part French and Catholic, and Upper Canada [is] British and Protestant, and the Lower Provinces [are] mixed, it [is] futile and worthless in the extreme ... In our own Federation we have Catholic and Protestant, English, French, Irish and Scotch, and each by his efforts and his success [will] increase the prosperity and glory of the new Confederacy. [W]e [are] of different races, not for the purpose of warring against each other, but in order to compete and emulate for the general welfare.[14]

Cartier's acknowledgment that distinctions between peoples will remain a significant part of our political reality contains an important insight when applied to the country's Indigenous nations. In deliberating about how we can ensure Canada's continued strength, these historically deep, constitutionally protected rights and traditions should not be ignored. They aim to foster unity amidst difference. They promote interdependence amongst our peoples and have great potential for application to Indigenous issues. Each of Canada's legal traditions must remain strong to ensure peace, order, and good government. Canadians must therefore strive to develop and extend societal cohesion through common allegiance to Confederation's historical and legal framework. At the same time, differences in traditions must not be sacrificed to overreaching attempts to enforce civic solidarity. The country's constitutional goal is to reconcile unity and diversity, to recognize continued interdependence even in the face of a measured independence.[15] Canada's democracy is fundamentally connected to these substantive goals. This includes the promotion of self-government through the accommodation of cultural and group identities.[16] These benefits that underlie Canada's constitutional order should be more widely available to Indigenous peoples.

Yet this message has detractors. Some say that the solution to Canada's challenge of diversity is to enforce a greater commonality, even absorption of minorities into an English-speaking majority. A number of suggestions are proposed to facilitate conformity: education, the media, targeted spending, propaganda, artistic and athletic excellence, and the creation of national institutions and symbols. Others concerned about difference often see the answer in assimilation.[17] Of course, the question of who should assimilate whom is not easily answered. The normal assumption is that minorities should be assimilated. Yet it is hard to justify why one group should be entitled to dominate and absorb others on solely numeric terms. Furthermore, it is also exceedingly difficult to secure agreement from groups facing assimilation.

Given the problems in overcoming differences, the melting pot metaphor may often appear to be an attractive one. This promotes the idea that cultures can be blended into a singular system of belief, practice, and approach to life. But this metaphor underestimates the inappropriate pressures this can place on individual identities and national development. This has particularly been the case with Indigenous peoples.[18] Despite Canada's constitutional embrace of European (French/English) cultural difference, respect for cultural difference has not always been extended to Indigenous peoples. Early legislation encouraged and endorsed their assimilation.[19] Duncan Campbell Scott, former Deputy Superintendent General of Indian Affairs, illustrated this approach in an address to Parliament in 1920. He stated: 'Our object is to continue until there is not a single Indian in Canada that has not been absorbed into the body politic and there is no Indian question.'[20]

But Indigenous assimilation has been an astonishing failure. A wealth of evidence makes it clear that assimilation is *the* most hated and resisted policy for Indigenous peoples.[21] Nothing will turn Indigenous peoples from the Canadian state with greater force than policies designed to assimilate them. Assimilation provokes resistance, confrontation, and strenuous objection. The policy has no credibility in contemporary debates for most Indigenous people. In the face of such strong repudiations, it would be unconscionable to force its application against their strongly expressed will. Assimilation must be rejected if Canada is to enjoy a healthy, vibrant democracy based on respect for the choice and free agency of individuals and groups under a non-coercive rule of law.

Too strong a push towards assimilation could destroy the country. The recent history of the Quebec secessionist movement illustrates these dangers.[22] English dominance was appropriately overthrown because French-speaking people in the province did not want to lose their deepest traditions.[23] Some still clamour for complete separation in order to more effectively resist assimilation.[24] People resist forced association and compulsion, especially if it is contrary to their deepest identities. As the Supreme Court of Canada has observed: 'If a person is compelled by the State or the will of another to a course of action or inaction, which he would not otherwise have chosen, he is not acting of his own volition and he cannot be said to be truly free.'[25] Of course, not all associations are voluntary, like the family or certain requirements of citizenship; they arise from the 'inescapable constraints of social life in modern society.'[26] But, to the extent possible, people should be free to choose and shape their community's practices and follow their underlying values.

As long as citizens are secure in their fundamental rights and freedoms, they should be entitled to live by their choices, customs, and traditions. Forced association inhibits the potential for self-fulfilment.[27] Democracy is enhanced when people can choose the rules and traditions under which they live. 'Democracy requires a continuous process of discussion.'[28] Mandatory assimilation is a recipe for resistance and continued conflict. Statutory assimilation (like we see in the *Indian Act*) should be rejected as being contrary to Canada's constitutional values. The protection of minority rights is an independent principle underlying our constitutional order.[29] As the Supreme Court of Canada observed: 'Although Canada's record of upholding the rights of minorities is not a spotless one, that goal is one towards which Canadians have been striving since Confederation.'[30]

Today, Canada is home to many more cultures and traditions than those that gave rise to Confederation.[31] A pressing contemporary challenge is how to stitch them together without shredding society.[32] Some people despair at the diversity of languages, cultures, and traditions in our midst.[33] But Aboriginal peoples occupy a special place in Canada's constitutional framework: they are not just another culture or minority group. Section 35(1) in Part II of the *Constitution Act, 1982* protects the existing culture, practices, and traditions of Aboriginal peoples. Section 35(1) safeguards Indigenous peoples as one of the country's founding political and legal groups. The embedding of Indigenous diversity in Canada's central legal texts provides a sound justification for recognizing their legal traditions.

A. The Recognition of Law in Historical Context

i. Aboriginal Land and Resources: Aboriginal-to-Aboriginal Relations

The recognition of Indigenous legal traditions alongside other legal orders has historic precedent in this land.[34] Prior to the arrival of Europeans and explorers from other continents, a vibrant legal pluralism sometimes developed amongst First Nations. Treaties, intermarriages, contracts of trade and commerce, and mutual recognition were legal arrangements that contributed to extended periods of peace and helped to restrain recourse to war when conflict broke out. When Europeans and others came to North America, they found themselves in this complex socio-legal landscape. Although it has not always been sufficiently acknowledged outside those who specialize in the area, contemporary Canadian law concerning Indigenous peoples partially originates in, and is extracted from, these legal systems.[35] While care must be taken to not overstate the point, evidence exists to show that Indigenous peoples were an important force in the Constitution of Canada.

For example, in the time before others arrived in North America, Aboriginal peoples had well-developed systems to oppose those who threatened access to land and resources.[36] Direct occupation of land was only one of a range of options that Aboriginal peoples employed to secure their resources.[37] There were wider systems of diplomacy in use to maintain peace through councils and elaborate protocols.[38] For example, First Nations and powerful individuals would participate in such activities as smoking the peace pipe, feasting, holding a Potlatch, exchanging ceremonial objects, and engaging in long orations, discussions and negotiations. Diplomatic traditions among Indigenous peoples were designed to prevent more direct confrontation. Intersocietal norms were developed to resolve conflict before people were placed in harm's way.[39] It was often easier to overcome disputes if each side's symbols and substantive concerns were acknowledged and reflected in diplomacy's process and product.

To formalize agreements, Aboriginal Nations might sometimes enter into treaties with one another. The purpose was to endorse an accord that might flow from diplomatic exchanges. Treaties are a form of agreement that can be very productive as a method for securing peace. An important Indigenous-to-Indigenous treaty occurred between the Haudenosaunee[40] and the Anishinabek[41] in 1701 near Sault Ste Marie.[42] The agreement was orally transacted and is recorded on a wampum belt. The 1701 belt has an image of a 'bowl with one spoon.' It references the fact that both nations would share their hunting grounds in order to obtain food. The single wooden spoon in the bowl meant that no knives or sharp edges would be allowed in the land, for this would lead to bloodshed.[43] This agreement is still remembered by the two nations today.

Peace was also pursued through intersocietal activities between First Nations to bridge division and discord. These less formalized paths to peace should not be underestimated; they contain lessons about how to effectively overcome problems today. Understanding between groups grew as diverse peoples and individuals interacted with one another in social and economic affairs that borrowed elements of each culture.[44] First Nations knew it was important to create a supportive social context to generate peace. The forging of personal ties was important, as friendship, intermarriage, and adoption helped to smooth tension.[45] Games, contests, dances, and other forms of recreation could bring whole groups together.[46] People would often learn one another's language to facilitate communication across cultural and political lines. Sometimes new languages would be developed, such as Chinook on the West Coast, to ease tension and encourage further communication and commerce.

Indigenous peoples from different nations could sometimes congregate together for spiritual sustenance and form stronger bonds of belonging. One example of the development of Indigenous-to-Indigenous intersocietal activities occurred in the Great Lakes area through the ancient Feast of the Dead.[47] There would be times when the Anishinabek and the Wendat[48] would gather together at such feasts to ceremonially cement ties. The parties would exchange food and other gifts, trade goods, discuss common issues, and conduct important business. At the centre of these gatherings was the exhumation of bones from recently deceased ancestors from each nation. These bones would then be reburied in a common grave symbolizing the mingling of the societies in this world and the next.[49] This powerful physical act of sharing and sociocultural/spiritual bonding is an example of how Indigenous peoples dealt with one another to overcome relational challenges.

If Indigenous peoples were not successful in maintaining amity through such national and individualized efforts, then steps were sometimes taken to separate groups from one another. Boundaries and neutral zones could be developed to buffer more intense conflict. Patrols and checkpoints could be utilized to identify and warn those who found themselves straying close to territorial- or resource-use conflict. In Anishinabek society, peace-keeping warriors, or *Ogijidah*, could be used to patrol and monitor such sites of conflict, and perhaps even occupy a contested site.[50] This physical occupation could extend to village sites, along with hunting, fishing, and gathering locations if others were not properly recognizing or affirming one party's rights.[51] As noted, these blockades – preventing others' access to a locale – were only one tool Indigenous peoples used to sustain important relationships to land and resources. These tools were embedded in a wider framework of law. Indigenous peoples' occupation of areas to which they maintain or claim rights is not merely a modern phenomenon. Like other nations and peoples of the world, Indigenous peoples have participated in civil disobedience within the context of their own and others' cultural norms and legal values for a long, long time.

As a last resort, if other methods of conflict resolution failed, Indigenous peoples would sometimes go to war over lands and resources. Though always tragic, most wars between Indigenous peoples in Canada were not fought on the scale found in Europe during the same period. Conflict between Indigenous nations in northern North America was often localized and based on Indigenous justice systems that required a life for a life.[52] However, there were rare occasions when armed conflict became more generalized and resulted in widespread violence and death. For example, there were catastrophic wars between the Haudenosaunee and Wendat in the 1640s. These battles led to the near extermination and brutal dispersion of the Wendat peoples from their traditional territories in southern Ontario.[53] This genocidal removal demonstrates why the failure of more peaceful methods of dispute resolution and the rule of law could be disastrous for entire peoples. The Wendat tragedy demonstrates the extreme consequences of armed confrontation if other forms of conflict resolution break down and the application of law breaks down. The failure of diplomacy, regulation, and dispute resolution on this scale is a severe tragedy, brutally removing people from their ancient territories. Indigenous peoples have long sought ways to avoid such calamities, thereby placing Indigenous law and diplomacy at the heart of much Indigenous experience with others in North America.

ii. The Arrival of Non-Aboriginal Peoples

When non-Aboriginal peoples ventured forth from their lands into North America, they encountered peoples with well-developed laws and duties related to land and resource use. In the first years of contact, many non-Aboriginal peoples adapted themselves to the existing Indigenous protocols.[54] Non-Aboriginal peoples would recognize Indigenous land and resource use through many of the same institutions with which Indigenous peoples were familiar: councils, feasts, ceremonies, orations, discussion, treaties, intermarriage, adoption, games, contests, dances, spiritual sharing, boundaries, buffer zones, occupations, and war.[55]

In the early 1700s, for example, the French entered into treaties with the Anishinabek of the Great Lakes by using Anishinabek forms, wampum belts, and ceremony.[56] From 1693 until 1779, the peace and friendship treaties between the Mi'kmaq, Maliseet, Passamaquoddy, and the British Crown used similar principles grounded in Indigenous protocols, procedures, and practices.[57] In 1764, when the British were able to assert an interest in North America after the Seven Years War, they used Indigenous legal traditions to transact their business and bind themselves to solemn commitments.[58] The Hudson's Bay Company entered into agreements with Aboriginal people during the fur trade.[59]

If their rights were not recognized, Indigenous peoples would take direct action and re-occupy areas recently claimed by others. They were willing to enforce their rights to land if necessary, illustrating the depth of their connections to land in North America. Perhaps one of the earliest known examples of this occurring was on the Great Lakes on 2 June 1763. The story is recorded as follows:

The Indians used a clever plan to capture Fort Michilimackinac. They knew that the British king's birthday was on June 4. A Chippewa chief suggested to the fort commander that the Indians and the British join together in a celebration. As part of the celebration, some visiting Sauk Indians would play a ball game against the Chippewa outside the fort.

On June 4 the soldiers came out of the fort to watch the game. Chippewa women stood around the fort wrapped in their blankets. The Chippewa and the Sauk began their game of *baggataway*, which was similar to lacrosse.

At one point, the wooden ball was thrown into the fort. The players rushed in after it. As they passed through the gates of the fort, the players grabbed the weapons that the women were holding under their blankets! Once inside, the Indians easily took control of the fort.[60]

At this point, violence ensued and the entire area once again fell under the control of the Indigenous peoples.

The relative ease with which Indigenous peoples could reoccupy their lands placed the British in a tenuous position after 1763. They had defeated the French in the Seven Years War, but the Indians threatened their power in North America.[61] The British were constrained to recognize Indigenous political and military might; aspirations for the development of North America would be thwarted if they did not acknowledge Indigenous rights. Therefore, the British agreed to preserve Indigenous peoples' possession of land and use of resources. They did this through the Royal Proclamation of 1763, the Treaty of Niagara of 1764, and subsequent agreements. The British approach committed the Crown to entering into treaties with Indigenous peoples if their lands were to be occupied by non-Aboriginal people. Indigenous peoples' actions and perspectives were important to this policy formulation. They persuaded the government to peacefully settle conflicts over land and resources in North America through treaties.[62] The Crown was bound to secure Indigenous consent before occupying Aboriginal lands.

Since that time, there have been hundreds of treaties and agreements in Canada, with many of them drawing on some form of Indigenous legal tradition, even in later eras when they enjoyed less political influence. Aboriginal laws, legal perspectives, and other Indigenous frameworks have been present throughout the entire span of the treaty-making process in Canada. Since 1982, existing treaty rights have been recognized and affirmed in section 35 of the *Constitution Act, 1982*, thus enjoying the highest possible status in Canada's legal order.[63] The continuation of treaty rights and obligations entrenches the continued existence of Indigenous legal traditions in Canada.

Yet treaties are not the only area where Indigenous traditions influenced Canada's Constitution and continue into the present day. When the British and Indians met in North America, diplomacy was not centralized, but diffuse.[64] The parties developed their own protocols and ceremonies, and these were rarely solely European.[65] They attempted to create a social context that supported peace. Diplomacy was conducted by many actors, including orators, headmen, war chiefs, peace chiefs, civil leaders, village and colonial councils, missionaries, traders, speculators, traditionalists, and dissidents, those with authority and those without.[66]

From the 1500s onward, a number of European individuals submitted themselves to Indigenous legal orders.[67] For example, many traders and explorers adopted Indigenous legal traditions and participated in their laws.[68] A perusal of the fur trade literature reveals that commercial transactions were often conducted in accordance with Indigenous traditions.[69] The giving of gifts, the extension of credit, and the standards of trade were often based on Indigenous legal concepts.[70] Traditionally, Indigenous peoples in Canada did not transfer goods by conducting their relations with other people in a static way.[71] Relationships were continually renewed and reaffirmed through ceremonial customs.[72] The idea of trade terms being 'frozen' through a contract written on paper was an alien concept.[73] The traders recognized this fact and conducted their affairs in accordance with Indigenous laws.[74] In the more personal sphere, many of the early marriage relationships between Indigenous women and European men were formed according to Indigenous legal traditions.[75] There were no priests or ministers in the northwest to officiate at weddings until 1818, and this meant that governing laws were found in the various Indigenous nations throughout the land.[76]

For example, in the first year of Canada's Confederation, the Quebec Superior Court affirmed the existence of Cree law on the prairies and recognized it as part of the common law. In arriving at this position, Justice Monk wrote:

> Will it be contended that the territorial rights, political organization such as it was, or the laws and usages of Indian tribes were abrogated – that

they ceased to exist when these two European nations began to trade with [A]boriginal occupants? In my opinion it is beyond controversy that they did not – that so far from being abolished, they were left in full force, and were not even modified in the slightest degree ...[77]

The legal doctrine applied by Justice Monk is known as the doctrine of continuity.[78] While the common law's original 'reception' and application in Canada is problematic if it is regarded as occurring without Indigenous consent, even in this view the common law did recognize the continuity of Aboriginal customs, laws, and traditions upon the Crown's assertion of sovereignty. Among the rights recognized by the Crown as continuing were Aboriginal rights to occupy and use their traditional territories and to conduct civil affairs.

Through time, however, these diverse forms of reconciliation and resistance at least partially founded upon Indigenous legal traditions and practices were attenuated. Interactions became more dependent on non-Aboriginal cultural and legal norms as these groups grew stronger in North America. In such circumstances, some Indigenous peoples found themselves increasingly adapting to non-Indigenous institutions and ideas to maintain their land and resources.[79] Despite these adaptations, Indigenous peoples never completely surrendered their approaches to law and conflict resolution.[80] Non-Aboriginal peoples have never achieved absolute dominance over Indigenous peoples in Canada in these matters. The aspirations of many Indigenous communities are still largely turned towards their own norms and values. Indigenous peoples' agency continues to exist. As such, Indigenous legal perspectives and traditions continue to shape Canadian law by being a part of it. In *Haida Nation v. British Columbia*, Chief Justice McLachlin wrote:

Put simply, Canada's Aboriginal peoples were here when Europeans came, and were never conquered. Many bands reconciled their claims with the sovereignty of the Crown through negotiated treaties. Others, notably in British Columbia, have yet to do so. The potential rights embedded in these claims are protected by s. 35 of the *Constitution Act, 1982*. The honour of the Crown requires that these rights be determined, recognized and respected.[81]

In *R. v. Mitchell*, Chief Justice McLachlin wrote for a majority of the Court:

European settlement did not terminate the interests of aboriginal peoples arising from their historical occupation and use of the land. To the contrary, aboriginal interests and customary laws were presumed to survive the assertion of sovereignty, and were absorbed into the common law as rights ... [82]

These statements are strong endorsements of the need to determine, recognize, and respect Aboriginal rights in Canada, and they reveal that Indigenous law is important to this venture. Chief Justice McLachlin noted Indigenous legal traditions continue to exist as rights in Canada unless: '(1) they were incompatible with the Crown's assertion of sovereignty, (2) they were surrendered voluntarily via the treaty process, or (3) the government extinguished them.'[83] Barring one of these exceptions, she wrote, the practices, customs, and traditions that defined the various Aboriginal societies as distinctive cultures continue as part of the law of Canada today.[84] While Indigenous peoples would strongly resist the limitations Chief Justice McLachlin placed on the continuity of their rights,[85] there are sound arguments that Indigenous rights, obligations, and conflict resolution procedures are compatible with the Crown's assertion of sovereignty. Indigenous peoples believe many of their rights were not surrendered by treaties and were not extinguished by clear and plain government legislation, if reconciliation is the lens through which the courts interpret the parties' relationships.[86] They believe that their laws coexist with common law and civil law traditions, and that they are a strong part of Canada's constitutional inheritance.

6 Challenges and Opportunities in Recognizing Indigenous Legal Traditions

Having developed a broader context for the recognition of Indigenous legal traditions in Canada's constitutional relationships, it is critically important to highlight the challenges and opportunities this recognition may encounter. While every attempt has been made to accurately convey the current relationship between Canadian legal traditions and their potential for future development, these positions are likely to be contested for different reasons. People will have different social, political, economic, psychological, ideological, and spiritual perspectives on the ideas presented thus far. This chapter chronicles some of the more pressing concerns which judges, lawyers, academics, politicians, journalists, theorists, and Indigenous community members might have about the recognition of Indigenous legal traditions.

One of the first challenges to the recognition and development of Indigenous legal traditions is the fact that law is never as tidy as we would wish. While I have sought to reveal more of the laws' complexity than is usual when discussing Canada's Constitution, the fact is there is never only one singular view of the law: it is always open to interpretation. As my colleague Professor Jeremy Webber has written:

> [I]t is always misleading ... to talk about 'the law' in a particular context as though the law's content were pre-determined and singular, at least until the mechanisms operative in that context have adjudicated the disagreement ... The hermeneutic character of normative argument means that law always has a measure of openness ... Any attempt to describe the law of a particular context should reflect this openness. It should not state the law as though it were singular. Instead it should aim to capture a legal culture, portraying the range of contending arguments on the one hand,

and practices, interests, patterns of historical experience and individuals' identifications on the other; the extant mechanisms for resolving social disagreement, and from an assessment of all these factors, the relative success of various normative assertions.[1]

In evaluating Canada's legal culture, I have concluded that it can accommodate Indigenous legal traditions. Yet law's open nature requires that we attend to contrary arguments. Since the relationships between common law, civil law, and Indigenous legal traditions are not fixed, the future shape of Canada's law (as these traditions interact) will be influenced by criticism about the reality or desirability of their coexistence.

Despite my best efforts, law's interpretive diversity leads me to acknowledge that it is simply not possible to definitively declare what 'the law' *is* or *should be* in the relationship between Canada's legal traditions.[2] Such answers will always be open for question and reinterpretation; that is the nature of legal reasoning. Therefore, in arguing for a greater respect between traditions, I must at the same moment be open to the view that Indigenous legal traditions do not or should not exist in Canada. As a result, this chapter will consider reasons why we should not recognize Indigenous legal traditions within Canadian law today, although it will be my conclusion that each of these objections can be overcome. I believe such objections can be moderated because, in line with Professor Webber's argument above, we possess powerful mechanisms to resolve disagreements about the place of Indigenous laws in our society. These supportive devices can be found in Canada's legal practices, the desire for peace with Indigenous people among our citizenry, patterns of historical experience, and in the power of individual innovation and creativity. To examine these issues, in the following pages I analyse questions related to the intelligibility, accessibility, equality, applicability, and legitimacy of Indigenous law.

A. Intelligibility

Laws are regarded as intelligible if those who must abide by their precepts 'can foresee, to a degree that is reasonable in the circumstances, the consequences which a given action may entail.'[3] On this basis, some people might question the legal intelligibility of Indigenous law. They may argue that Indigenous legal traditions are not precise enough to affect an individual's conduct. They may contend that it is not possible to foresee the consequences of inappropriate behaviour. Indigenous peoples and others who are supportive of their legal traditions should take this concern seriously. Since some Indigenous laws are framed as stories, songs, practices, and customs, they may be criticized as being unintelligible as a prescription of conduct. They could be construed as too open-ended to function as legal standards. It is reasonable to ask whether Indigenous citizens would have trouble understanding their own laws.

There are several approaches to this question. First, some Indigenous laws may need to be reframed to make them easier to understand. Every legal system is plagued with confusing jargon and vague concepts that produce a level of ambiguity that is sometimes intolerable. Indigenous legal traditions are no exception. Moreover, as is also the case with other legal traditions, some Indigenous laws contain too many anachronistic elements to be intelligible in our day. They may need to be made clearer by restating or revising them in ways that bring greater specificity or precision to assist with their eventual application. Furthermore, there are times when I have listened to an Indigenous person relate their law and I have come away from our meeting totally confused. Some of these occasions for misunderstanding were the result of my ignorance and failure to follow the intellectual subtleties of the presentation I was hearing. In such cases, it was not the law that was unintelligible but my reception of what was being communicated. However, there have been other times when it was apparent that it was not the law or cultural context that rendered an Indigenous legal principle unclear. Just as common law lawyers struggle to speak in plain English, without resorting to burdensome legalese, some Indigenous legal practitioners labour to communicate in ways that reveal rather than obscure the principles under discussion. This reality should add a note of caution concerning conclusions regarding the intelligibility of Indigenous laws. It may be that certain laws are intelligible, but the person responsible for articulating them experiences particular challenges in translating them for general consumption by those to whom they apply.[4] Despite this reminder, we must not lose sight of the fact that any legal system can benefit from giving greater attention to the intelligibility of principles, and Indigenous legal traditions are no exception. There is nothing inherently unintelligible within Indigenous laws but there may be a need to articulate, translate, or reinterpret some of them in particular instances to reduce their vagueness and imprecision.

A second point that should be remembered when examining the intelligibility of Indigenous law is that law is a cultural phenomenon. As a result, what may be unintelligible to those inexperienced with Indigenous culture may be quite intelligible to those familiar with it. A Eurocentric approach to legal interpretation must not be allowed to undermine Indigenous legal traditions. A leading historiographer of oral tradition, Jan Vansina, has observed that 'all messages are a part of a culture.'[5] As Vasina points out, in his seminal work, messages 'are expressed in the language of a culture and conceived, as well as understood, in the substantive terms of a culture.'[6] He therefore concludes that since culture shapes all messages, we must take culture into account when interpreting these messages. This is a challenging proposition. Since what constitutes a fact is largely contingent on the language and culture from which the information arises,[7] the person who decides what a 'fact' is inevitably defines it from the matrix of relationships they share with others.[8]

In practice, there are enormous risks for misunderstanding and misinterpretation when Indigenous laws are judged by those unfamiliar with the cultures from which they arise.[9] The potential for misunderstanding is compounded if each culture has somewhat different perceptions of space, time, historical truth, and causality.[10] The cultural specificity of what constitutes a fact may make it difficult for people from different cultures to accept the same information as a fact in their respective cultures.[11] Since variations between groups encode 'facts' with different meanings,[12] to be properly understood, they must be viewed through the lens of the culture that recorded them.

Those who evaluate the meaning, relevance, and weight of Aboriginal legal traditions must therefore appreciate the potential cultural differences in the implicit meanings behind explicit messages if they are going to draw appropriate inferences and conclusions.[13] They should attempt to grasp their unspoken symbolic aspects in order to evaluate their truth and value. Mastering both these facets of interpretation is a tremendously difficult and complex task. Even with the best of intentions, many simply may not be equipped to perform this role without further training. Each culture has its own shared imagery that conveys both meaning and emotion, as found in metaphors, stock phrases, stereotypes, and other clichés.[14] It is important to understand the particular imagery of a culture contained in these forms to appreciate 'the context of meaning' behind a legal standard.[15] Without this deeper knowledge, it may be difficult to understand and acknowledge the meanings that Aboriginal people give to their laws.[16] This evaluation will be especially fraught with danger if the interpreter does not recognize the cultural foundation of knowledge, and fails to acknowledge his or her own bias.[17]

Third, Indigenous peoples might also approach the issue of intelligibility by questioning the detail necessary for a formulation to be 'prescribed by law.'[18] Western courts have been deferential to Western governments in interpreting this phrase. In the European Court of Human Rights case of *Sunday Times v. United Kingdom*, the phrase 'prescribed by law' was interpreted flexibly under the European Convention on Human Rights to allow for a degree of vagueness. The Court wrote:

> In the Court's opinion, the following are two of the requirements that flow from the expression 'prescribed by law.' First, the law must be adequately accessible: the citizen must be able to have an indication that is adequate in the circumstances of the legal rules applicable to a given case. Secondly, a norm cannot be regarded as 'law' unless it is formulated with sufficient precision to enable the citizen to regulate his conduct: he must be able to foresee, to a degree that is reasonable in the circumstances, the consequences which a given action may entail. Those consequences need not be foreseeable with absolute certainty: experience shows this to be unreasonable. Again, whilst certainty is highly desirable, it may bring in its train excessive rigidity and the law must be able to keep pace with changing circumstances. Accordingly, many laws are inevitably couched in terms which, to a greater or lesser extent, are vague and whose interpretation and application are questions of practice. [19]

The phrase 'prescribed by law' does not require that an action's consequences be foreseeable with absolute certainty. This would lead to excessively rigid laws unable to keep pace with changing circumstances. Legal interpretation is a question of 'practice,' where potentially vague laws can be made intelligible by their application in a particular factual context.

In interpreting the phrase in the Canadian *Charter of Rights and Freedoms*, the Supreme Court of Canada took a similar approach to that in the *Sunday Times* case when it held that law cannot be characterized too rigidly. The Supreme Court noted 'prescribed by law' could set too high a standard for governments if interpreted too strictly. In *Irwin Toy v. Quebec (A.G.)* the Court observed:

Absolute precision in the law exists rarely, if at all. The question is whether the legislature has provided an intelligible standard ... The task of interpreting how that standard applies in a specific instance might always be characterized as having a discretionary element, because the standard can never specify all the instances in which it applies.[20]

This argument shows that the Supreme Court of Canada has interpreted 'prescribed by law' broadly. In matters 'prescribed by law,' 'discretion' and 'balance' are allowed.[21] The Supreme Court has held that a law is only 'impermissibly vague' if it does 'not provide a sufficient basis for legal debate.'[22] If broader Canadian law can describe 'debatable' legal standards as intelligible, Indigenous legal traditions should surely be given the same courtesy. Care must be taken to ensure that Indigenous legal traditions are not held to a higher standard of intelligibility than non-Indigenous law. Indigenous peoples may well be able to argue that their laws meet the standards of intelligibility as outlined by the courts, even if they are not immediately 'cognizable' to a judge trained in the common law or civil law systems, or if there is room for debate about their meanings.

B. Accessibility

Intelligibility is closely related to the issue of accessibility. Laws are accessible when people know where to find them, how to learn them, and who to speak to if they have questions about them. If too many people have difficulty understanding Indigenous laws because they are not readily available, steps should be taken to make them more accessible. Indigenous peoples would benefit if it were easier to obtain an understanding of their laws because they would have a better chance of grasping what was expected of them.[23] They would gain an even greater sense of control over their development and application. Expanding participation would enable Indigenous peoples to see that they have a hand in making their laws relevant amidst changing circumstances. Other Canadians would also benefit if Indigenous peoples' laws were more accessible. They would see that these laws can be learned and applied. They would develop a greater appreciation for the nature and scope of these laws. They would be less fearful of Indigenous legal traditions, and more willing to consider Canada as a multi-juridical society. This would further increase the accessibility of Indigenous laws because more respectful non-Indigenous recognition would provide an even greater incentive for Indigenous law to be communicated.

Steps to increase accessibility are important because there has been much socio-economic dislocation amongst Indigenous peoples in Canada as a result of colonialism. For some, this has produced a degree of alienation from both broader Canadian society and from their own Indigenous communities that makes questions of accessibility very real. Such disconnections may make it difficult for an Indigenous legal authority to clearly communicate laws to its citizens. This problem may lead to a lack of information amongst those to whom such laws are meant to apply. In these circumstances, people may not be aware of the consequences that flow from violating Indigenous law provisions. Such misunderstandings could lead to a lack of confidence and respect amongst Indigenous peoples concerning their own laws. At the same time, accessing Indigenous law is an issue for other Canadians, too. If the overall population is not able to easily learn about Indigenous law, it will be more difficult for our different legal traditions to coexist.

Increasing the accessibility of Indigenous legal traditions is thus necessary for Indigenous peoples and all other Canadians. There are many ways to place Indigenous legal traditions before the broader public. Indigenous laws could be codified and made available in written form. Registers of Indigenous laws could be created with rules regarding maintenance and access, as has happened under a recent land claims agreement.[24] Furthermore, decisions of Indigenous councils, courts, and traditional gatherings could be broadcast or publicized in a regularized and systematic way.[25] Law review articles and books could be published to describe and analyse the content of law for different Indigenous groups. Web-based audio and video recordings of Indigenous legal authorities could be archived and made available.[26] Two excellent examples of this form of legal communication are Fourdirectionsteachings.com and Nature's Laws.[27] More information could get into homes and institutions if these and other methods of distribution were more widely used.

Thus, enhancing both the written and oral distribution of Indigenous laws would make them much easier to learn. Yet the way these laws are communicated must be balanced and calibrated to the type of law being described or interpreted. Not all laws should be written. There will be examples where writing Indigenous law would deprive it of its force. In such instances, oral foundations must be maintained.

Therefore, when oral traditions are expressed in written form, it is important that steps be taken to ensure that their flexibility is not lost to preserve greater context. Fortunately, safeguards can be put in place to ensure wide communication without undue rigidity. Quebec's *Civil Code* has maintained an openness and flexibility despite its written nature. Flexibility can also be secured by making laws formed through oral tradition paramount over written laws. This occurred under the *Labrador Inuit Land Claim Agreement*. The agreement provides that if there is a conflict between an Inuit customary law and a law that has been passed by the Nunatsiavut legislative assembly, the customary law must be followed unless the assembly has said that they intend to vary or eliminate the Inuit customary law. Other Indigenous codes could contain preambles that help communities retain and reinforce local interpretative authority. In some respects, Canada itself has maintained flexibility with regard to its oral tradition in the preamble to its *Constitution Act, 1867*, where the constitution is said to be 'similar in principle to the United Kingdom.' The rooting of the written text of Canada's Constitution in unwritten constitutional principles has allowed Canadian courts to avoid the rigidities of textual absences or constraints on numerous occasions.[28] This example could be followed by Indigenous peoples to provide space for oral and written legal principles to be respected in their societies.

Indigenous peoples might also decide to make their laws more accessible by creating broader learning opportunities. This can be done through both general and detailed legal education programs which could take many forms: workshops, apprenticeships, classroom learning, written textbooks, public performances, and so on. Indigenous legal education could also be developed and expanded in our law schools, thus increasing its exposure to interested students and practitioners. New law schools with a focus on Indigenous legal traditions could be created. The teaching of Indigenous legal traditions within mainstream law schools and seminars could deepen practical and academic understandings of its features. The development of Indigenous legal education in a law school context will be explored in greater detail in a subsequent chapter.

However, at this point I want to indicate how I have experienced the importance of learning Indigenous legal traditions in a law school setting. When the territory of Nunavut was created there was an expressed desire to have more Inuit people work at all levels of the territorial public service. Article 23 of the *Nunavut Land Claims Agreement*

has as its stated objective: 'to increase Inuit participation in government employment in the Nunavut Settlement Area to a representative
level' which applies to 'all occupational groupings and grade levels'
within the government.[29] Article 23 presupposes that initiatives will be
taken to increase educational opportunities to allow more Inuit to
work within all levels of government.[30] The Nunavut government,
along with the Akitsiraq Law Society of Nunavut, determined that one
of the ways they could pursue this objective was by creating a law
school in the territory. The Akitsiraq Law Society approached the
Faculty of Law at the University of Victoria in British Columbia to set
up such a school. They soon partnered with the Nunavut Arctic
College and a four-year program was created to allow students to
receive a University of Victoria law degree. The Department of Justice
of Canada and the Gordon Foundation provided substantial financial
support for the initiative. This innovative legal education program
was called the Akitsiraq Law School.

One of the goals of the new law school was to make Inuit law more
intelligible and accessible to the students and, by extension, to the citizens of the territory and Canada as a whole. Thus, the program
worked to assist the residents of Nunavut to articulate their ancient
laws and present-day legal traditions in contemporary terms. The
Akitsiraq Law School attempted to be attentive to legal pluralism in
the North by integrating traditional Inuit law with the requirements of
Canada and the territory's constitutional and legislative provisions.
Students received all their classes in Iqaluit, the capital of Nunavut,
and at the end of four years received a law degree from the University
of Victoria. Inuit stories and values were a vital part of this education,
as were Elders and community leaders. This aspect of the program
grew in strength as the first four years progressed. Students also interacted with southern legal academics, judges, and lawyers to ensure
that Inuit law fit the needs of the residents of the new territory.

When I taught at the Akitsiraq Law School, I found that the students
were better equipped to understand law's cultural contours than is the
case with most southern law students. They were already bilingual
and bicultural before the program began, and Akitisiraq prepared
them to be bijuridical. They were outstanding students. They became
grounded in both the common law and Inuit law during their time at
the school. The use of Inuit law and language infused their courses at
each step along the way. For example, when I was teaching contract
law and remedies, the students would supplement their understand-

ing of the common law of obligations with the Inuit law of obligations. After I taught a concept, the students would often talk among themselves in Inuktitut to clarify and deepen their comprehension of what I was saying. In this way they took more active control of their legal education than is typical in a southern law school. It was impressive to watch them work, and it was the best formal educational experience I have ever had. In the classroom, we all felt a responsibility for translating common law concepts into an Inuit linguistic and cultural framework, although we, as southern faculty, were often secondary to this endeavour. The faculty did their best to introduce Inuit cases, context, and Nunavut legislation in each class. When I taught, I sought to demonstrate how I worked back and forth between Anishinabek law and the common law in my life, to provide analogies of how the students might work with Inuit law. However, the teachers trained in common law recognized that our efforts were somewhat inadequate to the students' needs when it came to their own legal traditions.

Fortunately, when the students were finished with classes that either I or others taught, they would go into an Inuit legal and language class under the direction of wise Inuit Elders. In this setting, they would then learn the law of obligations or other concepts immersed in an Inuit legal framework. They would also be able to further explore what they were learning in their common law education, but they would have someone much more knowledgeable in Inuit law than southern-trained law professors. Dr Lucien Ukaliannuk was exceptional in guiding the students through the interaction between Inuit legal traditions and the common law. He far exceeded anything we did as southern-trained legal academics and lawyers in making the law relevant to the students' eventual practice of law in the North. I also understand from the students that his classes were also very theoretically beneficial because their exploration of frameworks for integration and separation of the traditions made greater sense when it started from an Inuit world view.[31]

The Akitsiraq Law School is one example of the type of activity that might occur elsewhere in Canada to facilitate the development of legal processes and reasoning appropriate to Indigenous norms and needs. Indigenous legal traditions become more accessible to a greater number of people when they are taught in open and transparent ways. When the transmission and acquisition of legal knowledge is supported by governments, law schools, and community groups (like the Akitsiraq Law Society), it can more effectively convey the norms and values appropriate to the tradition's laws. Law is most successful when it expresses the normative order of the people whom it serves.

Indigenous laws also become more accessible when the government recognizes Indigenous law-making powers through treaties. Once again, events in Nunavut set an important example. As noted in chapter 2, in 1999, a new territory was created in Canada's North that makes Inuit law more intelligible and accessible to both Inuit and non-Inuit people. Called Nunavut, meaning 'our land,' the area covers almost one-fifth of Canada. It was established through the negotiation, vision, and hard work of Inuit leaders who wanted to determine their own place in the North. It is governed by and for the Inuit people who make up the majority in the region. In addition to the governance of the entire territory, the Inuit were also able to secure exclusive title to wide expanses of land, exclusive harvesting rights on lands and waters throughout the Arctic, control and participation on land use boards throughout the region, royalty payments for non-Inuit resource use, preferential employment status for government jobs in the terri-tory, and an exceptionally strong place in Canada's federal structure. This enables them to exercise law-making authority over many matters and express those laws in positivistic ways. There are many heads of power about which Inuit people proclaim their views. These laws are published in official reports, gazettes, and papers. The media covers law-making activities and there is widespread debate in Inuit and non-Inuit circles about the nature of these laws.

As both the Akitsiraq Law School and Nunavut territory example illustrate, Indigenous peoples' law can become more accessible when it is conveyed in modern forms. Indigenous peoples' cultural circum-stances are always in flux, and Indigenous law will not be accessible if this fact is not acknowledged. Understanding what Indigenous laws were like one hundred years ago is necessary but not sufficient to make these laws applicable today. Changes in traditional means of communication may be needed to increase legal understanding. These changes are acceptable as long as they are consistent with the tradi-tion's broader principles and in line with the community's contempo-rary aspirations. Thus, changing cultural circumstances will lead some Indigenous groups to embed common law or civil law principles in their traditions. If this is the self-determining response of the group, it could appropriately recognize the reality of their normative values in modern terms. Indigenous peoples have experienced other people's values for centuries, and they can be adapted to the extent the community desires them. Infusing Indigenous legal traditions with innovations from other systems does not necessarily negate the authenticity or autonomy of Indigenous traditions, as was seen in chapter 2. In fact, the careful development of Indigenous traditions that are consistent with ancient values, but relevant in today's circumstances, increases their intelligibility and accessibility.

On a related point, a discussion about accessibility would be incomplete without identifying potential dangers of making these laws more widely known. Indigenous peoples have many reasons to distrust the sharing of their ideas with greater numbers of people. Past attempts to communicate their laws to others have generated misunderstandings in some non-Indigenous communities. Misunderstandings arise when recipients do not place the full meaning of what is revealed into context, or when stereotypical assumptions determine the listener's interpretation.[32] Trust is destroyed when people demean Indigenous law or regard it as inferior or degraded. Responses of this kind can place Indigenous people in a consistently defensive role. This can lead to an inordinate amount of time being spent clarifying or justifying their legal position. Dealing with outdated stereotypes about Indigenous law and educating others about their wider context is frankly exhausting for many Indigenous peoples. If such debates occur in a setting where people are hostile to the very idea that Indigenous peoples have laws, this can also lead to a tremendous loss of trust of others by Indigenous peoples. The matter of trust between Indigenous and non-Indigenous people may need significantly more attention before Aboriginal people are willing to share their ideas in a more public, accessible way.

The matter of trust also relates to another barrier to the accessibility of Indigenous legal traditions. In the past, Indigenous culture has been wrongly appropriated and stolen. Some Indigenous peoples will be very hesitant to share their legal knowledge with people not of their community because of the potential for its inappropriate use. As discussed in chapter 1, for most of Canada's history Indigenous culture was considered inferior. Indigenous knowledge was thought to be degraded, static, decaying, and dying a slow but inexorable death. While many people within Canada were trying to eradicate Indigenous ideas, great effort was simultaneously expended in trying to catalogue Indigenous cultural expression, objects, and ideas before Indigenous peoples became extinct. Cultural interference took the form of the suppression of Indigenous institutions of government,[33] the denial of land,[34] the forced taking of children,[35] the criminalization of economic pursuits,[36] and the negation of rights of religious freedom,[37] association,[38] due process,[39] and equality.[40] Encouraged by government officials and religious leaders, feasts and dances were outlawed and made subject to criminal prosecution. Ceremonial masks, totem poles, bent boxes, wampum belts, clothing, baskets, and other objects were confiscated and placed in private collections and public institutions. As anthropologists stood by and took notes, bones, tissue, and other human remains were taken and studied in hospitals, universities, and museums, making the careers of archeologists, medical practitioners, and academics. Aboriginal songs, stories, and performances were appropriated. Non-Aboriginal musicians, literary guilds, and Hollywood were the beneficiaries. These practices were sanctioned by Canada's law and still create challenges at present.

It has been observed that Indigenous 'cultural appropriation is not just historical, it is happening today.'[41] Those who are attuned to Indigenous perspectives realize that issues of cultural appropriation are near-weekly news events. The impact at the community level is significant and presents an equally significant obstacle to expanding the accessibility of Indigenous legal traditions. People will not want to share their legal traditions if they believe that any exchange will only lead to appropriation, criticism, and extinguishment.

Thus, certain Indigenous legal knowledge can form part of a tradition that should be considered intellectual property. When this is the case, knowledge cannot be shared without following elaborate protocols that may purposely limit accessibility. For example, for many First Nations of the West Coast, only people who have earned the right to receive hereditary names are permitted to speak about and use certain knowledge. If others were to attempt to spread these traditions in a way in which they were not entitled, they would be breaking their deepest laws. Accessibility cannot be encouraged in a manner that undermines the very law you are trying to spread in order to increase its respect. In making Indigenous tradition more accessible, close attention must be paid to the specific cultural contexts in which it operates, and solutions must be crafted which skilfully address those contexts. Accessibility must be extended in accordance with a respect for the intellectual property of each Indigenous legal tradition.

C. Equality

Another challenge to the recognition of Indigenous legal traditions is the concern about equality. Some might view the recognition of Indigenous legal traditions as creating inappropriate special treatment for Aboriginal people within Canada's legal system. It might be said that the further implementation of Indigenous legal traditions would create separate but equal systems, or worse, separate but unequal treatment. It is true that the wider acceptance and affirmation of Indigenous laws could be done badly. There are many examples in this world of discrimination being exacerbated when differentiation between peoples becomes the basis of legal rules and is politically entrenched.[42] To appreciate the potential harm this might cause, one only has to remember the atrocities committed against the Jewish people under Nazi rule during the 1930s and 1940s, Jim Crow laws in the American South after the Civil War until the 1960s, or the appalling conditions that resulted from the creation of the so-called South African homelands during the latter half of the last century.[43] Applying distinct sets of laws to one group that are inapplicable to another group is, in many circumstances, a recipe for disaster and could lead to great human rights abuses.[44]

Furthermore, Indigenous peoples themselves have suffered in precisely such a manner because of attempts to segregate and separate them from the rest of Canada's population through the *Indian Act* and other such laws.[45] One of the great causes of poverty and psychological trauma in our country is the result of the *Indian Act* and associated policies so thoroughly disconnecting First Nations people from other Canadians.[46] Ironically, this was done under the guise of compassionate concern for Indigenous peoples with the intent of purging differences through assimilation. Distinctions were made with the goal that 'Indians' would eventually be eliminated, but the mechanisms to accomplish this purpose further distanced Indigenous peoples from those who subsequently came from other countries to live among them.[47]

The meaning of equality in the Canadian context should be fully appreciated when we hear allegations of special treatment. It is true that distinctions in treatment between people can encourage invidious discrimination and produce tremendous inequalities.[48] The Supreme Court has disapproved of laws that have this purpose or effect.[49] I would wholeheartedly support this view. Nothing in this book should be used to sanction ideas or practices that create or reproduce discriminatory distinctions that are contrary to Canada's *Charter* or to international human rights customs and conventions. I fully acknowledge there are a great many instances in which equality can be undermined if the law sanctions differential treatment. However, in agreement with the Supreme Court of Canada, I would qualify this with the thought that differential treatment can sometimes be necessary to produce equality. Although we should exercise great caution in this regard, there are instances in which distinctions in law are not only acceptable, they could become the means we need to achieve our equality ideals.

The Supreme Court of Canada has acknowledged that the recognition of difference can be a mechanism to achieve equality. For example, in the case of *Law v. Canada (Minister of Employment and Immigration)*, Justice Iacobucci observed that 'true equality does not necessarily result from identical treatment.'[50] He went on to note that formal distinctions in treatment will sometimes be necessary to accommodate differences between individuals and thus produce equal treatment in a substantive sense. 'Correspondingly, a law which applies uniformly to all may still violate a claimant's equality rights.'[51] Differential treatment does not always signal a denial of the equal benefit and protection of the law. Judgments about the fairness of differential treatment will always be contextualized; it will depend on the right at issue, a person's socio-economic status, and that of comparative groups. Applying these principles to Indigenous legal traditions, it can be argued that the mere fact of their difference does not necessarily raise concerns about equality, fairness, certainty, and so on. This will be the case so long as Canadian laws do not produce ideas or practices that regard or treat Indigenous or non-Indigenous Canadians as inferior or superior to others. Differential treatment only turns into invidious discrimination when distinctions are based on arbitrary presumptions that one group of people is more or less deserving of some public good than another, or when the effect of such treatment produces these results.

International legal principles also support the notion that equality can accommodate appropriate differential treatment. As early as 1934, the Permanent Court of Justice tackled the issue of discrimination in its opinion concerning the *Minority Schools in Albania*.[52] It held that a 'subtle form of persecution comes from measures which denies any members of a minority the capacity to be different from the majority, namely they are forced, to their disadvantage, to be the same as the majority.' Later, in the *South West Africa Case*,[53] the court further refined the meaning of discrimination. In Judge Tanaka's famous dissenting judgment in that case, he held:

> To treat different matters equally in a mechanical way would be as unjust as to treat equal matters differently.
>
> To treat unequal matters differently according to their inequality is not only permitted but also required.
>
> The principle of equality does not mean absolute equality but recognizes relative equality: namely differential treatment proportionate to concrete individual circumstances. Differential treatment must not be given arbitrarily; it requires reasonableness, or must be in conformity with justice, as in the treatment of minorities, different treatment of the sexes, regarding public conveniences, etc. In these cases, the differentiation is aimed at the protection of those concerned and is not detrimental and therefore not against their will.[54]

This position, that the principle of non-discrimination requires *both* the equal treatment of equals *and* the consideration of difference in assessing the need for differential treatment, is also accepted in the *International Convention for the Elimination of Racial Discrimination*.[55] Thus, if there are sound reasons for the implementation of Indigenous legal traditions that require some degree of differential treatment to allow them to flourish and grow, this would not be inconsistent with the Canadian Charter or international human rights laws.

However, at the deepest level, this book has consistently argued that the recognition of Indigenous legal traditions should not mean a completely separate system for Aboriginal peoples in Canada. The recognition of Indigenous legal traditions alongside common law and civil law traditions should be regarded as part of *the* same system. There is plenty of room for these traditions to interact within *one* framework. It is not segregation to more tightly associate Indigenous legal traditions with Canada's other tradition. A prominent idea in this book is that the failure to recognize the existence of Indigenous legal traditions as a part of Canadian law is in itself discriminatory. Indigenous peoples have constantly adjusted their laws to take into account the common law or civil law, but Canadian judges and lawmakers have rarely done the same when it comes to Indigenous legal traditions. With one side resisting adjustment to their legal relationships, and thus preventing further harmonization, it might be said that the resistant party is the one who is engaging in discrimination. Equality is not well served by denying Indigenous societies equal participation in the ongoing formulation of Canada's legal system.

Of course, the interconnection of our legal traditions does not imply absolute convergence and fusion between the traditions. Indigenous legal traditions should no more be subject to forced assimilation than the common law is to the civil law. Each can operate in conjunction with the other, and be harmonized to some degree. Despite differences between the civil law and the common law, we regard them as being part of the 'one law' for all Canadians. Indigenous laws must be placed in this same category. There would be fierce opposition if it were proposed to assimilate civil law within common law. Canadians do not generally label the status of civil law in the country as special treatment, segregation, or the creation of separate but unequal laws. We should not label Indigenous legal traditions any differently.

It must also be remembered that Canada is a federal system. There are ten provinces, three territories, and one central government; they both create and enforce a variety of legal rules throughout the country. Some of these laws even contradict one another. For example, some provinces permit state-funded denominational schools, while others prohibit them. Some provinces are required to fund religious schools through constitutional obligation, while others have no such constraint. Even the *Criminal Code*, a federal statute, is administered differently in each province. Provinces vary greatly in the application of criminal law, despite its common source.[56] The law in Canada unites uniformity with diversity. It is appropriate to want the country's laws (including Indigenous legal traditions) to be interconnected, balanced, and harmonized, and it is inappropriate to regard the law as undifferentiated and insist that exactly the same legal principles should apply to everyone in the same way when to do so would foment inequality.[57]

In this context, Judge Mary Ellen Turpel-Lafond's advice of a few years ago seems particularly appropriate:

> We spent several years in a distracting debate over whether justice reform involves separate justice systems or reforming the mainstream system. This is a false dichotomy and fruitless distinction because it is not an either/or choice. The impetus for change can be better described as getting away from the colonialism and domination ... Resisting colonialism means a reclaiming by Aboriginal people of control over the res-

olution of disputes and jurisdiction over justice, but it is not as simple or as quick as that sounds. Moving in this direction will involve many linkages ...[58]

There are many linkages that can be forged between Indigenous legal traditions and other Canadian laws. The larger question for Indigenous peoples in the implementation of their legal traditions is not whether they are separate. The implementation of Indigenous law is more of a matter of moving away from the domination and inappropriate control of Indigenous peoples based on presumptions that their laws and governing capacities are inferior. In this light, Canada and Indigenous peoples can create discrete yet interlocking laws consistent with our federal principles and our equality jurisprudence.

The fact that Canada has different, sometimes contradictory laws passed by different legal regimes does not bring our legal system into disrepute. In fact, its respect is heightened because the passage of different laws demonstrates a much-needed ability to respond to local circumstances. At times, provincial governments each pass different regulations under identical federal law (when given the responsibility to administer such statutes). This diversity is usually applauded because it allows legislators to be sensitive to matters of a purely local nature. Few would suggest that provincial and regional variation is a departure from the principle of one law for all Canadians.[59]

Moreover, pre-existing Indigenous laws aside, Canada has considerable experience in accommodating laws that do not emanate from central or provincial governments. As Geoff Hall pointed out in a *University of Toronto Faculty of Law Review* article, many different legal regimes operate within the country.[60] An example is the extraterritorial application of criminal law. Many countries have statutes that allow them to prosecute their citizens for crimes committed in another country.[61] Canada has accepted this principle.[62] Canada also recognizes the principle that tax obligations can be incurred to another country, even if one is working in Canada.[63] Another example is diplomats who have immunity from the operation of domestic law. The idea that countries can enjoy sovereign immunity is also a familiar concept. Similarly, naval and military law both operate extraterritorially.[64] These examples all show that the idea that Canadians live under one undifferentiated law is an overly simplistic view of how legal regimes interact.

It is important to judge the recognition and affirmation of Indigenous legal principles by equality standards. However, it is just as important that equality not be interpreted in a manner which is contrary to Canada's *Charter of Rights and Freedoms* as well as international human rights principles. The wider acceptance of differential Indigenous legal traditions and their existence within a singular framework could actually promote equality among our citizenry. As long as we do not create distinctions that have as their purpose or effect the idea or practice that Indigenous peoples are inferior or superior to other Canadians, equality need not be sacrificed in our law to recognize Indigenous legal traditions.

D. Applicability

A further challenge to the recognition of Indigenous legal traditions relates to questions of applicability. This concern is best addressed by reviewing some questions I received from a very good friend after making a presentation about the existence of Indigenous laws in Canada. He asked: 'To whom do these laws apply? If I were a First Nations citizen of your reserve, would I be obliged to obey every Anishinabek law? What if I, as a non-citizen permanently living on your reserve, broke Anishinabek law – would I be obligated to follow your laws? Finally, what about your laws off reserve but in your traditional territory and beyond – do your laws apply to people in these circumstances?' These are excellent questions because they reveal many appropriate concerns surrounding the reach of Indigenous laws. They deserve careful consideration and response.

One of the major issues surrounding applicability is that people could be obligated to follow laws over which they have no influence. If people are required to abide by particular laws, they usually insist that they should have some hand in potentially making those laws. This democratic principle is one that is deeply embedded in Canada's political culture. It should be respected as part of Indigenous law's applicability. The right to participate in the formulation, interpretation, and enforcement of laws ensures a measure of accountability that is imperative in our country. If laws operate without this feedback loop, we run a grave risk. Laws can become dictatorial and oppressive if they are detached from the average person's input. Therefore, as we consider the applicability of Indigenous laws, we should ensure that to the extent possible those who are bound by them have a potential role in creating and administering them.

Connecting the applicability of law with its administration is one of the reasons for this book. For too long, Indigenous peoples have been expected to follow laws over which they had little influence. As Indigenous legal traditions gain greater recognition throughout the country, Canada's democratic character is enhanced because Indigenous peoples will secure greater input over the common law and civil law's reach into their lives. As the common law and civil law are modified by Indigenous legal traditions, Indigenous peoples' participation in the law's development and enforcement can also grow. This has the potential to attenuate Canadian law's dictatorial and oppressive aspects by bringing the administration of law closer to Indigenous people.

However, at the same time as Indigenous peoples are achieving greater participation and gaining greater recognition within our legal systems, other Canadians must not be unduly prejudiced by this development. It is vital that the application of Indigenous law does not sever other Canadians democratic relationship to the laws which govern their behaviour. While there will always be unpopular laws, we must ensure that the reasons for their disfavour do not lie in any democratic deficit. Thus, in contemplating the reach of their laws, Indigenous peoples must be responsive to broader democratic values. Those who administer the common law and civil law should likewise judge the reach of their laws into Indigenous peoples' lives by similar standards.

With the foregoing principles in mind, we can return to the questions my friend asked following my presentation. His first inquiry was whether every citizen of my reserve should be obligated to obey Anishinabek law? In answer to his question I would say 'yes.' Every person who is a citizen of the Chippewa of the Nawash First Nation is entitled to live on the reserve and participate in the formulation of our laws; thus, democratic values are enhanced and preserved through each person's potential role in the identification, interpretation, and enforcement of Anishinabek law. In fact, since the case of *Corbiere v. Canada*, even those citizens of our First Nation who do not live on the reserve are entitled to vote in elections, serve on committees, and be actively involved in the development of our laws.[65] The principles animating the *Corbiere* case ensure that everyone who is formally registered on our membership rolls can have input into the standards that guide our actions. I also believe this is a norm embedded within older Anishinabek legal traditions.[66] Thus, at a minimum, I would consider the reach of Anishinabek law as being applicable to citizens of the Chippewa of the Nawash First Nation who live on reserve.

Of course, anyone who is familiar with First Nations reserves knows that there are many people who are living within their boundaries who are not citizens. They are often individuals married to Indians living on reserve, yet not entitled to Indian status, and therefore not granted citizenship in the Chippewas of the Nawash First Nation. These are our mothers, fathers, grandfathers, aunts, uncles, cousins, and friends. What should be their legal status in regard to the application of Anishinabek law? This is the second question my friend asked following my presentation: What are the legal obligations of non-citizens permanently living on your reserve towards Anishinabek law?

In answer to this question, it is my contention that First Nations should terminate definitions of citizenship that are based on the *Indian Act*. It is contrary to Indigenous constitutional values. Citizenship should be extended more broadly. *Indian Act* criteria for citizenship are flawed because they too often have reference to and incorporate racialized standards for membership.[67] There are many disturbing examples throughout the world of law being applied solely on racial lines. This practice is usually discriminatory and subordinates groups or individuals within society using arbitrary criteria. Applying Indigenous legal traditions on the basis of race should be rejected. This should lead us to extend citizenship to people of all so-called races who regularly reside on our reserves.[68] We should not deny people citizenship if they are willing to abide by First Nations citizenship laws and be fully participating members in our communities. This could enable many more people to become dual citizens of a First Nation and of Canada. With this approach as a guide, Indigenous laws should flow from the political character of our societies; they should not apply because of society's racialization of Indigenous peoples. Aboriginal peoples belong to distinct political bodies that have an existence that is broader than their familial and ancestral ties. As the Royal Commission on Aboriginal Peoples states:

> Aboriginal peoples are not racial groups; they are organic political and cultural entities. Although contemporary Aboriginal peoples stem histor-

ically from the original peoples of North America, they often have mixed genetic heritages and include individuals of varied ancestries. As organic political entities, they have the capacity to evolve over time and change in their internal composition.[69]

... Only when Aboriginal peoples are viewed, not as 'races' within the boundaries of a legitimate state, but as distinct political communities with recognizable claims for collective rights, will there be a first and meaningful step towards responding to Aboriginal peoples' challenge to achieve self-government.[70]

These ideas lead me to conclude that Indigenous peoples should apply their legal traditions as political bodies rather than as racial groups. Since Indigenous peoples have historic rules for adopting others into community, they could build upon these principles to grant people citizenship in the present day. The modernization and extension of citizenship to people from all parts of the world is a strong basis upon which to build the applicability of our laws.

Clauses in the recent Dogrib and Innu treaties recognize Indigenous peoples' authority to make their own citizenship decisions, and thus significantly depart from the *Indian Act*. These agreements allow communities to have anyone become a member 'if that person is accepted pursuant to the community acceptance process in the constitution.'[71] The Tlicho Constitution (section 4) states that citizenship is within the exclusive jurisdiction of their government and that the Tlicho assembly can set out the criteria for citizenship by a general assembly motion.[72] These provisions are much healthier than those of the *Indian Act*, which determine membership on the basis of rules designed to reduce the number of people who claim Indigenous community membership. Tlicho laws permit the community to set its own rules concerning membership, and thus create criteria for belonging to a political body that is not based on race. Since these laws are not aimed at assimilation like the *Indian Act*, they make room for others who are not defined as 'Indian' by the federal government. If a community moves away from race as a determinant of membership, many more people would join them based on the principles and traditions they espouse and apply.

Other First Nations could take the same approach as the Tlicho and regard themselves as legal and political entities, not ethnic groups. When Indigenous governments set criteria under their own laws to determine how people from other communities become citizens, democracy is facilitated. Indigenous groups should therefore loudly and clearly assert that they are *not* seeking race-based rights. This would help to overcome most problems of applicability of Indigenous legal traditions to those who are permanently living within Indigenous communities. Thus, the best answer I can give to my friend who wondered about the legal obligations to Anishinabek law for non-citizens permanently living on my reserve is that we should make them citizens if they desire to associate themselves with us in accordance with our community's self-determining criteria.

Of course, there will be some people living on reserves who do not wish to become First Nations citizens. There may also be people who visit a reserve for a short period, or who are only passing through as they do business or travel from one place to another. In this case my friend would ask me: Is Anishinabek law applicable to them, too? Should these people, who are unfamiliar with First Nations law and have little influence over its development and enforcement, also be obligated to obey Indigenous law? In this case, attention to democratic principles might seem to require a conclusion that Indigenous laws are inapplicable to people on reserves who are not First Nations citizens. It could be said that since non-citizens cannot participate in the administration of Indigenous law they should not be subject to the operation of that law.

However, we can be attentive to democratic values and still extend First Nations laws to the entire territory which encompasses the reserve. For example, municipalities make laws which residents of other cities must follow when they visit or do business in a locality that is not their own. These obligations are applicable even if such visitors do not have a direct hand in the administration of their host city's law. We see this principle in operation in other places in our country. Residents of the province of Ontario must abide by the laws of Alberta when they travel in that province. Citizens of the United States are subject to the laws of Canada when they visit this country. We find such practices consistent with democracy because they recognize that law has a jurisdictional component. Different majorities within our nation are responsible for administering law over different territories, but we do not consider law undemocratic if we do not directly participate in each of these majorities. Decentralized responsibilities for the law's creation and enforcement do not detract from our democracy but strengthen it, because such procedures allow the law to draw closer to the people who are most directly affected within any given jurisdiction. Thus, when a non-citizen breaks the law on an Indian reserve, the jurisdictional nature of law suggests that such persons be subject to those laws.

Furthermore, applying Anishinabek law to non-citizens on an Anishinabek reserve does not mean non-citizens would lack influence over the recognition of laws. One should not forget the colonial nature of Canada's history, which has affected and will continue to affect the application of Indigenous legal traditions, even as we try to decolonize our constitutional framework. Pushing back the oppressive bounds of past undemocratic intrusions of non-Aboriginal law on Indian reserves should not require the severance of Indigenous peoples' relationships with other Canadians. There will be a pervasive persistence of Canada's other legal traditions in their influence over Indigenous law no matter what we do. However, it is my hope that this influence is beginning to run in the other direction too, in strengthening the common law and civil law through incorporating Indigenous legal traditions. This interdependence should be the nature of legal discourse in a multi-juridical country. In fact, many Indigenous peoples will demand that protections developed through the common law and civil law's approach to regulation and dispute resolution be integrated into Indigenous law's application. I hope non-Indigenous peoples demand the same thing, and insist that protections developed from Indigenous law's insights be embedded within their laws. The challenge is to ensure that connections between the traditions are positive and constructive within Indigenous communities, rather than negative and destructive as they have been in the past.

Canadians could also have a more positive democratic relationship and influence over the application of Indigenous legal traditions if Parliament were to more explicitly recognize the scope of Indigenous law within reserves. If Canadians voted to accept the principles underlying this book's thesis, such action would accord greater democratic authority to the application of Indigenous laws to Canadian citizens when they are on Indian reserves or other recognized Indigenous jurisdictional spaces. This could be done through a constitutional amendment, a national treaty, or a Parliamentary act or statement of policy from the government of the day. If Canada's democratically elected officials were to acknowledge the scope of Indigenous law-making authority on reserves, this would ensure that Canadians had a representative voice in the application of First Nations law to non-citizens. Provincial legislatures could also make similar moves, although democratic recognition by the federal government would be doubly significant because they have constitutional jurisdiction relative to Indians and lands reserved for Indians.[73]

First Nations could also provide non-citizens of surrounding municipalities and provinces opportunities to comment on the development of their laws as they are being drafted. To that end, formalized mechanisms for mutual consultation between adjoining Indigenous and broader Canadian jurisdictions could be developed.[74] People who are not citizens of a reserve or Indigenous territory could also be guaranteed influence over the law's administration in other ways, such as through cross-deputization in policing agreements, where adjoining police forces delegate authority to one another to investigate, charge, and detain persons from the other jurisdiction when they reasonably suspect involvement in criminal activity.[75] Indigenous and off-reserve administrative agencies could rely on the expertise of one another in the development of their regulations and powers of enforcement.[76] Indigenous dispute resolution bodies and courts could also develop comity or full faith and credit agreements to provide official recognition and enforcement of decisions reached in each other's jurisdiction.[77]

These types of measures are important in considering law's applicability because limiting the reach of Indigenous law to citizens on reserve would not be administratively sound. A legal system will not be effective if enforcement turns upon distinguishing between citizens and non-citizens in a given territory when face-to-face encounters occur in the heat of an altercation. Such distinctions could lead to bias in the law's enforcement. Police officers or administrative officials might have negative incentives to treat one group or another in an inferior way if enforcement turned on citizenship.[78] Furthermore, the selective enforcement of law on the basis of a person's citizenship in an Indigenous community could lead to great problems of public safety on a reserve. For example, if laws against non-citizens were inapplicable on the reserve, this could create serious gaps in enforcement. Non-citizens could use the reserve as a haven for crime and other vices if it was difficult to apply First Nations' laws to them. This would undermine the rule of law on reserves and have negative spill-over consequences for surrounding communities. Imagine the chaos that would result if British Columbian authorities could only regulate or prosecute British Columbian residents. Indigenous communities should not have to face this kind of chaos in the application of their laws.

Thus, I think the best answer I can formulate in response to my friend's question about the applicability of laws to non-citizens is that Indigenous laws are best administered within Canada's constitutional framework on a territorial basis, giving strict heed to its broader democratic basis. On this principle, I would suggest that First Nations citizens and other people who reside on or visit the reserve should be obligated to follow the laws formulated for the reserve. Thus, not only would I recommend that First Nations citizens be bound by Indigenous law on my reserve, I would also extend such application to the people like my friend who are non-citizens when they are on our reserve land. Indigenous laws are best administered on a territorial basis because of the efficiencies this creates in regulating and enforcing the law, and because of consistency with our broader democratic traditions.

In making the foregoing observation, it should be recognized that Indigenous groups will not always exercise every aspect of their law-making powers. In such instances, Indigenous peoples could continue to have provincial or federal law apply on their reserves in accordance with currently recognized rules under section 91(24) of the *Constitution Act*, or section 88 of the *Indian Act*, which makes all provincial laws of general application extend to Indians.[79] It is important that people not consider that a legal vacuum exists on a reserve or Indigenous territory if a group does not immediately exercise the entirety of its authority. The Nisga'a, for example, refrained from exercising their authority to run a tribal court and yet there is no legally vacant space on their land. They have chosen not to run a court at present because priorities related to capacity-building and other socio-economic factors are more pressing. Other Indigenous groups may well take the same approach. In fact, they would be wise to do so if there were serious concerns related to under-developed capacity or resources within a community. In such cases, Indigenous peoples might place their jurisdictional powers in abeyance without relinquishing their authority over them. When this occurs, provincial or federal courts would apply the common law or civil law to Indigenous peoples, although in these cases they should be more attentive to principles discussed in this book by incorporating the continued vitality of Indigenous law as a source of authority in the resolution of disputes. There are many examples in the United States in which American Indian tribes have recognized authority to administer and develop law but do not use all their jurisdictional powers. There are also many examples of the U.S. Federal Court's deference to decisions of tribal councils and courts in the United States which Canadian courts could learn from.[80] Despite their jurisdictional entitlement, many tribes choose not to operate tribal courts; others willingly cede certain matters to federal or state courts so that they can pursue other priorities. Indigenous communities in Canada could also learn from these examples.

The final question my friend asked during my presentation related to the applicability of Indigenous laws off reserve in their traditional territories and beyond. He wondered whether Indigenous laws applied to people in these circumstances. There are a few issues to sort out in answering this question. First, in many instances, reserves were carved out of traditional territories without securing the consent of those whose lands were taken through the blunt force of colonial law. In other instances, particularly in the case of Métis and Inuit peoples, no lands were set aside and regarded as being notionally within Indigenous control (except for Métis settlements in Alberta). Thus, the severing of Indigenous peoples from their traditional territories without making provision for the extent of prior Indigenous legal relationships on them is something we are still trying to resolve. Indigenous territories must be significantly expanded to address the injustice of past losses at the hands of a voracious colonial state. We must account for this issue in answering my friend's question about the reach of Indigenous laws off reserve. Indigenous laws must also be used to enlarge the spaces within which Indigenous law operates. We should concede that there is much work ahead to more fully address the bounds in which Indigenous peoples would have recognized jurisdiction to apply their law off reserve.

However, assuming we can eventually come to some rough reconciliation that identifies the appropriate boundaries for reserves, or similar such creations, I believe my friend's question is best answered in the following way. Indigenous laws should have direct application on reserves in all cases. Off-reserve, provincial, or federal laws (as interpreted through the common law or civil law) should create the main obligations for Indigenous people and other Canadians, though these obligations will hopefully be influenced by Indigenous legal traditions. This is consistent with my earlier observations that hinge law's applicability on territorial boundaries to ensure the facilitation of a more fully democratic framework in Canada's legal system.

The recognition of somewhat bright (territorial-based) lines for the application of Indigenous laws does not foreclose the nevertheless important space for their mutual interaction. For example, Indigenous laws should have direct application off reserve in those cases related to the exercise of Aboriginal or treaty rights that spill over into provincial or federal spheres. This would be consistent with both section 35 of the *Constitution Act, 1982* and the dominant tide of Canadian federalism which allows for ancillary, secondary, or incidental effects of valid action in one field that may impact on another.[81] Furthermore, Indigenous laws should have an indirect and varying influence off reserve consistent with Canada's multi-juridical nature, just as the common law and civil law should influence laws on reserve. The variation in an Indigenous law's influence under this framework would depend upon whether a person or group was seeking to apply an Indigenous legal principle within a traditional territory or beyond. Thus, an Anishinabek legal principle should have greater sway in traditional Anishinabek territories than in Salish or Inuit territories that are thousands of miles distant, and located in completely different ecological niches.

As noted, this approach attempts to reinforce the territorial nature of law's application within Canada's constitutional framework. At the same time, this approach recognizes the interpenetrating nature of Canada's legal traditions, which infuse, infiltrate, and permeate one another's operation when they are not being directly applied in any dispute within their immediate sphere of application. This is the nature of multi-juridicalism. While some Indigenous laws would be personal, and follow an Indigenous person wherever he or she goes in the country, people best claim protection for personal rights for these practices as Aboriginal or treaty rights under section 35(1) of the *Constitution Act, 1982*, or as individual rights under Canada's *Charter of Rights and Freedoms*. Thus, to the extent that someone claims an aspect of Indigenous law that directly applies off reserve, the negotiation or application of treaties might best resolve such complexities. It is my belief that this approach most appropriately reconciles Canada's legal traditions, maintains a strong culture of certainty in securing law and order, and enhances the democratic relationship of citizens with their legal system.

E. Legitimacy

A final concern to explore in this chapter, related to the broader recognition and affirmation of Indigenous legal traditions, surrounds the question of legitimacy. This catch-all category addresses broader sociopolitical difficulties people might have in accepting Indigenous law. There are psychological and emotional objections to recognizing Indigenous legal traditions that must be addressed if Indigenous law is going to be more broadly received.

My desire to take account of these concerns is related to what I learned from a brief layperson's study of neuropsychology a few years ago. I was introduced to this field by an interesting *McGill Law Journal* article by Professor Jennifer Nedelesky entitled 'Embodied Diversity.'[82] In the piece, Professor Nedelsky explained that judgment is formed through the combination of intellectual and emotional processes working together. She drew on research from clinicians like Antonio Domasio, who concluded from his studies that emotion is an important element in our deployment of reason.[83] Domasio is joined by philosophers and other theoreticians who have recently devoted considerable attention to the role of emotion in structuring our ideas.[84] He explained that there is no significant separation between reason and emotion when we exercise what most would consider good judgment. Both are important in making rational judgments. This insight leads me to conclude that when we are making decisions about the recognition of Indigenous law, we must pay attention to both its emotional and intellectual elements. This is not to suggest for one moment that people discard reason when they make a choice. In fact, I have largely appealed to reason throughout this book, because I believe the intellectual justifications for the acceptance of Indigenous legal traditions in Canadian law are strong, and have largely been ignored. Nevertheless, Domasio's research suggests that the interaction of reason and emotion should be consciously acknowledged in our decision-making processes.

Thus, in being attentive to how people might feel about the ideas developed in this book, readers might want to identify whether they have strong negative or positive feelings that are not easily connected to logical argumentation. The identification of such feelings might reveal further issues that should appropriately defeat or support this book's thesis. Emotion can be a powerfully positive force if it leads us to identify lucid, cogent, rational arguments concerning a given course of action. I welcome the identification of such issues to the extent that they are based on fair and balanced argumentation. On the other hand, if our feelings cannot find a root or connection to intellectually persuasive justifications for denying or accepting the existence of Indigenous legal traditions, it may be we should harness such emotions in favour of a different approach.

In order to assist in this reflection, it may be helpful to identify some of the negative feelings people have expressed concerning the recognition and growth of Indigenous legal traditions. Some people may fear for their safety if Indigenous peoples exercise greater law-making power.[85] They understand that Indigenous people are over-represented in the country's jails and that Indigenous communities sometimes experience higher levels of interpersonal violence.[86] They may worry that such violence would spill over into other communities if Indigenous peoples are unable to properly administer their law.[87] Both Indigenous people and other Canadians are likely to express this concern. Of course, it may just be that peace is more easily attained and extended if Indigenous peoples have a greater sense of responsibility and accountability for the violence that occurs in their midst because they have the means to control it through access to their laws.

Others may worry that Indigenous peoples will drive a deeper wedge into our social fabric and foment civic alienation if Indigenous legal traditions are more prominent.[88] People do not want to see their country broken up and wracked with civil strife on these grounds. They will not or should not accept Indigenous legal traditions if they lead us down this path. The recognition and affirmation of multi-juridicalism should not be regarded as a justification for splitting up our territories. Resentment also might be a partial motivation for people's concerns about this book's thesis. Some Canadians might feel Indigenous peoples will be entitled to something they are not if Indigenous law grows stronger. Unfortunately, such feelings could generate irritation, fear, or bitterness towards Indigenous law. There may be other negative feelings at work. Greed, apprehension, discomfort, anxiety, envy, or paternalistic affection might all lead people to reject Indigenous legal traditions.[89] Any strategy to more widely recognize Indigenous law must address these emotional reactions.

From another perspective, some observers may worry about the legitimacy of working with Canadian legal systems when these structures have been so disrespectful of Indigenous traditions and ignored or denied their force. They may feel that Indigenous peoples cannot overcome oppression by working with the very instruments that help create oppression. People might feel that you cannot use the master's tools to take down the master's house.[90] In addressing these viewpoints, it is important to note secession is rarely regarded as an attractive goal amongst Indigenous peoples.[91] Secession would require leaving parts of their traditional territories behind and in the control of other people. It would mean separating themselves from their neighbours, when trade, intermarriage, and environmental interdependence characterize many relationships. Secession is largely a colonizer's activity.[92] It is rare for Indigenous peoples in Canada to talk about severing their relations with others. They usually speak of creating better relations. As such, it is not surprising that Indigenous peoples generally do not want to 'take down the master's house' by destroying the state in which they live.[93] It may even be contrary to many Indigenous legal systems to take this approach, given the emphasis on peacemaking, harmony, and reconciliation found in many Indigenous laws. Even if secession were consistent with Indigenous legal traditions, I have always doubted the utility of the 'master's tools' metaphor. A hammer, saw, and backhoe are instruments of creation *and* destruction. It is possible to use these tools to undo or renovate the thing that has been created. There are some countries in the world in which the so-called master's tools have remodelled oppressive regimes to accommodate diverse populations: the Soviet Union, South Africa, and Canada (as it concerns Quebec) spring to mind. While these examples illustrate that the end of one type of oppression does not completely terminate all other forms of subjugation, they do demonstrate that positive change can sometimes occur from within a society. Furthermore, if we judge reform or political change against the standard of perfection, then any action we take will always fall short of this unrealistic ideal. Despite these views, there will be some people who regard the interaction of Indigenous law with other laws as illegitimate. This may lead them to seek or support Indigenous peoples' complete separation from Canada's legal system because they feel that it would not be right to work with a country that has hurt Indigenous people so deeply.

In acknowledging these responses, I have tried to be pragmatic and recognize that the acceptance of Indigenous laws as a part of

Canadian law will *not* solve all problems. While I believe their extension could make a noticeable difference in many people's lives, some of these objections all too clearly foreshadow problems that will occur if we do not act in accordance with our highest traditions. For example, some Indigenous peoples might use their law to disrupt our country's aspirations for unity.[94] Furthermore, some Indigenous legal systems are and will be badly administered.[95] This could hurt those who are subject to them or live close to the jurisdiction, just as Indigenous peoples have been harmed by Canadian law. In the process, it is possible that Indigenous influence and power will grow at the expense of particular groups or individuals in Canada. This will cause distress, even if such a resource distribution is economically efficient and consistent with broader principles of justice. Of course, redistribution will hurt even more if non-Indigenous people are dispossessed and the result is both inefficient and unjust. Doubts about the wisdom of my ideas will be particularly poignant when miscarriages of justice occur in Indigenous systems, as they certainly will. No society is immune from error, miscalculation, vice, corruption, and distortion. *This is the reason all societies, including Indigenous societies, have need of law.* Law should be one of the tools we use to deal with issues of secession, maladministration, and injustice. Even though grave injustices periodically arise within Canada's other legal systems, similar injustices may be regarded more severely if Indigenous peoples create them. It is difficult to prevent Indigenous peoples from being held to a higher standard when they seek to administer their own affairs.

In recognizing negative feelings towards the ideas developed in this book, and giving them proper place, we should not give them wider scope or weight than they deserve. While our eyes should be wide open to the difficulties that lie before us, we should also be clear about the consequences of not opening our legal system to reflect Indigenous participation, norms, and values. This book attempts to show both the depths of the problems we experience in our law, and the height of potential to which we could aspire in improving relationships between Indigenous peoples and others. The recognition of Indigenous legal traditions could extend benefits to Indigenous peoples which others already enjoy, and simultaneously provide greater benefits to all Canadians. I have also tried to make the case that negative results will not inevitably flow from the application of Indigenous legal traditions. Whether we succumb to our worst fears depends upon whether we are prepared to creatively devote the resources necessary to accomplish the task outlined herein. Improvement also requires the creation of appropriate limits on constitutional, civil, and common law rules to enliven Indigenous peoples' participation in Canadian life. We will only overcome the very real fears that stand in the way of systematic reform to the extent that we continually work on constructively solving the conditions that give rise to them. I realize, however, that not everyone will see the issue in this light. There are those who may resist any expansion of the rule of law for Indigenous peoples in the way proposed in this work.

Since no one can guarantee that some of the scenarios envisioned by skeptics will not come to pass, we must at least ensure we do not base future decisions about Indigenous legal traditions on unexamined feelings that have questionable roots. Canadians have experienced a 500-year history that has portrayed Indigenous peoples as lower on the scale of social organization, and thus less capable of managing conflict. These messages run deep in popular culture and may be difficult to resist unless explicitly addressed. The Supreme Court of Canada has noted that racism against Aboriginal peoples is a part of the Canadian experience.[96] In *R. v. Williams,* Justice McLachlin found that people might exhibit bias when evaluating Indigenous peoples' claims. At a minimum, we must not let ideas nested in those experiences negatively affect our evaluation of Indigenous legal traditions in the present context.

The greatest challenge Indigenous peoples might encounter in accepting this book's thesis relates to potential feelings of resentment about the injustices they have endured in Canada. Deep and bitter feelings of anger, distrust, and betrayal reside in some Indigenous communities because of the centuries-long denial of their rights and traditions. In this context, it would be quite understandable if Indigenous peoples rejected this book's ideas. Canada's suppression of Indigenous rights and traditions has gone on for so long that Indigenous peoples might wonder how this book's arguments could possibly turn the tide. These views may be especially strong if Canada's past treatment of Indigenous law is denied as being real or relevant in moving forward in our relationships. If Canadians do not recognize that Indigenous peoples have experienced acute trauma they will likely dismiss much of this book's thesis.

When a group experiences severe suffering at the hands of another, this stands in the way of reform. When the historic causes and present consequences of such mistreatment are unacknowledged, this prevents constructive engagement in the present day. The denial of Indigenous legal traditions has been a painful and harrowing experience for many Indigenous people. The depth of this trauma has not been sufficiently accounted for in our legal system. As noted earlier, governmental interference with Indigenous law has been evidenced through the suppression of Aboriginal institutions of government,[97] the denial of land,[98] the forced taking of children,[99] the criminalization of economic pursuits,[100] and the negation of the rights of religious freedom,[101] association,[102] due process,[103] and equality.[104] The Canadian state continues to benefit from Indigenous losses through their possession of Indigenous lands and the exercise of virtually unconstrained legal power over them. The failure to acknowledge and remedy this situation is perhaps *the* underlying cause of conflict between Indigenous peoples and the Crown in this country. This conflict goes to the heart of why Indigenous legal traditions are not more widely recognized by courts, Parliament, and other Canadians. As such, this conflict reveals the central issue that lies at the foundation of our legal system: what is the meaning and significance of the *past* as it relates to the *present* configuration of law in Canada today, and who gets to determine the answer to this question in our official legal narratives?

In his work *Nineteen Eighty-Four*, George Orwell wrote: 'He who controls the present controls the past. He who controls the past, controls the future.'[105] Canadian courts and legislatures largely control historical interpretations of the past through official legal discourse. These institutions test Indigenous history and law against common law standards of proof. They measure Indigenous societies against non-Aboriginal sociopolitical norms and economic priorities. They often ignore or diminish Indigenous legal perspectives and do not give sufficient space for the operation of Indigenous legal traditions. In following this course, legislatures and the courts have been successful in claiming control of Canada's past. This stance places these institutions in a good position to control the future. Unfortunately, this approach has led to conflict in the past. Regrettably, continued non-recognition will likely lead to future conflict if Indigenous peoples are not given some measure of control over interpretations of the past. Since a contributing cause of our problems is the past denial of Indigenous legal traditions, this has prevented them from controlling their interpretations of how the future should unfold. This approach has injured

Indigenous societies, and Canada as an entire country. The acknowledgment and remedy for that harm has great significance for how we reconfigure the relationship between our legal traditions in Canada today.

Dr Judith Herman, Clinical Professor of Psychiatry at Harvard Medical School and Training Director of the Victims of Violence Program at Cambridge Hospital has recognized this point in another context. I want to apply her analysis to Crown/Indigenous relations in Canada. Dr Herman has written about how the denial of past atrocities is a cause of present dysfunctions. Her book *Trauma and Recovery* links literature and clinical studies involving women who have experienced domestic violence to the literature involving those who are veterans of combat and victims of political terror. Her work identifies parallels between so-called private terrors such as rape, and public traumas such as post-traumatic stress syndrome as a result of war. One of the major contributions of Dr Herman's research is that it places individual experiences of loss in a broader political frame. She argues that psychological trauma is best understood and remedied through a broader social context. This insight leads her to develop strategies for dealing with trauma that are attentive to wider societal responses. In this regard Dr Herman observes:

> [W]hen traumatic events are of human design, those who bear witness are caught in the conflict between victim and perpetrator. It is morally impossible to remain neutral in this conflict.
>
> It is very tempting to take the side of the perpetrator. All the perpetrator asks is that the bystander do nothing. He appeals to the universal desire to see, hear, and speak no evil. The victim, on the contrary, asks the bystander to share the burden of the pain. The victim demands action, engagement, and remembering ...
>
> In order to escape accountability for his crimes, the perpetrator does everything in his power to promote forgetting. Secrecy and silence are the perpetrator's first line of defense. If secrecy fails, the perpetrator attacks the credibility of his victim. If he cannot silence her absolutely, he tries to make sure that no one listens. To this end, he marshals an impressive array of arguments, from the most blatant denial to the most sophisticated and elegant rationalization. After every atrocity one can expect to hear the same predictable apologies: it never happened; the victim lies; the victim exaggerates; the victim brought it on herself; and in any case it is time to forget the past and move on. The more powerful the perpetra-

tor, the greater is his prerogative to name and define reality, and the more completely his arguments prevail.

The perpetrator's arguments prove irresistible when the bystander faces them in isolation. Without a supportive social environment, the bystander usually succumbs to the temptation to look the other way. This is true even when the victim is an idealized and valued member of society. Soldiers in every war, even those who have been regarded as heroes, complain bitterly that no one wants to know the real truth about war. When the victim is already devalued (a woman, a child), she may find that the most traumatic events in her life take place outside the realm of socially validated reality. Her experience becomes unspeakable ...

To hold traumatic reality in consciousness requires a social context that affirms and protects the victim and that joins the victim and witness in a common alliance. For the individual victim, this social context is created by relationships with friends, lovers, and family. For the larger society, the social context is created by political movements that give voice to the disempowered.[106]

It is usually easier to deny something happened than face up to the consequences of the past for the present. This response has been documented in many countries.[107] Herman's point regarding denial or forgetfulness helps explain why Indigenous grievances regarding Canadian law can rise to the point of conflict. There is little awareness in Canada's official history of the lived experience of trauma by Indigenous peoples and how this continues to consume present generations. There is a tendency to take the side of the Canadian government when viewing Indigenous claims, much as it is often easier to take the side of the perpetrator in other situations of abuse. 'All the perpetrator asks is that the bystander do nothing.' Preserving the status quo in legal relations between Indigenous peoples and the state can be like 'doing nothing' in Herman's analysis. Indigenous peoples often face situations in which they are told the thing they complain of never happened.[108] They might be told they never owned the land they claim,[109] never occupied it sufficiently to prove continuing legal title,[110] or did not have laws to substantiate their relationships.[111] They are often told they are lying or exaggerating, or that their views are incomplete, such that their testimony or views cannot be believed.[112] Sometimes Indigenous peoples are told they have brought their grievances upon themselves, and therefore are to blame for the tragedies they face.[113] They might encounter views that imply that if they had acted earlier, appropriate assistance would have been available, but that now others' subsequent claims are insurmountable.[114] Finally, Indigenous peoples may be told that, in any case, it is time to forget the past and move on, that past injustices cannot be cured today.[115] These reactions can cause Indigenous peoples to feel marginalized within Canadian society and turn away from constructive engagement with the state. This is one reason Indigenous peoples may not accept this book's thesis. In my view, such reactions would demonstrate the relevancy of Herman's thesis.

What Dr Herman says is required to overcome this situation is a social context that affirms and protects the victim, and reconnects him or her with healthy relationships in the present. Three things are required: action, engagement, and remembering. This result can be facilitated through the recognition and affirmation of Indigenous legal traditions, because this reconnects Indigenous peoples and other Canadians. These interactions have the potential to involve more people in a process of active engagement that acknowledges Indigenous experiences. This can create more respectful spaces where Indigenous peoples can tell their stories and extract meaning from them. In these circumstances, their grievances can be taken more seriously and not shuffled off to places where they have no control over their outcomes. Most Indigenous peoples do not feel it is safe to go to the courts as they are currently constituted. Their testimony and history are subject to discrediting cross-examinations and harsh burdens of proof.[116] Their legal traditions do not form standards for judgment in relation to their testimonies. Furthermore, Indigenous peoples do not find peace or security when raising their issues in the political sphere. They are outnumbered in the political process, and thus votes alone do not carry their concerns into action. In fact, some political parties are regarded as displaying outright hostility to any acknowledgment of Indigenous peoples' legal rights in Canada. It is even thought that the media is largely hostile because of the perceived bias of certain editorial boards. There is a noticeable absence of Aboriginal perspectives in newspaper columns and electronic media newsrooms.[117] Unfortunately, too many Indigenous people feel they generally face the same negative reactions to their aspirations when raised in corporations, unions, churches and other mainstream social organizations. Dr Herman's analysis suggests that this must change if Indigenous peoples are going to more strongly connect with Canada and overcome acute trauma. This requires a sociopolitical context that is more supportive of Indigenous peoples' perspectives. This is a major reason why I believe we should embrace multi-juridicalism in Canada. Indigenous peoples should be able to apply their laws within their own communities and have them influence broader Canadian legal analysis.

As Dr Herman counsels, when a supportive social context is established, those who have experienced trauma can then move on to remember and mourn their losses, and subsequently repair damaged relationships – for instance, to land and people – that are important to their well-being. These steps could reduce conflict in our country and breed the conditions for peace.[118] The wider acceptance of the legitimacy of Indigenous legal traditions could set us on a path to achieve this result.

F. Conclusion

While this entire book is devoted, in part, to identifying and overcoming challenges to the recognition and affirmation of Indigenous legal traditions, this chapter has addressed some of the more pressing concerns that may be expressed by politicians, journalists, judges, lawyers, academics, theorists, and Indigenous community members. While some of these issues can be answered by reference to historic experience, scholarly commentary, or legal principle, other concerns are less likely to be resolved through appeals to reason alone. There is an essential emotional and psychological component to human relationships that will influence the acceptance of my thesis no matter how rational my arguments may appear. Feelings, passions, deep-seated sentiments, and self-interest are always engaged when Indigenous legal issues are considered, and it is my hope this chapter has addressed each of these concerns in an appropriate way. It is deeply important to our peace and order that we attend to these broader issues in a positive manner, with a constructive approach, devoted to problem-solving and reconciliation.

As I was completing this book, a former student offered me an important insight that helped me remember this truth. I returned to Canada for spring break after teaching for the term at the University of Minnesota Law School. I had a meeting to attend at the University of Victoria and was making my way to the law school's boardroom. The halls were crowded with students as classes were let out for lunch. I was enjoying seeing familiar faces and listening to the way people's voices competed and mingled with one another in the air. I stopped a few times and had brief conversations with people whom I had taught in the previous year. As I was about to reach my destination, I saw a woman who had taken my course in Indigenous lands, rights, and governments. She had been raised in a blended family on an Indian reserve in northern Alberta. We had often talked about her experiences growing up as a Cree person in that setting, even though she was technically non-Aboriginal in the eyes of Canadian law. She saw issues from many angles and it was always insightful to visit with her regarding her ideas and experiences.

In our brief hallway conversation, she told me about a visit to Ottawa in the previous month. She was interviewed for a clerk's position at the Supreme Court of Canada. As the meetings progressed, she had a striking experience that recurred three times when asked about her long-term career goals. She told the judges that she wanted to do graduate work and eventually practise in the field of Aboriginal law. Upon hearing this response, each judge asked a similar question. Their inquiries were independent of one another and thus, to her, indicated a common concern. Each judge asked, in carefully measured tones: 'Is there any hope?' The student reported that she felt the question was heartfelt, honest, sincere, and searching. She thought it was posed in the most professional manner and with the utmost respect and dignity. She said she felt their goodness and understood more deeply the decency and honour that these people brought to their office. And yet, at an advanced and highly accomplished stage in their legal careers, an important question remained unanswered for them in relation to Indigenous peoples' relationship with the Canadian state: 'Is there any hope?' When the student had finished recounting her experience, she looked at me for a response.

This book tries to give reasons why I believe there is hope in our law as it relates to Indigenous peoples. While hope is only one part of the answer to finding our way out of the mess we are in, it is often the part we pay the least attention to in our formal legal circles. This must change. Subjects that are troubling to people must be honestly confronted if Indigenous legal traditions are to enjoy greater receptiveness. I find it very beneficial to read books, cases, and articles that confirm and critique the place Indigenous tradition has in contemporary Canada. It is my hope that in this book I am engaging in this debate in an affirmative and expansive way. In so doing, I hope I am opening up space for further debate and broader remedies. This chapter acknowledges that many issues must be resolved if we are to enjoy the full benefits that a vibrant multi-juridicalism can offer Canadians. At the same time, I believe we have the means to overcome these challenges if we draw upon one another's creativity and goodwill in addressing honest questions and in acknowledging our deepest fears. If we can take this path in further refining our legal relationships, there is hope – not just for Indigenous peoples, but for other Canadians as well.

7 The Role of Governments and Courts in Entrenching Indigenous Legal Traditions

How can governments and courts best facilitate the development and extension of Indigenous legal traditions in Canada? This question has been answered in numerous ways throughout this book. Chapter 1 explained that the fuller recognition of treaties would implement Indigenous law. Treaties often created Canada in their Indigenous territories by applying and referring to Indigenous legal traditions. A fuller understanding of their importance in Canada's constitutional framework exposes the deficiencies that lie behind other theories regarding the reception of law in this country. Chapters 2 and 3 demonstrated that Indigenous legal traditions were more likely to be implemented if their varied sources were more widely understood. Indigenous law's diversity of sources and social contexts reveals the living nature of Indigenous traditions and shows that their continued growth and development lies within the hands of Indigenous peoples themselves. Chapters 4 and 5 showed how Indigenous law could be strengthened through understanding the culturally contingent nature of the common law and civil law's authority in Canada. Canadians follow common law and civil law traditions because they were regarded as binding on people who came to this country from countries where these forms of law originated. In light of these choices, I argued that the implementation of Indigenous law could be facilitated if Elders, politicians, judges, lawyers, and academics from each of our communities drew analogies from bijuridicalism and recognized our country's multi-juridical character. Since Canada's early history and constitutional framework accommodated a *de facto* multi-juridicalism, I suggested that it is not completely novel or contrary to our legal order to more fully recognize Indigenous legal traditions in the present. Chapter 6 explained that Indigenous legal traditions could be more fully entrenched if we recognized their intelligibility, enhanced their accessibility, and understood that their implementation does not undermine but strengthens equality rights in our country. Chapter 6 also discussed the scope of Indigenous law's application and recommended that implementation should be the task of various Indigenous governments who have responsibilities over reservations and other Indigenous territories. I suggested that Indigenous law's application on a territorial basis could enhance the democratic nature of Canadian law. This could also provide a stronger foundation for having each legal tradition influence others across the land.[1]

The current chapter focuses on the specific role of governments and courts in strengthening legal traditions. These bodies are important in implementing Indigenous law in a Canadian context. Broadly speaking, governments formulate, authorize, and administer laws, while courts interpret and enforce them.[2] If these institutions function properly, they are a critical site for communication about the nature and scope of law in society. Unfortunately, if governments and courts are unresponsive, they can obscure the proper transmission and reception of legal values.[3] Sociopolitical chaos and disorder can result if legal institutions do not reflect a people's obligations or facilitate their participation. With few exceptions, Indigenous peoples in Canada experience these difficulties. They are not permitted to sufficiently control decisions within their own sphere. They rarely see their legal traditions reflected with sufficient strength across the country. Thus, they do not feel the same sense of obligation citizens usually experience when ruled by laws which strengthen their social bonds. As a result, Indigenous peoples do not enjoy the degree of peace, order, and security potentially available to them. This must change. Indigenous and other Canadian governments and courts can become a catalyst for constructive change if they appropriately build upon their highest traditions.

Thus, Indigenous legal traditions will more positively permeate our societies if their power is acknowledged by official state and community institutions.[4] It is for this reason that the present chapter examines steps that can be followed by governments and courts to implement Indigenous law. However, before we explore their role in enhancing multi-juridicalism, one caution is in order. A focus on formal state institutions should not cause us to discount the role of non-governmental organizations, families, or individuals in creating, interpreting, and enforcing Indigenous law. There is a tremendous danger that official state organs can overwhelm other institutions of civil society if they are regarded as exclusive legal agents in Canada. This would be a mistake and would undermine the vitality of Indigenous law. Governments and courts have been the cause of much dispossession and sorrow for Indigenous peoples.[5] They should be viewed with a healthy degree of suspicion because of their poor past performance. As we have seen, particularly in chapters 2 and 3, Indigenous legal traditions are strongly held by many different people and parties in Indigenous societies. In fact, their broad dispersal and decentralized force is one of the reasons they have survived colonialism's onslaught. Indigenous legal traditions have been more difficult to erase than would have been the case if their laws were intensely concentrated in highly formal offices. Indigenous law is often at its strongest when Elders, families, house systems, and other bodies have communicated their traditions in more diffuse and decentralized ways. This experience teaches us that we must be careful that Indigenous law's formal implementation by governments and courts does not undercut Indigenous civil society.

Thus, governments and courts will likely work best for Indigenous peoples when they are strong but limited in their powers and jurisdiction. As noted, of all peoples in Canada, Indigenous peoples should be especially suspicious of big government and overbearing courts. This is particularly the case where Indigenous peoples are likely to remain a numeric minority in their regions for the foreseeable future.[6] In such circumstances, they will not have sufficient clout at the ballot box to appropriately influence political decisions. They might not have enough persuasive power in judicial chambers if a majoritarian balance of interest were to be aligned against them in the courts. However, even if Indigenous peoples are in a majority in certain places, such as within their own communities, their governments and courts should still be somewhat limited. At some level, state-like institutions must be restrained because they tend to usurp vital functions that are often best performed by Elders, families, clans, and other bodies within Indigenous societies.[7] Governments and courts should not be trusted with more power than is necessary to create a sphere of recognition and enforcement for underlying community values. In the implementation of Indigenous legal traditions, we should ensure that governments and courts are supplementary and not at the centre of the resurgence of Indigenous law.

Furthermore, academic works or other commentaries should not displace the essential role of individuals, kin, clan, families, and community in making the most important judgments about how Indigenous law is lived. I make this point with full consciousness that this book is attempting to outline how and why we should recognize and affirm Indigenous legal traditions. Indigenous peoples will be poorly served if works like this become the standard against which Indigenous legal traditions are ultimately measured. People trained in multi-juridicalism should be somewhat distant from the daily identification, creation, interpretation, and enforcement of Indigenous law in Canada. If lawyers are given too great a role, '… it would not be too long before Indian customs and traditions, and the studied informality of [Indigenous law] and the particular attention that tribal [lawmakers] pay to family responsibilities would be replaced by a variety of model codes written by and for the convenience of the attorneys.'[8] While there is an important role for Indigenous lawyers and other assistants in expanding Indigenous legal traditions, this process must not become dominated by them. They are exceedingly poor substitutes for drawing peace and order from the living relationships and teachings found in families and communities. Their presence may foster an unhealthy reliance on so-called legal experts. This could fatally frustrate grass-roots community organization and family activism that should essentially drive regulation and dispute resolution with Indigenous communities.

While we should place governments, courts, lawyers, and academics in their proper place, we should not entirely discount their potential. They can play an important ancillary role in supporting individuals, families, and communities in the preservation and implementation of Indigenous legal traditions. Because of the strongly hierarchical nature of Canada's other legal traditions, Indigenous laws could be overlooked and undervalued if they are not championed by more centralized institutions within Aboriginal communities and Canadian society as a whole. Indigenous legal traditions will not receive the respect they deserve if governments, courts, lawyers, political scientists, and law professors fail to more fully articulate their place in our country. Effective governance and judicial decision-making thus requires that formal institutions work alongside Indigenous individuals and families to recreate a supportive context for Indigenous law's implementation. A strong yet limited role for governments, courts, and lawyers can help ensure that Indigenous legal traditions do not get lost in their interactions with the common law and civil law in Canada. Governments, courts, and lawyers should therefore help create the conditions for the more explicit implementation of Indigenous legal traditions and community values. Such action could unburden families and communities, thus enabling them to plan their lives according to their own priorities, freed from the *Indian Act* and other colonial fetters.

In the paragraphs that follow, therefore, I suggest that both Indigenous and other Canadian governments could enact legislation or undertake similar official acts that recognize and harmonize Indigenous legal traditions with the common law and civil law. I also suggest that Indigenous courts, along with federal and provincial courts, could better implement Indigenous law by developing appropriate interpretive mechanisms and ensuring that at least some of those who are appointed to the bench have a knowledge of or receptivity to Indigenous legal traditions. Indigenous governments and the Canadian Parliament should pass Indigenous law recognition legislation to facilitate the rule of law's development in Canada. Indigenous peoples' role in developing Recognition Acts will be considered before turning our attention to Canada's responsibility in this matter.

A. Indigenous Governments and Recognition Acts

While Recognition Acts could be very important in facilitating multi-juridicalism in Canada, it should be noted that Indigenous peoples do not require formal recognition to possess and exercise law. The very concept of recognition implies that such power already exists within a community. The word itself, recognition, describes a thought process that brings an accepted idea to awareness again. With this understanding, the primary reason for Recognition Acts within Indigenous communities would be to once more prominently bring Indigenous law to a society's attention. Formal recognition would remind Indigenous peoples of the Indigenous source of their rights and obligations. It would also make these facts more widely known to the various constituencies Indigenous governments regularly serve. There can be great value in a community formally remembering and proclaiming its highest legal values. The identification of Indigenous law as a primary source of regulation, decision-making, and dispute-resolution powers might even take the form of a constitution for some communities. Constitutions communicate a society's central organizing principles and convey overarching legal standards for judgment in order to evaluate a political society's future development.

Indigenous communities may also decide to participate in Recognition Acts or enact their own constitutions because they want other governments to understand the basis of their law-making authority. In this light, such acknowledgment could demonstrate to municipal, provincial, and national governments that an Indigenous community has occupied a field of law-making power appropriate to its jurisdiction. This action could also be important to subsequent acts of recognition for non-Aboriginal governments because it would provide an additional justification for the passage of their laws acknowledging Indigenous legal traditions. Additionally, the passage of Recognition Acts by Indigenous communities could provide a basis for subsequently harmonizing their laws with other legal traditions in Canada. There are many valid reasons why Indigenous peoples might want to pass laws recognizing the source and scope of their laws in their territories and beyond.

Furthermore, Indigenous governments may also want to include in their Recognition Acts an affirmation of the civil law and/or common law's scope of authority within their territories. As a part of this declaration, communities might decide to recognize the Crown's role as a source of law for other Canadians to whom they relate. Some Indigenous governments may even take the step of acknowledging that they have certain obligations to the Crown within their territories and that these obligations have a relationship to their own laws.

Recognizing the place of Canada's other legal traditions in this manner could be a huge challenge for Indigenous communities who have struggled under the weight of colonial oppression. They might wonder why they should recognize the common law's authority when the Crown has not extended similar courtesies in relation to Indigenous laws. It would not be a stretch to say it is unfair and overly one-sided for Indigenous peoples to act in this manner when they have experienced such great injustice under other legal traditions. For this reason, most communities would feel appropriately justified in choosing to withhold recognition of Canada's other legal traditions until the Crown takes steps to be more respectful of Indigenous law. Nevertheless, for many communities, the recognition of Crown law might appropriately seize the initiative and demonstrate to Canadian governments the generosity of spirit that Recognition Acts could encompass. Indigenous peoples could take the path of justice in their relations with others even in the face of the injustice they continue to experience. The recognition of other peoples' laws might even be an article of Indigenous law for some Indigenous communities, and thus be required within their legal system. It could be, in part, a generosity of heart that recognizes '*all* our relations,' a concept which undergirds many Indigenous legal values. In Anishinabemowin, the language of my community, the word that closely describes this concept is *n'bimi-gaedaugunuk* or *nindinawemaaganidog*. Today, our relations include more than the rocks, birds, animals, and Indigenous peoples that comprise our territories; a holistic view of our relations includes all beings resident in our territories, including those who have settled among us over the past 300 years, even if they have not always done so peacefully from our legal perspectives.

Embracing broader aspects of recognition would demonstrate the interdependence of Canada's legal traditions. As a collateral benefit, such legislation could perhaps alleviate fears that the recognition of Indigenous law would threaten other laws that aspire to create peace, order, and good governance in this land. If Indigenous peoples were to certify that the recognition of their legal traditions does not undermine common law and civil law traditions in their spheres this could create an even more stable base for the future growth and healthy interaction among the traditions. Additionally, the passage of recognition legislation or other such acts would enable Indigenous peoples to explicitly articulate their views about the sources of legal order in Canada. For many First Nations, this exercise would likely see them reference their treaties or other agreements that gave the Crown rights to have people from other parts of the world settle among them. Other First Nations might struggle with the basis for Crown recognition in their territories if Canadian law-making authority exists without their participation and consent (such as where treaties have not been executed or appropriately implemented). However, even in these circumstances, the formulation of principles upon which the recognition of other legal traditions is based could be important to subsequent Crown recognition of Indigenous legal traditions. As such, it could generate constructive alternatives, building Canada on an even firmer legal foundation. The recognition by Indigenous peoples of the place of the common and civil law in Canada would also be a legally accurate gesture. An Indigenous community's declaration of this type could help facilitate a culture of order and respect for people's entitlements and obligations no matter what the source in their lands might be. If First Nations and others desire the Crown to pass Indigenous law recognition legislation, their own actions could set the example needed to kick start the process of expanding the possibilities for the more formal interaction of laws in Canada.

When taking these steps, Indigenous law recognition legislation should be developed and instituted by the body within a First Nation, Métis, or Inuit territory that has the greatest legitimacy with the people in terms of their own legal traditions. For some communities, such legislation might be passed by a territorial legislature, such as in Nunavut where public governance is overwhelmingly controlled by the Inuit. Among the Métis, such legislation might be developed and promulgated by community settlement boards or representative political organizations, depending on the democratic will of people forming these organizations. First Nations might choose to have their national and regional organizations work together to create legal templates for internal community-based recognition. Once legislation is drafted at this level, it could be submitted to bands, house groups, clans, families, and other governmental bodies to rework in accordance with their own aspirations for eventual adoption in accordance with whatever form is most authoritative in their legal system. While such coordinated action might be helpful to some communities, other groups may already possess legal procedures or substantive rules for the recognition of other legal systems. In these cases, all that might be required is a gathering in the feast hall to make such a proclamation. In other settings, wampum belts might be circulated, or house poles raised, to reaffirm long-standing principles of legal recognition of the common law or civil law in relationship with Indigenous legal traditions in their territories. In other cases, a family or clan might gather in some authoritative way to express their fundamental principles. Whatever form recognition takes, communities must ensure that their acts accord with their community's desire to live in peace both within their community and with those who surround them.

If Indigenous peoples took these or similar steps, their legal traditions would be more securely protected. Indigenous peoples would be more likely to remain living cultural forces if they defined their law's parameters through formal Recognition Acts.[9] These acts must account for the totality of each group's relevant legal influences. As has been repeatedly stressed throughout this book, Indigenous legal traditions should not be frozen at some artificial moment in the past; they should continually develop to meet the needs of each generation. Indigenous law recognition legislation and other formal acts will not genuinely facilitate a community's normative order if they do not recognize this fact. No culture is free from so-called external effects and pressures. Indigenous legal cultures are no exception.[10] Laws do not automatically become non-Indigenous just because Indigenous peoples adapt and adopt practices found in other legal traditions.

When Recognition Acts are promulgated, Indigenous governments will likely draw upon their best practices and procedures in their law-making powers. They will generally seek appropriate guidance from other legal cultures whose practices and views accord with Indigenous aspirations. Indigenous law-making authorities can compare, contrast, accept, and reject governmental and legal standards from many sources, including their own. Therefore, Indigenous Recognition Acts must not be measured by how closely they mirror the perceived past, but by how consistent they are with current community values and future needs.[11]

The most effective types of recognition will abandon traditions that do not agree with contemporary mores. Recognition will be the strongest when it accords with international human rights law and is the contemporary product of the self-determining choice of Indigenous communities. This should come as no surprise to anyone familiar with how law operates. All legal traditions possess past practices that are no longer acceptable in light of modern values. The *Civil Code of Quebec* recently abandoned inequality between spouses, and added privacy rights, personality rights, and (trust-like) patrimony of affection powers. The common law no longer sanctions trial by ordeal, trial by battle, sexual or racial discrimination, and a host of other human rights abuses. Likewise, Indigenous legal traditions will be the subject of continual revision in order to ensure compatibility with contemporary communities and consistency with human rights values. Indigenous law Recognition Acts should explicitly reference this viewpoint.

B. Canadian Governments and Recognition Legislation

Along with Indigenous governments, Canadian governments also have a role to play in formally recognizing Indigenous law. In taking such steps, they should be guided by their own constitutional obligations to Indigenous peoples. Section 35(1) of the *Constitution Act, 1982* states: 'The existing Aboriginal and treaty rights of the Aboriginal peoples of Canada are hereby recognized and affirmed.' Aboriginal peoples could claim the practice of Indigenous law as a right requiring recognition and affirmation under this section and the government could recognize this fact. Section 35(1) therefore has significant implications for the Crown's acknowledgment of Indigenous legal traditions. This is the case because section 35(1) goes further than merely recognizing Aboriginal rights; it also affirms Crown obligations. As W.N. Hohfeld observed, '[A] duty is the invariable correlative of that legal relation which is most properly called a right or claim.'[12] Further, in *Lake & M.S.R. Co. v. Kurtz*, as cited by Hohfeld, 'A duty or a legal obligation is that which one ought or ought not to do. "Duty" and "right" are correlative terms. When a right is invaded, a duty is violated.'[13] This is the case with Aboriginal and treaty rights in Canada. Wherever an Aboriginal or treaty right exists, a correlative governmental obligation can be found. Section 35(1) must therefore be read in a way that incorporates reciprocity, particularly in relation to legal traditions.[14]

This view of section 35(1) means that whenever Aboriginal 'rights' are invoked, governmental 'duties' are summoned. This broader conceptualization of section 35(1) places the Crown more squarely in the picture if Aboriginal rights incorporate Indigenous law. It appropriately shifts the focus from Aboriginal peoples to the Crown in a more significant way in working out the section's scope, content, and meaning. The enactment of section 35(1) strengthened government obligations in relation to Aboriginal peoples; in the words of Justice Binnie: it converted them into 'sterner stuff.'[15] In *R. v. Sparrow*, the leading case interpreting section 35(1), the Supreme Court of Canada wrote that '... recognition and affirmation [of Aboriginal rights] ... import some restraint on the exercise of sovereign power.'[16] Governmental obligations flow from the limitations placed on Crown sovereignty under section 35(1). These limitations must be prescribed by law and be consistent with Canada's legal traditions.

The recognition and affirmation of Crown obligations under section 35(1) does not represent a break with Canada's constitutional order. Constraints on Crown sovereignty are consistent with Canada's democratic traditions. The Crown's subjection to the rule of law is at the centre of the nation's political values. Constraints on Crown sovereignty have often been heralded as great breakthroughs for furthering human rights and liberty. The same can be said for section 35(1) constraints, when placed in historical context. For example, many proclaim the date 1215 as significant because the issuance of the Magna Carta gave rights to certain classes of individuals relative to the Crown, which expanded through time.[17] Despite its limitations,[18] the Magna Carta is applied and commemorated, and is not seen as threatening but as supporting Canada's political order.[19] Similarly, the Glorious Revolution of 1688 in England, wherein the Crown's authority was made subject to Parliament, is held in high esteem in our democratic traditions. The English *Bill of Rights*, which flowed from the revolution, obligated the Crown to raise and spend money with the consent of elected parliamentary officials, and not of its own accord.[20] Judges, lawyers, politicians, and the public refer to the Glorious Revolution as an important source of political authority and regard it as a cornerstone of liberty. British North Americans enjoyed similar restraints to the exercise of Crown prerogatives when responsible government came to non-Aboriginal Canadians in the 1850s in the Canadas and in the Atlantic colonies. Furthermore, the American and French Revolutions of the late 1700s, which also purported to restrain Crown sovereignty relative to individual rights, are also regarded as essential steps in democracy's development. Canada's own *Charter of Rights and Freedoms* is in this tradition.[21]

Constraints on Crown actions under section 35(1) should be seen as flowing from this same tradition. The recognition of Indigenous law as potentially imposing limitations on the Crown could be viewed as a human rights triumph. There are sound reasons for ensuring that political authority is subject to proper checks and balances. Recognizing Crown obligations relative to Aboriginal peoples through Indigenous law could be a part of this process. The Supreme Court has been clear that Crown constraints are a part of the framework of section 35(1). As they observed in the leading case of *R. v. Sparrow:*

> Section 35 calls for a just settlement for aboriginal peoples. It renounces the old rules of the game under which the Crown established courts of law and denied those courts the authority to question sovereign claims made by the Crown.[22]

This holding makes clear the fact that Crown sovereignty is constrained by its obligations to Aboriginal peoples under section 35. These constraints on government action could be regarded in the same light as the Magna Carta, the Glorious Revolution, responsible government, and bills of rights. Each development significantly restricted the Crown's scope of authority relative to a noteworthy section of the body politic. Freedom was increased when the Crown was obliged to observe constitutional limitations on its power; section 35(1) falls within this tradition.

In dealing with Indigenous peoples, Parliament must therefore organize itself in accordance with its constitutional principles to meet its obligations. It would be a serious violation of the country's highest law if the federal government did not order itself in this way. Governmental actions that do not accord with the Constitution violate our most fundamental tenets. This is the nature of our constitutional democracy.[23] Section 52 of the *Constitution Act, 1982* states that 'any law that is inconsistent with the provisions of the Constitution is, to the extent of the inconsistency, of no force or effect.' The recognition and affirmation of Aboriginal rights and the proper exercise of federal responsibilities towards Indigenous peoples is not optional. Indigenous peoples must derive legal benefits from Canada's Constitution. The federal, provincial, and territorial governments must organize themselves in relationship to Indigenous peoples to abide by these higher precepts. This will more fully structure our society in accordance with its constitutional order. Regrettably, this is an area in which Canada has seriously failed to abide by its highest laws.

Fortunately, it would not be a completely groundbreaking stretch for governments to pass legislation recognizing the relationship between Canada's Constitution and Indigenous legal traditions. In fact, Parliament has been guided by a section 35(1) policy that implicitly embraces aspects of Indigenous law. To this end, the following policy statement was issued in 1995:

> The Government of Canada recognizes the inherent right of self-government as an existing right within section 35 of the *Constitution Act, 1982*. Recognition of the inherent right to self-government under the 1995 policy is based on the view that the Indigenous peoples of Canada have the right to govern themselves in matters that are internal to their communities, integral to their unique cultures, identities, traditions, languages and institutions, and with respect to their special relationship to their land and their resources.[24]

It is significant to note how each of these categories alludes to Indigenous legal traditions. It could be said that:

- Indigenous culture is partially created, preserved, and adapted through legal tradition.
- Indigenous identity is partially developed and passed on through Indigenous law.
- Indigenous language is an important medium through which Indigenous peoples create and interpret their law; it uniquely structures thought concerning binding norms and relationships.

- Indigenous institutions are held together by Indigenous laws.
- Indigenous peoples' special relationships with their lands and resources are best defined through their own legal traditions.

These and other facts lead to the conclusion that Indigenous legal traditions could be considered as existing Aboriginal rights in Canada, recognized and affirmed by section 35(1) of the *Constitution Act, 1982*. This shows that Canada's recent past policy holds some promise for the recognition of Indigenous legal traditions, if it could be made more explicit, that is, by the inclusion of specific written provisions.

To further the underlying recognition of Indigenous law, Parliament could pass legislation that translated the Inherent Rights Policy into a legally enforceable legislative instrument. Such law could make explicit the relationship of Indigenous law to governance in Canada. In this vein, Parliament could affirm that Indigenous governance includes the right of Indigenous peoples to implement their unique laws in order to continually strengthen their cultures, identities, traditions, languages, and institutions and thereby nurture their special relationships with lands and resources.

In developing Indigenous law recognition legislation, the federal government, with the participation and development of Indigenous governments, could take guidance from the recommendations of the Royal Commission on Aboriginal Peoples. The Royal Commission proposed the enactment of an *Aboriginal Nations Recognition and Government Act*.[25] Among other things, this Act would:

(a) Enable the federal government to vacate its legislative authority under section 91(24) of the *Constitution Act, 1867* with respect to core powers deemed needed by Indigenous nations. It could specify which additional areas of federal jurisdiction the Parliament of Canada is prepared to acknowledge as core powers to be exercised by Aboriginal governments.

(b) Provide enhanced financial resources to enable recognized Aboriginal nations to exercise expanded governing powers for an increased population base in the period between recognition and the conclusion or reaffirmation of comprehensive treaties.[26]

These are very helpful recommendations. Through legislative action, the federal government could confirm Indigenous peoples' law-making power and provide sufficient funds to support its proper exercise. Moreover, in my view, the passage of such legislation should be implemented with guidance from the following principles:

(a) A community must freely consent and elect to take advantage of any legislative provisions at their exclusive option, which should not be imposed or mandatory;

(b) The enabling legislation should be proposed and drafted on a nation-to-nation basis after wide-ranging consultation with First Nations, Métis organizations and Inuit communities;

(c) The legislation should also have the consent of the major Aboriginal organizations, including the Native Women's Association of Canada;

(d) The legislation should be rights-based; it should not undermine historical treaties, or abrogate or derogate from other section 35 rights;

(e) The legislation should not impose more bureaucratic control over Indigenous people; it should liberate them from assimilative supervision;

(f) The legislation should reflect the concerns of Indigenous women and reflect the principle of gender equality under s. 35(4) of the *Constitution Act, 1982*;

(g) The legislation should be drafted to enhance the best interests of Indigenous children;

(h) The legislation should also reject a 'one-size-fits-all' approach and thereby allow for the great diversity within Indigenous nations to find expression.

This is not an exhaustive list and many other matters could be added to guide parliamentarians in their task. The point is to draft legislation that accords with Canada's constitutional obligations, that implements Indigenous peoples' democratic aspirations, and ensures that those who may be vulnerable within Indigenous societies are appropriately served and protected by Indigenous legal traditions as well as by other Canadian laws. To further protect the political integrity of Indigenous communities, Indigenous law recognition legislation should create a framework for Indigenous communities within which to choose whether they want to accept the recognition offered by Parliament. Such legislation should also ensure that Indigenous peoples are not worse off after its enactment. The legislation will not be accepted by communities if the federal government uses this initiative to offload responsibility and increase costs of governance for Indigenous communities without an adequate *quid pro quo*. Legislation will most likely work if Indigenous peoples regard the bill as their own. The bill must not be seen to create Indigenous governance powers, but merely to provide a way for the federal government to formally acknowledge inherent Indigenous legal and governmental powers. The rights recognized must be also regarded as vesting in the proper Indigenous authorities, which is a matter for Indigenous peoples to choose.

i. *The Relevance of International Law to Recognizing*
   Indigenous Legal Traditions

Section 35(1) of the *Constitution Act, 1982,* is clear about who holds the rights: *peoples*. Indigenous groups should be able to claim organizational rights as *peoples*. This point is made by Professor Catherine Bell in an article about Métis rights.[27] She observes that section 35 came out of an international context in which there was 'growing activity at the United Nations aimed at ending colonial domination [which] resulted in increased international pressure on nation states to recognize and protect the human rights of colonized peoples.'[28] Section 35 should be placed in this broader human rights context and these principles should guide the development of recognition legislation. Since section 35 is a provision that is aimed at eradicating unconstitutional colonial domination, the principles of Indigenous law and governance should be acknowledged as an important part of our Constitution's purpose. Legislators must also remember that the stated purpose of section 35 is 'the protection and reconciliation of the interests which arise from the fact that prior to the arrival of Europeans in North America aboriginal peoples lived on the land in distinctive societies, with their own practices, customs and traditions.'[29] This statement makes it clear that reconciliation is a constitutional standard for the implementation of Aboriginal rights. If reconciliation were to be more broadly read in its international, anti-colonial, and human rights context, this could provide parliamentarians with essential guidance in their task of drafting recognition legislation. Seeing Aboriginal rights in this context could also lead drafters to draw upon principles within declarations prepared by the United Nations (UN) or the Organization of American States (OAS) that recognize the connection between Indigenous governance and Indigenous legal traditions.

International legal instruments contain norms that recognize the connection between Indigenous governance and law. The UN *Declaration on the Rights of Indigenous Peoples* (the *Declaration*) is clear about this relationship and could provide direction to those developing

Recognition Legislation. The *Declaration* is part of a fifteen-year-long intensive effort by members of the Working Group on Indigenous Populations of the Sub-Commission on the Promotion and Protection of Human Rights. The *Declaration*'s goal is to promote human rights for Indigenous peoples. It contains nine sections and numerous articles that deal with matters such as equality, self-determination, and freedom from threats of genocide or ethnocide, health, and the maintenance of distinct identity, history, religion, and cultural heritage. While the *Declaration* was finalized and enacted without the Canadian government's approval, and while International laws do not generally define 'peoples' who have a right of self-determination, this right nevertheless remains an important and widespread Indigenous goal. Governance and law are connected within the *Declaration*. It proclaims that 'Indigenous peoples have a right to self-determination.'[30] Furthermore, 'By virtue of that right they freely determine their political status and freely pursue their economic, social and cultural development.'[31]

The provisions within the *Declaration* are important guideposts to recognition legislation because they highlight the fact that Indigenous legal traditions can facilitate self-determination.[32] Article 9 of the *Declaration* asserts that 'Indigenous peoples have the right to belong to indigenous communities or nations *according to their own traditions and customs.*' Article 19 states, 'Indigenous peoples have the right ... to maintain and develop *their own decision making institutions.*' Article 33 recognizes that Indigenous peoples have the 'right to *maintain a justice system in accordance with their legal traditions.*'[33]

Other international instruments dealing with Indigenous peoples also acknowledge the connection between their governance and legal traditions. For example, in 1989, the International Labour Organization (ILO) adopted *Convention 169*, which contains provisions respecting Indigenous legal traditions. While the ILO primarily promotes and protects employee rights, it has been a long-time ally of Indigenous peoples. In the mid-1950s, the ILO *Convention 107* became the first international instrument to explicitly deal with Indigenous peoples. While the recognition of Indigenous rights was a positive step for an international organization, its assimilative premise did not coincide with Indigenous peoples' preferences. As a result, the ILO revised *Convention 107* by drafting *Convention 169* (the *Convention*), which was adopted in 1989.[34] Canada has not yet ratified the *Convention*. Nevertheless, its underlying philosophy is consistent with the premises listed in this chapter. The preamble of the *Convention* states its goal as being to recognize 'the aspirations of these peoples to exercise control over their own institutions, ways of life and economic development and to maintain and develop their identities, languages and religions.'[35]

In particular, Articles 8 and 9 of ILO's *Convention 169* are the provisions most applicable to the recognition and implementation of Indigenous legal traditions. Article 8.1 states that in 'applying national laws and regulations to the peoples concerned, due regard shall be had to their customs or customary laws.' This idea is certainly consistent with the thesis being developed in this book, which suggests 'due regard' can include the acceptance of Indigenous law not only for Indigenous peoples but also as a source of law for other Canadians. Article 8.2 of the *Convention* contemplates a procedure for ensuring that Indigenous legal traditions are compatible with fundamental international and domestic human rights. It states that Indigenous peoples 'shall have the right to retain their own customs and institutions where these are not incompatible with fundamental rights defined by the national legal system and with internationally recognized human rights.' Furthermore, it declares, 'Procedures shall be established, whenever necessary, to resolve conflicts which may arise in the application of this principle.' Article 9.1 reinforces the issues of compatibility of Indigenous legal traditions with human rights standards. It says states should respect Indigenous legal practices. It reads: 'To the extent compatible with the national legal system and internationally recognized human rights, the methods customarily practiced by the peoples concerned for dealing with offences committed by their members shall be respected.'[36] ILO *Convention 169* is important because it identifies the important relationship between governance and Indigenous law. Thus, it could also provide an important guidepost in the development of recognition legislation by the Canadian Parliament.

Finally, the OAS has also developed principles that are relevant for Canadian recognition legislation. The OAS is another international body that has promoted the recognition of Indigenous legal traditions as part of Indigenous and national governance. The OAS is a regional international organization of thirty-four member states, including Canada and the United States. The human rights component of the OAS is the Inter-American Commission on Human Rights (ICHR), whose primary mandate is to promote respect for and defence of human rights in the hemisphere. The OAS *Proposed Declaration on the Rights of Indigenous Peoples* (the *Proposed Declaration*) is the first international instrument to specifically have articles entitled 'Indigenous Law.' These articles were approved by the ICHR on 26 February 1997 at its 1333rd Session, 95th Regular Session.

Article 16 of the OAS *Proposed Declaration* acknowledges the importance of Indigenous law to the state's legal systems. It also recognizes the significance of Indigenous peoples' internal governance and dispute resolution systems. The draft contains the following declarations:

1 Indigenous law shall be recognized as a part of the states' legal system and of the framework in which the social and economic development of the states takes place.
2 Indigenous Peoples have the right to maintain and reinforce their Indigenous legal systems and also to apply them to matters within their communities, including systems related to such matters as conflict resolution, crime prevention and maintenance of peace and harmony.
3 In the jurisdiction of any state, procedures concerning Indigenous Peoples or their interests shall be conducted in such a way as to ensure the right of Indigenous Peoples to full representation with dignity and equality before the law. This shall include observance of Indigenous Law and custom and, where necessary, use of their language.[37]

These are important provisions because their acceptance could strongly support the extension of Indigenous legal traditions. They acknowledge the importance of Indigenous law for Indigenous peoples' social, economic, and communal development. They also confirm the idea that the state's acceptance of Indigenous law could enhance Indigenous people's equality and representative capacity within a country's jurisdiction.

Another section of the *Proposed Declaration* that could encourage parliamentarians to pass recognition legislation is Article 17. This article discusses the relationship between a state's legal system and those of Indigenous systems. It suggests the national incorporation of Indigenous legal and organizational systems within the state's systems. Article 17 of the *Proposed Declaration* says states should change their structures and practices to include Indigenous legal traditions. It reads:

1 The states shall facilitate the inclusion in their organizational structures, the institutions and traditional practices of Indigenous Peoples, and in consultation and with consent of the peoples concerned.

2 State institutions relevant to and serving Indigenous Peoples shall
   be designed in consultation and with the participation of the
   peoples concerned so as to reinforce and promote the identity,
   cultures, traditions, organization and values of those peoples.[38]

The *Proposed Declaration* makes it clear that the inclusion of Indigenous
law within state structures should be done with the consultation and
consent of Indigenous peoples. It also makes clear that such developments should be beneficial for those groups who are the subject of such
recognition. In facilitating Indigenous legal traditions, Parliament could
act in accordance with these international instruments to help Indigenous peoples more freely determine their civil, political, economic,
social, and cultural development. If Parliament followed this path,
Indigenous law could become the first line of protection for Indigenous
peoples' cultures; it could become the primary mechanism for the promotion of the values surrounding their most important relationships.

ii. The Royal Commission, Section 35(1) Jurisprudence, and
Canadian Government Recognition

When international human rights law is added to Canada's constitutional provisions, a strong argument can be made that the legal basis
for the recognition of Indigenous legal traditions already exists. These
arguments have been in circulation for some time, although they need
further formal action to bring them to even greater light. As already
noted, an important document relating to the recognition of Indigenous law is the *Final Report of the Royal Commission on Aboriginal Peoples*
(the *RCAP Final Report*). This document acknowledges that section
35(1) recognizes and affirms the Aboriginal right to self-government.
This has implications for Indigenous law because governments exercise law-making authority. The *RCAP Final Report* regards the Aboriginal right to self-government as one of the three orders of government
in Canada. In fact, the *Final Report* asserts that Aboriginals already
possess an inherent sphere of jurisdiction under section 35(1) related to
matters internal to their peoples (which could include legal orders).
According to the *Final Report*:

> In 1982, the inherent right of Aboriginal self-government was recognized
> and affirmed in section 35(1) of the *Constitution Act, 1982* as an Aborigi-
> nal and treaty-protected right. As a result, it is now entrenched in the
> Canadian constitution. Aboriginal peoples exercising this right constitute

one of three distinct orders of government in Canada: Aboriginal, federal and provincial. The sphere of inherent Aboriginal jurisdiction under section 35(1) comprises all matters relating to the good government and welfare of Aboriginal peoples and their territories.[39]

Indigenous peoples' desire for good governance would be facilitated if Indigenous law could structure peoples' internal community relations, their relations with the Canadian state, as well as Canada's own internal structures. The Royal Commission's observations are an important source of support for these aspirations. The Commission's recommendations regarding Aboriginal self-government could be built upon by Parliament and other Canadian governments. Aboriginal self-government could be implemented as an inherent right. This recognition would imply that Indigenous legal traditions could be more explicitly proclaimed and practised if the ideas found in this book were more widely accepted.

The Royal Commission was able to find that Indigenous peoples already possessed governance powers in Canada because it found that such powers were never extinguished. An important fact in the finding of non-extinguishment is the earlier and logical conclusion acknowledging that Indigenous peoples exercised governmental and law-making powers prior to assertions of sovereignty by the British Crown.[40] Support for this conclusion can be found in Canada's case law. In *Calder v. A.G.(B.C.)*, Justice Judson wrote, '... the fact is that when the settlers came, the Indians were there, *organized in societies* and occupying the land as their forefathers had done for centuries. This is what Indian title means.'[41] Organization is essential to governance. Indigenous peoples organized themselves through a set of understandings about what was appropriate and/or inappropriate in their day-to-day interactions. These understandings were given force through legal principles and customs that measured appropriate sanctions or commendations. The fact that Indigenous peoples were 'organized in societies' prior to the arrival of Europeans implies that their legal traditions were an important element of their 'pre-contact' societies.[42] It demonstrates that their power of self-organization existed before the Crown's assertion of sovereignty and was in fact strong enough to hold rights to land. These powers of governance and law-making were not voluntarily surrendered when the Crown asserted its own sovereignty in Canada.[43]

As has been explained in numerous ways throughout this book, Indigenous peoples continued to exercise their powers of governance after the Crown asserted its sovereignty in many ways.[44] These powers were evident in matters internal to their societies and in their external relationships with Canada, through treaties, trade, and conflict.[45] Indigenous peoples continue to live in organized societies to the present day. They are governed by ancient and contemporary customs, laws, and traditions that give meaning and purpose to their lives[46] despite the extensive regulation of these powers through instruments such as the *Indian Act*.[47] Fortunately, as the Supreme Court noted in *R. v. Sparrow*, 'that the right is controlled in great detail by the regulations does not mean that the right is thereby extinguished.'[48] The regulation of Indigenous law-making power does not extinguish it.

In *R. v. Van der Peet*, the Supreme Court of Canada held that Aboriginal rights were those practices that were integral to the culture and traditions of Aboriginal peoples prior to the arrival of Europeans.[49] *R. v. Pamajewon* held that governance powers would be tested according to the standard the Court developed in *R. v. Van der Peet*.[50] There are strong arguments that Indigenous law and governance were integral to the organization of the distinctive cultures of Aboriginal peoples throughout Canada prior to the arrival of Europeans.[51] There are strong arguments that this remains so today. An Indigenous society's legal traditions are inseparable from its governance powers. The ability of Indigenous peoples to express their legal traditions through governance does not depend for its existence on any grant of authority from the executive or legislative bodies in Canada.[52] The use of Indigenous law is a pre-existing right, vested in Indigenous groups prior to the arrival of the common law in Canada.[53] The exercise of governance power enables Indigenous peoples to use their legal traditions to pass on important names, divide territories, host feasts, raise memorials, engage in trade, sign treaties, participate in conflict resolution, exercise rights, keep the peace, facilitate development, build alliances, hold property, resist encroachments, and so on. Indigenous legal traditions enabled these peoples to be here 'when the settlers came, ... organized in societies and occupying the land as their forefathers had done for centuries.'[54] Indigenous law allows for the continuation of such organization.

In line with this viewpoint, the *RCAP Final Report* also emphasized that a major source of Indigenous governance was Indigenous law:

The laws of Canada spring from a great variety of sources, both written and unwritten, statutory and customary ... Given the multiple sources of law and rights in Canada, it is no surprise that Canadian courts have recognized the existence of a special body of 'Aboriginal rights.' *These are not based on written instruments such as statutes, but on unwritten sources such as long-standing custom and practice.* In the *Sparrow* case, for example, the Supreme Court of Canada recognized the Aboriginal fishing rights of the Musqueam people on the basis of evidence 'that the Musqueam have lived in the area as an organized society long before the coming of European settlers, and that the taking of salmon was an integral part of their lives and remains so to this day.' The court went on to hold that government regulations governing the Aboriginal fishing right were incapable of delineating the content and scope of the right.

Aboriginal rights include rights to land, rights to hunt and fish, special linguistic, cultural and religious rights, and *rights held under customary systems of Aboriginal law.*[55]

Aboriginal peoples hold rights under their legal systems. A particularly important right for the health and vitality of their legal orders is their inherent governmental power. Canada's multi-juridical status implies the existence of a multi-jurisdictional political order. Section 35(1) can facilitate the connection, growth, and development between Indigenous governance and Indigenous legal traditions. The recognition of Indigenous governance within Canada's Constitution is important because it can help heal the troubled relationship that Indigenous peoples have with the country.[56] Parliament could take significant steps through enacting recognition legislation to acknowledge this fact.

iii. A Caution about Section 35(1): Remembering Federalism

Despite the potential of section 35(1) to build stronger Indigenous legal orders, its provisions must not bear all the weight of reform in constructing recognition legislation. Aboriginal rights as articulated by the courts when interpreting section 35 of the *Constitution Act, 1982* can only go so far in building a harmonious nation state. Broader sociopolitical forces related to Indigenous peoples' place in Canada's federal structures must also be mobilized.[57] Reform should not be exclusively channelled through the language and categories of section 35(1) in implementing Indigenous law.[58] Even within the constitutional sphere, section 35(1) is necessary, but not sufficient, to accomplish legal reform. Other opportunities for reform might be missed, particularly in regard to federalism, if too much reliance is placed on section 35.

Section 35 has not been sufficiently directed towards the larger project of nation-building.[59] To put it bluntly, sections 25 and 35 have become focused on a few specific practices that the courts have decided were integral to Aboriginal peoples prior to the Europeans' arrival in North America, and those related rights that have not already been extinguished. Furthermore, from an Aboriginal perspective, the provisions in section 35 are increasingly used to justify government infringements of Aboriginal rights.[60] Section 35 should not be permitted to sidetrack all Canadians from the more fundamental work to be done to harmonize Indigenous peoples' relationships with their neighbours. Some Canadians are uncomfortable or at least unsure about whether they want to have in their midst Aboriginal nations that possess their own territories, speak their own languages, and administer their own laws. This is also a question of federalism. Canada needs to reinvigorate and reinterpret its federalism provisions in order that Indigenous legal traditions can receive fuller support.

Canada needs to move beyond narrow interpretations of the Constitution relative to Indigenous peoples. Parliament should take a leadership role in this regard. Section 35(1) as currently interpreted by the courts does not replicate jurisdictional powers for Aboriginal peoples as found in sections 91 and 92 of the *Constitution Act, 1867*. Aboriginal peoples do not have an Attorney General to protect their rights. There has been too little constitutional discussion of democracy, self-determination, and the rule of Indigenous law as they relate to Aboriginal peoples in Canada. In the 1998 *Quebec Secession Reference* case, the Supreme Court wrote that the federal system was only partially complete 'according to the precise terms of the *Constitution Act 1867*'[61] because the 'federal government retained sweeping powers that threatened to undermine the autonomy of the provinces.'[62] As a result, the courts have had to 'control the limits' of the federal and provincial governments' 'respective sovereignties' since 'the written provisions of the Constitution do not provide the entire picture'[63] of the Canadian federal structure. In this vein, the courts historically helped to facilitate provincial 'democratic participation by distributing power to the government thought to be most suited to achieving the particular societal objective,' having regard to the diversity of the component parts of Confederation.[64] The Court's historic approach has resulted in the sharing of political power in Canada between two orders of government: the provinces and the central government. Provincial power has been significantly strengthened under this interpretation. The Supreme Court of Canada justified this approach in an earlier era by writing,

> uniformity is not in the spirit of our Constitution. We have not a single community in this country. We have nine commonwealths, several different communities. This fact is embodied in the law. It may be wise or unwise, according to the preferences and predilection of everyone, but this is the basis of our Constitution. Diversity is the basis of our Constitution.[65]

These principles could be applied to Indigenous peoples if Parliament deferred to them in the realm of law and governance by passing recognition legislation. It should be possible to strengthen Aboriginal peoples' jurisdiction if we regard the federal system as only partially complete in relation to Aboriginal peoples.[66] In the context of the Court's interpretation of the applicability of provincial laws to Aboriginal rights, it could similarly be argued that the 'federal government retained sweeping powers' relative to Aboriginal peoples, 'which threatened to undermine the autonomy' of Aboriginal groups. Furthermore, since the 'written provisions of the Constitution do not provide the entire picture' relative to Aboriginal peoples, the courts could also 'control the limits of the respective sovereignties' by distributing appropriate powers to the Aboriginal governments. If provincial powers can be strengthened by drawing on federalism's unwritten principles to fill in the 'gaps in the express terms of the constitutional text,'[67] the same can be done for Indigenous peoples. We should remember the Supreme Court's statement in the *Canadian Western Bank* case, and apply it to Indigenous peoples: 'Canadian federalism is not simply a matter of legalisms. The Constitution, though a legal document, serves as a framework for life and for political action within a federal state, in which the courts have rightly observed the importance of cooperation among government actors to ensure that federalism operates flexibly.'[68] In keeping with this statement, we need to further develop the implications underlying Canada's constitutional framework in relation to Indigenous peoples. It is consistent with the country's constitutional ideals to enhance a flexible political federalism that included recognition and cooperation between Indigenous peoples' legal systems and those of other governments.

Perhaps our federalism would be more fully developed if we followed a process similar to that prescribed by section 37 of the *Constitution Act, 1982*, through which Canada's first ministers and Aboriginal representatives convened to fill in the meaning of section 35, particularly relative to Indigenous law and governance. Although this process failed to produce an outcome when it was applied in the mid- to late 1980s, it at least put the definition of Aboriginal rights at the centre of political debate. Since that time, the courts have been much too prominent in defining Aboriginal rights, although they have ultimately also provided little guidance on this issue as well. It is time that Canada's elected leaders and Indigenous peoples' chosen representatives did the necessary work in meeting to work out the contours of mutual recognition.

iv. Indigenous Law Harmonization Acts

After recognition legislation is enacted, other legislative mechanisms should be created to harmonize Canada's other legal traditions with Indigenous laws. Harmony is a value often associated with Indigenous societies.[69] It can be a positive goal in Indigenous–Crown relations as long as it is not coercively applied. Professor Val Napoleon has written that in some circumstances 'the promise of harmony may serve as another colonial tool to pacify resistance against the state in Indigenous and civil rights movements.'[70] However, harmony can have positive connotations if it encourages the mutual coexistence and blending of distinctive practices. Harmony's positive aspects were invoked by the Royal Commission on Aboriginal Peoples. According to the *RCAP Final Report*, 'Canada is a test case for a grand notion – the notion that dissimilar peoples can share lands, resources, power and dreams while respecting and sustaining their differences. The story of Canada is the story of many such peoples, trying and failing and trying again, to live together in peace and harmony.'[71] This vision of our country as one that promotes the simultaneous coexistence of similarity and difference is very much at the heart of the *Final Report*. At the same time, I share Professor Napoleon's concerns about the misuse of this notion. In this regard, the Royal Commission's caution is apropos: '[T]here cannot be peace or harmony unless there is justice.'[72]

Justice can be facilitated and peace thereby promoted through harmonization legislation. If properly applied, harmonization mechanisms could ease communication between Canada's other legal traditions and reduce conflict or inconsistencies between them. Harmonization mechanisms could address questions about the relationship of Indigenous law to federal statutes and create interpretive principles to ensure Indigenous laws are read in a wide, liberal, and generous manner. Where recognition legislation would acknowledge the existence of Indigenous legal traditions, harmonization legislation would provide ways to ensure this acknowledgment does not inappropriately disrupt settled interests under Canada's other legal traditions. Harmonization legislation would also help ensure that Canada's other legal traditions do not inappropriately unsettle interests developed under Indigenous laws.

It would not be completely novel to enact harmonization legislation in Canada. Such legislation already exists to deal with the interface between the civil law and the common law. The *Federal Law–Civil Law Harmonization Act (FLCLHA)* came into force on 1 June 2001, as chapter 4 of the Statutes of Canada. This act is the first in a series intended to harmonize hundreds of federal statutes and regulations. This exercise was the result of the coming into force of the *Civil Code of Quebec* in 1994, which substantially changed the concepts, institutions, and terminology of civil law. The *FLCLHA* was necessary because, since Confederation, the federal government has passed laws to regulate private law matters such as marriage and divorce, bankruptcy and insolvency, copyright and patents that, but for the division of powers in the *Constitution Act, 1867*, would likely be within the jurisdiction of provincial governments. The *FLCLHA* ensures that existing federal law provisions are brought into line with existing civil law provisions.[73] It also recognizes the common law and civil law as equally authoritative sources of law for property and civil rights. The act also contains provisions allowing statutes to be interpreted in a manner that applies the legal tradition closest to the source of the conflict. In this regard, sections 8.1 and 8.2 of the act state:

> 8.1 Both the common law and the civil law are equally authoritative and recognized sources of the law of property and civil rights in Canada and, unless otherwise provided by law, if in interpreting an enactment it is necessary to refer to a province's rules, principles or concepts forming part of the law of property and civil rights, reference must be made to the rules, principles and concepts in force in the province at the time the enactment is being applied.

8.2 Unless otherwise provided by law, when an enactment contains both civil law and common law terminology, or terminology that has a different meaning in the civil law and the common law, the civil law terminology or meaning is to be adopted in the Province of Quebec and the common law terminology or meaning is to be adopted in the other provinces.[74]

Similar principles and structures could be created for Indigenous legal traditions.[75] Harmonization legislation could ensure that federal law provisions are brought into line with existing Indigenous law provisions acknowledged in the recognition process. It could promote the equivalence of civil law, common law, and Indigenous law as equally authoritative sources of law for property and civil rights in Canada.

Harmonization legislation could be developed jointly with Aboriginal governments and organizations, possibly under the name the *Federal Law–Indigenous Law Harmonization Act*. This legislation could recognize the inherent rights of Indigenous peoples to property and civil rights within their legal traditions. This act could also borrow principles from the preamble of the *Federal Law–Civil Law Harmonization Act* and apply them to the Indigenous context. For example, as in the *Federal Law–Civil Law Harmonization Act*, Indigenous laws could be statutorily recognized as an equally authoritative and necessary part of law in Canada. Harmonization would also help remedy the fact that the Parliament of Canada has not always adequately included Indigenous legal systems and their languages when articulating private law standards. A *Federal Law–Indigenous Law Harmonization Act* could rework and adapt the preamble of the *Federal Law–Civil Law Harmonization Act* and proclaim that:

- All Canadians are entitled to access to federal laws in keeping with their legal tradition;
- Indigenous laws reflect the unique character of Indigenous societies;
- The harmonious interaction of federal and Indigenous legislation is essential; and
- The full development of our major legal traditions gives Canadians a window on the world and facilitates exchanges with the vast majority of other countries.

These principles would send a strong signal about the importance of Indigenous legal traditions throughout the country.[76] If the government can pass legislation harmonizing the civil law with federal law to facilitate these constitutional obligations, the same could also be done for Indigenous laws. Indigenous legal traditions deserve the same respect that is given to civil law. Therefore, to ensure equality in harmonization, the same administrative priority should be given to Indigenous law as to civil law. Thus, an associate or an assistant deputy minister should be given responsibility for the application and development of harmonization of Indigenous law, and be provided with resources comparable to those needed to harmonize the civil law.

A *Federal Law–Indigenous Law Harmonization Act* should also ensure that Indigenous laws and other Canadian legal traditions are consistent with international human rights standards. Harmonization must also protect individuals and groups against adverse discrimination. Therefore, harmonization legislation should contain provisions similar to recognition laws and include:

- a clause that the *Indigenous Law Recognition Act* would not abrogate or derogate from any Aboriginal or treaty right under section 35(1) of the *Constitution Act, 1982*;
- a clause that Indigenous legal traditions must treat men and women equally, and that any Indigenous legal traditions inconsistent with section 35(4) are of no force and effect;
- a clause that Indigenous legal traditions must be consistent with the provisions of the UN *Universal Declaration of Human Rights*, to be binding on any person or group;
- a clause noting that the act would only come into force with the consent of an Aboriginal community and its government.

Guidance for the development of harmonization legislation could also be drawn from studies of Indigenous legal traditions in other countries. For example, Australia's Law Reform Commission proposed recognizing and harmonizing Indigenous legal traditions. It even went so far as to recommend an *Aboriginal Customary Law Recognition Act* in its review of Indigenous legal traditions in that country.[77] Although the act was never implemented, it contained important provisions for protecting human rights, similar to those suggested in this book. Other countries also have laws recognizing and harmonizing Indigenous legal traditions that could provide assistance in drafting legislation. Those who draft these laws might look to those of many Pacific Island states,[78] South Africa,[79] Peru,[80] Bolivia,[81] Colombia,[82] and Ghana[83] for analogies about how Indigenous law might be treated in Canada. An examination of other countries' laws could provide appropriate mechanisms to secure Indigenous legal traditions while simultaneously protecting human rights.

The harmonization process would also have to eventually deal with issues of protocol between Indigenous peoples and the Crown. The act should also address the power imbalance that Indigenous peoples would encounter relative to the common law and civil law in the harmonization process. For example, the statute might contain an interpretative clause that directs decision-makers to give Indigenous law a large, liberal, and generous interpretation, following the canons of construction developed by courts in dealing with treaties and statutes concerning Indians. Furthermore, harmonization legislation should also create a process to address the following issues:

- the role of Elders in harmonization
- concerns about appropriation and culture property
- the impact of colonialism on Indigenous laws
- the problem of gender stereotyping, discrimination, or imbalance in Canadian and Indigenous laws
- the potential harm traditional laws and Canadian laws could cause for the vulnerable within Indigenous communities

As has been reiterated throughout this book, it is important that each of Canada's legal traditions embraces contemporary human rights concerns, including those with a colonial origin that have negatively affected Indigenous peoples. It is also important that human rights concerns do not become an excuse to further colonize Indigenous societies. Human rights can be protected within Indigenous and other Canadian communities without further extending the discriminatory practices and attitudes of earlier imperial policies. This is best done by Indigenous peoples and non-Indigenous Canadians reformulating their traditions in a manner that respectfully integrates traditional and contemporary normative values, and also protects and harmonizes their laws with international human rights standards.

The more comprehensive recognition of Indigenous legal traditions in Canada through recognition and harmonization legislation could give Canadians significant expertise in working with and assisting other countries that have mixed legal systems (civil, common, and Indigenous). This expertise in multi-juridicalism would allow Canadians to play an even greater role on the world stage. Furthermore, this explicit plurality would provide an even greater source of answers to pressing questions faced by Canadians. As Canadians compare and contrast the wisdom of many legal traditions, their legislatures are more likely to reflect the normative values of an increasingly diverse population.

C. The Role of Courts

At the same time as Indigenous and Canadian governments take steps to recognize and harmonize Indigenous law, Indigenous dispute resolution bodies and Canadian courts could also act to facilitate healthier interactions. Because courts often stand on a society's front lines in creating and interpreting law, they are important institutions in the recognition and harmonization of Indigenous law with other legal traditions. Courts are a special kind of public assembly that considers arguments about the resolution of disputes in accordance with a formalized set of procedures. Courts usually have presiding officers who are given a measure of deference during these meetings. Other people also play set roles in court, such as bringing issues forward for resolution, making arguments in relation to these issues, witnessing or recording the proceedings, and maintaining the decorum and order of the process. Courts do not have the authority to resolve every issue that is brought before them. They generally require a grant of jurisdiction from some external source to exercise their powers. For some courts, such jurisdiction comes from the parties to the dispute. For other courts, jurisdiction to settle an issue must come from a constitution, legislative act, political leader, or some other respected person or institution in society. However, there are times when courts might not find their jurisdiction in external sources. In such cases, they may discover that they have inherent jurisdiction which flows from the necessity of maintaining the integrity of their own proceedings.[84]

Each of Canada's legal traditions convenes special assemblies to resolve disputes in different ways. Common law assemblies are generally run on an adversarial model by means of which the parties and their lawyers are expected to present their evidence in a clash of opinions to establish the 'truth' of a matter. Judges in an adversarial system are presumed to be neutral in arbitrating between conflicting positions. As such, they can be at the mercy of parties in the gathering and receipt of evidence which forms the factual matrix of a dispute. In the civil law tradition, by contrast, courts are usually inquisitorial. This means that judges take a more active role in supervising the compilation of evidence and in testing that evidence before the parties to the dispute.

Within Indigenous legal traditions, special assemblies are also available to resolve disputes and they can take various forms. These meetings are neither wholly adversarial nor inquisitorial. There are as many different dispute resolution procedures and styles as there are Indigenous groups. As a result, Indigenous dispute resolution is in some ways distinct from the common law and civil law systems. In fact, the very idea that Indigenous legal traditions might have institutions that have functions similar to courts may come as a surprise to many people. This reaction would be understandable because it is true that Indigenous societies did not have courts that operated like Canada's other legal traditions. However, just because Indigenous peoples did not historically have courts does not mean that formalized dispute resolution was foreign to them. Special meetings were often convened to resolve disputes in accord with formalized procedures. Such gatherings could be presided over by those respected for their heightened powers of judgment. There were parties who brought issues forward for resolution, made arguments in relation to these issues, witnessed or recorded the proceedings, and maintained the decorum and order of the process. Furthermore, in more recent times, some Indigenous peoples have also developed courts that have drawn on adversarial or inquisitorial models of the common law or civil law in resolving disputes.

i. Indigenous Bodies and Dispute Resolution

There is much that can be done by Indigenous peoples to further develop mechanisms for communication between their laws and the laws of others. Indigenous governments could further encourage and empower dispute resolution institutions to takes steps down this path. Indigenous dispute resolution bodies could exercise primary legal jurisdiction over matters that are both internal to their communities and crucial to their relationship with other peoples. They could articulate principles about how these matters relate to the common law and civil law. Indigenous governments and courts could affirm their powers in the manner most consistent with their diverse legal traditions. This is important because Indigenous law must embrace a community's deeper normative values.

Indigenous law must be seen to be a fair and effective force in facilitating peace and order within Indigenous communities, so that it will be easier to convince others to eventually harmonize Indigenous and non-Indigenous laws. If Indigenous laws are not fair, they should be challenged and changed. When Indigenous laws are fair, which is often the case, they must be recognized and connected to our deepest legal structures. In the *Quebec Secession Reference,* the Supreme Court of Canada noted that the legitimacy of legal order within the country rests upon institutions that are accountable to their peoples' values.[85] This is an issue of harmonization. The Court wrote that, 'to be accorded legitimacy, democratic institutions must rest, ultimately, on a legal foundation. That is, they must allow for the participation of and accountability to the people, through public institutions created under the Constitution.'[86] Although not created under the Constitution, but enjoying the protection of it, Indigenous dispute resolution bodies must also meet these standards to be accorded legitimacy that is given to common law and civil law courts. This will help facilitate the harmonization process.

The further development of Indigenous dispute resolution is necessary because Canada's other legal traditions do not sufficiently engage Indigenous values and thus do not appropriately encourage Indigenous participation. This problem would be corrected by Indigenous adjudicative institutions applying Indigenous principles. Current constitutional structures too often frustrate the participation of Indigenous people since those structures falsely rest on public institutions such as the *Indian Act* that are constitutionally questionable. Such a result erodes Indigenous peoples' confidence in the rule of law in Canada.

The Supreme Court of Canada has noted that Canada's constitutional order will not tolerate 'chaos and anarchy.'[87] They have said the law will not accept a legal vacuum,[88] nor would it accept any part of Canada being without a valid and effectual legal system.[89] When Indigenous laws are not recognized and harmonized, Indigenous peoples experience conditions that resemble a legal vacuum. When their own laws are not respected, it creates chaos and makes the legal systems ineffectual for them.[90] As a result, there is a mounting crisis in the rule of law within Indigenous communities. The crisis does not exist because Indigenous peoples lack legal rules; Canadian law rests on shaky foundations within Indigenous communities because it pays so little attention to their values and participation. If Indigenous peoples could start to see themselves and their normative values reflected in how they conduct their day-to-day affairs, some of the legal challenges within Indigenous communities would diminish.

Furthermore, Indigenous governance would enjoy greater accountability and legitimacy if Indigenous peoples' own dispute resolution bodies were properly recognized as being able to resolve their disputes. The power to hold their own members accountable for their actions could be considered an Aboriginal right that was integral to Indigenous communities prior to the arrival of Europeans. The right to hold their own people responsible for their misdeeds has not been extinguished and can be exercised in a contemporary form.[91] Under section 35 of the *Constitution Act, 1982*, Indigenous peoples have the right to sit in judgment of their own citizens. They should be able to make them answerable for violations of rights and liable for failures to exercise appropriate responsibility and accountability. Indigenous dispute resolution bodies are in the best position to articulate legal principles that will have the deepest meaning and legitimacy in their communities.

This approach would be consistent with Indigenous legal values as well as with more general principles of Canadian constitutional law. Ultimately, accountability within Indigenous communities must flow from 'principles of constitutionalism and the rule of law [that] lie at the root of our system of government,' as the Supreme Court advised.[92] Protection and facilitation of the rule of law for Aboriginal peoples, as the *Quebec Secession* case suggests, 'requires the creation and maintenance of an actual order of positive laws which preserves and embodies the more general principle of normative order.'[93] Judging Indigenous peoples by norms that flow from within their legal traditions as well as by norms of Canadian law is essential to the facilitation of normative order. It would create a regime in which legality and legitimacy would coincide and which would bolster the respect and effectiveness of regimes of accountability.[94] The failure to permit Indigenous peoples to be governed and judged by principles that flow from their own normative prescriptions has not provided them with 'a stable, predictable and ordered society in which to conduct their affairs.'[95]

In the United States, tribal courts have played an important role in allowing Indigenous peoples to live by their own laws. They have been essential to explicitly identifying, applying, and creating a record of Indigenous legal decisions. While tribal courts were initially suspect because of their heavy reliance on the Bureau of Indian Affairs for the administration of justice,[96] they have grown in the last twenty-five years to become independent bodies capable of addressing the most challenging issues.[97] Many tribal courts have strong codes of conduct that include rigorous provisions regarding conflict of interest, tenure of officers, training, independence of the judiciary, and ethical behaviour.[98] They enforce tribal constitutions, codes, and customs in line with the histories, aspirations, and cultures of their people.[99] They vary in form and structure in accordance with the diverse theories and sources of law among Indigenous peoples.[100] As such, tribal courts are vital sites for the reproduction and harmonization of law in their spheres of influence.

While this book has focused on Indigenous legal traditions in Canada, the U.S. example is included to demonstrate what can happen when these traditions are given jurisdictional space by a nation state. Tribes in the United States have had greater experience in articulating and sharing their legal traditions with the wider world than is the case in Canada. There are lessons to be learned in understanding the American approach to recognizing Indigenous legal traditions. This is not because these traditions will necessarily be the same as Indigenous traditions in Canada, but because they have shown that it is possible to have a contemporary jurisprudence that draws on ancient values in a powerful Western democracy that is somewhat similar to Canada.

Thus, the development of Indigenous courts in Canada can lead to broader articulation of Indigenous laws, thereby increasing their intelligibility and accessibility. A sample of their legal rules shows the positive interaction between historic values and contemporary needs.[101] For example, the Navajo Nation Bar Association summarized important legal traditions in contracts, government, procedure, family law, property, and children's issues. Their principles show that Navajo law is not anachronistic but a living legal force. The Navajo Bar Association summarized some these principles as follows:

CONTRACTS

Oral agreement – A valid oral agreement, commitment, and/or contract is sacred and once made, is binding. *Tome v. Navajo Nation*, No. WR-CV-153-83, slip op. at 21 (W.R. Dist. Ct. 1984).

Execution – A person must follow through with an agreement made with another person. *Ben v. Burbank*, No. SC-CV-23-95 (Nav. Sup. Ct. 1996).

GOVERNMENT

Democracy & Power Abuse – A *naat'aanii* is chosen based upon his ability to help the people survive and whatever authority he has is based upon that ability and the trust placed in him by the people. If he lost the trust of his people, the people simply ceased to follow him or even listen to his words. *In re Certified Questions II (Navajo Nation v. Macdonald)*, A-CR-13-89, slip op. at 24–5 (Nav. Sup. Ct. 1989). See also *Downey v. Bigman*, No. SC-CV-07-95, slip op. at 3–4 (Nav. Sup. Ct. 1995).

Coercion – Navajo common law rejects coercion. *Navajo Nation v. Macdonald*, A-CR-10-90, slip op. at 27–8 (Nav. Sup. Ct. 1992). See also *Downey v. Bigman*, No. SC-CV-07-95, slip op. at 3–4 (Nav. Sup. Ct. 1995).

PROCEDURE/DUE PROCESS

Peacemaking – Controversies and arguments should be resolved by 'talking things out.' *Navajo Nation v. Crockett*, No. SC-CV-14-94, slip op. at 10 (Nav. Sup. Ct. 1996). See also *Rough Rock Community School v. Navajo Nation*, No. CC-CV-06-91, slip op. at 12 (Nav. Sup. Ct. 1995).

K'eh – includes equality and respect and leads to consensual solution. *Downey v. Bigman* … *Rough Rock Community School v. Navajo Nation*, No. SC-CV-06-94 (Nav. Sup. Ct. 1998). *K'eh* contemplates one's unique, reciprocal relationships to the community and the universe. It promotes respect, solidarity, compassion, and cooperation so that people may live in *hozho*, or harmony. *K'eh* stresses duties and obligations of individual relatives to their community. *Atcitty v. Dist. Ct. for the Judicial Dist. of Window Rock*, No. SC-CV-25-96, slip op. at 7–8 (Nav. Sup. Ct. 1996). See also *Ben v. Burbank*, No. SC-CV-23-95, slip op. at 5–6 (Nav. Sup. Ct. 1996).

Naalyeeh – owed to family, clan or person. *In re Claim of Joe*, No. A-CV-39-92, slip op. at 7–8 (Nav. Sup. Ct. 1993). One who inflicts harm must pay the victim to restore harmony. *Farley v. Kerr McGee*, No. SR-CV-103-95, slip op. at 7 (S.R. Dist. Ct. 1996). See also *Nez v. Peabody Western Coal Co., Inc.*, No. SC-CV-28-97, slip op. at 10 (Nav. Sup. Ct. 1999). It should be enough 'so there are no hard feelings' … If a person is hurt, he or she looks to clan relations for help. The tortfeasor and his or her relatives are expected to set things right in accordance with the hurt … *Nalyeeh* depends on restitution, reparation, restoring harmony or replacing the loss or paying back. The manner and amount of payback are not so crucial. *Benalli v. First Nat'l Ins. Co. of America*, No. SC-CV-45-96, slip op.

at 16–17 (Nav. Sup. Ct. 1998). See also *Navajo Nation v. Blake*, No. SC-CR-04-95, slip op. at 4–5 (Nav. Sup. Ct. 1996).

Punishment as last resort – Punishments were actions of last resort. *Navajo Nation v. Platero*, No. A-CR-04-91, slip op. at 7 (Nav. Sup. Ct. 1991).

DOMESTIC
Traditional Wedding – basket ceremony requirements. 9 N.N.C. 3(D) (1993).

Rejection of common law marriage – Unmarried couples who live together act immorally because they are said to 'steal each other.' *In re Validation of Marriage of Francisco*, No. A-CV-15-88, slip op. at 4 (Nav. Sup. Ct. 1989).

Traditional Wedding & Divorce – Husband moves in with wife at time of marriage. At divorce, husband returns to mother's unit. (Various methods to divide property discussed.) *Apache v. Republic National Life Insurance*, 3 Nav. 4. 250 (1982). See also *Naize v. Naize*, No. SC-CV-16-96, slip op. at 7–8 (Nav. Sup. Ct. 1997).

Traditional divorce – *Yoodeeyah* doctrine. *Begay v. Chief*, KY-FC-348-00 (2002); Traditional divorce outlawed. *In the Matter of Documenting the Marriage: Ellen M. Slim and Tom Slim*, 3 Nav. R. 218 (1982).

Navajo plural marriages – outlawed with exceptions. 9 N.N.C. 2 (1993). See also *Austin v. Smith*, KY-FC-178-02 (Kay. Dist. Ct. 2002).

Custody – Children are of the mother's clan or extended family. *Goldtooth v. Goldtooth*, 3 Nav. R. 223 (W.R. Dist. Ct. 1982).

In-laws – *Hadaane* has certain duties. *Means v. Dist. Court of the Chinle Judicial Dist.*, SC-CV-61-98, slip op. at 17–18 (Nav. Sup. Ct. 1999).

Respectful speech – People speak with caution and respect because speech is sacred. *Hosteen v. Tapaha*, No. SR-CV-77-92, slip op. at 9 (S.R. Dist. Ct. 1997).

PROPERTY / PROBATE
Communal ownership – Families hold land (grazing rights) in communal ownership. *Begay v. Keedah*, No. A-CV-09-91, slip op. at 9 (Nav. Sup. Ct. 1991). See also *In re estate of Benally*, 5 Nav. R. 174 (Nav. Sup. Ct. 1987). Private ownership is unknown to *Navajos*. *Hood v. Bordy*, No. A-CV-07-90, slip op. at 11–12 (Nav. Sup. Ct. 1991).

Property ownership – Property belongs to wife and her children. *In re Trust of Benally*, 1 Nav. R. 12 (1969). See also *Lenta v. Notah*, 3 Nav. R. 72 (1982).

Property distribution – 'Productive property' (sheep, land, land permits) is held for benefit of the individual and the camp, and upon death, such property is held for the benefit of those living in the camp. 'Non-productive property' (jewelry, tools, equipment, non-subsistence livestock) is held to belong to the individual. *In re estate of Boyd Apachee*, 4 Nav. R. 178 (1983).

Oral wills – must be in presence of family. *In re estate of Lee, in the matter of estate of Chisney Benally*, 1 Nav. R. 219 (1978).

Discussing Death – Death is not a proper and lively item to discuss. *In re Estate of Tsosie*, 4 Nav. R. 198, 200 (W.R. Dist. Ct. 1983).

CHILDREN'S CASES
Parent's obligation – A child's interests are paramount. A parent must provide for the child's needs until the child can support him/herself. *Burbank v. Clarke*, No. SC-CV-36-97, slip op. at 4 (Nav. Sup. Ct. 1999).

Father's obligation – A father of a child owes that child support. *Touchin v. Touchin*, No. CP-CV-237-87, slip op. at 5 (C.P. Dist. Ct. 1988). A man who fails to pay support is said to have 'stolen the child.' *Tom v. Tom*, 4 Nav. R. 12 (Nav. Ct. App. 1983).

Emancipation – A child is emancipated when self-supporting, independent, and free of parent control. *T'aabiak'inaaldzil* doctrine. *Burbank v. Clarke*, No. SC-CV-36-97, slip op. at 4 (Nav. Sup. Ct. 1999).

Adoption – Family members, aunts, grandparents obligated. *In re interest of JJS*, 4 Nav. R. 192 (W.R. Dist. Ct. 1993).[102]

Once again, I must stress that these examples are not given to propose an exact replication of American tribal courts in a Canadian context. Furthermore, Indigenous communities should not feel compelled to reorganize themselves along Western political lines in resolving their disputes (though important lessons can be drawn from that experience).[103] Nevertheless, this example shows that the recognition of Indigenous institutions of dispute resolution can even have a place in broader Canadian legal development and reform. Indigenous peoples can develop their own legal traditions and also participate in Canada's other institutions. Indigenous peoples are not prevented from serving as legislators, parliamentarians, government ministers, or judges just because aspects of their legal participation are particular to their

Indigenous citizenship. Participation in larger political communities does not have to suffer because Indigenous peoples belong to groups of which other Canadians are not a part. (But, as mentioned earlier, Indigenous peoples might productively consider developing citizenship laws to admit others fully into their communities.) People from Quebec are not prevented from participating in Canada because their dispute resolution procedures are based on the *Civil Code*. Navajo people in the United States can run for high political office in that country even though the tribe has its own justice system. Participating as an Indigenous person in Indigenous traditions (with a political identity, legal entitlements, and normative responsibilities) should not preclude other formal identities, entitlements, and responsibilities. Specifically, Indigenous peoples should not have to relinquish their participation in wider national and international communities just because they have separate dispute resolution systems.

Similarly, the existence of Indigenous dispute resolution bodies should not preclude the acceptance and application of Indigenous legal principles in broader matters. Indigenous law can influence the development of the common law and civil law and be an important source of guidance for other peoples. As I have written in another context:

> First Nations legal traditions are strong and dynamic and can be interpreted flexibly to deal with the real issues in contemporary Canadian law concerning Aboriginal communities. Tradition dies without such transmission and reception. Laying claim to a tradition requires work and imagination, and a certain degree of change, as particular individuals interpret it, integrate it into their own experiences, and make it their own. In fact, tradition is altered by the very fact of trying to understand it. It is time that this effort to learn and communicate tradition be facilitated, both within First Nations and between First Nations and Canadian courts. There is persuasive precedent in Canadian law recognizing the pre-existent aspect of Aboriginal rights and their associated laws. Furthermore, the courts have created an opportunity to receive these laws into Canadian law by analogy and through *sui generis* principles. Since First Nations possess the powerful ability to articulate their laws, it is time that these principles began to influence the development of law in Canada. When First Nations laws are received more fully in Canadian law, both systems of laws will be strengthened concurrently.[104]

ii. Canadian Courts

Canadian courts could also play an important role in recognizing and harmonizing Indigenous legal traditions. Of course, there is much work they could do on a doctrinal basis to further develop jurisprudence within section 35(1), and other sections of the Constitution, to describe the relationship between Canada's legal traditions. They would also have a significant task in interpreting recognition and harmonization legislation if such instruments were passed by Parliament and Indigenous communities. Furthermore, Canadian courts would engage in the essential work of declaring the common law's own position in relation to Indigenous legal traditions, as drawn from their inherent jurisdiction.

In particular, more Indigenous judges should be appointed to the bench in all common law and civil law jurisdictions in Canada. This would help to ensure that Indigenous traditions would develop by being understood and appropriately applied on a case-by-case basis. The appointment of Indigenous judges could spread to all levels of the court system, including the Supreme Court of Canada. It has been said that

> just as the recognition of the civil law of Québec makes it necessary that there be representation of Québec judges specifically on the Supreme Court, so too the recognition of Aboriginal laws and customs as living law in Canada makes Aboriginal representation necessary if the legitimate claim of the Supreme Court to be the final arbiter in cases concerning Aboriginal peoples is to be maintained.[105]

There has been support for this idea in Canada before. *RCAP Final Report* recommended that 'the Supreme Court of Canada should include at least one Aboriginal member.' Resolutions of support for this appointment have also been made by the Canadian Bar Association, the Indigenous Bar Association (IBA), the Canadian Association of Law Teachers, and the National Secretariat Against Hate and Racism in Canada. In their position paper produced for the IBA, Albert Peeling and Professor James Hopkins argued that 'the appointment of Aboriginal persons to the Supreme Court is philosophically consistent with Canadian Legal Pluralism.'[106] Appointing people with knowledge of Indigenous legal traditions to the courts in Canada is an issue of merit. A person with such knowledge would be more qualified to sit in judgment over cases involving Indigenous legal issues than a person not possessing this information.

The *Supreme Court Act* governs the Supreme Court appointment process. Section 5 of the Act states:

> Any person may be appointed a judge who is or has been a judge of a superior court of a province or a barrister or advocate of at least ten years standing at the bar of a province.[107]

Section 6 states that at least three of the Supreme Court justices must come from Quebec. Convention requires that an additional three be selected from Ontario, two from Western provinces, and one from Atlantic Canada. Indigenous legal traditions in Canada require that these conventions be revised to appoint a jurist knowledgeable in Indigenous bodies of law.[108] Such an appointment would also be consistent with section 35(1) of the *Constitution Act, 1982* and would recognize the unique constitutional status of Aboriginal peoples in Canada. The appointment of an Indigenous judge with Indigenous legal training would also facilitate the reconciliation framework that section 35(1) is designed to achieve. Appointing members of the Supreme Court with Indigenous law experience would increase its competence in strictly legal terms and develop its specific capacity to deal with Aboriginal issues.

It is also critical that Indigenous judges work at other levels within the judicial system. Canada has excellent examples of Indigenous judges working with Indigenous legal traditions. As noted in chapter 3, the creation of the Cree Court in Saskatchewan, presided over by the Honourable Judge Gerald Morin of the Provincial Court of Saskatchewan, was an important first step in reflecting Indigenous law in that province. The court's work in the Cree language compels the parties to frame their rights and obligations differently. Distinctive insights are generated when a problem is presented in a different language. Since the judge, legal aid lawyer, prosecutor, clerk, probation officer, and Aboriginal court worker all speak Cree in this court, they can be more creative than non-Cree speakers within a provincial-court framework. The small but important step in appointing an Indigenous judge to decide cases allows courts to dispense justice in a manner that is not always possible for those trained solely in the common law.

Alberta also showcases interesting innovations that result from the appointment of an Indigenous judge with a knowledge of Indigenous communities and their laws. Before he was appointed to the Federal Court of Canada, the Honourable Judge L.S. ('Tony') Mandamin, formerly of the Alberta Provincial Court, presided over the Tsuu T'ina First Nations Peacemaker Court on the Tsuu T'ina Nation on the outskirts of south-west Calgary. The court was inaugurated in October 2000; it is integrated with the Alberta Provincial Court and also with the Tsuu T'ina community and its traditions of justice. Judge Mandamin is a highly qualified Anishinabek member of the bar and is fully vested with the necessary authority for his role on the bench. He also possesses legal knowledge that enables him to bridge the cultural divide between Euro-Canadian and First Nations legal traditions. In addition, two Peacemakers who are Elders also sit as community witnesses to the proceedings and can provide Indigenous legal knowledge to the court. The Peacemaker coordinator calls on Peacemakers from the community who are trusted and respected. The peacemaking function could become more prominent within Canadian courts if Indigenous judges were appointed in greater numbers. They would use their knowledge of Indigenous legal traditions to chip away at problems within the communities in which they serve.

The most important reason for appointing people to the bench who have knowledge of Indigenous legal traditions is that they bring new ideas to their task in the context of a settled continuity of Canada's other legal traditions. A change of ideas when exercising judgment will bring broader reform than almost any other initiative. It is simply not enough to have Indigenous issues, individuals, and institutions become an integral part of the law. Until Indigenous *ideas* (ideologies) are part of the intellectual exchange, Canadians are just rearranging deck chairs on the *Titanic* as they deal with the ongoing problems of Indigenous peoples and the law. Nothing in the law changes if 'reform' simply means adding a few more issues, individuals, and institutional variations to the mix. Profound legal change requires that questions be examined from perspectives that at least partially emerge from sources outside Western legal discourses and that are motivated by considerations from Indigenous normative orders. Standards for judgment must not only flow from the common law but also from Indigenous legal values. Precedent should not be confined to dusty old law books; it should also be open to the authority of Indigenous teachings and lawways.

The criteria for measuring what is considered just, fair, and equitable should not solely be drawn from non-Indigenous sources. Indigenous codes of conduct need to be part of the law's formal and informal expressions. Indigenous traditions should guide how Indigenous people and other Canadians answer the problems they collectively encounter. Indigenous laws are necessary to meet challenges that lie in Canada's future. These traditions should be simultaneously compared, contrasted, combined with and distinguished from critical and constructive norms in the civil law and common law traditions. Judges with Indigenous legal training could perform this role. Progress in Indigenous law will be limited until the ideas by which people order and govern themselves include norms developed from these perspectives. This is why the appointment of Indigenous people to the courts is critically important. Their ideas could facilitate a unique exchange with Canada's other legal traditions. The exploration of new ideas may lead to answers not immediately apparent under conventional legal reasoning.

8 Indigenous Legal Institution Development

I have been building the case that the recognition and expansion of Indigenous legal traditions within Canada should not require submission to the current configuration of power that presently exists within the country.[1] Indigenous peoples should not be forced to accept and integrate into institutions that are designed to conform to the current structures of the colonial state.[2] Indigenous peoples must transform their relationships with Canada by practising their traditions throughout their territories, beyond the reserve and other colonial boundaries. Ancient teachings can be regenerated in a contemporary context if they are actively applied to all sites of struggle encountered by Indigenous peoples within their lives. In this vein it is important to re-emphasize that culture should not be essentialized. Fundamentalist interpretations of law should be rejected, within the common law, civil law, and Indigenous legal orders. Tradition must not be frozen in a past tense or within a reserve-only framework. In a legal context this means that an Indigenous logic must infuse the personal and political choices made by Indigenous peoples in all their relations. This includes those relationships within the Canadian state that have an adverse effect on Indigenous legal traditions.

In its *Final Report*, the Royal Commission on Aboriginal Peoples recommended that Indigenous peoples should reconfigure their affairs within all levels of the Canadian state. This includes challenging public institutions that contribute to Indigenous peoples' domination by not recognizing their identity, culture, and need for thoroughgoing participation throughout public life. In this vein the Royal Commission wrote:

Aboriginal peoples generally do not see themselves, their cultures, or their values reflected in Canada's public institutions. They are now considering the nature and scope of their own public institutions to provide the security for their individual and collective identities that Canada has failed to furnish.

This Commission concludes that a fundamental prerequisite of government policy making in relation to Aboriginal peoples is the participation of Aboriginal peoples themselves. Without their participation there can be no legitimacy and no justice. Strong arguments are made, and will continue to be made, by Aboriginal peoples to challenge the legitimacy of Canada's exercise of power over them. Aboriginal people are rapidly gaining greater political consciousness and asserting their rights not only to better living conditions but to greater autonomy.[3]

As the Royal Commission suggests, the Canadian state must be more fully built upon Indigenous foundations. Both Canada and Indigenous peoples become stronger and better able to develop healthy public institutions whenever this occurs. As has been argued throughout this book, the country changes for the better when Indigenous values, perspectives, and legal traditions become a more prominent part of our constitutional fabric.

This chapter takes this central insight one step further. It suggests that Indigenous participation has to expand not only in relationship to the larger structures of the Canadian state, but it must also be facilitated in more localized legal affairs. In particular, law societies and law schools should reflect Indigenous participation because they are important sites in conserving and developing Canada's legal traditions. Such institutions have important responsibilities in promoting high standards of legal education and conduct and these duties should extend to Indigenous legal traditions. In keeping with the Royal Commission's insight above, participation in these institutions could allow Indigenous peoples to see their laws more widely reflected in public life.

Broader recognition of Indigenous law would also facilitate greater autonomy within Indigenous communities. If law societies and law schools were more attentive to Indigenous law, Indigenous peoples would have greater incentives to develop and expand their own traditions. This could add further weight to the push felt by Indigenous communities from their own members to more boldly articulate their laws. The creation of a healthy institutional space into which Indigenous law could flow might lead to more focused efforts within Indigenous communities to explicitly reference their own laws when making decisions. As their laws are regarded with greater respect beyond reserve borders, this could give Indigenous peoples greater confidence in their interactions with other Canadians. Trust could grow if they knew that assimilation did not characterize their work with Canadian institutions. Such confidence is crucial because Indigenous peoples will not give up their deepest beliefs in order to work with others. As has been noted previously, Indigenous peoples do not want to be assimilated. Assimilation has been a dismal failure in Canada. It has contributed to the gross violation of Indigenous peoples' human rights. The recognition and development of Indigenous legal traditions across the Canadian landscape, within localized institutions, could provide an important bulwark against assimilation. To accomplish this goal, Indigenous peoples could use their own legal norms and work with law societies and law schools as a way to guide their interactions beyond their reserves and settlements so they can reoccupy their traditional territories and bring them into harmony with other people living in Canada.

A. Law Societies and Associations

Though law societies receive legislative authority to act in the public interest, they are independent from governments to ensure freedom from political interference.[4] An independent bar and legal professoriate work in tandem with an independent judiciary to implement the rule of law in Canada. As such, law societies could support the further extension of Indigenous law if they worked at this issue within their assigned spheres. If they pursued this objective through their own self-governing institutions they could greatly assist society in maintaining and advancing the cause of justice in the broadest public interest. With such power these institutions could implement fair and efficient procedures for acknowledging Indigenous legal practitioners' jurisdictional space for training, licencing, capacity, conduct, professional competence, complaints, and continuing education. In exercising these duties, they should not take such responsibilities away from Indigenous legal bodies. Instead they should search for ways to recognize and affirm Indigenous legal traditions in a manner that expands but does not compromise their central missions.

The exercise of these duties in relation to Indigenous legal traditions will require reform within these bodies. While law societies have expertise supporting the common law and the civil law traditions in regard to training, licensing, capacity, conduct, professional competence, complaints, and continuing education,[5] most do not have this experience in dealing with Indigenous legal traditions. As such, they will have to make some significant changes to ensure they appropriately deal with the unique circumstances presented by Indigenous law. Fortunately, many people recognize that the 'independence of the Bar is a dynamic rather than static concept.'[6] In this spirit, law societies could innovate ways that would more clearly acknowledge Indigenous legal traditions and help to implement them within Canada's legal system. As an independent and self-governing institution, they would not have to wait for governmental permission. They could act to advance Indigenous law without threatening their central missions: to promote education, the rule of law, and access to justice.[7] In this light, law societies could undertake activities to ensure that Indigenous legal practitioners have independence from outside regulation, independence from client control, independence from political control, and independence to pursue public purposes.[8] It should be expected that the search for practical mechanisms to implement multi-juridicalism will vary in accordance with the personality of each law society. Each one will devise its own methods to ensure that Indigenous legal traditions enhance its own legislatively mandated mission, while ensuring that Indigenous law is not adversely affected.

Building expertise in working with Indigenous legal traditions within law societies would have to be done with significant Indigenous participation. In fact, there would really be no other way to proceed in accomplishing this task. Canadian institutions have much to learn before they can adequately perform their role in enhancing Indigenous legal traditions. Without compromising their own independence, or that of Indigenous peoples, law societies will have to take direction from Indigenous communities because, at present, they do not have the necessary expertise with these issues. For example, law societies could create a special body of Indigenous benchers to sit in convocation and make decisions relating to Indigenous legal traditions. The election of Indigenous legal practitioners as benchers and the creation of special Indigenous-focused bodies within the law societies is one way to allow Indigenous peoples to more significantly participate in nation-wide procedures that enhance the rule of law and maintain the independence of the law societies. Such intersystemic legal engagement would allow Indigenous peoples to more fully contribute to Canada's broader legal education and practice.

Despite the attractiveness of provincial law societies acknowledging Indigenous legal traditions, there may be significant opposition to this concept. Many will worry that law societies will not be sufficiently independent from legislatures to create a legal profession that is truly at arm's-length from colonial governments. There will also be concerns that the common law or civil law bias of law societies will be hard to challenge and change because senior members of the profession may be distrustful towards or unfamiliar with Indigenous legal traditions. Some may even regard the recognition of Indigenous law as a challenge to their monopoly over legal services in the provinces. If this were the case, lawyers would have significant financial incentives to exclude Indigenous legal traditions as a recognized source of law in the country. If this were the case, such people might try to block Indigenous legal traditions to serve their own narrow interest despite the law societies' delegation of self-governing authority to serve the broader public interest.

As a result of these challenges, Indigenous peoples might not see immediate movement within the broader legal fraternity. Fortunately, this would not prevent Indigenous peoples from creating their own law societies. Such organizations could be developed by Indigenous peoples using their own political authority, without federal or provincial legislation. Alternatively such bodies could be recognized by federal or provincial authorities outside of provincial law society structures if existing bodies refused to act in accordance with their mandates. Furthermore, even if immediate acknowledgment is not forthcoming from other institutions, the creation of Indigenous law societies could incubate important bodies for future law society recognition.

It should be emphasized that Indigenous law societies are best organized in accordance with the legal structures and protocols that characterize their various systems. If an Indigenous system is clan or family based, institutions should recognize this fact. If communities want to cultivate structures that resemble administrative tribunals or courts, they might develop law societies that perform roles that ensure the practitioner's independence and professional responsibility.

I came to appreciate the importance of Indigenous law societies when I was teaching at law schools in the United States. Second- and third-year law students and practising attorneys would enrol in my federal Indian law class and tribal court courses because Native American Bar societies could require such courses for their practitioners. Even if such courses were not required by Indigenous law societies, students knew the information would be relevant to their search for eventual admission into a tribal bar. For example, the Bar of the Navajo Nation[9] tests its candidates on torts, contracts, domestic relations (9 NNC); criminal law, federal Indian law, the *Indian Child Welfare Act*, the *Navajo Nation Children's Code* (9 NNC § 1001, et seq.); District Court rules of civil and criminal procedure; business associations, including corporations and partnerships; model rules of professional conduct; Navajo Nation jurisdiction; the *Navajo Uniform Commercial Code* (5A NNC); Navajo Nation government (2 NNC); Navajo rules of evidence; the *Indian Civil Rights Act*; Navajo property law–personal/real property; Navajo employment and business preference laws; Navajo Nation Bill of Rights; Decedents' estates (8 NNC) and rules of probate procedure; the Treaty of 1868; administrative law; Navajo rules of civil and criminal appellate procedure; the *Navajo Sovereign Immunity Act* (1 NNC § 551 et seq.); and Navajo peacemaking. The Navajo Nation Bar examination includes a written test emphasizing the Navajo common law, the *Navajo Nation Code*, and Navajo Nation Supreme Court decisions, including the skills required to practise in the courts of the Navajo Nation. One can see how the creation of an effective Indigenous law society could enhance knowledge of the contemporary nature of Indigenous legal traditions for those who seek to practise in this context.

Indigenous law societies would also have an important role to play in outlining and regulating the behaviour expected of those who work with their legal traditions. The highest standards of ethical and professional responsibility should be articulated and upheld in any law society's creation and administration. In an Indigenous context, these principles should be developed in accordance with the traditions, values, philosophies, and beliefs of each community that adopts them. There are many examples of different approaches to tribal bar formation in the United States. One example can be found in the statement of purpose of the Navajo Nation Bar Association, which states its mission in the following terms:

- To promote and encourage the highest quality and professionalism in the practice of law in the Navajo Nation and in the judicial system thereof;

- To recommend to the Navajo Nation Supreme Court candidates for admission to practice of law before the Navajo Courts, so as to insure the competence of such practitioners and their scrupulous adherence to the ethical standards of the Navajo Courts and the Navajo Nation Bar Association, Inc.;
- To encourage and assist in the establishment of comprehensive training programs for persons desiring to practise in the Navajo Courts and to insure the maintenance of high standards for such training;
- To advise on and assist in the recruitment and selection of the most able practitioners to serve as judges in the Navajo Courts;
- To advise the Courts on rule changes and other measures which would improve the administration of justice in the Navajo Court system; and
- To recommend to the Navajo Courts legislation which would enhance and improve the Navajo Court system and the ability of the Navajo Nation effectively and fairly to govern those within its jurisdiction.[10]

Of course, other Indigenous law societies will express their purposes in other forms. If a First Nation does not have a tribal court, its focus will obviously be on other dispute-resolution practitioners and procedures that are particular to the community in question. The point to take from this example is that the creation of a body to augment the professionalism, ethics, and education of its practitioners can help in the administration of justice in an Indigenous context.

Despite the evident advantages in creating an Indigenous law society, its development may not be a priority within some communities because of the pressure to devote scarce resources to other more pressing matters. If your community is poor and has few human resources, it might not make sense to devote time and finances to legal structures when life-and-death issues occupy the bulk of a community administrator's time. Even though good governance might help funnel resources into a community, it can be difficult to create such structures if it is always in a reactive, crisis-management mode. Therefore, if Indigenous political bodies, the federal Parliament, provincial legislatures, or law societies do not or cannot develop Indigenous law societies (or mechanisms to work with them in the short term), there might be a role for Indigenous lawyers' organizations to take the first steps in promoting this form of governance.

For example, the Indigenous Bar Association (IBA) in Canada, with the participation and consent of Indigenous peoples who might want to opt into IBA management, could take on a role in the accreditation or coordination of lawyers or other practitioners who may be called on to participate in Indigenous legal systems. They could develop this function by accepting delegates from a First Nation community, a Métis settlement, or an Inuit community delegating authority to them. In this manner the IBA could be an educational and disciplinary body whose members bring to the organization expertise from most Indigenous groups in Canada. I have been associated with the IBA since it was founded over twenty years ago. Its members are often leaders at the bar within the provinces in which they practise, and many have strong Indigenous community connections with their own nations or those who they represent in various matters. The IBA has also devoted its resources to the development of Indigenous legal traditions over the years, which have frequently been the topic of discussion at conferences and seminars the IBA has hosted. The senior Indigenous Peoples' Counsel (IPC) group within the organization has encouraged its members to learn and respect Indigenous law as a vital part of their legal practice.

If the IBA were to create governance mechanisms that allowed communities to opt into a system for the recognition and governance of legal practitioners in an Indigenous context, it would be a step that is consistent with the aims of the organization. The IBA's stated objectives are:

1 To recognize and respect the spiritual basis of our Indigenous laws, customs and traditions.
2 To promote the advancement of legal and social justice for Indigenous peoples in Canada.
3 To promote the reform of policies and laws affecting Indigenous peoples in Canada.
4 To foster public awareness within the legal community, the Indigenous community and the general public in respect of legal and social issues of concern to Indigenous peoples in Canada.
5 In pursuance of the foregoing objects, to provide a forum and network amongst Indigenous lawyers: to provide for their continuing education in respect of developments in Indigenous law; to exchange information and experiences with respect to the application of Indigenous law; and to discuss Indigenous legal issues.

6 To do all such other things as are incidental or conducive to the attainment of the above objects.[11]

One can see that it would be consistent with the IBA's guiding philosophy if it developed mechanisms to assist Indigenous communities in building recognition for their legal traditions.

Aside from the IBA, other Canadian legal institutions could play a role in the recognition of Indigenous law as part of their central mission. For example, the Canadian Bar Association (CBA) has often played a supportive role in improving the rule of law and promoting access to justice for Indigenous peoples in the country. There are Aboriginal law sections of the CBA in most provinces whose role it is to educate their members about Indigenous legal issues. While these efforts are often focused on statutory, common law, and constitutional law developments related to Indigenous peoples, the CBA could expand its programs to more fully address Indigenous legal traditions. For example, it could develop and run continuing legal education programs on aspects of practice and policy pertaining to Indigenous legal traditions. The CBA could produce written materials for its membership explaining the implications of the recognition of Indigenous traditions in the practice of law. Codes of professional conduct could be drafted to ensure that any special issues of ethical practice in dealing with Indigenous issues are considered. The CBA's Standing Committee on Equity could consider Indigenous legal traditions as part of its mandate as expressed in *Touchstones for Change: Equality, Diversity and Accountability*, a document approved by the CBA Council in 1994 and 1995.[12] The committee promotes awareness in the legal profession of equity issues in relation to Indigenous legal traditions; it provides the means to eliminate discrimination about these traditions; it develops resources to assist the legal profession to achieve equity through the recognition of Indigenous legal traditions; and it monitors, on a national basis, the status of equity in Indigenous issues within the legal profession. Through these and other measures, the CBA could be an important institution in further developing understanding related to Indigenous legal traditions in Canada.

From the foregoing discussion one can see that law societies and associations could be helpful architects in the further design of multi-juridicalism throughout the land. Their independence and expertise could be a significant resource in constructing the law based on the highest and best principles of our public order. Since their structures do not generally require them to seek government authorization in order to act, law societies and organizations could take immediate steps to consider their role in the extension of Indigenous law. In fact, since these institutions are independent of government they could help to ensure that politics do not impede the healthy development of the concepts discussed in this book. It is vital to the rule of law in Canada that such organizations actively work to promote our legal traditions. If Indigenous peoples' own law societies also joined this coalition, they could build an important bulwark against the further erosion of Indigenous legal traditions.

B. Indigenous Legal Education

There are other institutions in Canadian society that are largely independent of government in their day-to-day operations. Universities are an important site for the exploration, critique, and construction of ideas in an intellectual space somewhat removed from the rough-and-tumble world of official political influence. The tradition of academic freedom permits professors and students to explore concepts and structures within society that may be unpopular or contrary to the aspirations of others around them.[13] Within this environment people can pursue inquiries that may not be welcome in other circles. For these reasons universities could have an important role to play in the further exploration of multi-juridicalism. The future development of scholarship and programs related to Indigenous law within a university law school setting is the focus of this section.

In particular, universities could work with Indigenous peoples to create law schools to teach multi-juridicalism. The richness of such a curriculum would enhance students' abilities to participate as citizens of a legally pluralistic and diverse world. They would learn how to compare and contrast sources of authority within legal systems that are committed to unity through understanding, critiquing, and applying deep jurisprudential diversity. A multi-juridical approach to education would highlight the choices available to students in further constructing our communities. Individuals and societies would benefit from people who know what is required to navigate many different traditions. In this way Indigenous law schools would effectively prepare students for future research or practise in Canada's legal traditions.

Obviously, multi-juridical Indigenous law schools would also teach Indigenous legal traditions alongside the common law or civil law.

Professors and students would learn from Elders, practitioners, and communities about the contours of ancient legal ideas in a contemporary setting. They would study Indigenous law in great depth and from a perspective that gives these traditions the respect they deserve. Of course, the respectful examination of any legal order includes thoroughgoing critique alongside appreciation and constructive application. This process helps to avoid dogmatism; it challenges those who hold a narrowly defined set of beliefs that are closed to the influence of other traditions. The desire of educators, practitioners, and students to improve Indigenous and other legal traditions would lead to recommendations for both reform and retrenchment. However, intense and rigorous intellectual debate over the strengths and weaknesses of a particular law does not have to be socially disagreeable.[14] As is the case within existing law schools, Indigenous law schools would work closely with their constituencies to ensure that law is taught in a way that is attentive to practical procedural and substantive concerns. At the same time, such a program of study would have to ensure that ideas and practices were always open to question and challenge. Independent individual thought and collective inquiry, along with respectful engagement, must lie at the heart of such an endeavour. The comparative nature of inquiry in an Indigenous law school should always be highlighted to encourage difficult and demanding questions of each tradition. Exposure to Indigenous law alongside other traditions would lead students to develop a broader, more refined understanding of the rule of law in Canada. If this process were followed, students would see more completely the choices available to them in the world of legal theory and practice.

While the creation of Indigenous law schools would facilitate learning without having to overcome potentially entrenched common law or civil law biases, it may be difficult to generate the resources to establish them. Therefore, in the short term, existing law schools may be in the best position to develop multi-juridical education programs. Many Canadian law schools already possess some experience working with Indigenous issues. It would be possible for some of these schools to build upon their successes to create new courses and programs. Existing schools could more readily introduce Indigenous law into legal education because they already possess resources to offer legal education programs. It also helps that current law schools enjoy broader credibility with the bench, the bar, and the community than do new law schools. The academic rigour and scholastic reputation of an existing law school could enhance the legitimacy of studying Indigenous law and ensure that such traditions are more widely understood. A newer Indigenous law school might initially have difficulty establishing its reputation with various constituencies and this could lead to a devaluation of its programs. While it is my hope that strong Indigenous law schools will one day come into existence, steps must be taken to prevent the 'ghettoization' of Indigenous legal education in Canada. The timing of an Indigenous law school's formation, and the resources devoted to it, must be carefully calibrated to ensure success.

In the meantime, it is possible to explore in greater detail the potential contours of Indigenous legal education in a contemporary law school setting. As noted, there is a good base to build upon. This is because in the last twenty years some law schools have developed a growing relationship and expertise in working with Indigenous communities.[15] Other law schools have developed admissions criteria and programs that help Indigenous students succeed at law schools.[16] Furthermore, most Canadian law schools already teach courses that examine how Canadian law affects Indigenous peoples. A few even specialize in training graduate students to further inquire into this field and have hired Indigenous law professors.[17] These programs and courses have played an important role in increasing student interest and scholarship about Indigenous issues more generally.[18] They have also encouraged a number of Indigenous academics to gain knowledge of their own legal traditions and pursue post-graduate legal training in a common law or civil law field. Furthermore, non-Indigenous academics with similar qualifications are also increasingly beginning to possess these skills. These experiences and skills have created a fertile ground for the future cultivation of Indigenous legal education.[19]

Thus, building on existing practices, the day may soon arrive when a Canadian law school will develop a degree program focused specifically on Indigenous legal traditions in a contemporary setting. For instance, the example of McGill Law School could be emulated in an Indigenous context. McGill University has a civil/common law program that integrates learning about the common law and civil law throughout its curriculum.[20] The dean of McGill Law School, Nicholas Kasirer, has written:

> A legal education at McGill is one that is marked by the mutually sustaining relationship between the common law and civil law as the Western world's two great legal traditions. It recognizes that the law flows from a broad range of sources and is predicated on the study of law

as an intellectual inquiry that ... is trans-systemic. While others watch the globalization of law and wonder about its impact on legal education, law teachers at McGill take it as a reason to be confident in their choice to teach law comparatively.[21]

The same reasons could be applied with even greater force if a law school made the decision to teach Indigenous legal traditions along-side the common law or civil law. Such a program would break new ground in the world of legal education and could be an important ingredient in helping Canadians to transform their view of the rule of law throughout the land.

One could take insight from McGill's experience and conceive of different models of legal education incorporating Indigenous law.[22] Though far from ideal, the following suggestion regarding multi-juridical legal education may prompt further teaching, scholarship, and planning towards an Indigenous law degree.[23] It may be possible to develop a joint Bachelor of Indigenous Law (BIL)/Bachelor of Law (LLB) degree program. If the program were to develop in Quebec it could deliver a joint BIL/Bachelor of Civil Law (BCL). The program should be designed to qualify students for the Bar Admission Course in all provinces. Combining Indigenous laws and the common law or civil law could increase students' understandings of the distinctive approaches available to regulation and dispute resolution within a Canadian context. Concepts from the common and/or civil law and Indigenous legal systems could be creatively conveyed through an integrated pedagogy designed to nurture critical analysis and practice. The comparative nature of such a program could sharpen analytical reasoning and enhance practical skills in research, writing, and practice. If such a path was followed students would obtain both an LLB and BIL degree after completing the appropriate number of academic units. This would move students beyond 'Western' legal traditions as described in the McGill Law School program guide and in this respect would offer an important challenge to fundamentalist ideas that would freeze our legal traditions.

The design of the program should be focused enough to ensure that resources are appropriately distributed within a law school. Given the current shortage of law teachers with knowledge of Indigenous legal traditions, there is a need to share qualified faculty among law schools. The University of Victoria law school followed this pattern when it conducted the Akitsiraq law school in Iqaluit, Nunavut. Students received a superior education as they learned from many of the leading judges, lawyers, and scholars in their fields, from across

Canada, who came and lived in Nunavut and taught there while the program was in progress. The Akitsiraq experience suggests that an efficient use of faculty resources would probably require running the program with only one group of students working their way through four years of law school at one time. If this model were followed, twenty-four students could move through the program as a single cohort over a four-year period. They could be taught by professors from the host law school, by Elders and traditional lawkeepers, and by visiting academics from other law schools.

As was the case with the Akitsiraq program, the cooperation and support of the Canadian Council of Law Deans and individual law schools would be vital to the program's success. They could ensure faculty and other academic resources were shared to meet the program's needs, and they would be valuable allies in helping other institutions understand the nature of educational multi-juridicalism. Furthermore, it may be the case that a joint LLB/BIL program would move between a couple of schools if there were a demand in different parts of the country. Again, this pattern has been discussed in relation to Inuit legal education: UVic offered the first Inuit law program, and Dean Bruce Feldthusen of the University of Ottawa Law School has been discussing hosting the next cohort of students with the university. Over the coming years, as expertise in Indigenous law grows in different parts of the country, there will be less of a drain on Indigenous and other faculty members. Furthermore, the first programs could service students who may have an interest in becoming law teachers. These graduates would then be in the best position to replicate and improve upon the education they received as they embark upon their legal teaching careers. Thus, the first cohort to be admitted to the program must be students who would like to become good teachers as well as excellent legal practitioners. In this regard, the program should be open to both Indigenous and non-Indigenous students who have these aptitudes and interests. This will help ensure that the knowledge is accessible to all students who are willing to work at understanding the contours of multi-juridicalism in Canada.

In putting into practice the ideas underlying this book, the curriculum of an LLB/BIL program would have to ensure that students learned in the classroom and through practical experience within Indigenous communities. With regard to classroom components, the course offerings and workload in the program's first year would be similar to those found in any Canadian law school, with one important difference. Each required first-year course would convey information in the context of an Indigenous legal tradition. Each course would alternately compare, contrast, critique, and construct an understanding of the materials from the perspectives of both common and Indigenous law (if offered in a common law school). For example, constitutional law could include Anishinabek law, criminal law could include Salish legal traditions, Inuit laws of obligation could be dealt with in tort law, Métis law could deal with contract law, and so on.

Throughout the first year, students would therefore be exposed to many of the same cases and statutory materials as other first-year students in a conventional curriculum.[24] At the same time, students enrolled in the program would receive the additional benefit of learning about Indigenous laws and legal traditions throughout their studies. In a typical first-year curriculum, courses could include (note: I have included a detailed description for each course in the endnotes for readers who want a better understanding of the content):

1 Constitutional Law Traditions (Anishinabek legal context)[25]
2 Criminal Law and Justice Traditions (Salish legal context)[26]
3 Comparative Indigenous Legal Traditions (multi-juridical Indigenous context)[27]
4 The Legal Process[28]
5 Voluntary Obligations/Contracts (Métis legal context)[29]
6 Involuntary and Hybrid Obligations/Torts (Inuit legal context)[30]
7 Property Law Traditions (Gitksan legal context)[31]

The first-year curriculum could also appropriately acknowledge and teach the legal traditions of communities that are close to where the law school is located. For example, if a Bachelor of Indigenous Law was offered at UVic or UBC, Salish law would be taught in recognition of the fact that these universities are located on Salish traditional territory. Aspects of Salish law would be taught through activities such as a traditional welcome to the territory, a Salish cultural awareness camp, and a legal process exercise in the second term of the first year involving Salish legal traditions. If the course were offered in Ontario, a similar structure could be used to address Anishinabek, Haudenosaunee, or Cree legal traditions. If the University of Saskatchewan or Manitoba Law School offered the program, it could include Anishinabek, Dene, Dakota, or Cree law. At Dalhousie, Mi'kmaq and Maliseet law could be taught. The programs could be adapted for each school depending on the desires of the Indigenous nations with which the schools have a relationship.

In the second year of the program, students could be required to take three courses directly related to the Indigenous legal traditions of the Indigenous territory on which the school is located. For example, Salish legal traditions could be taught at UVic or UBC if a joint degree were offered at either of these schools.[32] Salish Elders and lawkeepers from around the Strait of Georgia could teach courses in conjunction with teachers from Canadian law faculties. In this case, courses could include:

1 Salish Legal Traditions[33]
2 Salish Language and Law[34]
3 Salish Legal Writing and Advanced Legal Research[35]

Note how some initial exposure to an Indigenous language would be important in understanding Indigenous legal traditions. If students ever wanted to move beyond a bachelor's level in their work with an Indigenous legal tradition, they would have to go deeper into an Indigenous language at some point.[36] Furthermore, second-year students would also be required to enrol in three courses from the conventional LLB curriculum. This would recognize the importance of these areas for subsequent practice, especially in the Bar Admission Course upon graduation. The three courses are open to a faculty's own understanding of core student competencies, but could be designated as follows:

1 The Administrative Law Process[37]
2 Business Associations[38]
3 Family Law[39]

As with first-year courses, these courses would cover conventional LLB subject matter, but they would be enhanced to include common law and Indigenous legal perspectives.

In the third year of the program, students could be required to take three courses towards their Indigenous law degree. Once again, using UVic or UBC as an example, two of these courses could recognize two other major Indigenous legal traditions that are in close proximity to the school. The remaining special course would recognize and develop the importance of oral traditions within Indigenous law. The courses could be:

1 Nu-chah-nulth Legal Traditions[40]

2 Kwakwaka'wakw Legal Traditions[41]
3 Indigenous Moot: Indigenous Oral Advocacy Dispute Resolution[42]

Elders and lawkeepers could teach the courses from the Nu-chah-nulth and Kwakwaka'wakw traditions in conjunction with the host law faculty members. Third-year students would also be required to take three courses from the LLB curriculum in recognition of the importance of these areas for subsequent practice, should a student decide to enrol in a Bar Admission Course upon graduation. Once again, the precise courses to be offered could vary in accord with student's future needs and the strengths of the school, but could include:

1 Civil Procedure[43]
2 Evidence[44]
3 Secured Transactions[45]

These courses could also integrate conventional common law and Indigenous legal perspectives in some form. As is evident in this proposal, there are a few more required courses proposed in this model than in existing law degrees. This is done to ensure that the profession regards multi-juridical law students as competently prepared to take provincial bar admission courses.

Aside from these required courses, students would take the remainder of their courses from their law school's conventional LLB curriculum throughout their upper years. But they would have the option, if they so desired, of taking courses relevant to Indigenous law already within the LLB curriculum. These courses could include (if taught at UVic):

1 Indigenous Lands, Rights, and Governance[46]
2 Historical Foundations of Aboriginal Title and Government[47]
3 Comparative Indigenous Rights: The U.S. Experience[48]
4 Aboriginal Politics and Self-Government[49]
5 First Nations and Economic Development[50]
6 Self-Determination of Peoples[51]
7 Colonial Legal History[52]
8 Indigenous Women and the Law[53]

The fourth year of the program could be offered in at least two ways. One possibility is for students to spend their last year of study learning Indigenous legal traditions within Indigenous communities. They

could learn in context from Elders, leaders, and Indigenous law practitioners, with the assistance and guidance of professors from their
host law faculty who would be present during the immersion. Students could rotate in succession through three learning terms of four
months each over a twelve-month period. Each of the three terms
would be devoted to a single Indigenous legal tradition in order that it
could be explored in greater depth. Another possibility is to extend the
entire law school experience to allow for more course work within
Indigenous communities. If this option was chosen, the intensive
immersion in Indigenous legal traditions could occur in the three
summers between each of the four years. This would provide a full
year of legal instruction and immersion within a single Indigenous
legal tradition while still allowing for four years of classroom work.
This model would permit greater flexibility in the first year curriculum; it would allow a conventional first-year course (or two) to be
pushed into the second year to accommodate the trans-systemic
immersion into different legal traditions.

Immersion is important: a program would fail to adequately teach
Indigenous law if it did not provide learning opportunities outside of
law schools. While there is great value in formal classroom instruction,
Indigenous law must also be learned in an applied and practical
context. Indigenous laws are often the product of specific relationships
to land, plants, animals, water, people, and so on. To fully appreciate
Indigenous law, students need to live with the people whose law they
want to more fully understand. This is in accordance with the insights
found in chapters 2 and 3, which discussed the sources and context of
Indigenous legal tradition. This immersion must also be intensive, and
it must be focused on one tradition at a time in order to expose students
to each tradition's depth and complexity. Students' education in Indigenous law will be incomplete if they do not delve deeper into legal traditions of their choice for either three summer terms or one final year.

The intensive immersion experiences could have themes for each
term. Term one could focus on working with community Elders and
lawkeepers.[54] Term two could focus on learning Indigenous legal traditions within a political/community context.[55] Term three could place
students in an Indigenous court or a dispute resolution body, or with a
lawyer working with Indigenous law.[56] For evaluation purposes during
these immersion terms, students could be expected to write a reflective
daily journal and pass an oral exam. At the end of each placement, the
student would return to the school for a week to present his or her
knowledge before core faculty and other students in the program. As a

requirement of the Indigenous law degree, students would also produce a major paper in each term of the twelve-month period related to the Indigenous legal tradition in which they were immersed.

This pattern of learning builds on and extends the successful co-op program at UVic, where students are paid while they work in an applied context. Elders who practise Indigenous legal knowledge would be unable to pay students to work with them during these immersion experiences. It would therefore be appropriate for law schools to set aside funds for Elders salaries, and so on, which is the current practice for co-op placements at UVic where employers do not have the resources to fund the law students they receive. Furthermore, Indigenous laws may require an exchange of material goods before a student is permitted to take part in an apprenticeship opportunity. Students would have to be instructed on the precise requirements and protocols of a community to ensure Elders are properly approached and included in the program. Since Elders would be university instructors for the purpose of this program, they should be extended the resources and respect appropriate to their role.

The proposed program of study for a combined BIL and LLB could certainly be modified to meet the academic requirements of particular law schools, as well as the needs and protocols of the Indigenous communities with which they work. This course of study could also be offered with selected components if a law school or community were unable to support the program in full. It is possible to teach Indigenous law without being as ambitious as the program just outlined. For example, one first-year course could be taught in any law school: comparing, contrasting, critiquing and constructing Indigenous and other Canadian legal traditions. Alternatively, the intensive immersion component could be built into a law school's curriculum, similar to Osgoode Hall's intensive program in First Nations lands and resources. Other schools might want to introduce students to nearby Indigenous traditions through Indigenous legal language classes, cultural awareness camps, or Indigenous legal process exercises. Whatever methods are chosen, the point is that it is currently possible to teach Indigenous legal traditions with law school accreditation. All that is needed are willing Indigenous communities, academics, and academic institutions.[57]

C. Conclusion

There are many ways to constructively critique and respectfully change the current configuration of Canadian Confederation, in accordance with the rule of law. Indigenous peoples can work on their own, and with others, to transform their relationships by practising their laws and traditions throughout their territories. This chapter has discussed steps that lawyers, practitioners, and law professors might take to regenerate legal cultures in a contemporary context (Indigenous, common law, and civil law). It has shown how oppressively fundamentalist interpretations of law can be resisted to move us beyond essentialized ideas about tradition. The recovery and regeneration of any tradition involves working in a collective context, as well as being attentive to the larger philosophies and ideas of groups and individuals.[58] To be meaningful in peoples' day-to-day lives, tradition must be lived within the complex circumstances people encounter and challenge.

There are many institutions in society that could play a role in recognizing, critiquing, and facilitating Indigenous legal traditions. As this chapter has discussed, law societies and law schools are one particularly important site for development because of their centrality to the replication of the common law and civil law in Canada. Their independence from day-to-day government control is also significant because it could allow them to work with Indigenous communities and legal traditions without waiting for legislative approval. If there are people within these institutions who have the interest and skills to teach and practise Indigenous law in a multi-juridical context, they should be able to find space to apply their knowledge in these settings.

Canada's rule of law is enhanced when our legal traditions are brought into authoritative conversation with one another for the purposes of applying them to resolve pressing disputes that face us as a country. In fact, those who work with Indigenous legal traditions may find themselves claiming that such knowledge makes them better common law or civil law lawyers in certain contexts. They may say they are more attentive to the assumptions and contrasts available within the law when they are practising in their field. This awareness could highlight where choices between alternatives are culturally constructed, and therefore not as universal or neutral as other theorists and practitioners may be led to believe. As multi-juridical practitioners bring their insights to bear on our problems they, at times, may be in a better position to articulate a solution that has persuasive resonance in common law, civil law, and Indigenous legal traditions. The value of challenging, understanding, and working within a multi-juridical methodology is the next chapter's focus.

9 Living Law on a Living Earth: Religion, Law, and the Constitution

A. Introduction

This chapter attempts to apply the insights found throughout this book by demonstrating what legal analysis might look like if multi-juridicalism was a more prominent part of Canada's Constitution. As such, the arguments in this chapter test the recognition and harmonization of Canada's legal traditions in the context of whether Anishinabek beliefs concerning the Earth as a living being can be legally recognized and affirmed. An associated inquiry is what this question's answer reveals about the law's source, cultural commitments, institutional receptiveness, and interpretive competency. These questions explore matters that lay at the heart of Anishinabek spiritual life and at the centre of Canadian legal thought. Thus, this chapter further reveals where bridges and gaps, convergences, and inconsistencies exist within Canada's constitutional order.

The juxtaposition of Anishinabek legal traditions and current formulations of Canadian constitutional law reveals the country's profound legal pluralism at the same time that it highlights the law's failure to foster broader coexistence and application. To achieve a better balance, the current chapter furthers the argument that Anishinabek and Indigenous legal traditions should stand beside the civil law and common law in order to organize and structure society's relationships. Each tradition can provide guidance about how we should theorize, practise, and order our association with the Earth. It is therefore appropriate to address the Earth's legal personality from both Indigenous and Canadian constitutional law perspectives because both operate within the territories we call home.

As noted in chapter 4, the civil law and common law have force because Canadian legal authorities have chosen to bestow this authority upon them. These legal traditions are shaped by and subject to Canada's Constitution. Anishinabek law also has force when it accords with the earth's biological rhythms and where individuals and communities recognize and abide by its order. This legal tradition is shaped by Anishinabek teachings regarding the Creator, observations from nature, positivistic proclamations, deliberative practices and local customs.[1] The law's varied sources illustrate that not all legal power in Canada flows from legislation, regulation, and cases. Law can exist 'on the ground'; it does not always need cabinet approval, judicial endorsement, or lawyers' expertise to be relevant and functional.

In examining the law's composite character, Anishinabek spiritual beliefs about the Earth will be introduced briefly to provide context before turning to questions of Anishinabek law. After exploring how Anishinabek law deals with Anishinabek religion, Canadian constitutional law's current treatment of this issue will be examined, under section 2(a) of the *Charter of Rights and Freedoms* in Part I of the *Constitution Act, 1982* and in section 35(1) in Part II of the *Constitution Act, 1982*.

Interestingly, this chapter also serves as an illustration of how legal traditions could be taught in a trans-systemic perspective. The information below illustrates the types of inquiries that could be included in a constitutional law course teaching Indigenous legal traditions, alongside Canada's other laws. As such, this chapter reads a little like a lesson plan for highlighting the implications that legal pluralism might hold for Canadian constitutional law. In this respect, it builds upon the recommendations concerning Indigenous legal education in the last chapter. At the same time, this chapter highlights the significant challenge further development of multi-juridicalism presents to Canada's constitutional order. As such, it represents a self-reflexive critique of the ideas offered herein. While the following exploration makes for a messier thesis, I believe it is crucial to communicate that law is always fraught with conflicting and convergent ideas. This book is not a blueprint for Utopia; I do not believe the inclusion of Indigenous legal traditions in Canada's legal system will lead to a future free from strife, misery, and distress. Conflict will always be with us. Therefore, in order to emphasize that multi-juridicalism will not put an end to discord but only redirect it in new and more productive ways, it is important to further problematize the interaction of Canada's legal tra-

ditions. While legal pluralism is a better way to frame our legal relationships, because Indigenous peoples at least get to participate in constructing our collective world, conflict is at least diminished under this
approach by channelling it in ways that contests domination and facilitates agency. The test of this book's thesis should not hinge on
whether I have crafted a perfect solution to the problem addressed
herein. Perfection in practice or theory is not my aim. I believe a more
productive test of these ideas is whether they positively enhance or
negatively reduce our responsibilities and freedoms in the real world.[2]
Thus, this chapter seeks to illustrate how Canada's constitution could
be improved if we more explicitly adopted a trans-systemic approach
to legal interpretation. When analysing my conclusions, I hope others
will undertake their own analysis of Indigenous legal traditions in
comparison and contrast with other constitutional law principles. This
could lead to the development of a richer understanding of the choices
that are available to us within the law that will enable us to enhance
justice and the rule of law within our country.

B. Sacred Relationships:
The Earth and Anishinabek Spiritual Beliefs

As noted in chapter 3, the Anishinabek Nation surrounds the North
American Great Lakes and has occupied this territory for thousands of
years.[3] The Anishinabek are an Algonquian- and (more recently)
English-speaking people who historically organized themselves into a
loose confederacy of clans throughout the region.[4] Collectively, they
refer to themselves as 'Anishinabek,' meaning the 'good people.' In
more recent years, they have also been known as the Odawa,[5]
Potawatomi,[6] Ojibway, Chippewa,[7] Mississauga, or Saulteaux.[8] They
have a strong and long-standing attachment to the Great Lakes region
partially because their traditions indicate that this is where they originated as a people.[9] This is one of the Indigenous legal cultures, of
which I am a member.[10]

The Anishinabek regard Michee-Makinakong on the narrows
between Lake Huron and Michigan near Lake Superior as the world's
centre,[11] the place where the land above the water was formed.[12]
Michee-Makinakong was where Michabous recreated the upper Earth
by breathing life into soil that was brought up from the ocean's depths
by a muskrat.[13] The Earth grew as the soil was scattered around Michabous' raft and tread upon by this Great Being.[14] The Earth's ability to

respond to Michabous' actions provided enough space for plants and animals to find a home.[15] When these first animals died, the first Anishinabe arose from their corpses.[16] The Anishinabek take their identity and *dodem* or clan names from these ancestors.[17] Professor Heidi Bohaker has observed that '[t]his sacred story is part of what Anishinaabe peoples call *aadizookaanag*, or the grandfathers. Stories of this genre are set in time immemorial; they explain how the world came to have its present form and furnish embedded observations on how the beings who currently inhabit it should relate to one another.'[18]

For the Anishinabek, creation of the Earth did not end with Michabous' experience on the raft. The Earth grows and develops or dies and decays because it is a living being subject to many of the same forces as all other living creatures. Many Anishinabek people characterize the Earth as a living entity who has thoughts and feelings, can exercise agency by making choices, and is related to humans at the deepest generative level of existence.[19] As noted, I will address the legal and political implications associated with holding this world view.

The subject of the Earth's personality is a profound religious, political, and legal issue. Since the Anishinabek consider the Earth a sentient being that helps to generate life, religion is implicated in their beliefs concerning her existence.[20] While the Earth is considered sacred, Anishinabek people do not worship the Earth as one would a Creator, but she is regarded with great awe, respect, and wonder because of her ability to live a good life and reproduce in numerous forms. Anishinabek people believe in a Creator, Kitchee Manitou, who gave form and meaning to the Earth following a vision.[21] The first elements of Anishinabek creation stories explain how life came into being from a constellation of forces marshalled by the Creator. Later stories convey important spiritual insights by providing instruction about how the Earth must be honoured and respected. Within these teachings is the general recognition that the Earth has a soul (*chejauk*) that animates its many moods and activities. Many believe that the Creator, as the Great Master of Life, created a universal bond between all living things that placed the Earth at the centre of a vast web of kinship relations.[22] Great power can be attached to these relationships because of the spiritual energy that flows between, from, and through them.[23]

One does not need to belong to a formal religious community within Anishinabek society to regard the Earth as a living being. As I will discuss below, the very structure of the Anishinabek language depicts the Earth in this manner. Aside from the linguistic pervasiveness of Anishinabek thought regarding the Earth, there are strong and formalized Anishinabek structures to give this belief even greater coherence.[24] For example, the Medewiwin Society is regarded by some as the traditional Anishinabek religion. It teaches its members how to appropriately relate to the Earth and other living beings.[25] A large number of Anishinabek people who are nominal or dedicated Christians also hold a belief in a living Earth, either because it is taught within their congregations or because it is accepted as a syncretic practice within their belief structures and communities.[26] Furthermore, a number of Anishinabek people are neither Medewiwin nor Christian but hold a strong conviction of the Earth's agency and personality. In this mix, it must also be acknowledged that some Anishinabek people regard the Earth as inanimate, without a soul or spiritual life force. As with most societies, Anishinabek people have multiple viewpoints on religion and spirituality. Yet despite diverse perspectives, the land's sentience is a fundamental principle of Anishinabek law, one upon which many Anishinabek people attempt to build their societies and relationships. Of course, they have not always been successful in this regard; like most peoples, they often fall short of their highest ideals. Nevertheless, it is a present-day principle of central significance that has tremendous implications for how we live with one another on the Earth's surface.

Political issues are also implicated in the Earth's legal personality for many Anishinabek because they regard themselves as striving to live in community with the Earth. The political relationship between humans and rocks creates mutual obligations and entitlements that must be respected for this community to reproduce in a healthy manner.[27] This governmental structure requires humans both to consult with the Earth's Creator and to seek the Earth's receptiveness before important decisions are made.[28] The Anishinabek will listen to the Creator and/or the Earth through ceremonies, or they will elect to understand the Earth's requirements by observing her interactions with wind, water, fire, and other beings to which she relates.[29] Scientific understandings of how the Earth operates are also acknowledged and integrated into Anishinabek practices to form an important benchmark for respectful behaviour as communities develop greater knowledge about her through time.[30]

Like other political groupings, obligations between Anishinabek and the Earth have territorial aspects.[31] At one level, the political boundaries of Anishinabek relationships to the Earth coincide with the totality of the planet's surface. An Anishinabemowin word that describes this relationship is *aen-danee-yauk-kummikuak,* which means 'the nature of the land's character from which all derive sustenance.'[32] At this broadest level, we are all citizens with and of one land because we depend on its total existence to survive.

At the same time, this wider political ordering does not preclude Anishinabek or the land from being citizens of smaller polities: watersheds, islands, valleys, countries, tribes, cities, reserves, and so on. Anishinabek political community contemplates allegiances across global and smaller geographical units. The Anishinabemowin word for boundary is *ani-ishkawaek-kummikauk,* meaning 'the place along the way of the land's end according to her character.'[33] Within Anishinabek thought is the encouragement to determine the Earth's character to make decisions about how to best divide ourselves in ways that are most respectful of her. The ability to relate to the Earth on different scales feeds a multiplicity of citizenship rights and responsibilities for Anishinabek people and the Earth. A person could be simultaneously a clan (*dodem*) member, Anishinabek, Canadian, American, and world citizen. Likewise, the Earth can concurrently be a planet, geological plate, continent, or small rock.

C. Anishinabek Law and the Earth

Anishinabek legal traditions have ancient roots, but they are not stunted by time. They continue to grow and develop through observation, experience, and interaction with other people's more recent presence within their territories. Like other Indigenous legal systems, Anishinabek law is a living social order, developed through comparing, contrasting, accepting, and rejecting legal standards from many sources. Anishinabek legal traditions do not lose their Indigenous status if they adopt viewpoints that address matters not encountered before European contact. Law is not solely a matter of history because it is reinterpreted and reapplied in every generation to remain relevant amid changing circumstances. Furthermore, within Anishinabek jurisprudential thought there are usually various interpretations about the way law should be created, studied, and applied. Various perspectives within this law illustrate the tradition's vibrancy and vitality, just as is the case within the common law and civil law traditions. This diversity is healthy as long as mechanisms are present to authoritatively resolve disagreements at specific moments of height-ened conflict.[34]

Rocks are animate or living in verb-oriented Algonkian languages, of which Anishinabemowin is one. The very way in which Anishin-abek people conceive of the land as alive is hardwired through language. You cannot even describe the world without acknowledging this fact. The active nature of rocks means that they have an agency of their own that must be respected when Anishinabek people use them. As such, it would be inappropriate to use rocks without their acquies-cence and participation because such action could oppress their liberty in some circumstances.[35] Using rocks without their consent could be considered akin to using another person against his or her will. The enslavement of rocks could lead to great calamities for the Earth and her people. Therefore, to ensure that rocks and land are used appro-priately, particular ceremonies or legal permissions are required.

Under Anishinabek legal traditions, some rocks (or places on Earth) cannot be owned or allocated if such ownership or allocation implies control of the Earth without her involvement. However, a kind of own-ership can occur if undertaken in accordance with appropriate Anishinabek principles. The pipe ceremony is a particularly important certification-like process preceding the appropriate use or ownership of land. When one participates in a circle and handles the pipe under the guidance of proper leaders, the Earth's legal personality is acknowledged. While the smoke is said to ascend to the Creator and demonstrate thankfulness for existence, prayers of thanksgiving are expressed for the rocks, plants, animals, and other humans as the smoke rises from the pipe. The pipe itself represents Earth's different orders: '[T]he earth, whose elemental substance was rock, made up the pipe; the plant, tobacco, was the sacrificial victim; the animal, symbol-ized by feathers and fur, was appended to the sacred pipe of rock; man was the celebrant.'[36]

Use of the pipe is a token of peace between people and the land and between peoples settling on the land. The Earth is best used by cele-brating her contributions and consulting with her Creator in this way. This is why, when treaties were signed, Anishinabek people often included non-Indigenous people in this relationship, and treaty parties would use the pipe to register their mutual agreement concerning the use of the Earth. Anishinabek Elder Basil Johnston has observed that rocks are the elemental substance of life and must be continually acknowledged for their role in sustaining other orders of life.[37] While plants, animals, and humans all come to an end, the Earth lives on. It is contrary to certain interpretations of Anishinabek law to claim absolute ownership of the Earth, which is called a mother because of her role in bringing forth life.[38] In this vein, Dr Johnston has written,

> No man can own his mother. This principle extends even into the future. The unborn are entitled to the largesse of the earth, no less than the living. During his life a man is but a trustee of his portion of the land and must pass on to his children what he inherited from his mother. At death, the dying leave behind the mantle that they occupied, taking nothing with them but a memory and a place for others still to come.[39]

For many Anishinabek, 'ownership' is not regarded in the same light as in other Canadian legal traditions. Nevertheless, the analogy of a trustee when explaining limitations concerning Anishinabek land use is somewhat helpful in understanding Anishinabek law. A trust in equity, as merged through the common law, is a right held by one person (the trustee) for the benefit of another person (the beneficiary). Under Anishinabek law, land is held by the present generation for future generations. Land does not ultimately belong to a person or people in the sense that they have absolute discretion and control; land is provisionally held for (con)temporary sustenance and for those unborn.

However, analogies to trust law can also create confusion in understanding Anishinabek legal traditions if carried too far. Under Anishinabek law, while the Earth is somewhat dependent on other orders of life for its health and vitality,[40] plants, animals, and humans are much more reliant on the Earth for their survival.[41] In this sense, the Earth can be considered the trustee for its beneficiaries (plants, animals, and humans). This analogy may be a stretch for the common law legal imagination because, under the common law, the Earth is neither a living being nor does she possess a legal personality. Nevertheless, Anishinabek legal traditions recognize interdependence between rocks and humans because of their mutual agency. The concept of reciprocal obligations between rocks and humans is an important part of Anishinabek law. People are the beneficiaries of the Earth's care, and under Anishinabek law this creates duties for the beneficiaries as well as for the Earth (as the so-called trustee).

A contemporary applied example of these principles is provided by the Anishinabek people of the Bruce Peninsula, who live between the waters of Lake Huron and Georgian Bay. Ten years ago, the people of Neyashiingmiing, the Chippewas of the Nawash on the Cape Croker Indian Reserve (my home), had to make a decision about moving the site of an annual summer festival on their reserve. Each August a pow-wow is held in their park, drawing thousands of people in a celebration of Anishinabek resilience and culture. A move was contemplated to accommodate the increasing numbers of park users during this annual event. One suggestion was to move the pow-wow to 'the prairie,' a broad, flat, and largely treeless stretch of land lying below Jones Bluff just beyond the shores of Sydney Bay. The prairie had the advantage of being able to accommodate large crowds and offered easy access from the main road. The area affords beautiful views of the surrounding escarpments, lake, and ever-changing skies. The area is also easy to see from the park and other vantage points around the community. The idea to move the pow-wow to the prairie seemed to make sense by most principles of efficiency. To any casual observer, the land looked empty in terms of human use and did not seem to be productively used by most economic measures.

However, when it became apparent that a road would be built to facilitate access to the prairie, a significant community movement developed that drew on Anishinabek legal principles. The land is host to a significant alvar, a rock-barren or natural pavement-like feature with little or no brush or tree cover. The alvar is a limestone plain composed of dolostone bedrock with a surface that is almost completely exposed to the air. The alvar is among the oldest exposed stone in Ontario, having an age in excess of 440 million years. For many Anishinabek, the alvar is a storyteller who recounts the time when the land was younger and was covered by shallow tropical seas. It is related to the surrounding limestone escarpments and fossil-strewn beaches formed when the area once likely resembled the Great Barrier Reef of Australia's north-eastern coast. Furthermore, in those areas where a very thin layer of organic matter covers the alvar, it accommodates a unique community of resilient mosses, lichens, and plants that are well adapted to extreme conditions of intense cold, heat, drought, and flooding.

The alvar is also home to spiritually significant 'spirit trails' that wend their way through the area. Family stories among the Anishinabek speak of the place as having significant sacred power, with accounts of bear walkers, deceased relatives, and supernatural transformers traversing over the area. Armed with this knowledge, there was consultation, debate, discussion, direct experience on the land, prayer, and persuasion when making a decision about the use of the alvar. Scientists and Anishinabek lawyers, band councillors, grand-mothers, Elders, artists, medicine people, community employees, and others participated in a process that drew strongly on Anishinabek law respecting Anishinabek spiritual beliefs. Ceremonies were conducted and traditional teachings reviewed. This legal process, which is some-what akin to the Windigo example related in chapter 3, led to a deci-sion to stop the prairie's development. Community deliberation, natu-ralistic observations drawn from scientists and Elders and sacred teachings were all drawn upon to respect and show reverence towards the life force of what others might regard as barren rock. This led to a positivist law resolution whereby the band declared that the alvar would not host our annual pow-wows in the community.

This brief review of Anishinabek law demonstrates that Anishin-abek beliefs concerning the Earth as a living being can be legally rec-ognized and affirmed. It also shows how Anishinabek law can lead to land being accorded political citizenship with its other close relations. Attentiveness to the land's character and sacred power gives the Earth an important place within this jurisprudential system.

D. Section 2(a) of the *Charter*: Anishinabek Beliefs and Freedom of Religion

Like Anishinabek law, Canadian constitutional law has also developed principles to deal with matters of religion and land that have implica-tions for Indigenous peoples. One constitutional provision relevant to the protection of Indigenous spiritual beliefs and practices is section 2(a) of the *Charter of Rights and Freedoms* in Part I of the *Constitution Act, 1982*: 'Everyone has the following fundamental freedoms: (a) freedom of conscience and religion.' Like Anishinabek law, section 2(a) of the *Charter* can also provide answers to the question: Is an Anishinabek belief that the Earth is living capable of being recognized and affirmed? This inquiry will demonstrate that, while there is real poten-tial for protection within this section, there are also significant chal-lenges in shielding Anishinabek spiritual beliefs from government interference. These challenges are so profound that it is unlikely that courts would uphold Anishinabek beliefs unless they embraced broader conceptions of multi-juridicalism that have been developed in this book.

Canadian constitutional principles dealing with freedom of religion draw on ancient cultural traditions with their origins in the 'religious struggles of post-reformation Europe,' not in Indigenous North America.[42] The cultural context of constitutional protections potentially presents a problem for Indigenous peoples because their religious struggles with the Canadian state find their origins in the settlers' arrival from post-Reformation Europe. Those seeking religious freedom in the New World did not often understand Indigenous religions. Still others regarded these religions as pagan and frequently ridiculed and imposed cruel restrictions on Indigenous spiritual beliefs.[43] Indigenous peoples have a long and tragic history of severe persecution in the name of European religions.[44] One cannot help but wonder how contemporary, post-Reformation-inspired law will differ from historical, post-Reformation religion when dealing with Indigenous spiritual ideas and practices.

My colleague Professor Benjamin Berger makes the point that law has a cultural understanding of religion.[45] He notes that law has a difficult time escaping its liberal context and understands its subject through its own values. In particular, he says, this predilection means that 'Canadian constitutional law casts religion in accordance with its own informing commitments.' I would summarize my understanding of Berger's views as follows: law is a liberal god that creates religion in its own image. If the implications flowing from my analysis of his work are correct, then the Constitution will have difficulty protecting Anishinabek religious beliefs and practices if they are outside law's central commitments to individual choice, autonomy, privacy, and personal conviction.

Unfortunately, if beliefs about the Earth are not informed by a multi-juridical understanding, Anishinabek religion can be characterized as lying outside the Constitution's informing commitments. They can be seen as being alien to Western law, politics, and religion. Not many post-Reformation religious adherents or legal practitioners talk to the Earth, study her character, and expect to receive responses by observing her behaviour. The fact that Anishinabek religion and law treat the Earth as a living being with the power of choice, requiring respect for its autonomy, privacy, and personal convictions, might seem to fit within a liberal framework. Liberalism strives to protect these central values. However, the notion that *the Earth is the individual* possessing these characteristics probably propels Canadian constitutional law beyond its informing commitments. As a result, resorting to section

2(a) without a multi-juridical understanding would likely be unproductive for Anishinabek people because it would stretch the law beyond its cultural context.[46]

In contrast with this interpretation is another view of section 2(a) that accepts the law's current potential to protect diverse religious practices and beliefs. This view assumes that cultural constraints and biases may be overcome if greater emphasis is placed on section 2(a)'s doctrinal flexibility. In this regard, Professor Bruce Ryder develops the idea of equal religious citizenship, 'a relatively new and fragile concept' that seems to animate section 2(a)'s *Charter* jurisprudence.[47] He finds this concept present in a series of judgments from the Supreme Court of Canada dating from the middle of the 1980s up to the present day. Ryder's focus on equal religious citizenship could provide a strong check against law's cultural bias as identified by Berger. Ryder points to some brighter moments of jurisprudential possibility that seem to push the law beyond its originating context. Justice Iacobucci's statement in *Syndicat Northcrest v. Amselem* is viewed as representative of the aspiration for equal religious citizenship: '[R]espect for and tolerance of the rights and practices of religious minorities is one of the hallmarks of an enlightened democracy.'[48] If Ryder's view of section 2(a) is correct, then Anishinabek people may hope that the current tests might provide religious protection under the *Charter*. While this view has a degree of support within the jurisprudence, it remains untested in regard to the particularities of Anishinabek spiritual life.

To test section 2(a)'s potential, one can assume that an Anishinabek group might of necessity use this section for protection to practise their beliefs. For example, it is easy to imagine a case in which the federal government or a provincial government approved or constructed a road through a site such as the prairie alvar noted above. To claim section 2(a) *Charter* protection in these circumstances, Anishinabek people would have to prove that their religious beliefs and practices were infringed by such a development or that such an action offended matters of conscience. This is where their difficulty would begin. If they decided to make their case under section 2(a)'s religion clause, they would have to show that their beliefs were 'religious,' that interference with them was non-trivial, and that the infringement was not reasonable in a free and democratic society.

An Anishinabek claim could be defeated as not being religious. This was the problem encountered in the leading case of *Jack and Charlie v.*

The Queen, which asked whether the BC *Wildlife Act* interfered with Coast Salish rights to religious freedom.[49] While the *Jack and Charlie* case did not directly deal with section 2(a) of the *Charter,* because that section had not been enacted at the time the offence was committed,[50] it did consider the fundamental nature of religious freedoms. Religion was argued as a fundamental legal principle that ought to prevail over lesser statutory rights. The facts of the case turned on whether the killing of a deer contrary to the act in preparation for a religious ceremony could be a defence against the wildlife statute. The deer was killed to nourish a recently deceased ancestor through ritual burning of the meat. While the Supreme Court of Canada had a chance to consider the freedom-of-religion aspect of the case, it chose not to take this course; it found that the prohibited act of killing the deer was not a religious ritual.

The court did not regard the deer's death as part of a religious ceremony. It said that the ritual burning could have been carried out by using frozen deer meat retained in storage. By changing the appellants' characterization of the right, and substituting an alternative practice acceptable to the Court, the rights of religious freedom were evaded in this case. Justice Beetz wrote that '[t]here was no evidence that the use of defrosted raw deer meat was sacrilegious as is alleged in the appellants' factum.' Thus, since killing the deer was held to be separate from the deer's use, the court concluded that the deer's death was separate from any religious significance. The Court did not look deep enough; it failed to see the religious and Indigenous legal context of the Coast Salish ceremony. As Professor Len Rotman and I previously observed,

> There is no appreciation of the matrix of family responsibilities and relationships that are triggered by the requirement of obtaining fresh deer meat for this ceremony. There is no understanding of how the people plan for the trip, discuss its purpose, remember the great-grandfather, share their food and supplies, and experience nature together. There is no acknowledgment of the internal contractual and constitutional legal principles which govern the parties' conduct within Salish society. The event's narrow construction overlooks community participation that would accompany the preparation and dressing of a newly killed deer. The Court did not account for the people lifting the deer from the truck, taking it in the house or shed, skinning it, sitting around the table working at it, and discussing their routines and relationships in very specific ways.

Finally, the Court did not mention how the use of fresh deer meat for the ceremony would draw the community together in a way that retrieving frozen deer meat from a freezer never would. The immediacy of life and death would not be as culturally poignant if frozen deer meat were used.[51]

Failure to appreciate the spiritual significance of killing the deer led the court to accept an inappropriate analogy. It likened the distinction between purchasing and administering sacramental wine as part of a Holy Communion ceremony to a distinction between killing and burning the deer, arguing that both the sale of wine and the killing of deer are not ceremonial.[52] This analogy shows how Indigenous spiritual practices may flounder when judges fail to make appropriate distinctions between Indigenous religion and certain Christian practices. Common law understandings cannot always be appropriately read into Indigenous legal traditions. A multi-juridical approach would be more sensitive to the need to see this issue as one that involves a different legal, not just spiritual, construct. Unfortunately, the *Jack and Charlie* decision does not recognize the holistic practices of Salish legal tradition and thus fails to find a religious practice where one is present, at least from a Salish perspective. The case illustrates the problems that Anishinabek people can encounter when trying to bring their spiritual beliefs before the courts for protection under section 2(a) of the *Charter* that are not informed by multi-juridicalism.[53]

Without seeing the contemporary existence of Indigenous laws it may be hard for Canadian courts to detect the holistic religious practices of Anishinabek spiritual life. Anishinabek spiritual beliefs may not be labelled religious because they can lack many of the outward forms of other worship systems. They are not often taught in churches, synagogues, mosques, temples, or cathedrals. Of all Anishinabek religious experience, only the Medewiwin Society has a lodge where these teachings are more formally taught and practised. One can imagine the difficulty that an Anishinabek Christian would have in proving his or her religious beliefs where doctrines concerning a living Earth are submerged or not easily found written in a church's doctrinal canon. For many courts, Anishinabek Catholicism or Anglicanism would overshadow Anishinabek beliefs and practices. Similarly, an Anishinabek person not affiliated with any organized religion would have an equally difficult time convincing a court that his or her spiritual views and practices are religious when the collective nature of his or her 'worship' is difficult to pinpoint. Most Anishinabek spiritual expression differs substantially from what many people regard as religious, and this could prove problematic for protection under section 2(a) of the *Charter*.[54]

Fortunately, definitions of the religious nature of Anishinabek spiritual beliefs may not necessarily prove fatal to their claims. The *Charter's* standard for finding that a belief is religious is a 'nexus' with the divine or spiritual. This requirement is fortunately judged by subjective standards, meaning that a person's own declarations are seemingly sufficient to meet this test. In *Amselem*, the Supreme Court wrote, 'In essence, religion is about freely and deeply held personal convictions or beliefs connected to an individual's spiritual faith and integrally linked to one's self-definition and spiritual fulfillment, the practices of which allow individuals to foster a connection with the divine or with the subject or object of that spiritual faith.'[55] The court did not accept the dissenting judgment's view that '[r]eligious precepts constitute a body of objectively identifiable data that permit a distinction to be made between genuine religious beliefs and personal choices or practices that are unrelated to freedom of conscience.'[56] This is good news for Anishinabek people who may find it necessary to make a section 2(a) claim. The majority's broader view of religion might allow an Anishinabek Christian or non-church-going person to claim that his or her beliefs and practices regarding the Earth are religious.[57] Proponents could show that Anishinabek spiritual beliefs concerning the Earth are holistic, deeply held, linked to their self-definition and fulfilment, and foster a connection with the subject of their faith. Thus, despite potential difficulties proving that Anishinabek beliefs are religious, there is at least a chance that they might satisfy the Court's test on this front, thereby allowing an Anishinabek person to sincerely affirm a religious belief under section 2(a) of the *Charter*.[58]

Having met this hurdle, however, an Anishinabek person alleging government interference with his or her religion would have to show that the infringement was substantial or non-trivial.[59] In the example used in this chapter, the courts would have to be satisfied that building a road over an alvar was sufficiently significant to constitute an infringement of Anishinabek beliefs.[60] One wonders how some judges might regard the building of a road over old barren rock through an empty, unused field; it might appear to them to be trivial. Its impact could look insubstantial to certain judicial observers. Of course, the focus should be on the aggrieved person's faith, which is being interfered with, not the judge's perception or the impact on the Earth itself. The court is not expected or required to accept Anishinabek beliefs in order to protect them. The court would be concerned primarily with whether building a road over an alvar burdens Anishinabek beliefs and practices concerning the Earth in a non-trivial manner. In this analysis, while it is appropriate to the judicial role in a common law setting, the Earth is left out of political citizenship and lacks legal standing, although it is possible that courts would find impacts on Anishinabek beliefs substantial and non-trivial.

If an Anishinabek claimant were successful in meeting the first two hurdles in claiming section 2(a) protection, then he or she might still have to demonstrate that the right is 'summarily unassailable and receive[s] automatic protection under the banner of freedom of religion.'[61] The Supreme Court of Canada has said that freedom of religion is not absolute.[62] Rights are not automatically protected if they interfere with the rights of others. The Court put its concerns this way in *Syndicat Northcrest v. Amselem*:

> Even if individuals demonstrate that they sincerely believe in the religious essence of an action, for example, that a particular practice will subjectively engender a genuine connection with the divine or with the subject or object of their faith, and even if they successfully demonstrate non-trivial or non-insubstantial interference with that practice, they will still have to consider how the exercise of their right impacts upon the rights of others in the context of the competing rights of private individuals. Conduct which would potentially cause harm to or interference with the rights of others would not automatically be protected. The ultimate protection of any particular *Charter* right must be measured in relation to other rights and with a view to the underlying context in which the apparent conflict arises.[63]

Thus, Anishinabek beliefs and practices may not be automatically protected if the rights affect 'the rights of others in the context of the competing rights of private individuals.'[64] If Indigenous religious rights conflict with other constitutional rights, the Crown potentially gets two 'kicks at the can' in arguing that religious freedoms can be limited, both within section 2(a) and section 1 of the *Charter* (section 1, explored in subsequent paragraphs, permits governments to justify rights infringements). In other words, if another constitutional right conflicts or competes with Anishinabek religious rights, then those rights may not receive automatic protection within section 2(a).[65] Fortunately, since *Multani v. Commission Scolaire Marguerite-Bourgeoys* in 2006,[66] the Supreme Court has chosen to reconcile competing rights under section 1 of the *Charter* rather than within section 2(a). This approach has been taken to preserve individual rights in the first stage of analysis by resolving ambiguity surrounding them in a broad and liberal way. This then allows the Court to use section 1 in a more flexible way to balance competing rights in the second stage of analysis. Thus, it appears as though the court has resolved not to place internal limits on religious freedoms in its section 2(a) scrutiny. This is an important development because Anishinabek religious rights under section 2(a) could have a strong impact on the government or a third party's rights or interests.

Thus, in turning to a section 1 analysis, it is important to acknowledge that Anishinabek religious beliefs can be infringed upon if the government meets certain standards. Section 1 of the *Charter* allows the government to infringe upon religious rights if such interference is found to be a reasonable limit prescribed by law that can be demonstrably justified in a free and democratic society. Thus, governments are permitted to interfere with recognized individual rights if they are sufficiently important to warrant limiting a constitutional right and if the means chosen by the state authority are proportional to the objective in question. While testing governmental limitations of religious rights is difficult in the abstract, a preliminary observation should be made concerning this issue.

We must remember when balancing Anishinabek religious rights against potential infringements that the Supreme Court in *Amselem* and *Multani* said that governments will possess more compelling justifications for infringement where religious rights conflict or compete with other constitutional rights. The focus on competing rights might help to protect Anishinabek religious rights from interference because such rights will most likely conflict with non-constitutional interests. For example, in all likelihood, disputes involving property or contractual rights will most directly conflict with Anishinabek religious rights. However, contractual and property rights are not directly protected in Canada's Constitution;[67] therefore, if protecting Anishinabek beliefs increased transaction costs in the alienability and use of land on and off reserve, then this should not be sufficient to defeat their automatic protection. It is not enough that Anishinabek religious rights may interfere with other people's economic circumstances.

However, social, political, and contextual factors might limit Anishinabek religion despite *Amselem's* and *Multani's* focus on rights. In balancing religious rights against other factors, courts will find it difficult to ignore the economic costs of recognizing them if they have social or political implications. Courts could find reasons to weigh and favour non-Anishinabek economic interests against constitutionally protected rights by invoking the precept outlined in *Ross v. New Brunswick School District No. 15:* 'Freedom of religion is subject to such limitations as are necessary to protect public safety, order, health or morals and the fundamental rights and freedoms of others.'[68] If Anishinabek religious beliefs and practices threatened non-Anishinabek economic life, it would be easy to see how they might be regarded as matters of 'public safety, order, health or morals.' Restraints on the alienability of land and the government's ability to develop infrastructure over what to others looks like barren rock could bring other interests to the foreground, thus justifying government infringements upon Anishinabek religious rights.

The standard for proving whether the Crown has an important objective in passing legislation is often deferential in the government's favour.[69] This deference, while proper in respecting the nature of Canada's democracy, represents another hurdle for Anishinabek religious protection. Whether a court would find building a road across an alvar sufficiently pressing and substantial is context-dependent. For example, what difference, if any, would a court attribute to the alvar being on private land, public land, or land classified as an Indian reserve? Does something become more pressing and substantial if property rights diverge from or align with government or Indian objectives? If private property is given greater weight, then government interference may appear to be more compelling. All this potentially ignores the underlying land allocation scheme that largely favours non-Aboriginal owners. The fact that law's distribution of land after contact unjustly stripped Indigenous peoples of their land rights over an area might not enter into the court's evaluation.[70] In other words, the courts might not see government action in the creation of private property out of traditional Indigenous territories. If the government's role in creating private property is not recognized, then non-Aboriginal property rights might become a surrogate for making certain activities more pressing and substantial for governments, thus potentially constricting the scope of Anishinabek religious freedom. The cultural context of constitutional law is visible only if one is reminded of this fact, which again demonstrates the value of working in a multi-juridical context to remind judges of this fact.

Section one of the *Charter*, however, presses further. If the government is able to show a pressing and substantial objective, then other challenging issues arise concerning the proportionality of measures chosen by governments to meet their objectives. Legislation will be found proportional to its objectives if it is rationally connected to its goals, minimally impairs rights, and appropriately balances its positive effects against the legislation's burdens. In the circumstances of Anishinabek spiritual beliefs and practices that are interfered with by road building, it would likely be easy for governments to show that the exercise of zoning or expropriation powers for roads is rationally connected to legislative objectives. Presumably, all that the government would need to show is that the road connects point A to point B in a way that makes sense for its purpose.

When it comes to questions of minimal impairment, governments might encounter some real problems justifying religious infringement. For example, governments might not realize that they possess potential obligations towards Anishinabek religious adherents and thus inadvertently approve activities that are harmful to them.[71] However, once Anishinabek beliefs are brought to a government's attention, it might be possible to interfere with them if the government takes mitigative measures that are appropriate in a court's eyes. The road, for example, could make the smallest possible footprint on the alvar, and Anishinabek practices could be respected through pipe ceremonies, permissions, and prayers.[72] Although such measures resemble appropriate accommodation, one must not forget that the Earth might say no to development of the road, and yet the government might still decide to go ahead with construction. While the accommodation suggested is probably fair under Canadian law, one can see how it still likely offends religious beliefs. Thus, while minimal impairment might not be possible from an Anishinabek perspective, the Supreme Court's own test would presume that a reconciliation of government objectives and Anishinabek beliefs could be accomplished. This presumption would likely favour non-Anishinabek governmental objectives over Anishinabek beliefs and reveal the culturally constraining character of Canadian constitutional law. The minimal impairment test may be an example of a place where the law shows its inability to travel beyond its own informing commitments.

Finally, Anishinabek beliefs may be infringed upon if the salutary effect of the road's construction outweighs its deleterious effects on Anishinabek rights. Measured on the Anishinabek side is damage that the road may cause to their spiritual beliefs and practices. Weighed on the other side are the positive benefits of the infringement for the social, political, and economic lives of other Canadians. In making these judgments courts will have to work hard to avoid the following cultural biases without the guidance that a multi-juridical framework might provide. The idea that the Earth can form a purpose and is a teleological being is obviously open to criticism.[73] It does not accord with many people's perceptions of the Earth as inanimate. The Earth appears to have few of the characteristics of purposeful life; for most, there are no discernible thoughts, communication patterns, or conscious lifeways. Furthermore, the Earth's agency potentially threatens the core of North American economic organization in the twenty-first century. If the alienation and use of land are limited by one small group's spiritual beliefs, it could impose unacceptable costs on development for others. Furthermore, courts must be mindful of the potential for abuse that may arise from recognizing Anishinabek claims. The informal nature of Anishinabek spirituality can lead to potential manipulation despite the sincerity of a majority of adherents. There are untrustworthy people within Anishinabek society, just as within any community. Some Anishinabek might claim power to speak exclusively for the Earth to fraudulently advance their economic, social, or political agendas. It can be difficult for the judiciary to discern such charlatans, and thus the burden of proof can be even higher. As with many spiritual matters, beliefs are linked with faith, which is difficult to test in objective terms and should cause us concern.

Thus, when measuring deleterious effects that Anishinabek people might experience, judges will have to resist the temptation to measure favourably the law's salutary effects against their own cultural understandings of the law. Roads are generally seen as good or at least a necessary evil within Canadian society. They foster communication, commerce, and expansion. 'Empty' land is often seen as unproductive, inefficient, and of less value if roads do not service such sites. One might legitimately ask: Why should Anishinabek beliefs trump the social conveniences of enhanced mobility, municipal planning processes, and economic efficiencies that roads create? While it is possible that judges might be able to check their cultural biases in making these evaluations, they must still provide reasons for decisions drawn from Canadian constitutional law cases. If the law itself has embedded certain cultural commitments concerning land use that largely accord with non-Anishinabek organization, then it may be difficult for the law to move beyond its own parameters in such judgments. Anishinabek spirituality is very different from the Christian model of religion with which most judges are familiar. These differences shape an approach to religious freedom that does not sufficiently appreciate Anishinabek religious beliefs if multi-juridicalism is not present in judicial analysis.

The foregoing analysis illustrates that, while it may be possible for Anishinabek people to secure the protection of section 2(a) of the *Charter* for their religious beliefs and practices, achieving this protection may be exceedingly difficult without a more explicit call to incorporate Indigenous legal traditions into Canada's constitutional framework. Without the injection of Indigenous law, Professor Berger's interpretation of section 2(a) may better explain how Anishinabek religion would be currently treated under the *Charter* than does Professor Ryder's conception of equal religious citizenship. While section 2(a) might provide equal protection for Anishinabek spirituality, such arguments face significant challenges if Canada's constitutional tradition is constructed as culturally non-native, and therefore legally, 'neutral.' The theoretical possibility of protection may not easily translate into an actual result – possibility does not always equal probability in law. Anishinabek beliefs may not be regarded as 'religion,' interference with Anishinabek rights might be thought trivial, and infringement upon those rights may be found reasonable in Canada's 'free and democratic society.' Section 2(a)'s maze of doctrinal hurdles gives the courts many opportunities to forge religion in liberalism's image. If this occurs, then Anishinabek religion risks being cast out of constitutional law's presence because of its failure to follow liberalism's tenets.[74]

Thus, while Canadian constitutional law may on rare occasions transcend its cultural context and informing commitments,[75] it continues to draw significant inspiration from its common law parentage. Constitutional law will remain limited in its application to Anishinabek spiritual life until it regards its birth as also flowing from another source, outside its European and so-called neutral conception.[76] Unless the multi-juridical nature of law is recognized, Anishinabek religion will be better protected through Anishinabek law. This section shows that greater space must be found within our legal systems to recognize and affirm our complex and rich legal heritage.[77]

E. Section 35(1):
Aboriginal Rights, Land, and Religious Belief

The second constitutional category that Anishinabek people might use to protect their spiritual beliefs and practices is section 35(1) in Part II of the *Constitution Act, 1982*. This section states that '[t]he existing Aboriginal and treaty rights of the Aboriginal peoples of Canada are hereby recognized and affirmed.' While this section may be more likely to transcend common law's cultural footings, the courts have not yet achieved this result. Despite attempts to incorporate Indigenous perspectives and laws, section 35(1) remains securely tied to its non-Aboriginal foundations. There is no real Indigenous law cited in arriving at appropriate decisions. In fact, the Supreme Court of Canada has taken to translating Indigenous perspectives and practices into common law rights,[78] a sure sign of the problematic nature in this section's current configuration. Making common law the ultimate measure of ancient Indigenous traditions virtually ensures that non-Aboriginal cultural aspirations will predominate within section 35. If one were to translate Anishinabek words into English or French, many Anishinabek nuances, ideas, and understandings would be lost in the process. The same thing happens when one translates Anishinabek laws and legal perspectives into the Constitution's common law framework. A multi-juridical read of the constitution is needed to overcome this bias.

In 1990, the Supreme Court of Canada wrote that the recognition and affirmation of Aboriginal and treaty rights represented the 'culmination of a long and difficult struggle' that 'calls for a just settlement for aboriginal peoples' and 'renounces the old rules of the game.'[79] It is now fairly clear that section 35 did not end Indigenous peoples' struggle for 'a just settlement,' nor did it renounce the most problematic aspects of 'the old rules of the game' that give preferential treatment to non-Aboriginal cultural interpretations of Aboriginal and treaty rights. Indigenous peoples are still struggling for their rights, and the new rules of the game increasingly look like the old rules. After some initial promise, the common law as applied within section 35 seems to be collapsing back into itself and is interpreting Aboriginal and treaty rights through non-Aboriginal categories and principles. In fact, it might almost be argued that resort to its own contextual categorizations is 'integral to the distinctive culture' of common law's practices, customs, and traditions – since their 'contact' in North

America with Aboriginal peoples. Indigenous legal traditions are almost invisible in the current way problems are addressed under section 35(1).

The problems underlying the approach of section 35(1) can be illustrated by considering how this section might be used to protect Anishinabek spirituality. Once again, the Constitution's potential reach can be tested by taking the example of the construction of a road over a prairie alvar. Anishinabek people have many options, it might be argued, within section 35 for protecting the alvar. For example, the Anishinabek could try to assert an independent Aboriginal right to religion, they could claim Aboriginal title over territory considered sacred, they could attempt to prove a site-specific Aboriginal right to a religious practice, they could argue that they have an Aboriginal right to governance in relation to the alvar, or they might maintain that they possess a treaty right to territory, governance, or religion. Each argument and perhaps more can be relevant to the protection of Anishinabek religion.

While each of the foregoing arguments is significant on its own terms, in the remainder of this chapter I will deal only with Aboriginal rights to religion. I take this approach because of space limitations and my opinion that courts would insist on characterizing Anishinabek beliefs as religion if the most significant Anishinabek concern is the one underlying this chapter, that of a living Earth. However, one should note that these other section 35(1) arguments are potentially available and relevant for protection. For example, as was noted in chapter 2, many Indigenous nations regard their treaties as sacred.[80] They believe that treaties are a covenant made with the Creator with the participation of the Crown and thus imply deep religious obligations.[81] While the spiritual nature of Indigenous treaties is sometimes acknowledged in section 35(1) jurisprudence,[82] its implications for Indigenous spirituality must be explored in future research.[83]

In testing Aboriginal rights, the courts have ruled that they are subject to specific tests within section 35(1). Thus, to prove an Aboriginal right to religion, it has to be established first that Anishinabek religious practices or beliefs concerning a living Earth were integral to the distinctive culture prior to European contact. To receive constitutional protection, the Anishinabek belief cannot be the result of European contact. The court would expect to find that a belief in a living Earth truly made the society what it was, in 1615, at the moment Samuel de Champlain made contact with the Anishinabek of Georgian Bay. The

Supreme Court, curiously, does not seem to find it relevant if Anishin-abek practices, customs, or traditions developed in response to contact with other Aboriginal nations.

The 'integral to the distinctive culture' test has been criticized as inappropriately and arbitrarily freezing Aboriginal rights by reference to the arrival of European cultures. While this test is exceedingly prob-lematic when applied to Aboriginal hunting and fishing rights, its injustice becomes even more pronounced when Aboriginal religion is at issue. It is one thing to place constitutional limits on material culture's development, because doing so virtually drives that culture to physical poverty. However, when constitutional limits are placed on spirituality's development, the law stoops even lower. It denies Indigenous people protection of the inner means to cope with the physical impoverishment that often developed as a result of European contact. Indigenous peoples' religious freedoms should not hinge on historic non-Aboriginal contact, especially when non-Aboriginal Euro-peans were so harsh in their treatment of Indigenous religion after contact. Making Aboriginal religious rights dependent on whether practices, customs, and traditions were in existence before European arrival reveals the culturally chauvinistic roots of Canadian constitu-tional law relative to Indigenous peoples.

The 'integral to the distinctive culture' test also creates difficulties of proof. The focus on whether Anishinabek people believed that the Earth was living when Europeans arrived is not a straightforward inquiry. As noted earlier, some scholars believe that the concept of a 'Mother Earth' developed only in recent times, perhaps over the past fifty years. If Anishinabek people cannot marshal sufficient evidence about their religious beliefs and practices prior to the arrival of Euro-peans, then section 35(1) will fail to protect the foundational elements of their society's normative order. When Canadian constitutional law does not protect how Indigenous communities peacefully organize themselves in accordance with their own laws, then the Constitution becomes a potential threat to the very existence of Indigenous soci-eties. One can imagine scenarios in which the test in section 35(1) potentially undermines Anishinabek religion, particularly if it 'proves' that the belief in a living Earth is an 'inauthentic' modern invention contrary to the present perception of Anishinabek spiritual views. If the court's view is widely accepted within Anishinabek society, it could have devastating consequences for concepts at the heart of their legal order. Fortunately for those seeking to sustain their religion, it would likely take a lot more than a Supreme Court decision to over-turn Anishinabek beliefs. Aboriginal peoples have ignored laws in the past that threatened to assimilate their societies, and this tactic has ensured their survival. However, such a decision would not be without significance. The Supreme Court's stamp of disapproval would certainly constrict the socio-legal and political spaces within which Anishinabek laws could grow. Such a decision would hamper the further development of a healthy multi-juridicalism in our land.

Furthermore, the court's focus on the past when dealing with Anishinabek religious rights takes this institution onto exceedingly unsteady ground. It requires the judiciary to engage in inquiries that they are not willing to undertake in other constitutional cases. In *Amselem*, the Supreme Court held that '[i]t is important to underscore ... that it is inappropriate for courts rigorously to study and focus on the past practices of claimants in order to determine whether their current beliefs are sincerely held.'[84] Despite this concern, section 35(1)'s analytical framework would demand just such a determination. The Court's search would be for an 'authentic' pre-contact version of Anishinabek beliefs. If the courts were forced to delve into past Anishinabek religious practices under section 35(1), they would lose the benefit of insights relevant to section 2(a) of the *Charter:* 'Over the course of a lifetime, individuals change and so can their beliefs.'[85] The Supreme Court knows in other contexts that '[r]eligious beliefs, by their very nature, are fluid and rarely static.'[86] Section 35(1) would fail to take this insight into account because the 'integral to the distinctive culture' test requires a static view of Aboriginal societies.

The Supreme Court's test thus inappropriately encumbers and potentially distorts Indigenous spirituality and the constitutional pro-tection available to it under section 35(1). It misses one of the central points being made about multi-juridicalism in this book – Indigenous peoples have living legal systems that evolve through time. Protection for religion under these systems can change over the years even as individuals and societies attempt to maintain an acceptable degree of continuity with past beliefs and practices. Ironically, the Supreme Court has itself reinforced this observation within section 2(a): 'A person's connection to or relationship with the divine or with the subject or object of his or her spiritual faith, or his or her perceptions of religious obligation emanating from such a relationship, may well change and evolve over time.' The Court's recognition of the potential fluidity of spirituality under section 2(a) has therefore led the justices to focus on a person's sincerity at the time of the alleged interference with the beliefs. The Court does not focus on past beliefs or practices when testing other constitutional rights. The Supreme Court has summarized its position in this way: 'Because of the vacillating nature of religious belief, a court's inquiry into sincerity, if anything, should focus not on past practice or past belief but on a person's belief at the time of the alleged interference with his or her religious freedom.'[87] Unfortunately, the very structure of sections 35(1)'s inquiry into Anishinabek religion prevents this focus; the sincerity of an Anishinabek person's belief at the time of an alleged interference would be irrelevant if such a notion is found to be not 'integral to the distinctive culture' when Europeans arrived.

This test thus makes section 35 exceedingly inappropriate for the recognition and affirmation of Anishinabek religious freedoms. It can lead to potentially dangerous stereotypes and caricatures of Indigenous peoples as past tense cultures, with no right to expect protection for religious beliefs developed since Europeans arrived. This culturally biased categorization diminishes Indigenous religion's substance. It severely decreases the protection available for Indigenous practices in the modern world and degrades the court's role as a champion of human rights.

Similar problems will be encountered if protection for religious practices is sought through Aboriginal title. While the language of Aboriginal title does not often explicitly use the 'integral to the distinctive culture' test for proof, this test underlies the reason courts seek to protect title.[88] If Anishinabek people sought to protect their religious freedom through Aboriginal title, they would have to prove that they had exclusive occupation of the territory prior to the assertion of British sovereignty and that this occupation was continuous through time immemorial until the present day.[89] It might be difficult to establish these facts if certain pieces of land cannot be occupied in accordance with Anishinabek law because the Earth is living. It seems to be logically inconsistent to use evidence of non-occupation as proof of occupation for Aboriginal title.[90]

In any event, courts would likely resist attempts to protect Anishinabek religion through Aboriginal title or any other section 35(1) grounds. In *R. v. Pamajewon*, the Supreme Court wrote that it 'must first identify the exact nature of the activity claimed.'[91] Thus, the Court and not the claimants get the final word on the right's characterization. This would likely be fatal to claims brought on grounds other than Aboriginal rights to spiritual practice and expression if the living agency of the Earth is the core of the Anishinabek concern rather than occupation, site-specific, non-use, governance, or treaties. Any attempt to protect Indigenous peoples' spirituality through Aboriginal title or another section 35(1) category would likely be considered an indirect and more generalized claim for religious respect. The courts are loath to cast Aboriginal rights claims at broader levels of generality when more specific claims can be made; their search is for the appropriate level of specificity relative to the claim. These factors would probably lead the courts to recharacterize Anishinabek claims if they sought protection for the alvar on the ground of Aboriginal title. As noted, the Supreme Court's recharacterization of issues under section 35(1) is not unusual.[92] Recharacterization brings Aboriginal rights claims into line with the law's own image of Indigenous societies and reveals the cultural biases underlying Canadian constitutional law. There is a very limited conception of equal citizenship within section 35(1), unlike Ryder's identification of equal religious citizenship under section 2(a). Furthermore, there is also a very limited conception of multi-judicalism within section 35(1) which also brings Aboriginal rights claims into line with the common law, rather than Indigenous peoples' own legal conception of their relationships.

Furthermore, even if Anishinabek people are able to prove that their beliefs and practices related to a living Earth are integral to their distinctive culture prior to European contact, their struggle under section 35(1) is not over. They still have to prove that their rights were not extinguished prior to 1982.[93] If their beliefs or practices were extinguished prior to the Constitution's patriation, the Supreme Court has held that such rights are not revived by section 35(1) once they have been extinguished. Fortunately for Anishinabek people, the Crown has the burden of proving extinguishment, and the Supreme Court has written that the 'clear and plain' hurdle for extinguishment is 'quite high.'[94] Therefore, the overarching question in testing whether Anishinabek spiritual practices were extinguished hinges on what constitutes a 'high' standard of 'clear and plain' extinguishment and whether the Crown met this test for extinguishing Aboriginal and treaty rights prior to 1982.[95]

Unfortunately, one of the few cases to have considered extinguishment as it relates to Aboriginal religious rights construed the Crown's power in the widest possible manner, to the detriment of Indigenous religious freedoms. In R. v. Thomas and Norris, the court considered arguments about whether Coast Salish spirit dancing was protected under section 35(1) of the *Constitution Act, 1982*.[96] In this case, a Salish man was 'grabbed' and taken to a Salish Big House contrary to his will but for healing purposes in accordance with Salish spiritual beliefs and legal practices. Justice Hood of the British Columbia Supreme Court ruled that there was insufficient evidence to show that Salish spirit dancing was integral to the culture prior to European arrival. Furthermore, he held that, even if spirit dancing was once integral to the culture, it was extinguished through the operation of Canadian civil and criminal law. In arriving at this conclusion, Justice Hood relied on the notion that spirit dancing involved coercion against a person 'grabbed' against his or her will and thus was contrary to Canadian criminal and civil law.[97]

Justice Hood's reasons were based explicitly on the idea that the introduction of common law in Canada gave it 'supremacy' relative to Aboriginal religious practices. This finding is contrary to the central thesis of this book that has argued that Indigenous legal traditions survived the common law's introduction. Justice Hood found that spirit dancing 'did not survive the coming into force of that law, which occurred on Vancouver Island in 1846 or, at the latest, in 1866, when the two colonies of Vancouver Island and British Columbia were merged.'[98] This reasoning, if accepted, is potentially fatal to Indigenous peoples' religious claims under section 35(1) that are inconsistent with common law. Justice Hood found that '[i]t has never been the law of this Province that any person, or group of persons, Indians or non-Indians, had the right' to perform religious practices that were contrary to the civil or common law. 'This is so whether or not it is done under the umbrella of religion or some other tradition of long-standing or an Aboriginal right.'[99] This decision privileges the common law and civil law over Indigenous law by the raw power of judicial assertion. If these reasons were extended, it is possible that property law, being part of common law's civil order, extinguished Aboriginal rights to spiritual practices concerning a living Earth when it was introduced. It would be difficult to find a sharper illustration of how the scope of religious freedom under the Constitution can be forged in common law's image.

Without a multi-juridical reappraisal, the *Thomas and Norris* case represents a potentially insurmountable hurdle for Anishinabek spiritual beliefs because it reads extinguishment in the broadest possible light. Fortunately for the protection of Indigenous religious freedoms under section 35(1), strong doubts can be raised concerning the astonishingly low standard of extinguishment used in this case.[100] The Supreme Court has said that, for an Aboriginal or treaty right to have been extinguished prior to 1982, the Crown has the onus of proving that it possessed a 'clear and plain' intention to do so.[101] Thus, extinguishment should be narrowly construed. The standard required for extinguishment was best articulated by Madam Justice L'Heureux-Dubé in R. v. N.T.C. Smokehouse Ltd. She wrote that '[c]lear and plain means that the government must address the aboriginal activities in question and explicitly extinguish them by making them no longer permissible.'[102] The mere contours of common law rules concerning property, tort, or contract should not be regarded as sufficiently explicit to extinguish Aboriginal rights. Such an approach does not accord with the court's directive to interpret Aboriginal rights expansively, with a 'generous and liberal interpretation in favour of Aboriginal peoples.'[103] Furthermore, such an approach does not accord with the rule of law's spirit as developed in this book. Indigenous peoples' religious rights under section 35(1) hang under a cloud of general extinguishment unless the courts precisely and unequivocally reject the assumption of cultural superiority in Thomas v. Norris. The explicit recognition of multi-juridicalism in cases like this would be one way to dispel this bias.

Finally, Indigenous peoples have one last obstacle to overcome to secure their religious freedoms against government interference under section 35(1). This hurdle is present even if Anishinabek people are able to show that Anishinabek beliefs and practices regarding the Earth were integral to their distinctive culture and not extinguished. This is because the Crown can still argue that it has the right to infringe upon Anishinabek religion under section 35(1) through a justificatory process. The Crown can justify the infringement of Aboriginal rights if it has a valid legislative objective and its actions are consistent with the honour of the Crown.

It would likely be easy for the Crown to show that it has a valid legislative objective for the construction of roads, as discussed previously when dealing with pressing and substantial legislative objectives under section 1 of the Charter. Thus, if a road is being proposed over an alvar, it would not be too difficult for the Crown to show that it is acting in a constitutionally acceptable manner. For example, in the Delgamuukw case, the Supreme Court gave wide scope for finding valid legislative objectives, including 'general economic development' and 'the development of infrastructure,' to support colonization of lands and territories.[104] Building a road over an alvar would conceivably fall within this purpose, thus threatening the Earth's agency under Anishinabek beliefs.

In addition, it would be possible for the Crown to show that infringement of Anishinabek beliefs and practices is justified if procedures that uphold the Crown's honour are followed. Since 1982, the Crown's sovereignty has been constrained by numerous obligations to Aboriginal peoples when Aboriginal rights are at issue.[105] However, these constraints do not mean that governments are prevented from taking action that overrides Aboriginal rights if they follow proper procedures.[106] Nevertheless, these obligations can be a powerful tool for Anishinabek people to increase the scope of their rights. They place Indigenous peoples' relationship with the government in a reciprocal light, and show the Crown may have to defer to Indigenous legal orders in certain circumstances. Thus, the existence of Crown obligations could strengthen a multi-juridical analysis. In the context of interference with Anishinabek religious rights, these governmental obligations can include:

- recognition
- affirmation
- reconciliation[107]
- preventing the perpetuation of the 'historic injustice suffered by [Anishinabek] peoples at the hands of colonizers'[108]
- not imposing unjustifiably unreasonable limitations on religious rights[109]
- not imposing undue hardships on the exercise of religious rights[110]
- not unjustifiably denying the preferred means of exercising religious rights[111]
- minimally impairing Anishinabek religious rights[112]
- appropriately structuring administrative discretion in relation to interference with Anishinabek spiritual rights[113]
- giving priority to Anishinabek spiritual beliefs and practices when rights are infringed[114]
- consultation[115]
- accommodation[116]
- dispute resolution legislation to preserve Anishinabek religious rights[117]
- appropriate strategies to mitigate the impact of government action on Anishinabek rights[118]

- compensation for the loss of religious rights (which may be impossible)[119]

These rights could be a significant development for understanding Indigenous peoples' legal traditions. Their application calls upon Indigenous collective action to authoritatively deal with governments if rights are threatened. Recognition of the reality of Indigenous legal orders in such circumstances could strengthen the country's multi-juridical framework.

Unfortunately, governments may find appropriate ways to infringe upon Anishinabek religious rights and this may render nugatory these significant government obligations. Thus, while section 35(1) may contain a dim light at the end of the tunnel for protecting Anishinabek religion, such light may be ever receding if there is no possible way to build a road over an alvar without striking at the heart of Anishinabek spiritual life.

Thus, despite the potential of section 35(1) for recognizing and affirming Anishinabek spiritual beliefs and practices, it may have difficulty travelling beyond its own cultural commitments. Anishinabek rights might not be protected under section 35(1) if they are found not to be integral to the distinctive culture, if they are deemed to have been extinguished, or if the Crown is able to justify infringement through a valid legislative objective and the preservation of its honour.

F. Conclusion

This chapter has shown that Anishinabek religious beliefs and practices can be protected through law. Their protection depends on many factors, including the law's source, cultural commitments, institutional receptiveness, and interpretive competency. Protection is more likely to be accomplished when Anishinabek laws form the standards by which Anishinabek beliefs are judged. Anishinabek law exists 'on the ground' and can be relevant and functional to answer pressing needs. Anishinabek law provides guidance about how to theorize, practise, and order our association with the Earth, and can do so in a way that produces answers that are very different from those found in other sources.

Without a multi-juridical framework, Canadian constitutional law has much greater difficulty recognizing Anishinabek spirituality because of its different cultural sources, commitments, receptiveness, and institutional interpretive framework. Section 2(a) of the *Charter* might deny protection if Anishinabek people have difficulty convincing a court that their beliefs are 'religious,' that interference with them is non-trivial, that their scope is not limited by competing rights, and that their infringement is not reasonable in a free and democratic society. Section 35(1) of the *Constitution Act, 1982* might fail to protect Anishinabek spirituality if beliefs concerning the Earth are not regarded as integral to the distinctive Aboriginal culture prior to European contact, if they are thought to have been extinguished by common law, or if they are 'justifiably' infringed upon according to the Supreme Court's test regarding the Crown's valid legislative objectives and honour.

To better protect religious beliefs and practices, Anishinabek and Indigenous legal traditions should stand beside Canada's Constitution to organize and structure society's relationships. Greater space is needed within Canada's doctrinal fissures and formal legal structures to recognize and affirm this country's multi-juridical reality. Indigenous dispute resolution bodies, governments, and tribal courts could perform an important function in extending religious freedom within Aboriginal communities.[120] They could also provide greater visibility for Aboriginal law within Canadian constitutional structures and perhaps one day lead to a significant breakthrough in that forum. There are clear and contrasting alternatives for Canadians in construing their relationships to the land. Whether the Earth is thought of as living or dead, our laws have some distance to travel before they fully address the depths of our disagreements with one another. There is still much work to be accomplished before Canada's constitution can be regarded as rigorously multi-juridical.

10 The Work Ahead: Cultivating Indigenous Legal Traditions

This final chapter acknowledges that Indigenous legal traditions will not grow to their full potential unless we actively work at their further development. Traditions have the most relevance when each generation actively participates in their construction and application.[1] The root origin of the word 'tradition' is from the Latin verb *tradere*, which means 'to transmit.' Traditions must be both given *and* received to have any chance of application in a contemporary context. The relational nature of traditions means that they must constantly be re-taught and re-inscribed in people's lives through an active process of conveyance, reception, reformulation, and application. In this book, I have sought to participate in this transmission process by communicating ideas and practices that I think are crucial to properly reconstructing legal order in our territories. Because Indigenous peoples live all over Canada, and not just on reserves, I have tried to imagine how Canada's legal traditions could be reformulated to touch people's lives more fully, no matter where they live in the country. I have also sought to take this course because I believe non-Indigenous Canadians could also benefit from receiving these traditions and seeing their own laws in another light.

As noted in chapter 7, the acquisition, retention, and recreation of tradition is foremost an individual, family, and community affair. Nevertheless, more formal state-like institutions can also play a significant role in the reception of Indigenous legal traditions. Indigenous laws can be reinforced if people in positions of power actively seek to support them. Part of this support requires ensuring that state structures do not inappropriately displace the individual and family in the development of tradition. Fortunately, Canada's balanced, somewhat decentralized federal state is built on the principle of harmonized dis-aggregation. The ability to recognize difference in a synchronous framework is one of this country's great strengths, making it possible to reconcile diversity with unity. Canada's federalism creates the potential for experimentation in the 'social laboratory' that each con-stituent part of our federation encourages.[2] These principles should be extended beyond federal–provincial relations and applied to First Nations, Métis, and Inuit laws and governance.

The more explicit recognition of Indigenous legal traditions could lead to useful experimentation and innovation in solving many of Canada's pressing problems. Furthermore, the affirmation of Indige-nous legal traditions could strengthen Canadian democracy by placing decision-making authority much closer to the people within these communities.[3] Indigenous peoples would be better served in the federation if they had the recognition and resources to refine law in accordance with their perspectives. This is important because central and provincial governments are more physically and culturally remote from Indigenous peoples. They also tend to be less responsive to the Indigenous electorate than Indigenous governments would be if they could exercise greater responsibility for their own affairs.[4] A greater recognition of Indigenous legal traditions could provide some coun-terweight to the biculturalism and bi-elitism that sometimes infects Canada's polity.

The recognition of Indigenous legal traditions in the Canadian state is bound to be contested and create difficulties in law and policy.[5] The law dealing with Indigenous peoples must take account of the totality of cultural practices and expressions that belong to them.[6] As has been noted repeatedly in this text, the recognition and affirmation of Indige-nous legal traditions would develop the rule of law within Indigenous communities by allowing them to live closer to their values and prin-ciples. At the same time, it would permit them to more freely adapt the best ideas that press on their communities from other places. The recognition of Indigenous law would allow Indigenous peoples to exercise greater responsibility for their affairs, and to hold their gov-ernments and one another accountable for decisions made within their communities. It would strengthen individual rights and bolster collec-tive responsibility at the same time. If properly implemented and har-monized with Canada's other legal traditions, this approach would be consistent with their human rights as peoples, while ensuring that others' rights were not abrogated. Creating a national framework to facilitate the implementation of Indigenous legal traditions would help to ensure that non-Indigenous rights and interests are also respected. Laws are more fair and effective when rights are determined on more even playing field, with greater Indigenous influence and participation.

At their core, the ideas outlined in this book are directed at recognizing and creating practices that will find an appropriate harmonization between the interests of society as a whole and the rights, values, and laws of Indigenous peoples.[7] I have advocated formal Indigenous participation in the regulation of life and the resolution of disputes to extend recognition that the rule of law includes Indigenous peoples in Canada. It is problematic to treat questions about Indigenous knowledge as a discrete, decontextualized subject of inquiry to be used and judged by other normative systems. Indigenous law should rather be treated as an active system that contains its own values, norms, uses, standards, criteria and principles.

For this reason, intellectual methodologies that express Indigenous legal concepts must be embedded in and thereby change the very structure of Canada's law.[8] They should also be recognized and affirmed on their own terms as having force within Indigenous communities. Indigenous legal traditions must be at the root of Indigenous governments, courts, clan organizations, family relationships, and other important institutions within these societies. Indigenous vantage points should help shape the appropriate balance of rights and responsibilities when judging issues of Indigenous legal traditions. This book has suggested ways in which Indigenous norms could provide criteria for judgment of this kind. As Indigenous normative concepts are extended into regulatory and dispute resolution regimes at local, provincial, and national levels, a greater range of options will be available to tailor solutions to particular issues and disputes. This would be consistent with the *sui generis* approach to judging Indigenous rights outlined by the Supreme Court of Canada.[9] It would meet the task outlined in *R. v. Van der Peet*: 'The challenge of defining [A]boriginal rights stems from the fact that they are rights peculiar to the meeting of two vastly different legal cultures; consequently there will always be a question about which legal culture is to provide the vantage point from which rights are to be defined ... a morally and politically defensible conception of rights will incorporate both legal perspectives.'[10] Incorporating these varied legal perspectives in a morally and politically defensible manner is what I have attempted to do in this book. This task is a societal task but it can also have more personal applications.

A. Mandamin and the Law

A final account from my people, the Anishinabek, illustrates the nature of the work that lies ahead in realizing the vision expressed in this book. The following example relates how the Anishinabek came to have corn, or *mandamin*, in their midst. The report contains many legal principles, but for the purposes of this book, it will be recounted to demonstrate the kind of effort needed to encourage the growth of Indigenous legal traditions in Canada. The story of Mandamin was kept alive in our family by Verna Patronella Johnston, as is recounted in a book called *Tales of Nokomis*. Verna learned this and other stories from my great-great-grandmother Margaret McCleod. Margaret herself learned about these teachings from her great-grandmother. The story thus has deep personal meaning for our family and is a treasured memory, but I believe it also has much relevance for others as they consider the work required to grow Indigenous legal traditions. The version of the story retold in the following paragraphs also closely mirrors Basil Johnston's work in *Ojibway Heritage*. Dr Johnston is also from my reserve, the Chippewas of the Nawash First Nation, and he remains a great inspiration for those of us interested in understanding our traditions. His influences on the following ideas are direct and profound.[11] The Mandamin case unfolds in the following way:[12]

There was a young man who had been taught by his grandmother about how to live well. He had been taught about what it means to be good. This is a goal of many Anishinabek people, to gently teach our children and those around us how to be good. *Anishinabe* quite literally means 'good man.' This idea does not just apply to men. If you were describing a female from one of our communities, you would say *Anishinabequae*, which literally means 'good woman.' These were the concepts the young man learned from his grandmother. He was constantly reminded that the labels we have for ourselves remind us that extremely significant teachings are implanted in our languages. They provide direction and tell us what we should be: good. The young man learned that our collective name should always remind us that goodness lies at the heart of being a man or woman. He was taught to understand that the frequent use our own language in describing ourselves and the world around us gives great insight into how we should practise law.[13]

The young man enjoyed learning from his grandmother. Through countless unspoken actions, her life's good example was a great source of wisdom for him. She also instructed the young man through ceremony, word, and song. As he was growing, the young man's grandmother told him stories about how they were created and how they came to live around the Great Lakes. There were stories about the sky, sun, stars, moon, earth, plants, animals, and humans. He enjoyed these teachings and was always eager to hear more. They formed a backdrop against which he measured his experiences. Years came and went while he learned many lessons.

Then, one day, the young man's grandmother fell ill. She called her grandson to her bedside. She smiled and told him that it was her time to travel along the path of souls to the land of the dead. She counselled him to remember what he had learned and to look for opportunities to live by the ideas that lay behind her teachings. As she lay dying she said: 'You will meet those who will challenge all that you are. They will prey on your confidence and attempt to undermine your beliefs. They will try to destroy you by sowing doubt. Do not let their challenges destroy you. Stand up to them. You will have the strength to overcome.' He promised his grandmother he would remember her teachings. Then, with a tearful yet contented goodbye, she soon passed on.

The young man grieved for a long season. He missed his grandmother and the light she brought to the world. He would see her teachings in every rock, plant, and person he passed. However, he tried to retain the bright hope she saw in the world around her. As he constantly reminded himself of these things, in time he was able to resume his familiar rhythm of activity.

A few months later a stranger arrived in the village. He was a large, strident man, and he demanded to know if there were any good men in the community. He was loud, forceful, and boisterous in his bearing. He wanted to test the people of the village to see if they were good. He wanted to find out if they were worthy of the gifts they might receive from the Creator if they worked for them. The stranger easily attracted the attention of the people. He was eventually brought to the Elders and leading figures of the community. He told them he was searching for an adversary to test their strength and goodness. After much discussion, the Elders eventually sent him to the young man, who was down by the lake shore repairing his nets. They said they thought the young man was good.

The large man immediately headed to the water to find him.

When they met, the young man was kind to the stranger. They greeted one another and the young man left his work to show the visitor around the village. The young man introduced the stranger to his family, friends, and kin. The visitor was fed, clothed, and sheltered. The young man extended his guest every kindness and was a generous host. The visitor stayed some time with the young man, listening and learning about his views of the world. They sat up many long nights together discussing the world, and what made it beautiful.

After a few weeks together, the young man asked the stranger why he had come to the village. The stranger replied: 'I have been sent to find a good man. But in all my years, I have not yet found one among all the peoples I have visited. I understand from your reputation that you may be such a man. I hope for your sake, and for the good of your people, that you are a good man.'[14]

In response, the young man was curious but cautious. He replied, 'I do not know why you speak as you do. My grandmother told me about many people in the world who are good. I think you are mistaken if you believe there is no good. Look around. Have you not seen this place? We are far from perfect, but you can see people who live well. We know who we are. We know how to take care of ourselves and others. Can't you see their goodness?'

The stranger laughed at the young man. 'You are naïve. You think goodness is found in what you see. Where I come from, goodness is found in much deeper places. I'm Mandamin, sent by the Creator to test the worth of your people.'

The young man looked at the visitor incredulously.

The stranger continued, 'Your Elders have judged you as good. I have no reason to disbelieve them, but I must also know for myself. I must therefore test your strength to learn whether you or your people are worthy. And the most fitting way to test your inner strength is through battle. You must fight me to prove your merit. If you win, you live; if you lose, you die, and I will judge your people unworthy of the gifts I bear.'[15]

The young man was shocked. He took some time to gather his composure before replying. After a few minutes he said, 'I remember my grandmother taught me there would be people like you. I think strength is found in resisting your invitation. I do not wish to fight; your taunts do not move me.'

Mandamin spit on the ground in front of the young man. He stomped about him and bellowed in derision, 'You cannot be counted as good if you refuse my challenge. If you do not fight me, I will return and tell others that the Anishinabek are cowards. I will say that they do not fully live, and that they turn their backs on anything new and potentially threatening. I will say they are deluded, not fully living as they profess. What kind of people feel satisfied in who they are, without testing themselves against the unknown? If you do not rise to my challenge, your Elders' professions of goodness will be hollow and meaningless. If you do not meet my challenge you and your people will surely die.'

The young man took in his words and felt their sting. He was not so much concerned for his own life and reputation as he was of that of his people's. He was disturbed by Mandamin's words concerning his Elders. He was particularly alarmed by his threats to the community's existence.

The young man took a long moment before he replied. 'I will fight you, but not for my sake. I know my people are good. My grandmother told me there would be people like you. I am not scared by your threats. I have nothing to fear from those in the world outside our lands. Let's begin.'

The two circled one another, looking for a weakness in the other's stance and preparation. Some minutes passed before the first took a swing at the other. The fight was then engaged. There was a long and bitter battle that went on for four days. Neither could seem to gain the advantage over the other. They were bloodied and worn, and it seemed as though the contest would last indefinitely. Finally, the young man spotted a weakness in Mandamin's approach. He was not very quick to adapt to changes the young man made to his fighting style.

Pressing this weakness, the young man slew Mandamin.

At the stranger's death, the weight of the four-day war fell upon the young man. He was struck with sorrow and wept beside Mandamin's body. He had not wanted to fight, but felt he was left with little choice. He wanted to honour Mandamin for his strength, even though he did not fully understand why his adversary had picked this fight. The young man lay still on the ground for a long time before taking further action. When he had sorted through some of his feelings, he buried Mandamin beside his grandmother and then sought the village medicine man to relate the events of the previous days.

When the young man found the medicine man, he told him what had transpired. The old man received the account in stillness. He eventually took up his pipe, offered prayers, then shared an hour's silence with the young man. After what felt like an eternity to the young man, the older man finally spoke, 'You did well to listen to your grandmother. You must care for Mandamin's grave as you would your grandmother's.'

The young man walked back to the place Mandamin was buried. He followed the directions of the old man and brought gifts, offerings and prayers to the grave every day. He fasted and sought meaning from his experience in the battle, and from his earlier visits with the stranger. He reflected on what his grandmother taught him, and rehearsed the fight and its purpose in his mind almost every day. He could not immediately find any meaning. Yet he obeyed the medicine man's instructions for an entire year.

Next spring, as the young man was tending the grave he noticed a new plant growing from the soil. He was not familiar with it and sought the medicine man once again. The medicine man came to the site and examined the new growth but did not recognize it either. All he said was, 'Continue as you have commenced. You will soon understand.'

The days lengthened and the sun strengthened. Life-giving rains fell to the earth through the spring and into summer. Summer's humidity coursed throughout the land and the strange plant grew. It was tall, slender and green, with golden tassels crowning its height. Large husks grew at angles from its stalk. The young man once again sought the medicine man's advice. He had never observed such a plant as this. The medicine man came to the site and inspected the mysterious plant. He pulled one of its pods from the stalk and tore back its leaves. Underneath these sheaves, large yellow kernels of seed reflected the sun. The medicine man cautiously dislodged a seed and placed it on his tongue. A smile came to his face, and he offered a kernel to the young man. The sweet goodness of the plant was strong.

The medicine man told the young man that the plant was 'Mandamin – Food of Wonder.' 'Your actions will change the course of our history. They will bring great joy and success. Remember how you achieved them and teach this to your children. It will feed us in many ways. You have not killed Mandamin; you have given him life in a new form. Generations of our people will live because you were not afraid to meet a challenge. We must never think we are immune from struggle and change. Your work, care and thought will benefit us all. Mandamin has given life to the Anishinabek. Our whole nation will be rewarded for your obedience and goodness. Your deeds have demonstrated our worth. We will live.'

Mandamin's message has implications for the development of Indigenous law. Just like the young man, Indigenous peoples face many challenges from outside their communities. They have many choices about how they will deal with the challenge of developing their laws. There must be adaptation to change, but this must occur within a context that respects our grandparents' good teachings. Challenges regarding change must be met with goodness at the centre point of judgment. The young man was fortunate to have the opportunity to listen and ponder upon his grandmother's teachings before she died. Some Indigenous people have not had this opportunity, but they should not despair. As this book has demonstrated there are people willing to teach these ideas if they are sought out.

Mandamin's message also teaches that Indigenous peoples have successfully encountered change in the past and this has helped sustain them. We have experience in receiving new people and ideas in our lives, and these experiences of receiving them have been a part of our traditions for a long time. There was a time when corn was not among the Anishinabek. It was introduced from another place. The struggle the young man had to go through in cultivating the corn indicates that change is not always easy. The development of Indigenous law in a contemporary context requires similar struggle. There are risks involved. Survival is sometimes on the line. Indigenous peoples cannot approach legal development without realizing that sometimes they will fail. There will be times they do not succeed in making their values the core of judgment in their communities and in having these norms also impact on wider Canadian society. Mandamin's message stands as an example, however, about what is necessary to achieve success. Not only did the young man have to spend days defeating his adversary; when Mandamin died it took over a year to see corn grow from the ground. The young man was not sure any benefit would flow to himself or community from his tending of the graves; he was merely following the medicine man's advice and honouring his grandmother and Mandamin. So it is with the continued development of Indigenous legal traditions. There are kernels of goodness with the common law and civil law traditions. It we want to receive them in a way which will nourish our future the way will not always be easy. It may take some long periods of time to see results.

There is a further principle in this chronicle that may have some troubling connotations. The positive consequences of the young man's action flowed from a very negative event: Mandamin's death. How can death in violent circumstances give rise to such goodness? Some legal practices must die in order for them to be transformed into a more nourishing way of living – the death of threatening traditions must take place in all legal systems. Another approach to this issue would be to focus on the idea that the young man acted in self-defence because Mandamin threatened the community's existence. While this may be true, one should be careful not to solely focus on death-related aspects of this story to the exclusion of others, and thereby judge Indigenous peoples in a less than favourable light. Of course, there are many examples of violence in Indigenous peoples' lives, as there are in the lives of any other group of people. This must be fully acknowledged and appropriate actions must be taken to address these problems. However, in making this observation, other messages in Mandamin's story should not be lost. For example, the case teaches a lot about the role of struggle in bringing forth benefits for yourself and others. While other chronicles will teach that competition must be tempered by other values, the fact remains that struggle is important to Indigenous law's development. The young man defeated Mandamin through a contest. If this illustration is examined figuratively, rather than literally, it will be seen that Anishinabek people knew the importance of striving against others to secure favourable results. Indigenous peoples must not shy away from competitive behaviour in their quest to develop their laws, particularly when many would love to defeat them in their quest to bring these traditions to contemporary application. Of course, while we are struggling we must also remember other teachings and ensure that respect is maintained; extreme, hyper-competitive behaviour in all situations would contravene wider cultural norms. Nevertheless, to succeed in bringing about positive change, Indigenous peoples will find themselves battling forces that would like to defeat Indigenous law.

As noted, this story was kept alive in our family by Verna Patronella Johnston, my great-great aunt.[16] You can also find the story in Basil Johnston's book *Ojibway Heritage*.[17] Both writers are Elders and citizens of Cape Croker Indian Reserve on Georgian Bay, where I have my band membership. They tell the story in a slightly differently manner than I do. This demonstrates that there are often varied approaches to legal meaning within the law of a single tradition. Some of these differences are shaped by gender, perspective, life experience, and age. We must not expect Indigenous jurists to speak with unanimity in their articulation of the law, just as we do not expect this of Parliaments, judges, and legal scholars. The common law tradition allows for dissenting and concurring opinions. Canada's democratic processes allow for shifting majorities and minorities in drafting legal principles. Likewise, Indigenous peoples have variation within their traditions and can incorporate differences of opinion and dissent within their law. In explaining the differences between the accounts of Basil and Aunt Verna, the following variations are present. First, the version of the story told by Verna has the battle between Mandamin and the young man occur during a Vision Quest (dream), rather than in real time. Second, Verna's version has the young Anishinabek man leaving the plant as it matures, rather than cultivating it, as was the case in Basil's account.

The first lesson that might be drawn from these different versions is that Verna's version places greater emphasis on the act of imagination and vision in creating something new. The creation of better legal relationships is not only a matter of physical struggle it is also a question of will. As a result, in Verna's version, competition not only takes place with other beings but also involves inner struggle with oneself: the struggle is in the dream, rather than through a physical contest. I believe Verna's message is an important complement to the ideas found in Basil's account. Not only must Aboriginal peoples take physical steps to overcome barriers to legal development, we must prepare ourselves emotionally and spiritually to accomplish our objectives. This takes imagination and creativity, as well as hard physical work.

We can also find significant lessons in the second difference between the stories, concerning the attention paid to the plant as it grows. In Basil's chronicle, the plant was closely tended as it matured, which represents the importance of active monitoring and control over the legal development process. It is important that Indigenous peoples do all they can to assert a measure of control over their legal futures. Verna's story presents another consideration to be taken into account when pondering control. In Verna's version, the counsel to leave the plant as it ripens represents the real role of other factors in law's development. While Indigenous peoples can do much to influence the law's direction and pace of development, these matters are often beyond a community's control. Once the forces of creation and change are in motion, some matters cannot be contained. The lesson we can take from this as it relates to the law's development is that while Indigenous peoples can do much to create better futures, it must also be acknowledged that development always contains a degree of risk. Indigenous communities cannot control all aspects of the law's development and this caution must be a part of any message suggesting paths forward. Acknowledging this fact does not mean that Indigenous peoples should forsake their quest for peace and order in their own communities and in their relationships with others. Rather, it means they must also recognize that the paths towards a better future will not always be ones they can completely create on their own.

B. Conclusion

Indigenous peoples face many challenges in developing their legal traditions in a contemporary context. This book has discussed the opportunities that must be embraced, and the trials that must be faced, to further bring our laws to life. Like the young man's experience with Mandamin, Indigenous peoples and others have a fight on their hands to bring multi-juridicalism to its fullest fruition. They will have to work hard and exercise care and patience in cultivating the grounds for broader acceptance. Part of this process will involve rooting traditions in contemporary community values that are consistent with our country's most revered legal teachings.

If the broader legal system does not acknowledge Indigenous laws, the rule of law will be more severely constrained in the process. Unfortunately, the burden will be weightier for Indigenous peoples if this occurs. The formal space for their operation will be smaller than that under common law and civil law traditions if there is no official recognition. In working to expand our traditions it must be remembered that Canadian law derives its authority from appeals to precedent, consensus, reason, and consistency. It should also be remembered that Canadian law also derives its authority from force.[18] Its application can be hard to wrest from the biases of wealth, status, social convention, and established Western traditions. If Indigenous peoples and others choose to take advantage of opportunities noted in this book, these cautions should be amplified and heeded. While busy working for recognition and affirmation of Indigenous laws within Canada, supporters must also remember that such victories can be hollow if Indigenous peoples' own traditional authorities are permanently subjugated in the process. This warning is not to counsel against working with Canadian law in every case but is meant to simultaneously keep our attention on its collateral consequences. We must continue to speak many languages of law, as I have tried to illustrate in a companion book, written simultaneously with this work.[19] Canadian law can sometimes be used with great effect, but only if Indigenous cultural values, traditions and authorities are simultaneously part of this process. Canadian law can also be a problem. If Indigenous peoples cannot practise their traditions in light of the conceptions developed in this book, they will be rightly rejected.

Fortunately, we have a choice about how we will respond to our multi-juridical heritage. We can choose to recognize, affirm, and apply Indigenous legal traditions alongside the common law and civil law, or we can choose to deny their historic reality and contemporary force. The consequences of this choice will mark our country as progressive and open to legal guidance from the best of our traditions, or as oppressively fundamentalist and frozen in our orientation to law. There should be no doubt about my choice between these alternatives. I choose openness and freedom. Legal cultures are fluid. Law is in the process of continual transformation, and Indigenous peoples must participate in its changes. In the midst of the constructively critical nature of this book, I hope that readers of this work will see the complimentary and complementary nature of my arguments. Our legal traditions have great wisdom, durability, and flexibility in their ability to generate stability and order across this land. Multi-juridicalism must receive the support it needs to nourish these strengths. Indeed, our Constitution depends upon it.

Reproduction

An otter scrambles along a rock-strewn shore. One otter and the law. Black flies swarm in clouds above Nigig's head. Their incessant energy infuses the morning air, driving him crazy. Nigig scuttles over obstacles along his path, climbing over boulders and sliding around stones. The fish in his mouth writhes in the last throes of death.

It's been a hard year as an otter. Nigig's companions have all been slain – tangled in nets, hunted by predators, and poisoned by men. Being an otter is not as peaceful as Nanabush imagined. Life is marked by constant conflict, no matter the form you assume. Nigig misses his companions; their absence is a persistent reminder of his own shifting, unstable existence.

He continues picking his way along the beach, negotiating each slope, incline, and barrier with nimble feet. Trouble is not just before him, along the broken surface; he also senses danger above. It is everywhere. The fish and flies attract unwanted attention, stealing his last shred of serenity. A band of crows swirl just out of reach, occasionally diving towards him, hoping to snatch his meal.

Nigig pauses on a spit of sand, and puts his catch on the earth. The crows move closer but Nigig strategically places himself between the birds and his quarry. He lunges forward and rips the belly from the fish before throwing it down his throat. His teeth and claws tear at its flesh as Nigig quickly devours his prey. Bones, blood, and sinew mingle with the shore, and in his mouth, as he crushes the life from the small silver herring. In so doing, Nigig replenishes his own life. Death demands this exchange; nourishment ever arises from decay.

Nigig remembers this teaching as he looks across the bay.

The thought works a change deep within him. Thinking of his old self, Nigig stretches out, paws extended, transforming himself back to Nanabush.

Looking around, he yawns.

He sees a limestone escarpment rising out of the bay, across the sound in front on him. It looks permanent, ever constant, until you see it through the corridor of time. Nanabush remembers it was once a complex living being, a coral reef. Thousands of tiny creatures made it their home as they built on each other's death. This was during the time that the earth was covered in water, when he had to take refuge on the turtle's back. The divers plumbed the depths for him then, retrieving small particles of soil, so he could grow this present world. Muskrat died bringing mud to the surface. That was many years ago, but life had always demanded death, even at that time. The world continually draws sustenance from decay. Like the escarpment, life's appearance of permanence is deceiving.

Now the escarpment's white stone face basks in the rising sun and reflects on the shimmering waves. Its ancient death still feeds life. Cedar, birch, and poplar grow from the old rocks. They host a thousand species under their expansive green canopies. Sea life has turned to stone, and eventually turned into trees, birds, and insects. Animals feed on each, and humans follow this same pattern. Transformation is the law of life.

Seeing all this, and making connections, Nanabush remembered he couldn't escape the law, no matter how hard he tried or what form he took. Law was just like him   a peaceful, vicious being. It was all around him, continually in motion, never stable, always changing. It needed conflict and it needed resolution, so new conflict could arise and devour resolution. There was no way to escape its grasp, though many tried. Transformation is the life of law.

Notes

1 Living Legal Traditions

1 Aharon Barak, 'Judicial Philosophy and Judicial Activism' (1992) 17 *Tel Aviv University Law Review* 483.
2 For a contrary view, suggesting we should not question a legal system's roots, see Immanuel Kant, *The Metaphysics of Morals*, trans. Mary J. Gregor (Cambridge: Cambridge University Press, 1991), 129–30:

> A people should not inquire with any practical aim in view, into the origin of the supreme authority to which it is subject, that is, a subject ought not to rationalize for the sake of action about the origin of this authority, as a right can still be called into question with regard to the obedience he owes it. For, since a people must be regarded as already united under a general legislative will in order to judge with rightful force about the supreme authority, it cannot and may not judge otherwise that as the present head of state wills it to. Whether the state began with an actual contract of submission as a fact, or whether power came first and law arrived only afterward, or even whether they should have followed this order: For a people already subject to civil law these rationalizations are altogether pointless and moreover, threaten a state with danger.

Kant's approach does not align with our legal system's demand for rationality and the provision of reasons in its operation. As the Supreme Court of Canada wrote in the *Quebec Secession Reference*, [1998] 2 S.C.R. 217 at para. 68: 'a functioning democracy requires a continuous process of discussion.'

3 The methodology of this book does not search for an abstract and universal idea of justice, but seeks for greater understanding about its meaning
   and development by questioning what may appear to be self-evident to
   lawyers, judges, law students, journalists, chiefs, and legislators in regard
   to the sources and structures of Canada's laws. In characterizing my
   approach in this work I have benefited greatly from my colleague James
   Tully's ideas. Drawing on the writings of Michel Foucault, Professor
   Tully partially describes what I feel I am trying to do, which is to develop
   an historical analysis of the limits that are imposed on us [in Canadian
   law] while at the same time experiment with the possibility of going
   beyond them. See James Tully, *Public Philosophy in a New Key*, vol. 1,
   Democracy and Civic Freedom (Cambridge: Cambridge University Press,
   2008), 71–131. As such, I do not view myself as trying to dissolve relations of power 'in the Utopia of a perfectly transparent communication';
   rather, I hope to suggest an alternative that would 'give oneself the rules
   of, the techniques of management, and also the ethics, the *ethos*, that
   practice of the self, which would allow these games of power [in relation
   to Indigenous peoples in Canada] to be played with a minimum of domination,' quoting Michel Foucault, *The Final Foucault*, ed. James Bernauer
   and David Rasmussen (Cambridge, MA: MIT Press, 1988), 18, cited in
   James Tully, *Public Philosophy in a New Key*, vol. 1, *Democracy and Civic
   Freedom* (Cambridge: Cambridge University Press, 2008), 121. I hope this
   book enables us 'to see our island of disputation and negotiation as it is,
   in the rough and agonistic sea of relations of power, rather than from the
   point of view of a utopia free of power. With this toolkit in hand we will
   be in a position not only to think differently but to begin the cautious
   experiments in acting differently, in modifying our rules of interpretation
   and practices of self-formation in such a way that the specific game in
   question can now be played with a "minimum of domination." In so
   doing, we may overlook something universal in what we are thinking
   and doing, and we will always find that we have to begin again. This is
   the risk ... we take in exchange for this "patient labor" on actual existing
   limits in the present by means of an approach that gives form to our
   "impatience for liberty."' Ibid., 130–1.
4 H.W. Arthurs, *Without the Law: Administrative Justice and Legal Pluralism in
   Nineteenth-Century England* (Toronto: University of Toronto Press, 1985);
   Ronald Dworkin, *A Matter of Principle* (Cambridge, MA: Harvard University Press, 1985); Lon Fuller, *The Morality of Law* (New Haven, CT: Yale
   University Press, 1968); Lon Fuller, *The Anatomy of Law* (New York:
   Praeger, 1968); H.L.A. Hart, *The Concept of Law*, 2nd ed. (Oxford: Claren-

don, 1994); L. Nader and H. Todd, *The Disputing Process: Law in Ten Societies* (New York: Columbia University Press, 1978); G. Postema, *Bentham and the Common Law Tradition* (Oxford: Clarendon, 1983); F. Shaer, *Playing By the Rules: A Philosophical Examination of Rule Based Decision-Making in Life and Law* (Oxford: Clarendon Press, 1991); J. Shklar, *Legalism: Law, Morals and Political Trials* (Cambridge: Cambridge University Press, 1983); Michael Walzer, *Spheres of Justice* (New York: Basic Books, 1983); A. Watson, *The Making of the Civil Law* (Cambridge: Cambridge University Press, 1981); J.B. White, *Acts of Hope: Creating Authority in Literature, Law and Politics* (Chicago: University of Chicago Press, 1994). In my experience, Indigenous laws are those procedures and substantive values, principles, practices, and teachings that reflect, create, respect, enhance, and protect the world and our relationships within it.

5 Roderick Alexander Macdonald, *Lessons of Everyday Law* (Montreal: McGill-Queen's Press for the Law Commission of Canada and the School of Policy Studies, Queen's University, 2002).

6 Bronislaw Manilowski, 'Introduction' to H.L. Hogbin, *Law and Order in Polynesia* (New York: Harcourt, 1934), xiii; Lon Fuller, 'Human Interaction and the Law' (1969) 14 *American Journal of Jurisprudence* 1.

7 Law is one way in which some degree of beneficial predictability can be encouraged through principles, practices, and patterns of regulation and dispute resolution; Gerold Postema, 'Implicit Law' (1994) 13 *Law and Philosophy* 361. See Jeremy Webber, 'The Grammar of Customary Law' [unpublished]. On file with the author.

8 H. Patrick Glenn, *Legal Traditions of the World: Sustainable Diversity in Law* (Oxford: Oxford University Press, 2004); Martin Krygier, 'Law as Tradition' (1986) 5 *Law and Philosophy* 237.

9 J.H. Merryman, *The Civil Law Tradition: An Introduction to the Legal Systems of Western Europe and Latin America*, 2nd ed. (Stanford, CA: Stanford University Press, 1985), 1.

10 M.B. Hooker, *Legal Pluralism* (Oxford: Clarendon Press, 1975).

11 A.W.B. Simpson, *Leading Cases in the Common Law* (Oxford: Oxford University Press, 1996), 11.

12 A.W.B. Simpson, 'Legal Systems and Legal Traditions,' in *Invitation to Law* (London: Blackwell, 1988), chap. 3. The legal tradition relates the legal system to the culture of which it is a partial expression. It puts the legal system into cultural perspective. Systems of legal thought are not necessarily coterminous with nation-state boundaries and can be divided into groups or families.

13 Andre-Jean Arnaud, 'Legal Pluralism and the Building of Europe,'

retrieved 28 August 2009 from www.reds.msh-paris.fr/communications
/texts/arnaud2.htm. For a discussion of 'tribalism' and legal pluralism,
see Leon Shaskolsky, *The Future of Tradition: Customary Law, Common Law
and Legal Pluralism* (New York: Routledge, 2000). For a critique of legal
pluralism, see Brian Tamanhana, 'The Folly of the Social Science Concept
of Legal Pluralism' (1993) *Journal of Law and Society* 192.

14 See Robert Cover, 'Nomos and Narrative' (1983) 97 *Harvard Law Review* 4
at 9:

> A legal tradition ... includes not only a *corpus juris*, but also a language
> and a mythos – narratives in which the *corpus juris* is located by those
> whose wills act upon it. These myths establish the paradigms for
> behavior. They build relations between the normative and material
> universe, between constraints of reality and the demands of an ethic.
> These myths establish a repertoire of moves – a lexicon of normative
> action – that may be combined into meaningful patterns culled from
> meaningful patterns of the past.

15 See Katherine T. Bartlett, 'Tradition, Change and the Idea of Progress in
Feminist Legal Thought' (1995) *Wisconsin Law Review* 303, 331.

16 See also Jaroslav Pelikan, *The Vindication of Tradition* (New Haven, CT:
Yale University Press, 1984), 54.

17 Martin Krygier, 'Law as Tradition' (1986) 5 *Law and Philosophy* 237.

18 Andrew Halpin, 'Glenn's Legal Traditions of the World: Some Broader
Philosophical Implications' (2006) 1 *Journal of Comparative Law* 116.

19 Ibid., 118, drawing on the work of Stanley Fish, *Doing What Comes Naturally: Change, Rhetoric and the Practice of Theory in Literary and Legal Studies*
(Oxford: Clarendon Press, 1989).

20 As Michel Foucault has written: 'The critical ontology of ourselves must
be considered not, certainly, as a theory or a doctrine; rather it must be
conceived as an attitude, an ethos, a philosophical life in which the critique of what we are is at one and the same time the historical analysis of
the limits imposed on us and an experiment with the possibility of going
beyond them.' In Michel Foucault, 'What Is Enlightenment?' in *The Politics of Truth*, ed. Sylvere Lotringer and Lysa Hochroth (New York: Semio-
text(e), 1997), 133.

21 For a discussion of how law can be studied from the outside of inside,
see Jeremy Webber, 'The Past and Foreign Countries' (2006) 10 *Legal
History* 1, 2.

22 For an excellent summary of readings and approaches in the field of law
and society, see John Monahan and Laurens Walker, *Social Science in Law:*

Cases and Materials, 5th ed. (Westbury, NY: Foundation Press, 2002). There are also many excellent journals that examine law from social science perspectives, see *Law and Society Review, Canadian Journal of Law and Society, Law and Human Behavior, Political and Legal Anthropology Review, Law and History Review, Journal of Law and Economics, Canadian Journal of Criminology and Criminal Justice, Canadian Journal of Women and the Law,* and *Social and Legal Studies.* For a critique, see Brian Z. Tamanaha, 'The Folly of the "Social Scientific" Concept of Legal Pluralism' (1993) 20 *Journal of Law and Society* 192.

23 The various studies on Aboriginal peoples in the criminal justice system have generously drawn on social science insights; see *Royal Commission on the Donald Marshall Jr. Prosecution* (Halifax: Government of Nova Scotia, 1989); *Report of the Osnaburgh/Windigo Tribal Council Review Committee,* Prepared for the Attorney General (Ontario) and Ontario Minister Responsible for Native Affairs and the Solicitor General (Ontario, 1990); Law Reform Commission of Canada, *Aboriginal Peoples and Criminal Justice: Equality, Respect and the Search for Justice,* Report No. 34 (Ottawa: Law Reform Commission of Canada, 1991); Aboriginal Justice Inquiry, *Report of the Aboriginal Justice Inquiry of Manitoba,* vol. 1, *The Justice System and Aboriginal People* (Winnipeg: Province of Manitoba, 1991); *Justice on Trial: Report of the Task Force on the Criminal Justice System and Its Impact on the Indian and Metis People of Alberta* (Edmonton: Attorney General and Solicitor General, 1991); Judge Patricia Linn and Representatives of FSIN, Saskatchewan and Canada, *Report of the Saskatchewan Indian Justice Review Committee* (Regina: Saskatchewan Justice, 1992); Judge Anthony Sarich, *Report on the Cariboo-Chilcotin Justice Inquiry* (Victoria: Attorney General of British Columbia, 1993); *Bridging the Cultural Divide: Report on Aboriginal People and Criminal Justice in Canada* (Ottawa: Supply and Services, 1996); Commission on First Nations and Metis Peoples and Justice Reform, *Final Report,* vol. 1, *Legacy of Hope, and Agenda for Change* (Saskatoon: Saskatchewan Justice, December 2003); Larry Chartrand and Celeste McKay, *A Review of Research on Criminal Victimization and First Nations, Métis and Inuit Peoples, 1990 to 2001* (Ottawa: Department of Justice, 2006).

24 For a representative sample of this literature in other countries, see Sally Falk Moore, *Law As Process: An Anthropological Approach* (New York: Routledge, 1978); Laura Nader, *Harmony Ideology: Justice and Control in a Zapotec Mountain Village* (Stanford, CA: Stanford University Press, 1990); Roy Rappaport, *Pigs for Ancestors: Ritual in the Ecology of a New Guinea People* (New Haven, CT: Yale, 1968).

25 For a discussion of issues Indigenous peoples might have towards research about their traditions, see Linda Tuhiwai Smith, *Decolonizing Methodologies: Research and Indigenous Peoples* (London: Zed Books, 1999).

26 William Twining, 'Law and Anthropology: A Case in Inter-Disciplinary Collaboration' (1972–3) 7 *Law and Society Review* 561. For a general discussion of how communities can function as interpretive bodies, see Clifford Geertz, *Local Knowledge: Further Essays in Interpretive Anthropology* (New York: Basic Books, 1983).

27 Law Commission of Canada, ed., *Indigenous Legal Traditions in Canada* (Vancouver: UBC Press, 2008). For discussions about Indigenous legal traditions, see selected articles in the *Indigenous Law Journal*, edited by faculty and students at the University of Toronto. In New Zealand a similar phenomenon is occurring; see the work of the Te Matahauariki Research Institute and the leading law reform papers, available at http://lianz.waikato.ac.nz/publications-internal.htm, retrieved 15 October 2008.

28 John Borrows, *Recovering Canada: The Resurgence of Indigenous Law* (Toronto: University of Toronto Press, 2002); John Borrows (Kegedonce), *Drawing Out Law* (Toronto: University of Toronto Press, 2010).

29 This book flows from research undertaken while I was a Virtual Scholar in Residence for the Law Commission of Canada in 2005–6. Research was funded by the Social Sciences and Humanities Research Council.

30 Law Commission of Canada, *Indigenous Legal Traditions* (Vancouver: UBC Press, 2007).

31 James Tully, *Public Philosophy in a New Key*, vol. 1, *Democracy and Civic Freedom* (Cambridge: Cambridge University Press, 2008), 185–219.

32 *Quebec Secession Reference*, [1998] 2 S.C.R. 217 at para. 68.

33 H. Patrick Glenn, 'Are Legal Traditions Incommensurable?' (2001) 49 *American Journal of Comparative Law* 133.

34 The need to recognize the contemporarily entangled nature of Indigenous relationships is discussed in James Clifford, 'Dialogue: Indigenous Articulations' (2001) 13:2 *Contemporary Pacific* 467 at 473.

35 The potential of Indigenous laws to appropriately conflict in Canada was one of the themes of my previous book, John Borrows, *Recovering Canada: The Resurgence of Indigenous Law* (Toronto: University of Toronto Press, 2002).

36 'Conflict is an integral and necessary aspect of human societies. The challenge is not to prevent conflict or even to resolve it, but rather, to effectively manage it so that it does not paralyze people.' Val Napoleon, 'Ayook, Gitskan Legal Order, Law and Legal Theory' (PhD diss., University of Victoria, 2009), iii.

37   My own people, the Anishinabek, possess many accounts of bitter conflicts in the past within our societies and in our relations with others. See
William Warren, *History of the Ojibway People* (St Paul: Minnesota Historical Society, 1984). Furthermore, any time spent in an Anishinabek community today would quickly reveal that conflict continues to be a part of
our lives.

38   Sidney Harring, *White Man's Law: Native People in Nineteenth Century
Canadian Jurisprudence* (Toronto: University of Toronto Press, 1998), 8–10.

39   *R. v. Van der Peet*, [1996] 2 S.C.R. 507 at para. 40.

40   Ibid.

41   Ibid. at para. 42.

42   *R. v. Mitchell*, [2001] 1 S.C.R. 911 at para. 8.

43   For further discussion of this idea in my work, see John Borrows, 'Creat-
ing an Indigenous Legal Community: 5th Annual John Tait Memorial
Lecture' (2005) 50 *McGill Law Journal* 3; 'Ground Rules: Indigenous
Treaties in Canada and New Zealand' (2006) 22 *New Zealand Universities
Law Journal* 188.

44   John Borrows, 'Tracking Trajectories: Aboriginal Governance as an Aboriginal Right' (2005) 38 *UBC Law Review* 285, 300–7.

45   *Constitution Act, 1982*, Schedule B to the *Canada Act, 1982*, (U.K.) 1982,
c. 11.

46   Editorial, 'One Tier Justice,' *National Post*, 23 November 2004, A19.

47   John Austin, *The Province of Jurisprudence Determined*, vol. 1, 2nd ed., ed.
W. Rumble (1832; reprint, Cambridge: Cambridge University Press, 1995),
176. Thanks go to Professor Sakej Henderson for bringing these references to my attention in his 'Indigenous Jurisprudence and Aboriginal
Courts' (unpublished).

48   John Finnis, 'On the Incoherence of Legal Positivism' (2000) 75 *Notre
Dame Law* 1597.

49   Lon Fuller, 'Positivism and Fidelity to Law' (1958) 71 *Harvard Law Review*
630–72; E. Erlich, *Fundamentals Principles of the Sociology of Law* (Cambridge, MA: Harvard University Press, 1936), 24; John Griffiths, 'What Is
Legal Pluralism?' (1986) 24 *Journal of Legal Pluralism* 1.

50   *Milirrpum v. Nabalco Pty Ltd* (1971) 17 FLR 141 at 267. For a discussion of
the marginalization of custom, see Patrick H. Glenn, 'The Capture,
Reconstruction and Marginalization of "Custom"' (1997) 45 *American
Journal of Comparative Law* at 613.

51   See Adamson Hoebel, *The Law of Primitive Man* (Cambridge, MA:
Harvard University Press, 1967), 28: '[a] social norm is legal if its neglect
or infraction is regularly met, in threat or in fact, by the application of
physical force by an individual or group possessing the socially recog-

nized privilege of so acting.' For further descriptions of customary law, as going beyond force to normative agreement, see James B. Murphy and Amanda Perreau-Suassine, eds., *The Nature of Customary Law* (New York: Cambridge University Press, 2007).

52 John Austin, *The Province of Jurisprudence Determined*, vol. 2, 2nd ed., ed. W. Rumble (1832; reprint, Cambridge: Cambridge University Press, 1995), 178.

53 Ibid., 178; John Austin, *Lectures on Jurisprudence*, vol. 2 (London: John Murray, 1885), 568.

54 Thus, at law school we were basically told that the regularized practices that people followed to maintain order in their lives were first subject to the constitution, then to parliamentary or legislative sovereignty, then to judicial interpretation of these sources measured through the common law, next to learned commentaries by professors (dead ones being more authoritative than those who were living), and finally to custom.

55 Gerald Gall, *The Canadian Legal System* (Scarborough: Thomson, 2004), 35–53; George Alexandrowicz et al., eds., *Dimension of Canadian Law: Canadian and International Law in the Twenty-first Century* (Toronto: Emond Montgomery, 2004), 48; Peter Hogg, *Constitutional Law of Canada* (Scarborough: Thomson, 2005), 1–28.

56 Of course, Canada was not uninhabited and there were competing legal systems when the country was settled by Europeans. Despite the existence of Indigenous laws, the leading article entitled 'Reception of English Law,' written by J.E. Cote, states that the 'aborigines of the New World were always disregarded for these purposes also, no matter how numerous they might be,' (1977) 25 *Alberta Law Review* 29 at 38.

57 Ibid., 38.

58 For an excellent examination of how Aboriginal peoples are labelled as inferior in the present context, see Wayne Warry, *Ending Denial: Understanding Aboriginal Issues* (Toronto: University of Toronto Press, 2008).

59 The date of 'reception' depends upon how and when a colony was acquired.

60 Peter Hogg, *Constitutional Law of Canada* (Scarborough: Thomson, 2005), 29.

61 Ibid., 32.

62 Margaret McCallum, 'Problems in Determining the Date of Reception in Prince Edward Island' (2006) 55 *U.N.B.L.J.* 3.

63 Peter Hogg, *Constitutional Law of Canada* (Scarborough: Thomson, 2005), 29.

64 Jim Tully reformulates an idea of reception of laws as being based on

'two confederations.' He says: 'The "first" confederation (or federation) is the treaty confederation of the First Nations with the Crown and later with the federal and, to some extent, provincial governments. The second confederation (or federation) is the constitutional federation of the provinces and federal government. The basis of the first confederation is the sets of relations that the First Nations, Inuit and Metis have established with the Crown, federal governments and provincial governments over the centuries by mutual agreement.' See James Tully, *Public Philosophy in a New Key*, vol. 1, *Democracy and Civic Freedom* (Cambridge: Cambridge University Press, 2008), 236–7.

65 John Borrows, 'A Genealogy of Law: Inherent Sovereignty and First Nations Self-Government' (1992) 30 *Osgoode Hall Law Journal* 2 at 291–354.

66 Brian Slattery, 'Aboriginal Sovereignty and Imperial Claims' (1991) 29 *Osgoode Hall Law Journal* 1.

67 Peter Hogg, *Constitutional Law of Canada* (Scarborough: Thomson, 2005), 30.

68 *R. v. Van der Peet*, [1996] 2 S.C.R. 507 at para. 263.

69 Peter Hogg, *Constitutional Law of Canada* (Scarborough: Thomson, 2005), 30.

70 For further development of this point, see John Borrows, *Recovering Canada: The Resurgence of Indigenous Law* (Toronto: University of Toronto Press, 2002), 115.

71 *Amodu Tijani v. Secretary, Southern Nigeria*, [1921] 2 A.C. 399 at 402–4 (JCPC).

72 Ibid.

73 Peter Sack has written: 'It is my perception of the relations between law, culture and language was based on three assumptions: firstly, that all human societies had some form of law; secondly, that all forms of law were cultural constructs; and, thirdly, that all human cultures used language as their central medium of construction. Taken together, these three assumptions seemed to rule out the possibility of a culturally neutral language of law, because law appeared to be not only culture-specific but also firmly tied to a particular "neutral" language in which it expressed itself.' Peter Sack, 'Law, Language, Culture: Verbal Acrobatics and Social Technology' (1998) 41 *Legal Pluralism & Unofficial Law* 15, 15, cited in Val Napoleon, 'Ayook, Gitskan Legal Order, Law and Legal Theory' (PhD diss., University of Victoria, 2009), 28.

74 Lon Fuller, 'The Law's Precarious Hold on Life (1968–1969)' 3 *Georgia Law Review* 530. For further critiques of legal positivism's view of customary

law, see Henry Sumner Maine, *Ancient Law* (London: Dent, 1864), 6; Lon
Fuller, 'Human Interaction and the Law' (1969) 14 *American Journal of
Jurisprudence* 1; K.N. Llewellyn and E.A. Hoebel, 'The Cheyenne Way:
Conflict and Case Law,' in *Primitive Jurisprudence* (Norman: University of
Oklahoma Press, 1941); E. Adamson Hoebel, *The Law of Primitive Man*
(New York: Atheneum, 1974); Karl N. Llewellyn and E. Adamson Hoebel,
The Cheyenne Way: Conflict and Case Law in Primitive Jurisprudence
(Norman: University of Oklahoma Press, 1941); Max Gluckman, *Politics,
Law and Ritual in Primitive Society* (Chicago: Aldine Publishing, 1965);
Rennard Strickland, *Fire and the Spirits: Cherokee Law from Clan to Court*
(Norman: University of Oklahoma Press, 1982); Antonio Mills, *Eagle
Down is Our Law: Witsuwit'en Law, Feasts and Land Claims* (Vancouver:
UBC Press, 1994).

75 *Calder v. A.G.B.C.*, [1973] S.C.R. 313 at 346–7.

76 This reasoning was derived from doctrines of the United States Supreme
Court in *Mitchell v. United States,* 34 U.S. (9 Pet.) 711 (1835); *Worchester v.
Georgia*, 31 U.S. (6 Pet.) 515 (1832); *Cherokee Nation v. Georgia*, 31 U.S. (5
Pet.) 1 (1831); *Johnson & Graham's Lessee v. M'Intosh*, 21 U.S. (8 Wheat) 543
(1823); *Fletcher v. Peck*, 10 U.S. (6 Cranch) 87 (1910). For an analysis of the
transformation of law from recognizing to undermining Aboriginal prop-
erty rights through the doctrine of discovery, see Stuart Banner, *How The
Indians Lost Their Land: Law and Power on the Frontier* (Cambridge, MA:
Harvard University Press, 2005). My arguments in the next nine para-
graphs have previously appeared in John Borrows, 'Ground Rules:
Indigenous Treaties in Canada and New Zealand' (2006) 22 *New Zealand
Universities Law Journal* 188; John Borrows 'Creating an Indigenous Legal
Community: 5th Annual John Tait Memorial Lecture' (2005) 50 *McGill
Law Journal* 3; 'Tracking Trajectories: Aboriginal Governance as an Abo-
riginal Right' (2005) 38 *UBC Law Review* 285.

77 *R. v. Guerin*, [1984] 2 S.C.R. 335 at 378: 'The principle of discovery which
justified these claims gave the ultimate title in the land in a particular
area to the nation which had discovered and claimed it. In that respect at
least the Indians' rights in the land were obviously diminished; but their
rights of occupancy and possession remained unaffected.'

78 *R. v. Sparrow*, [1990] 1 S.C.R. 1075 at 1103.

79 John Borrows, 'Constitutional Law from a First Nations Perspective: Self-
Government and the Royal Proclamation' (1994) 28 *University of British
Columbia Law Review* 1–48.

80 For strong critiques of the doctrine of discovery, see R.A. Williams Jr., *The
American Indian in Western Legal Thought: The Discourses of Conquest* (New

York: Oxford University Press, 1990); Peter Fitzpatrick, '"No Higher Duty": *Mabo* and the Failure of Legal Foundation,' (2002) 13 *Law and Critique* 233; B. Clark, *Native Liberty-Crown Sovereignty* (Montreal: McGill-Queen's University Press, 1990); A.C. Hamilton and C.M. Sinclair, eds., *Report of the Aboriginal Justice Inquiry of Manitoba* (Winnipeg: Queen's Printer, 1991), 130–42.

81 David E. Wilkins and K. Tsianina Lomawaima, *Uneven Ground: American Indian Sovereignty and Federal Law* (Norman: University of Oklahoma Press, 2001), 19–63.

82 This is the thesis in Kent McNeil, *Common Law Aboriginal Title* (Oxford: Oxford University Press, 1989). The High Court of Australia has characterized the doctrine of discovery, tied to *terra nullius*, as 'unjust and discriminatory.' See *Mabo v. Queensland*, (1992), 107 A.L.R. I (H.C. Aust.) at 42. The doctrine of discovery was rejected in *Island of Palmas* (1928) 2 R.I.A.A. 829.

83 *Mabo v. Queensland*, (1992), 107 A.L.R. I (H.C. Aust.) at 42.

84 Richard Lillich, Hurst Hannum, S. James Anaya, and Dinah Shelton, *International Human Rights: Problems of Law, Policy and Practice*, 4th ed. (New York: Aspen, 2006), 31–4.

85 *R. v. Marshall; R. v. Bernard*, [2005] 2 S.C.R. 220 at para. 132.

86 See Royal Commission on Aboriginal Peoples, *The Final Report of the Royal Commission on Aboriginal Peoples*, vol. 1., *Looking Forward and Looking Back* (Ottawa: Supply and Services Canada, 1996), recommendation 1.16.2 at page 696:

> Federal, provincial and territorial government further the process of renewal by: (a) acknowledging that concepts such as *terra nullius* and the doctrine of discovery are factually, legally and morally wrong ...

87 Joe Singer, 'Sovereignty and Property' (1991) 86 *Northwestern University Law Review* 1.

88 According to the *Island of Palmas* case, a claim based on occupation was incomplete until accompanied by 'effective occupation of the region claimed to be discovered.' The term 'effective occupation' incorporates the notion of 'uninterrupted or permanent possession.' Based on this rule, the only ones capable of successfully advocating a claim of discovery and occupation of British Columbia at the time of Confederation were the Aboriginal peoples themselves. The *Western Sahara* case (1975) I.C.J. 12 precludes a region from being termed uninhabited if nomadic or resident tribes with a degree of social and political organization are present in the area.

89 *R. v. Calder*, [1973] S.C.R. at 328.
90 James Tully, *An Approach to Political Philosophy: Locke in Contexts* (Cambridge: Cambridge University Press, 1993).
91 *R. v. Marshall; R. v. Bernard*, [2005] 2 S.C.R. 220.
92 William Wicken, *Mi'kmaq Treaties on Trial: History, Land and Donald Marshall Junior* (Toronto: University of Toronto Press, 2002); John Mack Faragher, *A Great and Noble Scheme: The Tragic Story of the Expulsion of the French Acadians from Their American Homeland* (NewYork: W.W. Norton, 2005); L.F.S. Upton, *Micmacs and Colonists: Indian-White Relations in the Maritimes, 1713–1867* (Vancouver: UBC Press, 1979); Stephen E. Patterson, '1744–1763: Colonial Wars and Aboriginal Peoples,' in *The Atlantic Region to Confederation: A History*, ed. Phillip A. Buckner and John G. Reid (Toronto: University of Toronto Press, 1995), 1254; Stephen E. Patterson, 'Indian-White Relations in Nova Scotia, 1749–61' (1993) 23 *Acadiensis* 23.
93 See *Amodu Tijani v. The Secretary, Southern Provinces* at 410: 'There is a tendency, operating at times unconsciously, to render that title conceptually in terms which are appropriate only to systems which have grown up under English law. But this tendency has to be held in check closely.'
94 John Locke, *Two Treatises of Government: A Critical Edition with an Introduction and Apparatus Criticus*, ed. Peter Laslett (New York: Cambridge University Press, 1965), 329.
95 Thomas Flanagan, *First Nations, Second Thoughts* (Montreal: McGill-Queen's University Press, 2000).
96 An example of an Indigenous group who 'mixed their labour with the soil' includes the Wendat; see Bruce Trigger, *The Children of Aataentsic: A History of the Huron People to 1660* (Montreal: McGill-Queen's University Press, 1976).
97 *Milirrpum v. Nabalco Pty. Ltd.* 1971, 17 Federal Law Reports, 141 at 201, per Justice Blackburn. See William Blackstone, *Commentaries on the Laws of England*, 21st ed., vol. 1 (London: Sweet, Maxwell and Stevens and Norton, 1844), 36–7: society required authority 'whose commands and decisions' all members were bound to obey, otherwise it would 'still remain as in a state of nature.'
98 For a more general critique on this approach, see Alex Frame, *Property and the Treaty of Waitangi: A Tragedy of the Commodities?* (Hamilton, NZ: Te Matahauariki Institute, 2001); Michael Asch, 'From Terra Nullius to Affirmation: Reconciling Aboriginal Rights with the Canadian Constitution' (2002) 17 *Canadian Journal of Law and Society* 23.
99 Kent McNeil, 'The Post Delgamuukw Nature and Context of Aboriginal Title,' retrieved 28 August 2009 from www.delgamuukw.org/research. On page 36 at footnote 143 McNeil has written: 'Acquisition of title to

Crown land by adverse possession was first allowed by *The Crown Suits Act*, 21 Jac. I (1623), c.2. The *Nullum Tempus Act*, 9 Geo. III (1769), c.16, set the limitation period for this at 60 years. The latter Act has been held to be applicable in overseas dominions of the Crown, including Canada: see *Attorney-General for British Honduras v. Bristowe* (1880), 6 App. Cas. 143 (P.C.); *Attorney-General for New South Wales v. Love*, [1898] A.C. 679 (P.C.); *Hamilton v. The King* (1917), 35 D.L.R. 226 (S.C.C.) ... For discussion, see *Common Law Aboriginal Title* (Oxford: Oxford University Press, 1989), 87–92.'

100 Winter King, 'Illegal Settlements and the Impact of Titling Programs' (2003) 44 *Harvard International Law Journal* 433.

101 A.C. Hamilton and C.M. Sinclair, *The Justice System and Aboriginal People: Report of the Aboriginal Justice Inquiry of Manitoba* (Winnipeg: Queen's Printer, 1991), 130–5.

102 Sidney Linden, *Report of the Ipperwash Inquiry,* vol. 2, *Policy Analysis* (Toronto: Queen's Printer for Ontario, 2007), 20–41.

103 *Haida Nation v. British Columbia*, [2004] 3 S.C.R. 511 at para. 25.

104 See *Status of Eastern Greenland Case* (1933) 3 W.C.R. 148 at 171: '[The doctrine of conquest] only operates as a cause of lack of sovereignty when there is a war between two states, and by reason of the defect of one of them sovereignty over territory passes from the loser to the victorious state.'

105 Ibid.

106 *Campbell v. Hall* (1774) 1 Cowp. 204, 98 E.R. 1045.

107 *R. v. Van der Peet*, [1996] 2 S.C.R. 507 at para 133, per Lamer. Madam Justice L'Heureux-Dube in *R. v. N.T.C. Smokehouse Ltd.* held: 'Clear and plain means that the government must address the aboriginal activities in question and explicitly extinguish them by making them no longer permissible.' [1996] 2 S.C.R. 672 at para. 78.

108 See Sakej Henderson, 'Empowering Treaty Federalism' (1994) 58 *Saskatchewan Law Review* 241; Thomas O. Hugelin, 'Exploring Concepts of Treaty Federalism: A Comparative Perspective' (paper prepared for the Royal Commission on Aboriginal Peoples, 1994).

109 The ideas in these paragraphs were previously explored in John Borrows, 'Ground Rules: Indigenous Treaties in Canada and New Zealand' (2006) 22 *New Zealand Universities Law Journal* 188.

110 For a discussion of the use of Maori law in Maori governance, Tikanga, in Aotearoa/New Zealand, see Caren Wickcliffe and Matui Dickson, 'Maori and Constitutional Change' (1999) 3 *Yearbook of New Zealand Jurisprudence* 9.

111 Ani Mikaere, a highly respected Maori scholar, cautions that Indigeneity

is not achieved without recognizing Tikanga Maori as the starting point of human relationships in Aoteatoa. See 'Are We all New Zealanders Now? A Mäori Response to the Päkehä Quest for Indigeneity,' lecture delivered at Maidment Theatre, Auckland, Monday, 15 November 2004, retrieved 28 August 2009 from www.brucejesson.com/lecture2004.html:

> For Päkehä to gain legitimacy here, it is they who must place their trust in Mäori, not the other way around. *They must accept that it is for the tangata whenua to determine their status in this land, and to do so in accordance with tikanga Mäori. This will involve sorting out a process of negotiation which is driven by the principles underpinning tikanga, a process which Päkehä do not control. There is no doubt that many Päkehä will find this challenging: their obsession with control over the Mäori-Päkehä relationship to date could almost be categorised as a form of compulsive disorder. Giving up such control requires a leap of faith on the part of Päkehä. In my view, however, nothing less will suffice if they truly want to gain the sense of belonging they so crave, the sense of identity that until now has proven so elusive.* (Emphasis mine.)

Under this view, treaties may be a necessary but certainly not sufficient condition for undermining colonialism in Canada and New Zealand.

112 James Tully, *Strange Multiplicity: Constitutionalism in an Age of Diversity* (Cambridge: Cambridge University Press, 1995), 198–209.

113 James Tully, *Public Philosophy in a New Key*, vol. 1, *Democracy and Civic Freedom* (Cambridge: Cambridge University Press, 2008), 160.

2 Sources and Scope of Indigenous Legal Traditions

1 Vernon Palmer, ed., *Mixed Jurisdictions Wordwide* (Cambridge: Cambridge University Press, 2001); J.E. Du Plessis, 'Comparative Law and the Study of Mixed Legal Systems,' in Mathias Reimann and Reinhard Zimmermann, eds., *Oxford Handbook of Comparative Law* (Oxford: Oxford University Press, 2006); R. Evans-Jones, 'Receptions of Law, Mixed Legal Systems and the Myth of the Genius of Scots Private Law' (1998) 114 *Law Quarterly Review* 228; E. Örücü et al., eds., *Studies in Legal Systems: Mixed and Mixing* (The Hague: Kluwer, 1996).

2 Some common law/civil law bijuridical countries include Botswana, Burkina-Faso, Burundi, Buthan, Chad, Chile, China, Congo, Cyprus, Japan, Lesotho, Malta, Mauritius, Namibia, Philippines, Puerto Rico, Saint Lucia, Saudi Arabia, Scotland, Seychelles, South Africa, Thailand, Vanuatu, and Yemen.

3   Some countries that combine customary law and other legal traditions
    are Cameroon, Côte D'Ivoire, Guinea, Eritrea, Ethiopia, Gabon, Gambia,
    Hong Kong, Indian, Indonesia, Israel, Jordan, Kenya, Korea (North and
    South), Lesotho, Liberia, Madagascar, Malawi, Malaysia, Mali, Microne-
    sia, Myanmar, Nepal, Niger, Nigeria, Rwanda, Senegal, Sierra Leone,
    Solomon Islands, Sri Lanka, Swaziland, Taiwan, Tanzania, Uganda,
    Vanuatu, Western Samoa, Zambia, and Zimbabwe. For an interesting
    study of Indigenous law's interactions with European law, see Joan
    Church, 'The Place of Indigenous Law in a Mixed Legal System and a
    Society in Transformation: A South African Experience' (2005) *ANZLHS
    E-Journal* 94; D. Visser, 'Cultural Forces in the Making of Mixed Legal
    Systems' (2003) 78 *Tulane Law Review* 41.
4   For a discussion of legal pluralism, see Sally Engle Merry, 'Legal Plural-
    ism' (1988) *Law and Society Review* 2 at 869.
5   James Tully, *Strange Multiplicity: Constitutionalism in an Age of Diversity*
    (Cambridge: Cambridge University Press, 1995).
6   The earliest practitioners of law in North America were its Indigenous
    inhabitants. These peoples are known as the 'Aboriginal' or 'Native'
    peoples of the continent. 'Aboriginal' in Canadian law includes Indian,
    Inuit, and Métis people: see s. 35(2) of the *Constitution Act, 1982*
    (Canada), enacted as Schedule B to the *Canada Act*, 1982 (U.K.) 1982, c. 11.
    They include, among others, the ancient and contemporary nations of
    the Innu, Mi'kmaq, Maliseet, Cree, Anishinabek, Haudenosaunee,
    Dakota, Lakota, Nakoda, Assinaboine, Saulteaux, Siksika, Secwepemec,
    Nlha7kapmx, Salish, Nuu-Chah-Nulth, Kwakwaka'wakw, Haida,
    Carrier, Tsimshian, Nisga'a, Gitksan, Tahltan, Tlingit, Gwichin, Dene,
    Inuit, and Métis. In relation to this diversity, I wrote in *Recovering
    Canada: The Resurgence of Indigenous Law* (Toronto: University of Toronto
    Press, 2002), 3–4:

> The traditions of these Indigenous peoples can be as historically differ-
> ent from one another as other nations and cultures in the world. For
> example, Canadian Indigenous peoples speak over 50 different Aborig-
> inal languages from 12 distinct language families that have as wide a
> variation as those of Europe and Asia. The linguistic, genealogical,
> political, and legal descent of these nations can be traced back through
> millennia to different regions or territories in northern North America.
> This explains the wide variety of laws found in Indigenous groups.

7   Gerald Postema, 'On the Moral Presence of Our Past' (1991) 36 *McGill
    Law Journal* 1153.

8 Jeremy Webber, 'Legal Pluralism and Human Agency' (2006) 44 *Osgoode Hall Law Review* 167.

9 Philip Bobbit, 'Constitutional Law and Interpretation,' in *A Companion to Philosophy of Law and Legal Theory*, ed. D. Patterson (Oxford: Blackwell, 1996); Philip Bobbitt, *Constitutional Interpretation* (New York: Blackwell, 1991).

10 Michael Hadley, *The Spiritual Roots of Restorative Justice* (Albany: SUNY Press, 2001); R.H. Helmholz, *The Spirit of the Classical Canon Law* (Athens, Georgia: University of Georgia Press, 1996); Wael B. Hallaq, *The Origins and Evolution of Islamic Law* (Cambridge: Cambridge University Press, 2005); Neil S. Hecht, *An Introduction to the History and Sources of Jewish Law* (New York: Oxford University Press, 1996); Wener F Menski, *Hindu Law: Beyond Tradition and Modernity* (New Delhi: Oxford University Press, 2003); Rebecca French, *The Golden Yoke: The Legal Cosmology of Buddhist Tibet* (Ithaca, NY: Cornell University Press, 1995); Y. Liu, *Origins of Chinese Law: Penal and Administrative Law in its Early Development* (New York: Oxford University Press, 1998).

11 Immanuel Kant, *The Metaphysics of Morals*, trans. Mary J. Gregor (Cambridge: Cambridge University Press, 1996).

12 Harold J. Berman, *The Interaction of Law and Religion* (New York: Abingdon Press, 1974); Peter Radan, Denise Meyerson, and Rosalind Frances Croucher, eds., *Law and Religion: God, the State and the Common Law* (New York: Routledge, 2005); Brian Young, *The Politics of Codification: The Lower Canadian Civil Code of 1866* (Montreal: McGill-Queen's University Press, 1994), 113–20.

13 For further information, see M.H. Ogilvie, *Religious Institutions and the Law in Canada*, 2nd ed. (Toronto: Irwin Law, 2003), chap. 7.

14 Jonathon Penney and Robert Jacob Dannay, 'The Embarassing Preamble? Understanding the Supremacy of God and the Charter' (2006) 39 *UBC Law Review* 287; George Egerton, 'Trudeau, God, and the Canadian Constitution: Religion, Human Rights, and Government Authority in the Making of the 1982 Constitution,' in *Rethinking Church, State, and Modernity: Canada Between Europe and America*, ed. David Lyon and Marguerite Van Die (Toronto: University of Toronto Press, 2000), 90–112.

15 See John Borrows, 'Peace and Order: Describing and Implementing Treaty Justice in Saskatchewan' (paper prepared for the Office of the Treaty Commission, Saskatoon, 2003).

16 In 2001 I was approached by the Office of the Treaty Commissioner to produce a 'Blue Sky' Report about justice in the Saskatchewan Indian treaties. In undertaking this task I was encouraged to be innovative in

my research and to speculate in my findings about what justice jurisdiction and delivery might require under the treaty relationship. As such, I was directed to 'look outside the box,' in keeping with the exploratory nature of the parties' Treaty Table process. I was asked to see if relationships of justice could be different in the province if the treaties formed a central part of the parties' relationships. My terms of reference were to 'lead discussions on the present justice system, identify key issues and options based on a review of existing justice system studies, inquiries, and recommendations, and to focus on justice delivery in the future based on the treaty relationship.' I was also to provide an overview of the Crown's views on justice issues at the time of the treaty, and to give an overview of First Nations' views on law and traditional justice concepts discussed at the time of the treaty. To accomplish this work I facilitated two symposia over a two-year period, involving many people representing various interests in the treaty process. I wrote three draft reports before completing a Final Report in 2005 which was approved by the Elders, but remains unpublished because of concerns about the Crown's treatment of oral history in the courts.

17 Treaties 4, 5, and 6 reads as follows:

> The undersigned chiefs, on their behalf and on behalf of all other Indians inhabiting the tract within ceded do hereby solemnly promise and engage to strictly observe this treaty and also to conduct and behave themselves as good and loyal subjects of Her Majesty The Queen. They promise and engage that *they will in all respects obey and abide by the law; that they will maintain peace and order between each other, and also between themselves and other tribes of Indians or whites*, now inhabiting or hereafter to inhabit any part of the said tract, or that they will not molest a person or property of any inhabitants of such ceded tract or the property of Her Majesty The Queen, or interfere with or trouble any person passing or travelling through the said tract or any part thereof, and that *they will aid and assist the officers of Her Majesty in bringing to justice and punishment any Aboriginal offending against the stipulations of this treaty or infringing the laws in force in the country so ceded*. (Emphasis mine.)

The text of Treaties 8 and 10 is only slightly different:

> And the undersigned Cree, Beaver, Chipewyan and other Indian Chiefs and Headmen, on their own behalf and on behalf of all the

Indians whom they represent, DO HEREBY SOLEMNLY PROMISE and engage to strictly observe this Treaty, and also to conduct and behave themselves as good and loyal subjects of Her Majesty the Queen.

THEY PROMISE AND ENGAGE that they will, in all respects, obey and abide by the law; that they will maintain peace between each other, and between themselves and other tribes of Indians, and between themselves and others of Her Majesty's subjects, whether Indians, half-breeds or whites, this year inhabiting and hereafter to inhabit any part of the said ceded territory; and that they will not molest the person or property of any inhabitant of such ceded tract, or of any other district or country, or interfere with or trouble any person passing or travelling through the said tract or any part thereof, and that they will assist the officers of Her Majesty in bringing to justice and punishment any Indian offending against the stipulations of this Treaty or infringing the law in force in the country so ceded.

18 Alexander Morris, *The Treaties of Canada with the Indians of Manitoba and the North West Territories Including the Negotiations on Which they were Based* (Toronto: Belfords and Clark and Co., 1880).
19 Harold Cardinal and Walter Hildebrandt, *Treaty Elders of Saskatchewan: Our Dream Is that Our Peoples Will One Day Be Clearly Recognized as Nations* (Calgary: University of Calgary Press, 2000), 6–7.
20 Elder Jacob Bill, cited in John Borrows, 'Peace and Order: Describing and Implementing Treaty Justice in Saskatchewan' (paper prepared for the Office of the Treaty Commissioner, Saskatchewan, 2003), 105–6. Paper on file with the author.
21 Robert S. Allen, *His Majesty's Indian Allies: British Indian Policy in the Defense of Canada, 1774–1815* (Toronto: Dundurn Press, 1992); Carl Benn, *The Iroquois in the War of 1812* (Toronto: University of Toronto Press, 1998).
22 For more information about the resettlement of British Columbia by non-Aboriginal peoples, see Cole Harris, *The Resettlement of British Columbia: Essays on Colonialism and Geographical Change* (Vancouver: UBC Press, 1997); Cole Harris, *Making Native Space: Colonialism, Resistance and Change in British Columbia* (Vancouver: UBC Press, 2002).
23 Noel Lyon and Elder Jacob Bill, cited in John Borrows, 'Peace and Order: Describing and Implementing Treaty Justice in Saskatchewan' (paper prepared for the Office of the Treaty Commissioner, Saskatchewan, 2003), 105–6. Paper on file with the author.

24 An interesting example of how natural law might develop and be operative within Indigenous communities is found in the writings of Professor Julie Cruickshank. See Julie Cruickshank, *Do Glaciers Listen? Local Knowledge, Colonial Encounters and Social Imagination* (Vancouver: UBC Press, 2005).

25 Cree Elder Wayne Roan speaks about nature's laws from a Cree perspective on the website Nature's Laws, retrieved 19 September 2008 from www.abheritage.ca/natureslaws/index2.html.

26 Nancy J. Turner, *The Earth's Blanket: Traditional Teachings for Sustainable Living* (Vancouver: Douglas and McIntyre, 2005), 11–40.

27 Aristotle, *Politics*, ed. Trevor Saunders, trans. T.A. Sinclair (New York: Penguin, 1962), Book I, chap. 2.

28 Andrew Dyck, *A Commentary on Cicero, De Legibus* (Ann Arbor: University of Michigan Press, 2004), Book I, chap. 13; Cicero, *The Republic*, trans. Clinton W. Keyes (Cambridge, MA: Harvard University Press, 1928), Book III, chap. 22.

29 Thomas Hobbes, *Leviathan* (London: G. Routledge and Sons, 1887); Jean Jacques Rousseau, *The Social Contract* (London: Dent, 1973); John Locke, *Two Treatises on Government* (New York: New American Library, 1965).

30 For a critique of Western ideas of natural law, see Myres S. McDougal et al., *Human Rights and World Public Order* (New Haven, CT: Yale University Press, 1980). For an excellent discussion of European conceptions of natural law and its application to Indigenous peoples, see James Anaya, *Indigenous Peoples in International Law*, 2nd ed. (Oxford: Oxford University Press, 2004), 16–19. See also James Tully, *A Discourse on Property: John Locke and his Adversaries* (Cambridge: Cambridge University Press, 1980); James Tully, *Strange Multiplicity: Constitutionalism in an Age of Diversity* (Cambridge: Cambridge University Press, 1995), particularly part 3.

31 *Delgamuukw v. A.G.B.C.* (1991), 79 D.L.R. (4th) 185; [1991] 3 W.W.R. 97; [1991] 5 C.N.L.R. 5 (B.C.S.C.).

32 One such story, related to butterflies, is found in John Borrows, 'Creating an Indigenous Legal Community: 5th Annual John Tait Memorial Lecture' (2005) 50 *McGill Law Journal* 3.

33 *R. v. Jones and Nadjiwon*, [1993] 3 C.N.L.R. 182 (Ont. Prov. Div.).

34 For further context, see Edwin Koenig, *Culture and Ecologies: A Native Fishing Conflict on the Saugeen-Bruce Peninsula* (Toronto: University of Toronto Press, 2005).

35 Gisday Wa and Delgam Uukw, 'Delgam Uukw Speaks,' in *The Spirit in the Land* (Gabriola Island, BC: Reflections, 1992), 7–9. For general commentary about the *Delgamuukw* case, see Dara Culhane, *The Pleasure of the*

Crown: Anthropology, Law and First Nations (Vancouver: Talon Books, 1998).

36 Don Monet and Skanu'u, *Colonialism on Trial: Indigenous Land Rights and the Gitksan and Wet'suwet'en Sovereignty Case* (Gabriola Island, BC: New Society Publishers, 1992), 1.

37 Ibid., 26.

38 For another account of this event, see William Robinson as told by Walter Wright, *Men of Medeek*, 2nd ed. (Kitimat, BC: Northern Sentinel Press, 1962).

39 *Delgamuukw v. A.G.B.C.*, [1991] 5 C.N.L.R. 5 at 52–3 (B.C.S.C.).

40 Ibid., 49. See Val Napoleon, *'Delgamuukw*: Legal A Straight-Jacket for Oral Histories?' (2005) 20 *Canadian Journal of Law and Society* 2.

41 Richard Daly, *Our Box Was Full: An Ethnography for the Delgamuukw Plaintiffs* (Vancouver: UBC Press, 2004); Frank Cassidy, ed., *Aboriginal Title in British Columbia: Delgamuukw v. the Queen* (Lantzville, BC: Oolichan Press, 1991), 4, 51, 53, 58, 62, 199.

42 Frances Widdowson and Howard Adams, *Disrobing the Aboriginal Industry: The Deception behind Indigenous Cultural Preservation* (Montreal: McGill Queen's University Press, 2008).

43 Thomas Flanagan, *First Nations, Second Thoughts* (Montreal: McGill-Queen's University Press, 2000).

44 A.C. Hamilton and C.M. Sinclair, 'Aboriginal Women,' in *The Justice System and Aboriginal People: Report of the Aboriginal Justice Inquiry of Manitoba*, ed. A.C. Hamilton and C.M. Sinclair, vol. 1 (Winnipeg: Queen's Printer, 1991), 475–87; Amnesty International, *Stolen Sisters: Discrimination and Violence against Indigenous Women in Canada, A Summary of Amnesty International's Concerns* (London: Amnesty International Secretariat, October 2004); First Nations Child, and Family Caring Society of Canada, *Wen'de: We Are Coming to the Light of Day* (Ottawa: First Nations Child and Family Caring Society of Canada, 2005), 14–15; Suzanne Fournier and Ernie Crey, *Stolen from Our Embrace* (Vancouver: Douglas and McIntyre, 1997).

45 John Borrows, *Seven Generations, Seven Teachings* (Vancouver: National Centre for First Nations Governance, 2007).

46 J. White and P. Maxim, 'Social Capital, Social Cohesion, and Population Outcomes in Canada's First Nations Communities,' in *Aboriginal Conditions: Research as a Foundation for Public Policy*, ed. J. White, P. Maxim, and D. Beavon (Vancouver: UBC Press, 2003), 18.

47 See Robert Putnam, *Bowling Alone: The Collapse and Revival of American Community* (Toronto: Simon and Schuster, 2000).

48 S. Callahan, 'The Capital that Counts' (1996) 123(20) *Commonweal* 123
    (November 22, 1996), 7 at 7; J. Coleman, 'Social Capital in the Creation of
    Human Capital' (1988) 94 *American Journal of Sociology* 98.
49 Robert Odawi Porter, *Sovereignty, Colonialism and Indigenous Nations: A
    Reader* (Durham, NC: Carolina Academic Press, 2005), especially 503–675.
50 In his *Ending Denial: Understanding Aboriginal Issues* (Toronto: University
    of Toronto Press, 2008), 4, and citing Sally Engel Merry, 'Human Rights
    and the Demonization of Culture' (February 2003) *Anthropological News*,
    anthropologist Wayne Warry has written:

> [T]he idea of cultural relativism is often seen as an anathema to human
> rights activists, because they work with an out of date notion of
> culture. For those who see culture as a 'coherent, static and unchanging
> set of values' culture is a problem. Cruel and inhuman behaviors – for
> example, female genital mutilation, or female circumcision, or 'honour
> killings' sanctioned by tribal elders as punishment for having an affair
> – are immoral by any standard and need not be reformed. But only
> those who assume a model of culture as static would suggest that these
> practices be protected in the name of culture or tradition. As Merry
> notes, this antiquated view of culture 'is increasingly understood as a
> barrier to the realization of human rights.'

51 *Indian Act*, R.S.C. 1985, c. I-5. For further critique about the human rights
    limitations of the *Indian Act*, see Menno Boldt, *Surviving as Indians: The
    Challenge of Self-Government* (Toronto: University of Toronto Press, 1993).
52 Sonia Harris Short, 'The Road to Hell: Indigenous Child Welfare in Inter-
    national Context' (unpublished paper on file with the author).
53 There can also be sacred elements to the way circles are conducted. Cree
    Elder Jacob Bill from Saskatchewan has observed:

> At our time when our Elder used to speak to us he used to make us sit
> in a circle, used to take the pipe first and he used to pray to the Creator
> first so that we would understand, us young people, anything that he
> was going to relate, that the Creator would place the words that were
> going to be passed on to the young people. I guess that's the way,
> that's the way we received the knowledge that we carry, since that is
> where it comes from. Life comes from the Creator. We could under-
> stand that language what our grandpa had told us. We can see that
> today what is happening today. Our Elders used to foresee a long ways
> because the Creator used to help them, the Creator used to show them

a future; that is what I see today. The Elders used to say you are not to fight with the white man, tell him, tell him, remind him to remember the treaty. You don't have to give him hard words, just tell him in good words, soft words, understandable words. If you talk to somebody using a low tone of voice they will understand that, but if you get mad nobody will understand. But get along with him; tell him what you want to tell him in a good way what you need. Eventually, a little bit further down the road he will start to listen to you.

Elder Jacob Bill in John Borrows, 'Peace and Order: Describing and Implementing Treaty Justice in Saskatchewan' (paper prepared for the Office of the Treaty Commission, Saskatoon, 2003), 102.

54 Institute for the Advancement of Aboriginal Women, *Can you Hear Me? How to Get Your Voice Heard for Aboriginal Women*, retrieved 30 March 2005 from Institute for the Advancement of Aboriginal Women website, www.iaaw.ca/Pubs/Can%20you%20Hear%20Me.pdf; Sarah Deer, Bonnie Clairmont, Carrie A. Martell, and Maureen White Eagle, eds., *Sharing Our Stories of Survival: Native Women Surviving Violence* (Lanhan, MD: Altamira Press, 2007); Wendy Stewart, Audrey Huntley, and Fay Blaney, *The Implications of Restorative Justice for Aboriginal Women and Children Survivors of Violence: A Comparative Overview of Five Communities In British Columbia* (Ottawa: Law Commission of Canada, 2001).

55 For further information about Aboriginal Legal Services of Toronto, see Craig Proulx, *Reclaiming Aboriginal Justice, Identity and Community* (Saskatoon: Purich Publishing, 2003).

56 Ibid., 47–52.

57 The ALST vision statement reads as follows:

- We seek a community which deals with justice issues in an assertive, constructive and respectful way.
- A community which provides support and guidance to its citizens when they need to interact with the justice system.
- A community involved in developing and implementing justice initiatives and alternatives which are culturally based and community controlled.
- A community where our youth have the opportunities and abilities to deal with justice issues affecting them.
- A community where its citizens have minimum exposure to the existing legal system and are less vulnerable to acts of aggression, of racism and ignorance of who we are.

- A community which resolves its conflicts internally with minimal need for outside involvement.
- A community which promotes a positive environment related to justice issues – an environment based on mutual understandings with non-aboriginal groups/services such as schools, police, and other enforcement agencies.
- A community where its agencies work together to ensure justice and related services and issues are provided in holistic and integrated way.
- A community where its citizens have the confidence and self-esteem to deal with issues in a constructive way.

58 Craig Proulx, *Reclaiming Aboriginal Justice, Identity and Community* (Saskatoon: Purich Publishing, 2003), 41–52.

59 ALST also works with the Gladue (Aboriginal Persons) Court, which sits all day Tuesdays and Fridays in Courtroom 126 at the Old City Hall Courts in Toronto. The court derives its name from the 1999 decision of the Supreme Court of Canada, *R. v. Gladue*, [1999] 1 S.C.R. 688, that set out the parameters of section 718.2(e) of the *Criminal Code* regarding the sentencing of offenders, and in particular, Aboriginal offenders. At present, the Court only hears cases from Aboriginal people whose matters are going through the Old City Hall Courts; charges cannot be brought into the Gladue Court from other Toronto Courts. The Court accepts guilty pleas, sentences offenders, and does bail hearings. Eventually it is anticipated that the Court will also take on trials as well. ALST has three staff, Gladue Caseworkers who write reports at the request of defence counsel, the Crown counsel or the judge on the life circumstances of an Aboriginal offender. These reports also contain recommendations that the court can consider in sentencing in light of the circumstances of the offender. These Gladue Reports (as they are often called) can be made for Aboriginal offenders in any court in Toronto as well as for Aboriginal offenders in the Hamilton and Brantford area. When I visited with ALST along with Dawnis Kennedy, we were of the opinion that it was the most successful and sophisticated legal clinic dealing with Aboriginal issues of which we were aware. ALST has an Aboriginal Courtworker Program to explain legal rights and obligations to their clients. Courtworkers assist in securing legal counsel, finding interpreters if they are needed, and also assist with pre-sentence reports, bail hearings, and referrals. The ALST Clinic serves people in a variety of areas including: housing problems and tenant rights, Ontario Works and Ontario Disability Support Plan, *Indian*

Act matters, Canada Pension Disability applications, Employment Insurance and Employment Standards, Police Complaints, Criminal Injuries Compensation, Human Rights issues, and referrals to lawyers on other matters including criminal and family law. The clinic is also involved in law reform, community organizing, public legal education, and test case litigation. They do an impressive amount of work in changing the law and its interpretation as it relates to Aboriginal peoples in Canada, particularly in an urban context.

ALST has made it a priority to become involved in test case litigation. In some cases, this means bringing cases forward on behalf of individuals or groups. In other cases, ALST intervenes in cases that have been brought by other parties. In an intervention, ALST's main concern is that the perspectives of Aboriginal people, particularly urban Aboriginal people, are brought to the attention of the court. Some of the matters in which it has intervened are the leading cases affecting urban Aboriginal people's rights in the Criminal Justice system. ALST has filed factums and made representations before the Supreme Court of Canada in the following cases: *Corbiere* (granted non-reserve resident voting rights), *Gladue* (recognized special circumstances of Aboriginal offenders in sentencing), *Golden* (strip searches could not be routine police practice), *Powley* (recognition of Métis rights for first time at the Supreme Court), *Suave* (denial of prisoner's voting rights violated Charter), *Wells* (further clarification of the *Gladue* case), and *Williams* (identified racism as a problem faced by Aboriginal people in getting a fair trial).

Finally, ASLT involves itself in Law Reform work in the areas of policing, youth criminal justice, the International Convention of the Elimination of All Forms of Racial Discrimination, Legal Aid, section 718 (e) of the *Criminal Code* (Aboriginal considerations in sentencing), and inquests.

60 Uuli Steltzer, *A Haida Potlatch* (Vancouver: Douglas and McIntyre, 1984); Margaret Seguin and Margaret Halpin, eds., *Potlatch at Gitsegukla* (Vancouver: UBC Press, 2000); Pamela Amoss, *Coast Salish Spirit Dancing: The Survival of an Ancestral Religion* (Seattle: University of Washington Press, 1978); A. Jonaitis, D. Cole, I. Jacknis, and W. Suttles, *Chiefly Feasts: The Enduring Kwakiutl Potlatch* (Seattle: University of Washington Press, 1994); Sergei Kan, *Symbolic Immortality: The Tlingit Potlatch of the Nineteenth Century* (Washington: Smithsonian Institution Press, 1989); Christopher Bracken, *The Potlatch Papers: A Colonial Case History* (Chicago: University of Chicago Press, 1997); Antonia Mills, *Eagle Down Is Our Law: Witsuwit'en Law, Feasts and Land Claims* (Vancouver: UBC Press, 1994); Dale Hunt, '"We Are All Different, Still Living Under the Same Culture": A

Kwakwakw'wakw Perspective on Dispute Resolution and Relationship Building' (Master's in Dispute Resolution, University of Victoria, BC, 2005).

61 For example, the Gitksan and Wet'suwet'en are organized into Houses and Clans in which hereditary chiefs preside over the allocation, administration, and control of traditional lands. Within House structures the chiefs pass on important histories, songs, crests, lands, ranks, and properties from one generation to the next. The passage of these legal, political, social, and economic entitlements is performed and witnessed through Feasts. These Feasts substantiate the territories' relationships. A hosting House serves food, distributes gifts, announces the House's successors to the names of deceased chiefs, describes the territory, raises totem poles, and tells the oral history of the House. Chiefs from other Houses witness the actions of the Feast, and at the end of the proceedings validate the decisions and declarations of the Host House. As such, the Feast is an important 'institution through which the people [have] governed themselves' and it confirms the relationship between each House and its territories. See John Borrows, *Recovering Canada: The Resurgence of Indigenous Law* (Toronto: University of Toronto Press, 2002), 79–80.

62 Douglas Cole and Ira Chaikin, *An Iron Hand Upon the People: The Law against the Potlatch on the Northwest Coast* (Vancouver: Douglas and McIntyre, 1990).

63 Antonia Mills, ed., *Hang Onto These Words: Johnny David's Delgamuukw Evidence* (Toronto: University of Toronto Press, 2005), 360.

64 Ibid., 361.

65 Jo-Anne Fiske and Betty Patrick, *Cis Dideen Kat, When the Plumes Rise: The Way of the Lake Babine Nation* (Vancouver: UBC Press, 2000), 101.

66 Warner Adam, Travis Holyk, and Parry Shawana, 'Whu Neeh Nee (Guiders of Our People): Carrier Sekani First Nations Family Law Alternative Dispute Resolution' (paper presented at the 6th International Conference on Restorative Justice, 1 June 2003), retrieved 5 July 2007 from www.sfu.ca/cfrj/fulltext/adam.pdf.

67 Phil Lucas, producer/director/writer, *Voyage of Rediscovery*, The National Film Board of Canada, 1993, 25 min., video 2 of First Nations, *The Circle Unbroken*.

68 Wet'suwet'en, Burns Lake Band, Cheslatta Carrier Nation, Stellat'en, Naudleh Whu'ten, Takla lake, Nee Tahi Buhn, Saik'uz, Lake Babine Nation, Skin Tyee (formerly a part of Nee Tahi Buhn), and Yekochee.

69 Warner Adam, Travis Holyk, and Parry Shawana, 'Whu Neeh Nee (Guiders of Our People): Carrier Sekani First Nations Family Law Alter-

native Dispute Resolution' (paper presented at the 6th International Conference on Restorative Justice, 1 June 2003), retrieved 5 July 2007 from www.sfu.ca/cfrj/fulltext/adam.pdf.

70 Ibid., 109–10.

71 John Hurley, *Children or Brethren: Aboriginal Rights in Colonial Iroquoia* (Saskatoon: Native Law Centre, 1985), 40.

72 See *Henco Industries Ltd. v. Haudenosaunee Six Nations Confederacy Council* (2006), 273 D.L.R. (4th) 284 (Ont. C.A.); *1536412 Ontario Ltd v. Haudenosaunee Confederacy Chiefs Council et al.* (2008) CanLII 28041 (Ont. S.C.) Court file No.: CV-08-82; Date: 2008-06-10.

73 John Borrows, 'A Genealogy of Law: Inherent Sovereignty and First Nations Self-Government' (1992) 30 *Osgoode Hall Law Journal* 2 291–354.

74 *Indian Act*, R.S.C. 1985, c. I-5.

75 *Indian Band Council Procedures Regulations*, C.R.C. 1978, c. 950.

76 Sometimes Indigenous laws find their articulation in ceremony. Ceremonies often consist of formalized rituals that enable its participants to directly participate in law. Each group created its own distinctive ceremonies and formalities to renew, celebrate, transfer, or abandon their legal relationships. As such, the ceremonies of the Potlatch on the West Coast produced entirely different legal relationships from those of the Sundance on the prairies, or the Midewiwin and False Face societies of central Canada. The stories told in the Big Houses of the Salish fundamentally differ from those told in the teepees of the Assinaboine, and these could be very different again from those spoken in the longhouses of the Haudenosaunee, or in the lodges of the Mi'kmaq. Some ceremonies required special initiation in order to participate, thus creating a realm of sacred knowledge with some traditions. Each group's ceremonies and stories varied according to its history, material circumstances, spiritual alignment, and social structure.

77 Leland Donald, *Aboriginal Slavery in the Northwest Coast of North America* (Berkeley: University of California Press, 1997).

78 It is also my view that Canadian law as currently formulated and practised also restricts Indigenous peoples' participation in the creation of Canadian law.

79 Robert Cover, 'The Supreme Court, 1982 Term – Foreword: Nomos and Narrative' (1983) 97 *Harvard Law Review* 1 at 40–4.

80 John Tobias, 'Protection, Civilization, Assimilation: An Outline History of Canada's Indian Policy,' in *As Long as the Sun Shines and Water Flows: A Reader in Canadian Native Studies*, ed. Ian Getty and Antoine Lussier (Vancouver: University of British Columbia Press, 1990), 29.

81 *Indian Act*, R.S.C. 1985, c. I-5. See John Borrows, 'A Genealogy of Law: Inherent Sovereignty and First Nations Self-Government' (1992) 30 *Osgoode Hall Law Journal* 2 at 291–354.

82 Indians could not vote for the first seventy-five years of Confederation. See, for example, British Columbia's *Qualification and Registration of Voters Amendment Act*, 1872, s. 13. Indians did not generally enjoy federal voting rights until 1960, when the federal franchise was finally extended to them without qualification. The provinces extended the franchise to Indians at different dates: British Columbia 1949, Manitoba 1952, Ontario 1954, Saskatchewan 1960, Prince Edward Island and New Brunswick 1963, Alberta 1965, Quebec 1969. The Inuit were excluded from the federal franchise in 1934 but had the vote restored to them in 1950. Métis were always considered citizens able to vote in federal and provincial elections.

83 Indigenous law creates relationships between people by addressing the consequences of their actions. Arthur Ripstein, 'Justice and Responsibility' (2004) 17 *Canadian Journal of Law and Jurisprudence* 361–86.

84 John Austin, *Lectures on Jurisprudence and the Philosophy of Positive Law* (St Clair Shores, MI: Scholarly Press, 1977), 88.

85 Tim Schouls, *Shifting Boundaries: Aboriginal Identity, Pluralist Theory, and the Politics of Self-Government* (Vancouver: UBC Press, 2003).

86 When laws flow from this source, people might merely obey an injunction because those who continue to proclaim it are regarded with a measure of respect. Of course, obedience might even be given for less healthy reasons, such as the fear of a negative consequence if they fall out of favour with those who are regarded as the law-makers within a community.

87 Robert Cover, 'Violence and the Word' (1986) 95 *Yale Law Journal* 1601.

88 Robert A. Williams Jr., 'Taking Rights Aggressively: The Perils and Promise of Critical Legal Theory for People of Color' (1987) 5 *Law and Inequality* 103; Duncan Kennedy, *Legal Education and the Reproduction of Hierarchy: A Polemic Against the System: A Critical Edition* (New York: New York University Press, 2004).

89 Andree Lajoie, Henry Quillnan, Rod Macdonald, and Guy Rocher, 'Legal Pluralism at Kahnawake,' in *Aboriginality and Governance: A Multidisciplinary Perspective*, ed. Gordon Christie (Penticton, BC: Theytus Books, 2006), 239.

90 'The body of rules, whether proceeding from formal enactment or from custom, which a particular state or community recognizes as binding on its members or subjects,' *Oxford English Dictionary*, 2nd ed. (Oxford: Clarendon Press, 1989), 712. Articles commenting on First Nations law include Bradford Morse and Gordon Woodman, eds., *Indigenous Law and the State* (Providence, RI: Foris, 1988); Michael Coyle, 'Traditional Indian

Justice in Ontario: A Role for the Present?' (1986) 24 *Osgoode Hall Law Journal* 605. For a contrary view, see Roger F. McDonnell, 'Contextualizing the Investigation of Customary Law in Contemporary Native Communities' (1992) 34 *Canadian Journal of Criminology* 299; *Delgamuukw v. British Columbia* (1991), 79 D.L.R. (4th) 185 (B.C.S.C.) at 455: 'What the Gitksan and Wet'suwet'en witness[es] describe as law is really a most uncertain and highly flexible set of customs which are frequently not followed by the Indians themselves.' For criticism of this view, see Michael Asch, 'Errors in Delgamuukw: An Anthropological Perspective,' in *Aboriginal Title in British Columbia: Delgamuukw v. The Queen*, ed. Frank Cassidy (Lantzville, BC: Oolichan Books, 1992), 221. For a fuller description of Wet'suwet'en law, see Antonia Mills, *Eagle Down Is Our Law: Witsuwit'en Law, Feasts and Land Claims* (Vancouver: UBC Press, 1994).

91 For further information about Indigenous diversity in Canada, see Tim Schouls, *Shifting Boundaries: Aboriginal Identity, Pluralist Theory, and the Politics of Self-Government* (Vancouver: UBC Press, 2003).

92 The laws of England largely operated through custom until precedent and consolidation took place through the 1700s. Patrick Glenn, 'The Common Law in Canada' (1995) *Canadian Bar Review* 261. Even today, the common law method uses customs and traditions to fill gaps when interpreting written rules, *Reference re Secession of Quebec*, [1998] 2 S.C.R. 217.

93 Rudolf B. Schleinger et al., *Comparative Law*, 4th ed. (New York: Foundation Press, 1980), 669–70, 690–4; Stephen McCaffrey, *Understanding International Law* (Newark, NJ: LexisNexis, 2006), 44–55.

94 General definitions of customary law can be found in J. Brierly, *The Law of Nations*, 4th ed. (Gloucestershire, UK: Clarendon Press, 1949), 60; *Black's Law Dictionary*, 6th ed. (St Paul, MN: West Publishing, 1990), 384.

95 Gerald Postema, 'Implicit Law,' in *Rediscovering Fuller: Essays on Implicit Law and Institutional Design*, ed. Willem Witteveen and Wibren Van der Burg (Amsterdam: Amsterdam University Press, 1999), 255.

96 (1993) 106 D.L.R. (4th) 720 (B.C.C.A.).

97 Ibid., para. 13.

98 Ibid., para. 42.

99 *R. v. Nan-E-Quis-A-Ka* (1889), 1 Terr. L.R. 211; 2 C.N.L.C. 368 (N.W.T.S.C.); *R. v. Bear's Shin Bone* (1899), 4 Terr. L.R. 173 (N.W.T.S.C.); *Re Noah Estate* (1961), 32 D.L.R. (2d) 185 (N.W.T.S.C.); *Re Katie's Adoption Petition* (1961), 32 D.L.R. (2d) 686 (N.W.T.T.C.); *Re Beaulieu's Petition* (1969), 3 D.L.R. (3d) 479 (N.W.T.T.C.); *Re Deborah*, (1972), 27 D.L.R. (3d) 225 (N.W.T.S.C.); *Aboriginal Custom Adoption Recognition Act*, S.N.W.T. 1994, c. 26. For further commentary, see Professor Norman Zlotkin, 'Judicial Recognition of

Aboriginal Customary Law in Canada: Selected Marriage and Adoption Cases' [1984] 4 C.N.L.R 1.

100 Subsection 2(1) of the *Indian Act* defines the 'council of the band' as being chosen either by the procedures set out in section 74 of the act or according to the custom of the band. Section 2(1)(b) states 'in the case of a band to which section 74 does not apply, the council chosen according to the custom of the band, or, where there is no council, the chief of the band chosen according to the custom of the band.'

101 *R. v. Delgamuukw*, [1997] 3 S.C.R. 1010, para. 141.

102 *R. v. Van der Peet*, [1996] 2 S.C.R. 507, para. 46.

103 *Labrador Inuit Land Claims Agreement Act*, S.N.L. 2004, c. L-3.1; *Labrador Inuit Land Claims Agreement Act*, S.C. 2005, c. 27.

104 See section 3 of the *Labrador Inuit Land Claims Agreement Act*, S.C. 2005, c. 27. See also *Labrador Inuit Land Claims Agreement*, Chapter 2, 2.1.1., schedule A to the *Labrador Inuit Land Claims Agreement Act*, S.N.L. 2004, c. L-3.1.

105 Section 9.1.2 of the *Labrador Inuit Constitution*, retrieved 11 September 2007 from www.nunatsiavut.com/pdfs/Constitution.pdf.

106 *Labrador Inuit Land Claims Agreement*, Chapter 1, 1.1.1.

107 Part 9.1 of the *Labrador Inuit Constitution*, retrieved 11 September 2007 from www.nunatsiavut.com/pdfs/Constitution.pdf.

108 There are no criminal justice protections within the Constitution because the *Labrador Inuit Land Claims Agreement* does not include general criminal justice jurisdiction as part of the Nunatsiavut government; see Part 17.28.2 of the *Agreement*.

109 Part 2.2.3. of the *Labrador Inuit Constitution*, retrieved 11 September 2007 from www.nunatsiavut.com/pdfs/Constitution.pdf.

110 Section 9.1.4 of the *Labrador Inuit Constitution* states:

If a Labrador Inuit customary law applies to a matter for which an Inuit law has been made:
   (a) both laws are equally operative to the extent that they do not conflict with each other; and
   (b) Labrador Inuit customary law will prevail to the extent of any conflict with an Inuit law unless the Inuit law expressly extinguishes, replaces or varies the Labrador Inuit customary law.

111 Part 9.1.5 of the *Labrador Inuit Constitution*, retrieved 11 September 2007 from www.nunatsiavut.com/pdfs/Constitution.pdf.

112 *Labrador Inuit Land Claims Agreement*, Chapter 17.5.1., schedule A to the *Labrador Inuit Land Claims Agreement Act*, S.N.L. 2004, c. L-3.1.

113 The Labrador Inuit Constitution states:

> Labrador Inuit customary law may be recognized by any judicial or administrative authority and in any proceeding the existence and content of any Labrador Inuit customary law may be established:
>   (a) if the Labrador Inuit customary law has been codified under section 9.1.5, with reference to the code; or
>   (b) as a question of fact in relation to the specific matter or matter at issue in the proceeding.

Part 9.1.6 of the *Labrador Inuit Constitution*, retrieved 11 September 2007 from www.nunatsiavut.com/pdfs/Constitution.pdf.

114 *Quebec Secession Reference*, [1998] 2 S.C.R. 217 at para. 49; John Merryman, John Henry Merryman, and Rogelio Pérez-Perdomo, eds., *The Civil Law Tradition: An Introduction to the Legal Systems of Europe and Latin America* (Palo Alto, CA: Stanford University Press, 2003), 112–24.

115 For more general information about Indigenous oral traditions, see Peter Nabakov, *A Forest of Time: American Indian Ways of History* (Cambridge: Cambridge University Press, 2004).

116 This list is taken from Jan Vansina, *Oral Tradition as History* (Madison: University of Wisconsin Press, 1985), 13–27.

3 Indigenous Law Examples

1 Many Indigenous legal systems could be identified. However, it would be exceedingly difficult to outline Indigenous legal traditions within their own internal categories. At the same time, it would be inappropriate to force Indigenous law examples into common law and civil law boxes. This could mischaracterize Indigenous systems by organizing their legal relationships in terms of other legal cultures. The best way to provide examples seems to lie in sensitively providing descriptions that find resonance for Indigenous and non-Indigenous legal systems in Canada.

Civil law categories in the Quebec Civil Code provide analogies: persons, the family, successions, property, obligations, prior claims, evidence, prescription, publication of rights, private international law. S.Q., 1991, c. 64.

Common law analogies can be taken from law school or law society divisions of subject matter: property law, tort law, contracts law, criminal law, constitutional law, legal process, administrative law, evidence, civil procedure, corporate and commercial law, family law, trusts, wills and estates, and so on. The categorizations chosen in this chapter are borrowed from broad comparisons and contrasts in civil law, common law, and Indigenous legal systems. The Professional Legal Training Course of British Columbia breaks law down into the following categories: civil litigation, estates, family, real estate, commercial, company, creditors remedies, criminal procedure, professional responsibility, and law office management.

2 Clifford Gertz, *Local Knowledge: Further Essays in Interpretive Anthropology* (New York: Basic Books, 1983), 167.

3 The examples of Indigenous legal traditions in this chapter do not permit sufficient detail to represent a comprehensive view of any one system. This is best left to those with the proper knowledge and authority. A legal commentary should never be confused with a legal judgment. Care must also be taken to ensure that the written word is not considered superior to oral and other forms of literacy. The living application of Indigenous legal traditions remains their best representation.

4 Karl N. Llewellyn and E. Adamson Hoebel, *The Cheyenne Way: Conflict and Case Law in Primitive Jurisprudence* (Norman: University of Oklahoma Press, 1941), 11.

5 For a discussion of Indigenous legal traditions in the U.S. context, see Justin Richland and Sarah Deer, *Introduction to Tribal Legal Studies* (Lanham, MD: Altamira Press, 2004).

6 Sakej Henderson, 'Ayukpachi: Empowering Aboriginal Thought,' in *Reclaiming Indigenous Voice and Vision*, ed. Marie Batiste (Vancouver: UBC Press, 2000), 264.

7 Sakej Henderson, 'First Nations' Legal Inheritances: The Mikmaq Model' (1995) 23 *Manitoba Law Journal* 12.

8 Ibid.

9 Ibid. For further discussion of the *Santé Mawíomi,* see Royal Commission on Aboriginal Peoples, *The Final Report of the Royal Commission on Aboriginal Peoples,* vol. 1, *Looking Forward, Looking Back* (Ottawa: Supply and Services, 1996), 48–9.

> The Mawíomi, which continues into the present time, recognizes one or more *kep'tinaq* (captains; singular: *kep'tin*) to show the people the good path, to help them with gifts of knowledge and goods, and to sit with the whole Mawíomi as the government of all the Mi'kmaq. From among themselves, the kep'tinaq recognize a *jisaqumow* (grand chief) and *jikeptin* (grand captain), both to guide them and one to speak for them. From others of good spirit they choose advisers and

speakers, including the *putu's*, and the leader of the warriors, or *smaknis.*

10 James (Sakej) Youngblood Henderson, 'First Nations' Legal Inheritances in Canada: The Mikmaq Model' (1996) 23 *Manitoba Law Journal* 1 at 13.
11 Ibid., chap. 4. See Royal Commission on Aboriginal Peoples, *Report of the Royal Commission on Aboriginal Peoples*, vol. 1, *Looking Forward, Looking Back* (Ottawa: Supply and Services, 1996), 50. At the annual meeting, the *kep'tinaq* and *Mawíomi* saw that each family had sufficient planting grounds for the summer, fishing stations for spring and autumn, and hunting range for winter. Once assigned and managed for seven generations, these properties were inviolable. If disputes arose, they were arbitrated by the *kep'tinaq* individually or in council.
12 James (Sakej) Youngblood Henderson, 'First Nations' Legal Inheritances in Canada: The Mikmaq Model' (1996) 23 *Manitoba Law Journal* 1.
13 James (Sakej) Youngblood Henderson, '*Ayukpachi*: Empowering Aboriginal Thought,' in *Reclaiming Indigenous Voice and Vision*, ed. Marie Batiste (Vancouver: UBC Press, 2000), 256.
14 Kiera L. Ladner, 'Governing within an Ecological Context: Creating an AlterNative Understanding of Blackfoot Governance' (2003) 70 *Studies in Political Economy* 125 at 150.
15 Sakej Henderson, 'First Nations' Legal Inheritances in Canada: The Mikmaq Model' (1996) 23 *Manitoba Law Journal* 14.
16 Christie Jefferson, *Conquest by Law* (Ottawa: Supply and Services, 1994), retrieved 28 August 2009 from http://ww2.psepc-sppcc.gc.ca/publications/abor_policing/Conquest_by_Law_e.asp.
17 See the following story in Wilson Wallis and Ruth Wallis, *The Micmac Indians of Eastern Canada* (Minneapolis: University of Minnesota Press, 1954), 175:

> One night a man went to hunt moose, gave the moose call, and heard an answer. He was wearing, as a disguise, antlers of bark, in imitation of a moose. He called again, and this time was sure that the answer came from a moose. The other, who was in fact a man, saw the antlers in the bushes and shot at it. He heard a fall, and went over to look at his kill. He peeled off a piece of bark, lighted it, held it up as a torch, and saw a fallen man, shot through the heart. He carried the body home, and explained how the misadventure had happened. He was not punished.

See also Bernard Hoffman, *The Historical Ethnography of the Micmac of the Sixteenth and Seventeenth Centuries* (Berkeley: University of California Press, 1946), 515.

18 Ibid., 10–27.

19 Royal Commission on Aboriginal Peoples, *The Final Report of the Royal Commission on Aboriginal Peoples*, vol. 1, *Looking Forward, Looking Back* (Ottawa: Supply and Services, 1996), 47–9. The Royal Commission reproduced *A Mi'kmaq Creation Story* as follows:

> On the other side of the Path of the Spirits, in ancient times, *Kisúlk*, the Creator, made a decision. Kisúlk created the first born, *Niskam*, the Sun, to be brought across *Sk•tékmujeouti* (the Milky Way) to light the earth. Also sent across the sky was a bolt of lightning that created *Sitqamúk*, the earth, and from the same bolt *Kluskap* was also created out of the dry earth. Kluskap lay on Sitqamúk, pointing by head, feet and hands to the Four Directions. Kluskap became a powerful teacher, a *kinap* and a *puoin*, whose gifts and allies were great.
>
> In another bolt of lightning came the light of fire, and with it came the animals, the vegetation and the birds. These other life forms gradually gave Kluskap a human form. Kluskap rose from the earth and gave thanks to Kisúlk as he honoured the six directions: the sun, the earth, and then the east, south, west and north. The abilities within the human form made up the seventh direction.
>
> Kluskap asked Kisúlk how he should live, and Kisúlk in response sent Nukumi, Kluskap's grandmother, to guide him in life. Created from a rock that was transformed into the body of an old woman through the power of Niskam, the Sun, Nukumi was an elder whose knowledge and wisdom were enfolded in the Mi'kmaq language.
>
> Nukumi taught Kluskap to call upon *apistanéwj*, the marten, to speak to the guardian spirits for permission to consume other life forms to nourish human existence. Marten returned with their agreement, as well as with songs and rituals. Kluskap and his grandmother gave thanks to Kisúlk, to the Sun, to the Earth and to the Four Directions and then feasted. As they made their way to understand how they should live, Kluskap then met *Netawansum*, his nephew, whom Kisúlk had created in his human form from the rolling foam of the ocean that had swept upon the shores and clung to the sweetgrass. Netawansum had the understanding of the life and strength of the underwater realms and he brought gifts from

this realm to Kluskap, including the ability to see far away. They again gave thanks and feasted on nuts from the trees.

Finally they met *Níkanaptekewísqw*, Kluskap's mother, a woman whose power lay in her ability to tell about the cycles of life or the future. She was born from a leaf on a tree, descended from the power and strength of Niskam, the Sun, and made into human form to bring love, wisdom and the colours of the world. As part of the earth, she brought the strength and wisdom of the earth and an understanding of the means of maintaining harmony with the forces of nature.

They lived together for a long time, but one day Kluskap told his mother and nephew that he and his grandmother Nukumi were leaving them to go north. Leaving instructions with his mother, Kluskap told of the Great Council Fire that would send seven sparks, which would fly out of the fire and land on the ground, each as a man. Another seven sparks would fly out the other way and out of these seven sparks would arise seven women. Together they would form seven groups, or families, and these seven families should disperse in seven directions and then divide again into seven different groups.

Like the lightning bolts that created the earth and Kluskap, the sparks contained many gifts. The sparks gave life to human form; and in each human form was placed the prospect of continuity. Like Kluskap before them, when the people awoke naked and lost, they asked Kluskap how they should live. Kluskap taught them their lessons, and thus he is named 'one who is speaking to you' or the Teacher-Creator.

Source: This segment is based on a story taken from the ancient teachings of Mi'kmaq elders. The ancient creation story was compiled by Kep'tin Stephen Augustine of Big Cove, New Brunswick. See *Introductory Guide to Micmac Words and Phrases*, compiled by Evan Thomas Pritchard, annotations by Stephen Augustine, observations by Albert Ward (Rexton, NB: Resonance Communications, 1991). Another version is recounted by Reverend D. MacPherson in *Souvenir of the Micmac Tercentenary Celebration* (St Anne de Restigouche: Frères Mineurs Capucins, 1910).

20 James (Sakej) Youngblood Henderson, 'Mikmaw Tenure in Canada' (1995) 18 *Dalhousie Law Journal* 195 at 217–36.
21 Ibid.
22 Ibid., 239–44.
23 Ibid.
24 Ibid.

25 John Borrows, 'Listening for a Change: The Courts and Oral Tradition' (2001) 39 *Osgoode Hall Law Journal* 1.
26 Alison Prentice et al., *Canadian Women: A History* (Toronto: HBJ-Holt Canada, 1988), 207–8, 282–3.
27 *Edwards v. A.G. Canada* [1930] 1 DLR 98 (JCPC) at 105, citing *Rex. v. West Riding of Yorkshire County Council*, [1906] 2 K.B. 676.
28 Ibid.
29 Ibid., 106.
30 Ibid.
31 Ibid., 106–7.
32 The Supreme Court of Canada's decision in this case is styled *R. v. Marshall; R. v. Bernard*, 2005 SCC 43 (CanLII).
33 *R. v. Marshall*, (2001), 191 N.S.R. (2d) 323; [2001] 2 C.N.L.R. 256 at para. 57:

> Chief Augustine testified about stories passed down to him by his family. The most important of the stories were the Mi'kmaq creation story and the Getoasaloet story his grandmother told him when he was young. His grandmother said she had learned the creation story from his grandfather whom she had married while she was very young and his grandfather was very old. Chief Augustine said he had told the story at meetings of the Grand Council.

34 Ibid. at para. 58: 'The defence offered those stories as evidence of ancient connections between the Mi'kmaq and their territory and of the ancient roots of the seven districts into which that territory is divided ...'
35 *R. v. Marshall*, (2001), 191 N.S.R. (2d) 323; [2001] 2 C.N.L.R. 256 at para. 56–65.
36 Ibid.
37 The Nova Scotia Supreme Court (2002), 202 N.S.R. (2d) 42; [2002] 3 C.N.L.R. 176 at paras. 115–16, restated the Provincial Court's decision as follows at:

> [115] [...] There is also reference in Judge Curran's decision to the oral tradition and evidence of Stephen Augustine, a Hereditary Mi'kmaq Chief from New Brunswick and member of the Mi'kmaq Grand Council. The Learned Trial Judge acknowledged that Chief Augustine knows a great deal about Mi'kmaq culture and history. The Trial Judge did not appear to doubt the truthfulness of Chief Augustine. The evidence would appear to support a determination by the Trial Judge to

the effect that while Chief Augustine was telling the truth as he knew it, much of Chief Augustine's evidence was not historically accurate and Judge Curran specifically ruled:

I was not persuaded by him that Grand Council or seven districts were ancient Mi'kmaq traditions. I refer to other evidence which supported the Trial Judge's conclusion. Dr. Von Gernet referred to evidence Chief Augustine gave in relation to a wampum belt at the Vatican Archives. Chief Augustine suggested this was a representation of the linking of the Mi'kmaq nation with Christianity when Membertou was baptized in the early 1600's. Dr. Von Gernet went to the Vatican Archives and studied the belt, finding conclusive evidence that it had been made by Aboriginals in Québec as a gift for the Pope more than 200 years after Membertou's baptism. It was conceded by the Appellant's counsel at trial that the belt had nothing to do with Nova Scotia or the Mi'kmaq. Dr. Von Gernet cautioned about neo-traditionalism in relation to proof of historical events. He recognized that many traditions are very important to many modern native societies. That does not necessarily mean they are rooted in history. [116] Both *Van der Peet* and *Delgamuukw* make it clear that oral evidence is important in terms of conveying Aboriginal perspective. That does not mean it must be accepted as being historically accurate if there is convincing evidence to the contrary. Oral tradition is not any better than documentary evidence and it is not to be blindly accepted over a mountain of documentary evidence. The risks associated will oral history or oral tradition become very apparent when as in the present case it became obvious that the wampum belt was not part of Mi'kmaq history. In spite of this lack of connection the self-proclaimed interpreter of wampum belts in this case testified as to his reading of the belt and what it meant to the Mi'kmaq people.

38 Thanks go to Benjamin Berger and Hamar Foster for suggesting these possible analogies.
39 *Woolmington v. D.P.P.*, [1935] A.C. 462 (H.L.). For commentary, see Benjamin Berger, 'Trial by Metaphor: Rhetoric, Innovation and Juridical Text' (2002) 29 *Court Review* 30.
40 *Woolmington v. D.P.P.*, [1935] A.C. 462 (H.L.), 481.
41 Bruce P. Smith, 'The Presumption of Guilt and the English Law of Theft, 1750–1850' (2005) 23 *Law and History Review* 133. For a discussion of this principle in the United States, see William S. Laufer, 'The Rhetoric of Innocence' (1995) 70 *Washington University Law Review* 329.
42 Benjamin Berger, 'Peine Forte et Dure: Compelled Jury Trials and Legal Rights in Canada' (2003) 48 *Criminal Law Quarterly* 207.

43 Benjamin Berger, 'Criminal Appeals as Jury Control: An Anglo-Canadian Historical Perspective on the Rise of Criminal Appeals' (2005) 10 *Canadian Criminal Law Review* 1.

44 William Blackstone, *Commentaries on the Laws of England: A Facsimile of the First Edition of 1795–1769*, vol. 3 (Chicago: University of Chicago Press, 1979), 379.

45 Hamar Foster, 'Trial By Jury: the Thirteenth Century Crisis in Criminal Procedure' (1979) 13 *UBC Law Review* 280.

46 See Lewis H. Morgan, *League of the Ho-He-No-Sau-Nee or Iroquois*, vol. 1 (New York: Burt Franklin, 1901).

47 'The Last Speech of DeskaHeh, March 25, 1925,' in John Borrows and Len Rotman, *Aboriginal Legal Issues: Cases, Materials and Commentary*, 3rd ed. (Scarborough: LexisNexis, 2007), 45.

48 Francis Jennings, *The Ambiguous Iroquois Empire* (New York: W.W. Norton, 1990).

49 Taiaiake Alfred, *Peace, Power, Righteousness: An Indigenous Manifesto* (Toronto: Oxford University Press, 1999)

50 Donald A. Grinde Jr. and Bruce E. Johansen, *Exemplar of Liberty: Native America and the Evolution of Democracy* (Los Angeles: American Indian Studies Centre 1991); Bruce E. Johanesen, *Forgotten Founders: How the American Indian Helped Shape Democracy* (Boston: Harvard Common Press, 1982); Elizabeth Tooker, 'The United States Constitution and the Iroquois League,' in *The Imaginary Indian: Cultural Fictions and Government Policy*, ed. James Clifton (New Brunswick, NJ: Transactions Publishers, 1996), 108.

51 John Borrows, 'Wampum at Niagara: Canadian Legal History, Self-Government, and the Royal Proclamation,' in *Aboriginal and Treaty Rights in Canada*, ed. Michael Asch (Vancouver: UBC Press, 1998), 155–72; Victor Lytwyn, 'A Dish with One Spoon: The Shared Hunting Grounds Agreement in the Great Lakes and St Lawrence Valley Region,' in *Papers of the 28th Algonquian Conference*, ed. David H. Pentland (Winnipeg: University of Manitoba, 1997), 210–27.

52 William Fenton, *The Great Law and the Longhouse* (Norman: University of Oklahoma Press, 1998).

53 *Reading the Great Law of Peace*, Jake Thomas Learning Centre, 1992, 120 min., 10 videocassettes.

54 The structure of this overview follows the outline of the Great Law of Peace found at www.sixnations.org/Great_Law_of_Peace/.

55 Wampum was made traditionally of clam shells, which were drilled and threaded into strings or woven into belts. Wampum of various colours carried different symbolic meanings. Wampum strings and belts eventu-

ally came to be used as aids to memory and to validate the authority of persons carrying messages between communities and nations.

56 John Hurley, *Children or Brethren: Aboriginal Rights in Colonial Iroquoia* (Saskatoon: Native Law Centre, 1985), 40.

57 Henry Lewis Morgan, *League of the Ho-De-No-Sau-Nee or Iroquois* (Rochester: Sage, 1851), 77.

58 Ibid., 109–10.

59 William Fenton, 'Structure, Continuity and Change in the Process of Iroquois Treaty Making,' in *The History and Culture of Iroquois Diplomacy,* ed. Francis Jennings et al. (Syracuse: Syracuse University Press, 1985).

60 However, see *Logan v. Styres* (1959), 20 D.L.R. (2d) 416 (Ont. H.C.) on upholding forcible eviction of traditional Haudenosaunee government. For more information on the differing interpretations of the Two Row Wampum and the Silver Covenant Chain, see Kathryn V. Muller, 'The Two "Mystery" Belts of Grand River: A Biography of the Friendship Belt' (2007) 31 *American Indian Quarterly* 129–64.

61 See the following works by Taiaiaike Alfred: *Peace, Power, Righteousness: An Indigenous Manifesto* (Toronto: Oxford University Press, 1999); *Heeding the Voices of our Ancestors: Kahnawake Mohawk Politics and the Rise of Native Nationalism* (Toronto: Oxford University Press, 1999); *Wasáse: Indigenous Pathways of Action and Freedom* (Peterborough: Broadview Press, 2005).

62 For example, in 1876, the year the first consolidated *Indian Act* was passed, thirty-three Onondaga Chiefs from the Oshweken Council House of the Six Nations Indians wrote in a letter dated 17 August:

> To the Honourable Mr. D. Laird Superintendent of Indian Affairs: We the undersigned Chiefs & Members of the Six United Nation Indian Allies to the British Government residing on the Grand River, Township of Tuscarora, Onondaga and Oneida, in the counties of Brant and Haldimand Ont., to your Honourable our Brother by the treaty of Peace we thought it is fit and proper to bring a certain thing under your Notice which is a very great hindrance and grievance in our council for we believe in this part it is your duty to take it into consideration with your government to have this great hindrance and grievance to be removed in our council and it is this, one says we are subjects to the British Government and ought to be controlled under those Laws which was past in the Dominion Parliament by your Government you personally and the others (That is us) says we are not subjects but we are Allies to the British Government; and to your Honourable our Brother we will now inform you and your Government,

personally, that we will not deny to be Allies but we will be Allies to the British Government as our forefathers were; we will further inform your Honourable our Brother and to your Government that we do now separate from them henceforth we will have nothing to do with them anymore as they like to be controled under your Laws we now let them go to become as your own people, but us we will follow our Ancient Laws and Rules, and we will not depart from it.

NAC RGIO, Red Series, volume 1995, file 6897, MR C11130, 17 August 1876 (original spelling and punctuation preserved); cited in the Royal Commission on Aboriginal Peoples, *The Final Report of the Royal Commission on Aboriginal Peoples,* vol. 1, *Looking Forward, Looking Back* (Ottawa: Supply and Services, 1996), 182.

63 For example, the Haudenosaunee Confederacy at Six Nations on the Grand River represents the community in negotiations with other governments and has re-established its sittings in their traditional longhouse. This fact became more prominent because of a long unresolved dispute over land with their neighbours. On 28 February 2006 a group of Haudenosaunee people occupied a portion of a forty-hectare site in Caledonia, near Hamilton, Ontario, on which residential property development had commenced. They sought to reclaim their land and exercise their rights of governance over it. The developers sought and obtained an injunction to remove the Haudenosaunee occupiers, who had constructed a barricade to control access to the impugned site. The Ontario Provincial Police were called in and arrests were made, but the barricade and the protest remained. The Ontario government later purchased the land in question from the developers and the injunction against the occupiers was vacated, but the land is being held in trust pending the negotiated outcome of the dispute. Both the federal and Ontario governments appointed prominent former politicians as their negotiators; the elected chief of the Six Nations relinquished control over the negotiations to the Six Nations' hereditary chiefs.

64 This is illustrated by the Haudenosaunee submission to the United Nations at San Francisco, California, on 13 April 1945, cited from E. Lauterpacht, *International Law Reports* (Toronto: Butterworths, 1963), 243–4, as follows:

On behalf of the people of the Six Nations Indians settled upon part of the territory granted to them pursuant to the pledge given by the British Crown and granted under the terms of the Haldimand

Treaty of March 1784, we, the representatives of the above named
people of the Six Nations Indians, appeal to the conscience of the
democratic nations for action to correct the deep injustice under
which we are suffering ...

In accord with the terms of the proposal made to us by representatives of the English Crown, we as a sovereign people accepted the
terms of the Haldimand Treaty and settled upon the territory
thereby granted to us. A few years after our occupation of the territory and before it was fully settled a large part of the territory was
alienated from us by methods and on terms which did a deep injustice to our people and all their descendants ....

We appeal to the representatives of the governments and peoples
of the United Nations gathered here in this historic conference at
San Francisco to aid the people of the Six Nations Indians in securing these fundamental rights. Our appeal for restoration of the
property rights guaranteed to us in 1784 is based first of all upon
our duty, as parents, to protect the rights and the futures of our children, but it is based also upon our solemn obligation to protect the
rights of our people as a whole. We, the people of the Six Nations
Indians, who fought as allies of the British Crown during the American revolutionary war, accepted the grant of lands described in the
Haldimand Treaty and came to Canada from the United States to
settle on those lands in the spirit and in the understanding that we
were doing so as a sovereign people. As a nation we now appeal to
the conscience of the nations of the world. We appeal for the
restoration of those lands which the terms of the Haldimand Treaty
guaranteed the people of the Six Nations and their posterity are to
enjoy forever.

Verification of all the above statements is to be found in the copy
of Sessional Paper No. 151 tabled in the House of Commons
Canada on April 5th, 1945, which is attached.

ON BEHALF Of the people of the Six Nations Indians on the Grand
River at Brantford, Ontario ...

65 Robert Odawi Porter, 'A Proposal to the Hanodaganyas to Decolonize
    Federal Indian Control Law' (1998) 31 *University of Michigan Journal of
    Law Reform* 899.
66 'Haudenosaunee Confederacy Land Rights Statement, July 27, 2007,'
    retrieved 21 March 2008 from http://reclamationinfo.com/
    ?p=60#more-60.

67 The Haudenosaunee have in times past invited others to seek shelter in
their confederacy and under their Great Law. See William Fenton, *The
Great Law and the Longhouse: A Political History of the Iroquois Confederacy*
(Norman: University of Oklahoma Press, 1998), 73.

68 See Helen Hornbeck Tanner, *Atlas of Great Lakes Indian History* (Norman:
University of Oklahoma Press, 1982), 58–9.

69 See Diamond Jenness, *The Indians of Canada* (Ottawa: Queen's Printer,
1967), 277.

70 The Odawa are also known as Otaouan or Ottawa. I refer to these people
as the Odawa because that is what they prefer to be called. Historically,
the Odawa had four known subdivisions: the Sinago, Kiskakon, Sable,
and Nassauakueton. Christian A. Feest, 'Ottawa,' in *Handbook of North
American Indians*, vol. 15, ed. Bruce G. Trigger (Washington: Smithsonian
Institute, 1978), 772. See also Vernon Kinetz, *The Indians of the Western
Great Lakes* (Ann Arbor: University of Michigan Press, 1940), 246.

71 For a history of the Potawatomi, see R. David Edmunds, *The Potawatomis,
Keepers of the Fire* (Norman: University of Oklahoma Press, 1978).

72 Ojibway is the common title applied to these people in Canada, and
Chippewa is the name most frequently used in the United States.
Throughout their history, the Ojibway have gone by different European
descriptions in various regions of the Great Lakes. Contemporary Western
terminology still applies some divisions to the Ojibway. On the north
shores of Lakes Ontario and Erie, the Ojibway are called Mississaugas, on
the south shore of Lake Huron they are sometimes named Saugeens,
while at the confluence of Lakes Huron and Superior around Sault Ste
Marie they are often known as the Saulteaux. Ojibway are further classified by their geographical location: the Southeast Chippewas of Michigan's lower peninsula and adjacent Ontario, the Chippewas of Lake Superior, the Southwest Chippewas of interior Minnesota, the Northern
Chippewa of the Laurentian uplands above the Great Lakes, and the
Plains Chippewa or Bungees. See Edmund Jefferson Danziger Jr., *The
Chippewa of Lake Superior* (Norman: University of Oklahoma Press, 1978).

73 People of the Three Fires are now found in other places in North
America. Odawa people live in Kansas and Oklahoma because of the
Removal Policies of the U.S. government in earlier periods. Potawatomi
people also live in Oklahoma for the same reason, though there are still
some communities in their traditional territories in Michigan and Wisconsin. Contemporary Ojibway communities can also be found surrounding Lakes Superior and Michigan, and on the north shores of Lakes
Erie and Ontario.

74 'Each family of this tribe has a certain hunting region, to which the members of the family have a particular or exclusive right.' Rev. Frederick Baraga, *Chippewa Indians: As Recorded by Rev. Frederick Baraga in 1847* (New York: Studicia Slovenica, 1976), 25.

75 'A Band Civil Chief had no coercive force. Control over affairs depended entirely upon personal prestige and the demands of the moment ... Civil Chiefs, usually men who inherited their position, also presided at band councils and represented their people at common and grand councils. All men and women past the age of puberty were included in open discussions of the band council.' Edmund Jefferson Danziger Jr., *The Chippewa of Lake Superior* (Norman: University of Oklahoma Press, 1978), 23.

76 Though sometimes totems were chosen rather than inherited if the circumstances were expedient for it. See Richard White, *The Middle Ground: Indians, Empires and Republics in the Great Lakes Region, 1650–1815* (Cambridge: Cambridge University Press, 1991), 16–20.

77 William Warren, *History of the Ojibway Nation* (St Paul: Minnesota Historical Society, 1885; reprint, Minneapolis: Ross and Haines, 1970), 42.

78 See C. Callender, *Social Organization of the Central Algonkian Indians,* Pub. No. 7 (Milwaukee: Milwaukee Public Museum, 1962), cited in Leo Waisberg, 'The Ottawa: Traders of the Upper Great Lakes, 1715–1800' (MA thesis, McMaster University, 1977), 128–31. For a more general description of the clan or totem system of organization, see William Warren, *History of the Ojibway Nation* (St Paul: Minnesota Historical Society, 1885; reprint, Minneapolis: Ross and Haines, 1970), 41–53.

79 William Cronon has described First Nations' distribution of fishing rights in a way that harmonizes with the above communal methods of resource distribution, and corresponds to the traditional fishing practices used by the Odawa and Ojibway. While describing other groups which resembled the Anishinabek in social and cultural practices, he has written: '[I]n the case of extraordinarily plentiful fishing sites – especially major inland waterfalls during spawning runs – several major villages might gather at a single spot to share the wealth. All of them acknowledged a mutual right to use the site for that specific purpose, even though it might otherwise lie within a single village's territory. Property rights, in other words, shifted with ecological use.' See William Cronon, *Changes in the Land: Indians, Colonists, and the Ecology of New England* (Toronto: McGraw-Hill Ryerson, 1983), 63. See also J.H. Coyne, *Galinee's Narrative 1670–71,* vol. 4 (Toronto: Ontario Historical Society, 1903), 73, for a description of this phenomenon occurring among the Ottawa and Ojibway at Sault Ste Marie.

80 The framework of allocation that was based on specific ecological uses was also reflected in the distribution of property between village sites:

> In order to use the sparse resources of the north woods efficiently, members of the Ottawa and Chippewa bands migrated seasonally to locations where they could find adequate resources. In time, these movements settled into well-established patterns, an annual round. The pattern varied from place to place, depending on the flora and fauna and the amount of farming practised by a band or a group, but its basic rhythms remained. From late spring through early fall, the Ottawas and the Chippewas lived in relatively large groups on the shores of the Great Lakes, where fish provided plenty to eat ... In the fall these large gatherings separated into smaller kin-linked groups ... migrating to family hunting grounds usually located about fifty miles inland along the banks of a river ... The same families appeared to have used the same winter camps year after year and had developed a sense of ownership.

Robert Doherty, *Disputed Waters: Native Americans and the Great Lakes Fishery* (Lexington: University Press of Kentucky, 1990), 481–3.

81 H.P Biggar, ed., *The Works of Samuel de Champlain*, vol. 3 (Toronto: University of Toronto Press, 1936), 210 and 319.

82 One has to be careful about assuming that observations about Aboriginal resource-use by post-contact writers are valid for pre-contact Aboriginal society. There is a debate in the anthropological literature that states that the allocations to be described in the next few pages developed as a result of the fur trade, and were not practised before contact. See T.G. Brasser, 'Group Identification along a Moving Frontier,' *Verhandlungen des XXXVIII Internationalen Amerikanischenkongresses* (Munich: BndII, 1971), 261. While there is no doubt that contact had significant ramifications on Aboriginal customs, the effect was usually to intensify pre-existing uses, before changing them over a longer period of time. See Bruce G. Trigger, *Natives and Newcomers: Canada's Heroic Age Reconsidered* (Kingston: McGill-Queen's University Press, 1985), 214–28. As an Anishinabe person, I have been taught that the types of resource allocations I am describing existed long before contact.

83 Robert Doherty, *Disputed Waters: Native Americans and the Great Lakes Fishery* (Lexington: University Press of Kentucky, 1990), 15–16.

84 Baron De Lahontan and Reuben Thwaites, eds., *New Voyages to North America*, vol. 1 (Chicago: McClurg, 1905), 210 and 319. For a critique of

his work, see Percy Adams, *Travelers and Travel Liars, 1660–1800* (Berkeley: University of California Press), 1.

85 Robert Doherty, *Disputed Waters: Native Americans and the Great Lakes Fishery* (Lexington: University Press of Kentucky, 1990), 11–12.

86 Ibid., 59.

87 Basil Johnston, personal correspondence to the author, 20 June 2008.

88 Michael Coyle, 'Traditional Indian Justice in Ontario: A Role for the Present?' (1986) 24 *Osgoode Hall Law Journal* 605–33.

89 Jennifer Nedelsky, 'Reconceiving Rights as Relationship' (1993) 1 *Review of Constitutional Studies* 1–26; Joseph Singer, 'The Legal Rights Debate in Analytical Jurisprudence from Bentham to Hohfeld' (1982) *Wisconsin Law Review* 975.

90 Wesley Newcomb Hohfeld, *Fundamental Legal Conceptions*, ed. Walter Wheeler Cook (New Haven, CT: Yale University Press, 1919), 35–64.

91 *Lake Shore & M. S. R. v. Kurtz* (1894) 10 Ind. App., 60; 37 N.E., 303, 304.

92 I found this excellent rendition of the Anishinabek creation story at 'Creation Story,' retrieved 28 March 2008 at www.ancestraltrails.org /ojibwe.html:

> When the Earth was new, it had a family. The moon, or Grandmother and the sun, called Grandfather. The Creator of all of this said that the Earth was a woman – Mother Earth – because all living things came from her. Water (the oceans, lakes, rivers and streams) are her life blood nourishing and purifying her. Mother Earth was given four directions – East, South, West and North, each with physical and spiritual powers.
>
> When Mother Earth was new Creator filled her with beauty. He sent singers in the form of birds who also carry the seeds of life to all Directions. There were swimmers in the water. He placed plants, trees, insects, crawlers and four-leggeds on the land. And everyone lived in harmony with everyone else.
>
> Creator, or Kitchi-Manitoo as Ojibwe people call him, then blew into four parts of Mother Earth using the sacred Megis Shell. From the union of these four sacred elements and his breath, two-leggeds or man was born. Thus, man was the last form of life to be put on Earth. From this original man came the Anishinabe – or The People.
>
> There came a time when the harmonious way of life did not continue. Men and women disrespected each other, families quarreled and soon villages began arguing back and forth. This saddened Kitchi-Manitoo greatly, but he waited. Finally, when it seemed there was no

hope left, Creator decided to purify Mother Earth through the use of water. The water came, flooding the Earth, catching all of creation off guard. All but a few of each living thing survived. How could life begin again?

Nanabush, or the spirit of the original people, found himself floating on a log in the water covering Mother Earth. As he floated, some of the other animals still alive would come and rest on the log. All would take turns and through this sharing they saved themselves and each other. After floating for a long time and not seeing land, Nanabush finally said, 'I'm going to swim to the bottom of this water and grab a handful of Earth. With this and help from Creator, I believe we can create a new land.' He dived and was gone a long time. Finally he surfaced but was so out of breath he could not speak. Then he said, 'It's too deep. I can't swim fast enough to reach the bottom.'

Everyone on the log was silent. Finally a loon, who was swimming alongside the log, spoke: 'I can dive a long ways for my food. I will dive to the bottom and bring some of Earth up in my beak.' Loon dived and was gone a long time. Just when the others thought she'd drowned she surfaced very weak and out of breath. 'I couldn't make it. There doesn't seem to be a bottom.'

The grebe then came forward and offered to try. Grebe was gone a long time too and just when everyone was about to give up hope, they saw him float to the top. He was unconscious but alive. When he awoke he said, 'I am very sorry my brothers and sisters, I too couldn't reach the bottom.'

Many more animals offered themselves to do the job, important to the survival of all. Mink tried but couldn't make it; otter tried and failed. Even Turtle tried but didn't make it. Just when all seemed hopeless, a soft voice spoke up. 'I'll try,' it said. When everyone turned to look, Muskrat stepped forward. 'I'll try,' he said again. Some of the others laughed at him, but Nanabush said, 'Hold it, it is not our place to judge another. That belongs to Creator and if little Muskrat wants to try I think we should let him.'

With that, Muskrat dived down and disappeared. Nanabush and the others were sure Muskrat had given up his life trying to reach the bottom. Muskrat made it to the bottom. He grabbed some Earth in his paw and with his last bit of strength pushed toward the surface. One of the animals on the log saw Muskrat as he floated to the top and they pulled him onto the log. Nanabush looked him over and said, 'It seems our brother went without air for too long. He's dead.' A song of

mourning and praise began and floated over the water. Then
Nanabush said, 'Look! Muskrat has something in his paw.' Carefully
they opened it and there in Muskrat's paw was a piece of Earth. Everyone cheered. Muskrat had given up his life so that the others could
begin again.

   Nanabush took the piece of Earth from Muskrat's paw just as Turtle
came swimming up. 'Use my back to bear the weight of this piece of
Earth. With Creator's help we can make a new Earth,' she said. When
the Earth was placed on Turtle's back the winds began to blow from
each of the Four Directions. The tiny piece of Earth began to grow.
Larger and larger it grew until it formed an island. And still Turtle bore
the weight on her back. Nanabush began to sing and all the animals
began to dance in a circle. Finally the winds ceased and water was
calm and a huge island sat right in the middle of the great water.

See also Basil Johnston, *Ojibway Heritage* (Toronto: McClelland and
Stewart, 1996), 11–17. I draw heavily on the work of Basil Johnston in the
following sources because his research is well respected in many Ojibway
communities, and he grew up and resides on my reserve. For another
prominent version of Anishinabek creation, see Edward Benton-Banai,
The Mishomis Book: The Voice of the Ojibway (Hayward: Indian Country
Communications, 1988).

93 'Out of nothing Kitche Manitou made rock, water, fire, and wind. Into
each he breathed the breath of life. On each he bestowed with his breath
a different essence and nature. Each substance had its own power which
became its soul-spirit. From these four substances Kitche Manitou created
the physical world of sun, stars, moon and earth. Then Kitche Manitou
made the plant beings. These were four kinds: flowers, grasses, trees and
vegetables. To each he gave a spirit of life, growth, healing and beauty.
Each he placed where it would be most beneficial, and lend to earth the
greatest beauty and harmony and order. After plants, Kitche Manitou
created animal beings conferring on each special powers and natures.
There were two-leggeds, four-leggeds, wingeds and swimmers. Last of
all he made man. Though last in order of creation, least in the order of
dependence, and weakest in bodily powers, man had the greatest gift –
the power to dream. Kitche Manitou then made The Great Laws of
Nature for the well being and harmony of all things and all creatures.
The Great Laws governed the place and movement of sun, moon, earth
and stars; governed the powers of wind, water, fire and rock; governed
the rhythm and continuity of life, birth, growth and decay. All things

lived and worked by these laws.' Basil Johnston, *Ojibway Heritage* (Toronto: McClelland and Stewart, 1996), 13–14.

94 For Anishinabek to speak of accountability detached from notions of to whom duties are owed (acknowledgment), how they should be exercised (accomplishment), and the consequences that flow from such exercise (approbation) is to speak of a hollow, almost meaningless concept. Accountability is given context by its relationship to larger principles of stewardship. It draws its significance from the fact that the Creator, the earth, plants, animals, and other beings are those to whom responsibility flows. Accountability is thus given meaning by the knowledge one has about how to prepare to exercise and implement this responsibility. Stewardship is only effective when people recognize that specific consequences flow from how duties are acknowledged and accomplished. Part of the *acknowledgment* necessary for Anishinabek peoples in exercising contemporary stewardship is to admit that people who originally came from other parts of the world now form a part of our network of associations. Just as Anishinabek once acknowledged a stewardship towards the Creator, earth, plants, animals, and other beings in a time prior to their arrival, they must now acknowledge that non-Indigenous peoples form a part of their current web of life. In this light, there are four important considerations that should form a part of discussions about stewardship and accountability.

95 For a discussion of these stories describing people's stewardship responsibilities and associated ceremonies, see generally, Basil Johnston, *Ojibway Ceremonies* (Toronto: McClelland and Stewart, 1980). Historically, Aboriginal peoples would learn how to *accomplish* their stewardships through instruction and practice. Learning would be assisted by participation in ceremonies that taught people how best to *acknowledge* 'all their relations.' This period of preparation was vital to understanding the laws and customs upon which stewardship was based. When students had solid background knowledge of what their responsibilities required, they would receive a specific responsibility in the community. They would learn the specific duties required to *accomplish* each particular job they undertook in accordance with the values learned earlier. They would be expected to live according to their preparation to put those teachings into practice. Through such preparations, First Nations peoples learned that stewardship was *accomplished* by following principles such as loyalty, bravery, courage, generosity, and love towards other beings that were part of their world. Currently, much of the government's response to securing accountability within First Nations is focused on taking legisla-

tive action to codify technical rules of behaviour. There is no talk of
preparation in accordance with ancient ceremonies and teachings. There
is no discussion *acknowledging* the source of First Nations stewardship,
nor the means by which this stewardship should be *accomplished*.
Missing are words and stories that incorporate Aboriginal principles
about faithfulness, valour, kindness, resolve, affection, and steadfastness
towards the Creator.

 96 Ibid., 21–58, 119–33.
 97 Ibid., 80–93, 134–48.
 98 Ibid., 94–118.
 99 Verna Petronella Johnston, *Tales of Nokomis* (Toronto: Stoddart, 1975), 25.
100 Edward Higgins, *Nookomis O Dibajamonwin, Grandmother Tell Me a Story*
     (Cobalt: Highway Book Shop, 1986), 7–10.
101 Basil Johnston, 'Animoosh w'gauh izhitchigaet,' in *Star Man and Other
     Tales* (Toronto: Royal Ontario Museum, 1997), 44–51.
102 Basil Johnston, *The Manitous: The Spiritual World of the Ojibway* (Toronto:
     Key Porter, 1995), 195–220.
103 Basil Johnston, *Ojibway Heritage* (Toronto: McClelland and Stewart,
     1996), 61.
104 See, generally, George Laidlaw, 'Ojibway Myths and Tales,' *Twenty-Seventh
     Annual Archeological Report 86* (Ontario: Ministry of Education, 1915), 30–5.
105 Compiled by Emerson Coatsworth and David Coatsworth, and told by
     Sam Snake, Chief Elijah Yellowhead, Alder York, David Simcoe, and
     Annie King, *Adventures of Nanabush: Ojibway Indian Stories* (Toronto:
     Doubleday Canada, 1979).
106 Basil Johnston, *Ojibway Heritage* (Toronto: McClelland and Stewart,
     1996), 17.
107 For further information about the symbolism and role of Odaemin, see
     Benton-Banai, *The Mishomis Book: The Voice of the Ojibway* (Hayward:
     Indian Country Communications, 1988), 57.
108 Jarvis Papers, Metro Toronto Reference Library, Collection # S-125,
     Volume B57. Jarvis was superintendent of Indian Affairs in the 1840s.
109 *Rodriguez v. B.C. (A.G.)*, [1993] 3 S.C.R. 519 at 54.
110 Fikret Berkes, *Sacred Ecology: Traditional Ecological Knowledge and Resource
     Management* (Philadelphia, PA: Taylor and Francis, 1999).
111 Harold Cardinal and Walter Hildebrandt, *Treaty Elders of Saskatchewan:
     Our Dream Is That Our Peoples Will One Day Be Clearly Recognized as
     Nations* (Calgary: University of Calgary Press, 2000).
112 These words have the following meaning: *wahkohtowin* – laws govern-
     ing all relations; *miyo-wicehtowin* – having or possessing just relations as

in the way Cree will conduct their lives individually or collectively; *pastahowin* – a transgression of spiritual or natural law, sin, use of bad medicine, or evil doings all of which will be responded to by the Creator; *ohcinewin* – part of the concept of *pastahowin*, to suffer in retribution for an action against Creation; and *kwuyaskitotamowin* – doing things in a right way, treating Creation in a good way, a just or legal dealing.

113 Kathleen O'Reilly-Scanlon, Kristine Crowe, and Angelina Weenie, 'Pathways to Understanding: Wahkohtowin as a Research Methodology' (2004) 39 *McGill Journal of Education* 1 at 29.

114 Elder Dolly Neapetung, cited in Harold Cardinal and Walter Hildebrandt, *Treaty Elders of Saskatchewan: Our Dream Is That Our Peoples Will One Day Be Clearly Recognized as Nations* (Calgary: University of Calgary Press, 2000), 6.

115 Harold Cardinal and Walter Hildebrandt, *Treaty Elders of Saskatchewan: Our Dream Is That Our Peoples Will One Day Be Clearly Recognized as Nations* (Calgary: University of Calgary Press, 2000), 34.

116 Ibid., 14.

117 Ibid.

118 Shalene Jobin, 'Guiding Philosophy and Governance Model of Bent Arrow Traditional Healing Society' (Master of Arts in Indigenous Governance thesis, University of Victoria, 2005) retrieved 28 August 2009 from http://web.uvic.ca/igov/research/pdfs/Bent%Arrow%20%Governance-Final.pdf.

119 Harold Cardinal and Walter Hildebrandt, *Treaty Elders of Saskatchewan: Our Dream Is That Our Peoples Will One Day Be Clearly Recognized as Nations* (Calgary: University of Calgary Press, 2000), 14–15.

120 Ibid.

121 Robert Brighton, *Grateful Prey: Rock Cree Human-Animal Relations* (Berkeley: University of California Press, 1993), 104: '*pastahow* (verb): "someone brings retribution on himself."'

122 Chief Wayne Roan and Earle Waugh, *Nature's Laws* (Heritage Community Foundation, 2004), retrieved 19 September 2008 from www.abheritage.ca/natureslaws/spiritual/index9.html.

123 Paul Driben, Donald J. Auger, Anthony N. Doob, and Raymond P. Auger, 'No Killing Ground: Aboriginal Law Governing the Killing of Wildlife among the Cree and Ojibwa of Northern Ontario' (1997) 1 *Ayaangwaamizin* 101.

124 Robert Brighton, *Grateful Prey: Rock Cree Human-Animal Relations* (Berkeley: University of California Press, 1993), 197.

125 Rupert Ross has observed: 'Storytelling as a means of law-giving seems

to be based on the same understanding – that law can be known to
everyone through reciting the consequences of acts alone, not through
communicating judgmental labels for either the act or, worse still, the
actor.' Rupert Ross, *Return to the Teachings: Exploring Aboriginal Justice*
(Toronto: Viking/Penguin, 1996), 171.

126 In addition to Michif, there is a Gaelic-influenced language called
Bungee. Chinook is also arguably a Métis language.

127 'Among the historical Métis people, entire families participated in
buffalo hunting expeditions. As there were large numbers of participants to organize, some of the activities within family units were supplemented by a quasi-military organization in the camp as a whole.
Alexander Ross, in an 1856 account, described the discipline enforced
during a buffalo hunt involving 1,210 Red River carts and 1,630 men,
women, boys and girls. The movement of the camp was under the direction of 10 captains, among whom a senior was named. Under the captains were 10 soldiers and 10 guides, the latter taking turns bearing the
flag used to signal directions to move or to stop the entourage. While
the flag was up, the guide was chief of the expedition and in command
of everyone. The moment the flag was lowered, the captains and soldiers were on duty.' See Royal Commission on Aboriginal Peoples, *The
Final Report of the Royal Commission on Aboriginal Peoples*, vol. 3, *Gathering
Strength* (Ottawa: Supply and Services, 1996).

128 Alexander Ross, *The Red River Settlement: Its Rise, Progress, and Present
State* (Minneapolis: Ross and Haines, 1957), 249–50.

129 See Royal Commission on Aboriginal Peoples, *The Final Report of the
Royal Commission on Aboriginal Peoples*, vol. 3, *Gathering Strength* (Ottawa:
Supply and Services, 1996). The Commissioners wrote: 'Métis families
similarly divided responsibilities between men and women as they
ranged on extended hunting expeditions from permanent settlements,
such as Red River. A woman from a Montana Métis settlement, who
lived a mobile lifestyle with a group that migrated from Manitoba to
Montana following the buffalo, recalled camp life in the early part of the
twentieth century: "Our men did all the hunting, and we women did all
the tanning of the buffalo hides, jerky meat making, pemmican and
moccasins. For other supplies, we generally had some trader with us …
who always had a supply of tea, sugar, tobacco and so on."' Obituary of
Clemence Gourneau Berger, *Democrat-News*, Lewistown, Montana, 31
December 1943, quoted in Verne Dusenberry, 'Waiting for a Day that
Never Comes: The Dispossessed Métis of Montana,' in *The New Peoples:
Being and Becoming Métis in North America*, ed. Jacqueline Peterson and

Jennifer S.H. Brown (Winnipeg: University of Manitoba Press, 1985), 125.

130 See Janna Promislow, *Toward a Legal History of the Fur Trade: Looking for Law at York Factory, 1714–1763* (LL.M. thesis, Osgoode Hall, 2004).

131 George F.G. Stanley, *The Birth of Western Canada: A History of the Riel Rebellion* (Toronto: University of Toronto Press, 1960).

132 The Dominion's unilateral attempt to add the old north-west to Canada was legislated in the *Rupert's Land Act, 1868,* 1868, (U.K.), c. 105. For historical context, see Maggie Siggins, *Riel: A Life of Revolution* (Toronto: Harper Collins, 1994).

133 *Manitoba Act,* 1870 (U.K.) 32 & 33 Vict., c. 3. The act provided for the creation of the Province of Manitoba, French-language rights, protection for settled and common lands, distribution of 1.4 million acres of land to Métis children, and amnesty for those who participated in the provisional government.

134 The Imperial Parliament passed the *Constitution Act, 1871,* 1871, (U.K.), c. 28 to give effect to the provisions embodied in the *Manitoba Act.*

135 See *R. v. Dumont,* (1988) 52 D.L.R. (4th) 25 (Man. C.A.); rev'd (1990) 67 D.L.R. (4th) 159 (S.C.C.).

136 Joanne Pelletier, *Gabriel Dumont* (Saskatoon: Gabriel Dumont Institute of Native Studies and Applied Research, 1985).

137 Fred Shore and Lawrence Barkwell, eds., *Past Reflects the Present: The Métis Elders' Conference* (Winnipeg: Manitoba Métis Federation, 1997).

138 *Métis Settlements Act,* R.S.A. 2000, c. M-14.

139 See Cathy Bell, *Contemporary Métis Justice* (Saskatoon: Native Law Centre, 1999).

140 Carrier clans are bear, caribou, grouse, frog, small frog, fireweed, wolf, and beaver. Linguistic dialects are Babine, Cheslatta, Nakazd'li, Saik'uz, Lheidli-T'enneh, and Wit'suwit'en. See Diamond Jenness, 'The Carrier Indians of the Bulkley River: Their Social and Religious Life,' *Bulletin #133, Bureau of American Ethnology, Anthropological Papers No. 25* (Washington, DC, 1943), 469–586.

141 Factum of the Appellants, 'The Wet'suwet'en Heriditary Chiefs, in the Supreme Court of Canada,' No. 23799, Native Law Centre of Canada (n.d.), retrieved 19 September 2008 from www.usask.ca/nativelaw /factums/W.html at para. 31. The house in historic times was literally a plank-walled house, where the chief would provide leadership to people living under one roof. The house controlled its own territories for food, social, ceremonial and commercial purposes, trade and ceremonial purposes. See Ken Rabet, 'The Past into the Present: Cultural Her-

itage Resource Review of the Bulkley Timber Supply Area' (2000), at 32, retrieved 19 September 2008 from http://66.102.7.104/search?q=cache:5lq7hnWu2dkJ:www.for.gov.bc.ca/dss/cultural/CHRRE-VIEW.pdf+Babine+kun gax&hl=en#22.

142　Ibid.
143　The Carrier name (*Porteur*) comes from a historic law that required widows to carry their deceased husband's ashes from their winter to their summer village, so that a ceremonial rite could be performed to acknowledge and fulfil important legal obligations.
144　Margaret Tobey, 'Carrier,' in *Handbook of North American Indians,* vol. 6, *Subarctic*, ed. June Helm (Washington, DC: Smithsonian Institution, 1981), 413–42.
145　Antonia Mills, *Eagle Down Is Our Law: Witsuwit'en Feasts and Land Claims* (Vancouver: UBC Press, 1994), 122.
146　Ibid., 74.
147　Ibid., 75.
148　Warner Adam, Travis Holyk, and Perry Shawana, 'Whu Neeh Nee (Guiders of Our People): Carrier Sekani First Nations Family Law Alternative Dispute Resolution' (paper presented at the 6th International Conference on Restorative Justice, 1 June 2003), retrieved 28 August 2009 from www.sfu.ca/cfrj/fulltext/adam.pdf.
149　Ibid., 3.
150　Antonia Mills, *Eagle Down Is Our Law: Witsuwit'en Feasts and Land Claims* (Vancouver: UBC Press, 1994), 157–8.
151　Ibid.
152　Ibid., 157.
153　Diamond Jenness, 'The Carrier Indians' (1943) 25 *Anthropological Papers* 547.
154　Antonia Mills, *Eagle Down Is Our Law: Witsuwit'en Feasts and Land Claims* (Vancouver: UBC Press, 1994), 157.
155　Diamond Jenness, 'Myths of the Carrier Indians of British Columbia' (1934) 47 *American Folklore*, 203.
156　Ibid.
157　Jo-Anne Fiske and Betty Patrick, Cis Dideen Kat, *When the Plumes Rise: The Way of the Lake Babine Nation* (Vancouver: UBC Press, 2000).
158　Warner Adam, Travis Holyk, and Parry Shawana, 'Whu Neeh Nee (Guiders of Our People): Carrier Sekani First Nations Family Law Alternative Dispute Resolution' (paper presented at the 6th International Conference on Restorative Justice, 1 June 2003), retrieved 28 August 2009 from www.sfu.ca/cfrj/fulltext/adam.pdf.

159 Jo-Anne Fiske and Betty Patrick, Cis Dideen Kat, *When the Plumes Rise: The Way of the Lake Babine Nation* (Vancouver: UBC Press, 2000), 57.

160 Warner Adam, Travis Holyk, and Perry Shawana, 'Whu Neeh Nee (Guiders of Our People): Carrier Sekani First Nations Family Law Alternative Dispute Resolution' (paper presented at the 6th International Conference on Restorative Justice, 1 June 2003), retrieved 28 August 2009 from www.sfu.ca/cfrj/fulltext/adam.pdf, 3.

161 Ibid.

162 Antonia Mills, *Eagle Down Is Our Law: Witsuwit'en Feasts and Land Claims* (Vancouver: UBC Press, 1994), 138.

163 Ibid., 38.

164 W. Naziel, 'Wet'suwet'en Traditional Use Study Report' (Moricetown, BC: Office of Wet'suwet'en Hereditary Chiefs, 1997), n.p.

165 Antonia Mills, *Eagle Down Is Our Law: Witsuwit'en Feasts and Land Claims* (Vancouver: UBC Press, 1994), 38.

166 Ibid.

167 Ibid.

168 Ibid.

169 Warner Adam, Travis Holyk, and Perry Shawana, 'Whu Neeh Nee (Guiders of Our People): Carrier Sekani First Nations Family Law Alternative Dispute Resolution' (paper presented at the 6th International Conference on Restorative Justice, 1 June 2003), retrieved 28 August 2009 from www.sfu.ca/cfrj/fulltext/adam.pdf, 3.

170 Jo-Anne Fiske and Betty Patrick, Cis Dideen Kat, *When the Plumes Rise: The Way of the Lake Babine Nation* (Vancouver: UBC Press, 2000), 57.

171 Neil Sterritt, Susan Marsden, Robert Galois, Peter Grant, and Richard Overstall, *Tribal Boundaries in the Nass Watershed* (Vancouver: UBC Press, 1998), 12.

172 Ibid.

173 A. Rose, ed., *Nisga'a: People of the Nass River* (Vancouver: Douglas and McIntyre, 1993), 22.

174 Ibid., 15.

175 T. Molloy, *The World Is Our Witness* (Calgary: Fifth House, 2000), 121.

176 For a summary of *Ayuukhl Nisga'a* by Nisga'a Elder Bert McKay, see A. Rose, ed., *Nisga'a: People of the Nass River* (Vancouver: Douglas and McIntyre, 1993), 125–9.

177 Ibid. Elder Bert McKay has said:

     [T]he Settlement of the Estate ... happens when a person dies. And it's the only time a name of a chieftain can be transferred to a person.

Ayuukhl Nisga'a dictates that to be a chieftain, you have to be reared for it. You have to be disciplined and you have to have the approval of your people before you can take that rank. And today, that's still in place. Under the chieftainship too is our property rights. Again, this was in place before the advent of our western counterparts. There were very strict laws regarding property rights so that there was no need for our people to be going beyond their boundaries to take someone else's property because it was never allowed under our laws. I'm a Raven and my father was a Wolf chieftain. According to our law, I was privileged because I was his son, or any of my brothers and sisters were allowed, to harvest from his resource areas as long as he was alive. And the minute he died that privilege was given back; I had no claim on his property then. I'm married to a Killer Whale princess and they have resource areas so when we married I was told that because of the children that we were going to have, they will be Killer Whales so I was privileged to feed them from that resource area. As long as my wife lives that will happen. And it's reciprocal. My people would say the same to my wife, but the minute I die that property goes back to us. Our laws, perhaps, are edicts, really much more refined because they are constant. They are still observed today.

Ibid., 127–8.

178 Ibid.
179 Ibid., 125.
180 Ibid., 15.
181 Chief Joseph Gosnell, 'Nisga'a Treaty Sends Signal of Hope and Reconciliation around the World,' retrieved 28 August 2009 from www.kermode.net/nisgaa/speeches/gosnell3.html.
182 A. Rose, ed., *Nisga'a: People of the Nass River* (Vancouver: Douglas and McIntyre, 1993), 129.
183 R.S.C. 2000, c. 7; S.B.C. 1999, c. 2. Within Nisga'a Lisims Government there are two legislative houses known as the Wilp Si'ayuukhl Nisga'a and the Nisga'a Lisims.
184 Nisga'a Final Agreement Act, S.B.C. 1999, c. 2.
185 Ibid.
186 Neil Sterritt, Susan Marsden, Robert Galois, Peter Grant, and Richard Overstall, *Tribal Boundaries in the Nass Watershed* (Vancouver: UBC Press, 1998). The authors argue that the Nisga'a have breached Indigenous law in making such a large claim over territory that belongs to others.
187 During Wilp Si'ayuukhl Nisga'a meetings, all members are able to make

statements, participate in question periods, introduce petitions, raise urgent matters, and debate Nisga'a bills that are introduced. Legislation is enacted by Wilp Si'ayuukhl' Nisga'a when there is an introduction of a bill; consideration of the bill; final vote of the bill; and the signing of the bill by the president.

188 The Nisga'a Lisims Government is composed of the Nisga'a Lisims Government executives; members of the Nisga'a village governments in the villages of New Aiyansh, Gitwinksihlkw, Laxgalts'ap, and Gingolx; and representatives elected by the Nisga'a urban locals of Vancouver, Terrace, and Prince Rupert/Port Edward.

189 The Nisga'a Lisims Government executive consists of all the officers, the chief councillor of each Nisga'a village government, and one representative from each Nisga'a urban local.

190 See the Nisga'a Lisims Government website at www.nisgaalisims.ca /legislation.html.

191 Edmond Wright, 'Self-Government: The Nisga'a Experience,' in BC Treaty Commission, *Speaking Truth to Power III: Self-Government Options and Opportunities* (Vancouver: BC Treaty Commission, 2002), 21–30. Available online at www.bctreaty.net/files/pdf_documents/truth _3_book.pdf.

192 Matters that are internal to the Nisga'a people are membership in the Nisga'a Nation, Nisga'a Lisims Government institutions, marriage, social services, health services, child and family services, child custody, adoption and education; management of Nisga'a lands, including the development and management of a Nisga'a land title system, control over access to Nisga'a lands and highways and the use, management, planning, zoning, and development of Nisga'a lands; management of resources on Nisga'a lands, including forest, fisheries, wildlife, and resources.

193 The following is a list of powers under the Nisga'a Final Agreement Act, S.B.C. 1999, c. 2: Use, possession and management of assets located off of Nisga'a Lands, of the Nisga'a Nation, Nisga'a Villages or Nisga'a Corporations; Public order, peace and safety on Nisga'a Lands; Regulation of traffic and transportation on Nisga'a Roads; Solemnization of marriages; Provision of social services by Nisga'a Government to Nisga'a citizens; Health services on Nisga'a Lands; Prohibition of, and the terms and conditions for, the sale, exchange, possession or consumption of intoxicants on Nisga'a Lands; Emergency preparedness; Sale, in accordance with the Final Agreement, of fish or aquatic plants harvested under the Final Agreement or the Harvest Agreement; Sale of wildlife or

migratory birds harvested under the Final Agreement; Environmental assessment of projects on Nisga'a Lands; Environmental protection on Nisga'a Lands; Own source revenue administration.

194 Edmond Wright, 'Self-Government: The Nisga'a Experience,' in BC Treaty Commission, *Speaking Truth to Power III: Self-Government Options and Opportunities* (Vancouver: BC Treaty Commission, 2002), 4. Available online at www.bctreaty.net/files/pdf_documents/truth_3_book.pdf.

195 Ibid. 'Other areas where Nisga'a law prevails are timber resources and non-timber forest resources on Nisga'a Lands, if Nisga'a laws meet or exceed provincial standards (subject to transitional provisions); Nisga'a Nation's rights and obligations in respect of fish and aquatic plants under the Final Agreement, if Nisga'a laws are consistent with this Agreement and the harvest Agreement and are not inconsistent with Nisga'a annual fishing plans approved by the Minister; Nisga'a Nation's rights and obligations in respect of wildlife and migratory birds under the Final Agreement, if Nisga'a laws are consistent with this Agreement and are not inconsistent with the annual management plans approved by the Minister; establishment of a Nisga'a Police Board and Nisga'a Police Service, if Nisga'a laws include provisions in substantial conformity or are compatible with provincial standards set out in the Final Agreement, and with the approval of the Lieutenant Governor in Council; establishment of a Nisga'a Court, if Nisga'a laws include laws to ensure fairness, independence and accountability, and with the approval of the Lieutenant governor in Council; direct taxation of Nisga'a citizens on Nisga'a Lands to raise revenue for Nisga'a Nation or Nisga'a Village purposes; implementation of taxation agreements with Canada or British Columbia.'

196 Mariano Aupilaarjuk, Marie Tulimaaq, Emile Imaruittuq, Lucassie Nutaraaluk, and Akisu Joamie, *Interviewing Inuit Elders*, vol. 2, *Perspectives on Traditional Law*, ed. Jarich Oosten, Frédéric Laugrand, and Wim Rasing (Iqaluit: Nunavut Arctic College, 1999).

197 Ibid., 2. *Malik* means 'to follow a person, an animal, an idea, an object.'

198 Ibid., 2.

199 Ibid., 13.

200 Ibid., 24.

201 John Bennett and Susan Rowley, eds., *Uqalurait: An Oral History of Nunavut* (Montreal: McGill-Queen's University Press, 2004), 110.

202 For more on these, see ibid., 131, 310, 391, 402.

203 Law Commission of Canada, *Final Report: Transforming Relationships through Participatory Justice* (Ottawa, 2003), chap. 2.

204 Jaypetee Arnakak, 'Commentary: What is Inuit Qaujimajatuqangit?' *Nunatsiaq News*, 25 August 2000, n.p.
205 Nu. 2001, c. 7.
206 Legislative Assembly of Nunavut, Fifth Session, *Hansard*, 24 May 2001, available online at www.assembly.nu.ca/old/english/hansard/final5/010524.html. See, generally, the work of the Integrity Commissioner of Nunavut at www.integritycom.nu.ca/English/index.html.
207 For example, the opening session of 2004 on Tuesday, 16 November 2004, restated government commitments to *Inuuqatigiitsiarniq*, healthy communities; *Pijarniniqsaq qattujjiqatigiitsiarnirlu*, simplicity and unity; *Nangminiq makitajunnarniq*, self reliance; and *Illipallianginnaqniq*, continuous learning.
208 Under the consensus system, ministers are chosen by the legislative assembly, not by the premier. The premier, however, is in charge of assigning departmental jobs.
209 Research and Statistics Division, *Review of the Nunavut Community Justice Program: Final Report* (Ottawa: Department of Justice, 2004), retrieved 28 August 2009 from http://canada.justice.gc.ca/en/ps/rs/rep/2005/rr05-7/p0.html, appendix I.
210 See generally, Nunatsiaq News Archives available at www.nunatsiaq.com/archives/archives.html.

4 Learning from Bijuridicalism

1 Marie-Claude Gervais, 'Harmonization and Dissonance: Language and Law in Canada and Europe,' in Department of Justice, *Bijuralism and Harmonization: Genesis* (Ottawa: Minister of Justice and Attorney General of Canada, 2001), 10.
2 J.F. Gaudreault-Desbiens, 'The Québec Secession Reference and the Judicial Arbitration of Conflicting Narratives about Law, Democracy and Identity' (1999) 23 *Vermont Law Review* 793.
3 There is even an argument to be made that all Canadian law is customary and arises out of the social practices of society. See Jeremy Webber, 'The Grammar of Customary Law' (unpublished paper on file with the author).
4 *Reference re Secession of Quebec*, [1998] 2 S.C.R. 217.
5 Ibid., para. 54.
6 Ibid.
7 *Delgamuukw v. British Columbia* at 1068 (S.C.C.), quoting from Royal Com-

mission on Aboriginal Peoples, *The Final Report of the Royal Commission on Aboriginal People,* vol. 1, *Looking Forward, Looking Back* (Ottawa: Minister of Supply and Services Canada, 1996).

8 Quoted from *Delgamuukw v. British Columbia* at 1068, paraphrasing Clay McLeod, 'The Oral Histories of Canada's Northern Peoples, Anglo-Canadian Evidence Law, and Canada's Fiduciary Duty to First Nations: Breaking Down the Barriers of the Past' (1992) 30 *Alberta Law Review* 1276.

9 William Tetley, 'Mixed Jurisdictions: Common Law and Civil Law (Codified and Uncodified)' (1999) 4 *Uniform Law Review* 591.

10 Melanie Brunet, *Out of the Shadows: The Civil Law Tradition at the Department of Justice* (Ottawa: Supply and Services, 2000), 5.

11 Robin Elliot et al., *Canadian Constitutional Law,* 3rd ed. (Toronto: Emond Montgomery, 2003), 64.

12 John Brierly and Roderick Macdonald, eds., *Québec Civil Law: An Introduction to Québec Private Law* (Toronto: Emond Montgomery, 1993).

13 W.J. Eccles, *France in America* (Toronto: University of Toronto Press, 1972), 234.

14 1. persons (e.g., basic individual rights, residence rules, privacy); 2. the family (e.g., marriage, parentage, adoption); 3. successions (e.g., wills, inheritance, estates); 4. property (e.g., possession, land boundaries, right-of-way); 5. obligations (e.g., contract law, civil liability [tort law], sales, leasing); 6. hypothecs (e.g., mortgages and the sale of land); 7. evidence (e.g., burden of proof, rules of evidence); 8. prescription (e.g., statutes of limitations); 9. publication of rights (e.g., registration of property); 10. private international law (governs the resolution of legal issues involving persons outside Canada).

15 Rod MacDonald, 'Encoding Canadian Civil Law,' in Department of Justice Canada, *The Harmonization of Legislation with Quebec Civil Law and Canadian Bijuralism* (Ottawa: Supply and Services, 1997), 159; see also J. Carbonnier, 'Le Code Civil,' in *Les Lieux de Memoire,* ed. P. Nora, vol. 2 (Paris: Gallimard, 1986).

16 A.W.B. Simpson, *An Invitation to Law* (Oxford: Blackwell, 1998), 23.

17 See Patrick Glenn, 'The Common Law in Canada' (1995) 74 *Canadian Bar Review* 265 at 276; Matthew Hale, *The History of the Common Law of England,* ed. Charles M. Gray (Chicago: University of Chicago Press, 1971), 39–43. The cultural diversity in the development of the United Kingdom is nicely detailed in Norman Davies, *The Isles: A History* (New York: Oxford University Press, 1999).

18 See John H. Baker, *An Introduction to English Legal History,* 2nd ed. (London: Butterworths, 1979).

19 See Frederic W. Maitland and Francis C. Montague, *A Sketch of English Legal History* (London: G.P. Putnam and Sons, 1915), 1–130.

20 See Frederic W. Maitland, *The Forms of Action at Common Law* (Cambridge: Cambridge University Press, 1948), 11.

21 Ibid., 100–1.

22 See M.P. Furmston, ed., *Cheshire, Fifoot and Furmston's Law of Contract*, 11th ed. (London: Butterworths, 1986), 2.

23 Henry Campbell Black, *Black's Law Dictionary*, 5th ed. (St Paul, MN: West Publishing, 1979), 587.

24 Ibid.

25 See Albert K.R. Kiralfy, ed., *Potter's Historical Introduction to English Law and its Institutions* (London: Street and Maxwell, 1962), 293–7.

26 See Margaret H. Ogilvie, *Historical Introduction to Legal Studies* (Carswell: Toronto, 1982), 70, 101, 106–7.

27 See Stroud F.C. Milsom, *Historical Foundations of the Common Law*, 2nd ed. (Toronto: Butterworths, 1981), 11–36.

28 Peter Hogg, *Constitutional Law of Canada* (Toronto: Carswell, 1997), 1–17.

29 Patrick Glen, 'The Common Law in Canada' (1995) 74 *Canadian Bar Review* 265 at 266.

30 See, generally, France Allard, 'The Supreme Court of Canada and its Impact on the Expression of Bijuralism,' in Justice Canada, *The Harmonization of Federal Legislation with the Civil Law of the Province of Quebec and Canadian Bijuralism* (Ottawa: Department of Justice, 2001). See also J.M. Brisson and A. Morel, 'Droit fédéral et droit civil : complémentarité, dissociation,' in Department of Justice, *The Harmonization of Federal Legislation with Quebec Civil Law and Canadian Bijuralism* (Ottawa: Supply and Services, 1997), 213, 231.

31 D. Howes, 'From Polyjurality to Monojurality: The Transformation of Québec Law, 1875–1929' (1987) 32 *McGill Law Journal* 523.

32 *Quebec Railway, Light, Heat and Power Co. v. Vandry*, [1920] A.C. 662; *Town of Montreal West v. Hough*, [1931] S.C.R. 113.

33 Lloyd Brown-John and Howard Pawley, *When Legal Systems Meet: Bijuralism in the Canadian Federal System* (Barcelona: Institut de Ciencies Politiques I Socials, 2004), 12, retrieved 1 January 2006 from www.diba.es/icps/working_papers/docs/wp234.pdf.

34 Ibid., citing P.B. Mignault, 'Les Rapport entre le droit et la common law au Canada spécialement dans la province de Québec' (1932) 11 *Revue de Droit* 201; P Azard, 'La Cour Suprême du Canada et l'application de droit civil de la Province de Québec' (1965) 43 *Canadian Bar Review* 553; J.L. Baudoiin, 'Le Code Civil du Québec: Crise de croissance ou crise de vieil-

lesse' (1966) 44 *Canadian Bar Review* 391; S. Normand, 'Un thème dominant de la pensée juridique traditionelle au Québec: La Sauveguarde de
l'integrité de droit civil' (1987) 32 *McGill Law Journal* 559.

35   *Béliveau St-Jacques v. Fédération des employées et employés de services publics
Inc.*, [1996] 2 S.C.R. 345; *Québec (Public Curator) v. Syndicat national des
employés de l'Hôpital St-Ferdinand*, [1996] 3 S.C.R. 211; *Godbout v. City of
Longueuil*, [1997] 3 S.C.R. 844; *Aubry v. Éditions Vice-Versa*, [1998] 1 S.C.R.
591.

36   Patrick Glenn, 'The Common Law in Canada' (1995) 74 *Canadian Bar
Review* 261; C.D. Gonthier, 'L'influence d'une cour suprême nationale sur
la tradition civiliste québécoise,' in *Journées Maximilien-Caron 1990, Enjeux
et valeurs d'un code civil moderne* (Montreal: Thémis 1991), 8.

37   Patrick Glenn, 'Le droit comparé et la Cour suprême du Canada,' in
Mélanges Louis-Philippe Pigeon, ed. E. Caparros et al. (Montreal: Wilson
and Lafleur, 1989), 197.

38   See Department of Justice, 'The Supreme Court of Canada and Its Impact
on the Expression of Bijuralism,' retrieved 29 August 2009 from
http://canada.justice.gc.ca/en/dept/pub/hfl/fasc3/fascicule3_ptitre
.html.

39   Ibid., 19–20.

40   I express my appreciation for an anonymous reviewer, commissioned by
the University of Toronto Press, who brought this to my attention.

41   James Boyd White, *Justice as Translation* (Chicago: University of Chicago
Press), xiii, 80.

42   See ibid.

43   Based on a story by Phil Lane Jr., Four Worlds Development, University
of Lethbridge in Lethbridge, Alberta, as retold by Richard Wagamese, in
Royal Commission on Aboriginal Peoples, *The Final Report of the Royal
Commission on Aboriginal Peoples*, vol. 2, *Restructuring the Relationship*
(Ottawa: Supply and Services, 1996), chap. 3.

44   Nancy L. Cook, 'Outside the Tradition: Literature as Legal Scholarship'
(1994) 63 *University of Cincinnati Law Review* 95, 116–39; Robert M. Cover,
'The Folktales of Justice: Tales of Jurisdiction' (1985) 14 *Capital University
Law Review* 179, 182; Valerie Karno, 'Bringing Fiction to Justice: Including
Individual Narrative in Judicial Opinions' (1990) 2 *Hastings Women's Law
Journal* 77, 79; Thomas Ross, 'The Richmond Narratives' (1989) 68 *Texas
Law Review* 381, 385–6.

45   The recognition of Indigenous legal traditions and their application
within Indigenous communities could also provide stronger connections
to land for Indigenous peoples. Their stories, ceremonies, teachings,

customs, and norms often flow from very specific ecological relationships, and are interwoven with the world around them. For example, the
West Coast Potlatch systems depend on the vast wealth that flows into
their territory with the return of the salmon each year. This abundance
made possible the accumulation of material resources that became an
important part of the give-away ceremony and feast that accompanied
the Potlatch. Relationships of family law, the law of obligations, and
property law hinged upon these connections to land and resources. The
symbols of the Potlatch system also reflected a specific location, as cedar
bent boxes, house posts, and big houses provided the setting and gifts
that permitted the memorialization of West Coast Indigenous laws.
Similar observations about the connectedness of Indigenous laws to land
could be made elsewhere in Canada. See Antonia Mills, *Eagle Down Is
Our Law: Witsuwit'en Feasts and Land Claims* (Vancouver: UBC Press,
1994); Robin Riddington, *Little Bit Know Something* (Vancouver: Douglas
and McIntyre, 1990); Darwin Hanna and Mavis Henry, *Our Tellings: Inte-
rior Salish Stories and the Nlha7kapmx People* (Vancouver: UBC Press, 1996);
Harold Cardinal and Walter Hildebrandt, *Treaty Elders of Saskatchewan:
Our Dream Is that Our Peoples Will One Day Be Clearly Recognized as
Nations* (Calgary: University of Calgary Press, 2000); Basil Johnston,
Ojibway Ceremonies (Toronto: McClelland and Stewart, 1982); William
Fenton, *The Great Law and the Longhouse* (Oklahoma City: University of
Oklahoma Press, 1998); J. Oosten, F. Laugrand, and W. Rasing, eds., *Inter-
viewing Inuit Elders*, vol. 2, *Perspectives on Traditional Law* (Iqaluit:
Nunavut Arctic College, 2000).

46 It would probably also be dangerous to only have Indigenous law apply
within a community, because many community members would expect
elements from common law or civil law to also guide answers to their
disputes.

47 *Reference re Secession of Quebec*, [1998] 2 S.C.R. 217, and *Manitoba Language
Rights Reference*, at [1985] 1 S.C.R. 721.

48 *United States v. Winans*, 198 US 371 (USSC).

49 *Delgamuukw v. British Columbia*, [1997] 3 S.C.R. 1010.

50 *R. v. Van der Peet*, [1996] 2 S.C.R. 607.

51 Robert Rotberg and Dennis Thompson, eds., *Truth vs. Justice* (Princeton:
Princeton University Press, 2000).

52 However, there are a few other countries that could claim to have multi-
juridicalism at their roots; see E. Adamson Hoebel, *The Law of Primitive
Man* (New York: Atheneum, 1974); Karl N. Llewellyn and E. Adamson
Hoebel, *The Cheyenne Way: Conflict and Case Law in Primitive Jurisprudence*

(Norman: University of Oklahoma Press, 1941); Max Gluckman, *Politics, Law and Ritual in Primitive Society* (Chicago: Aldine Publishing, 1965); Anne Salmond, *Between Worlds: Early Exchanges Between Maori and Europeans 1773–1815* (Honolulu: University of Hawaii Press, 1997); Anne Salmond, *Two Worlds: First Meetings Between Maori and Europeans 1642–1772* (Toronto: Viking, 1991); Judith Binney, *Redemptive Songs: A Life of a Nineteenth Century Maori Leader* (Honolulu: University of Hawaii Press, 1997); Michael Kwaioloa and Ben Burt, *Living Tradition: A Changing Life in the Solomon Islands* (London: British Museum Press, 1997); Roger Keesing, *Custom and Confrontation: The Kwaio Struggle for Cultural Autonomy* (Chicago: University of Chicago Press, 1992); Keith Basso, *Western Apache Raiding and Warfare* (Tucson: University of Arizona Press, 1971).

5 Recognizing a Multi-Juridical Legal Culture

1 These traditions have grown to include Aboriginal peoples in the past thirty years; see Michael Asch, ed., *Aboriginal and Treaty Rights in Canada: Essays on Law, Equality, and Respect for Difference* (Vancouver: UBC Press, 1997); Patrick Macklem, *Indigenous Difference and the Constitution of Canada* (Toronto: University of Toronto Press, 2001); The Right Honourable Chief Justice of Canada Beverley McLachlin, 'The Civilization of Difference: LaFontaine-Baldwin Symposium' (2003), retrieved 29 August 2009 from www.operation-dialogue.com/lafontaine-baldwin/e/2003_speech_1.html.
2 The guarantee of rights in Canada's *Charter of Rights and Freedoms*, Schedule B to the *Canada Act 1982*, (U.K.) 1982, c. 11, is subject to 'reasonable limits prescribed by law as can be demonstrably justified in a free and democratic society.'
3 *Dunmore v. Ontario (Attorney General)*, [2001] 3 S.C.R. 1016; *Delisle v. Canada (Deputy Attorney General)*, [1999] 2 S.C.R. 989; *Canadian Egg Marketing Agency v. Richardson*, [1998] 3 S.C.R. 157; *Lavigne v. Ontario Public Service Employees Union*, [1991] 2 S.C.R. 211; *Professional Institute of the Public Service of Canada v. Northwest Territories (Commissioner)*, [1990] 2 S.C.R. 367; *Reference Re Public Service Employee Relations Act*, [1987] 1 S.C.R. 313; *Public Service Alliance of Canada v. The Queen*, [1987] 1 S.C.R. 424; *Government of Saskatchewan v. Retail, Wholesale and Department Store Union*, [1987] 1 S.C.R. 460.
4 Section 2 of the *Charter* guarantees: 'Everyone has the following fundamental freedoms: *a*) freedom of conscience and religion; *b*) freedom of thought, belief, opinion and expression, including freedom of the press

and other media of communication; *c*) freedom of peaceful assembly; and
d) freedom of association.'
5 Ian Angus, A *Border Within: National Identity, Cultural Plurality, and
Wilderness* (Montreal: McGill-Queen's University Press, 1997); Will Kym-
licka, *Finding Our Way: Rethinking Ethnocultural Relations in Canada*
(Toronto: Oxford University Press, 1998); Charles Taylor, *Reconciling the
Solitudes: Essays on Canadian Federalism and Nationalism* (Montreal: McGill-
Queen's University Press, 1993); Stephen Tomblin, *Ottawa and the Outer
Provinces: The Challenge of Regional Integration in Canada* (Toronto: James
Lorimer, 1995); Jeremy Webber, *Re-imagining Canada: Language, Culture,
Community and the Canadian Constitution* (Kingston: McGill-Queen's University Press, 1994); Robert Young, ed., *Stretching the Federation: The Art of
the State in Canada* (Kingston: Institute of Intergovernmental Affairs, 1999).
6 See sections 3–15 of the *Canadian Charter of Rights and Freedoms*.
7 Ibid., sections 16–22.
8 Ibid., section 27.
9 Ibid., section 1. Leading cases interpreting section 1 of the *Charter* are *R.
v. Oakes*, [1986] 1 S.C.R. 103; *Thompson Newspapers v. Canada (Attorney
General)*, [1998] 1 S.C.R. 877; *Dunmore v. Ontario (Attorney General)*, [2001]
3 S.C.R. 1016; *Irwin Toy v. Québec (Attorney General)*, [1989] 1 S.C.R. 927;
Libman v. Québec (Attorney General), [1997] 3 S.C.R. 569; *R.J.R. v. Canada
(Attorney General)*, [1995] 3 S.C.R. 199; *Ross v. New Brunswick School District*, 1 S.C.R. 825.
10 Arthur Silver, *The French-Canadian Idea of Confederation, 1864–1900*
(Toronto: University of Toronto Press, 1982).
11 Of course, there were also other factors that led to Confederation; see
Garth Stevenson, *Unfulfilled Union*, 3rd ed. (Toronto: Gage Publishing,
1989), 20–33.
12 Arthur Silver, *The French-Canadian Idea of Confederation, 1864–1900*
(Toronto: University of Toronto Press, 1982), 33–50.
13 See section 93 of the *Constitution Act, 1867 (British North American Act,
1867)* 30 and 31 Victoria, c. 3: ' ... each Province the Legislature may
exclusively make Laws in relation to Education, subject and according to
the following Provisions:

(1) Nothing in any such Law shall prejudicially affect any Right or
Privilege with respect to Denominational Schools which any Class of
Persons have by Law in the Province at the Union:
(2) All the Powers, Privileges and Duties at the Union by Law conferred and imposed in Upper Canada on the Separate Schools and

School Trustees of the Queen's Roman Catholic Subjects shall be and the same are hereby extended to the Dissentient Schools of the Queen's Protestant and Roman Catholic Subjects in Québec:

(3) Where in any Province a System of Separate or Dissentient Schools exists by Law at the Union or is thereafter established by the Legislature of the Province, an Appeal shall lie to the Governor General in Council from any Act or Decision of any Provincial Authority affecting any Right or Privilege of the Protestant or Roman Catholic Minority of the Queen's Subjects in relation to Education:

(4) In case any such Provincial Law as from Time to Time seems to the Governor General in Council requisite for the Execution of the Provisions of this Section is not made, or in case any Decision of the Governor General in Council on any Appeal under this Section is not duly executed by the proper Provincial Authority in that Behalf, then and in every such Case, and as far as the Circumstances of each Case require, the Parliament of Canada may make remedial Laws for the due Execution of the Provisions of this Section and of any Decision of the Governor General in Council under this Section.'

14 *Parliamentary Debates on the Subject of Confederation, 8th Provincial Parliament of Canada* (Quebec City: Hunter, Rose and Co., Parliamentary Printers, 1865), 60.

15 *Reference re Secession of Quebec*, [1998] 2 S.C.R. 217.

16 Ibid., para. 64.

17 An early example of assimilation is found in G. Craig, ed., *Lord Durham's Report, 1839* (Toronto: McClelland and Stewart, 1963), where Lord Durham argues that French Canadians should be assimilated into English Canadian culture. Duncan Campbell Scott spoke to Parliament in 1920 and stated, 'Our object is to continue until there is not a single Indian in Canada that has not been absorbed into the body politic and there is no Indian question.' J. Leslie and R. Maguire, ed., *The Historical Development of the Indian Act*, 2nd ed. (Ottawa: Treaties and Historical Research Centre, Indian Affairs and Northern Development, 1978), 115. For greater context on the policy of assimilation of Aboriginal peoples, see Andrew Armitage, *Comparing the Policy of Aboriginal Assimilation: Australia, Canada and New Zealand* (Vancouver: UBC Press, 1995).

18 John Tobias, 'Protection, Civilization and Assimilation: An Outline History of Canada's Indian Policy,' in James Miller, ed., *Sweet Promises: A Reader on Indian-White Relations in Canada* (Toronto: University of Toronto Press, 1991), 127.

19 For a detailed overview of these policies, see 'Displacement and Assimi-
    lation,' in Royal Commission on Aboriginal Peoples, *The Final Report of
    the Royal Commission on Aboriginal Peoples*, vol. 1, *Looking Forward Looking
    Back* (Ottawa: Supply and Services, 1996), chap. 6.
20 J. Leslie and R. Maguire, eds., *The Historical Development of the Indian Act*,
    2nd ed. (Ottawa: Treaties and Historical Research Centre, Indian Affairs
    and Northern Development, 1978), 115.
21 J. R. Miller, *Lethal Legacy: Current Native Controversies in Canada* (Toronto:
    McClelland and Stewart, 2004).
22 David Cameron, *The Referendum Papers: Essays on Secession and National
    Unity* (Toronto: University of Toronto Press, 1999); Joseph Carens, ed., *Is
    Québec Nationalism Just? Perspectives from Anglophone Canada* (Montreal:
    McGill-Queen's University Press, 1995).
23 Jocelyn MacLure, *Quebec Identity: The Challenge of Pluralism* (Montreal:
    McGill-Queen's University Press 2003); Louis Balthazar, 'La Dynamique
    du Nationalisme Québécois,' in *L'État du Québec en Devenir*, ed. Gérard
    Bergeron and Réjean Pelletier (Montreal: Boréal Express, 1980), 37–8.
24 Robert Young, *The Secession of Quebec and the Future of Canada*, 2nd ed.
    (Montreal: McGill-Queen's University Press, 1998); Robert Young, *The
    Struggle for Quebec: From Referendum to Referendum* (Montreal: McGill-
    Queen's University Press, 1999).
25 *R. v. Big M. Drug Mart Ltd.*, [1985] 1 S.C.R. 295 at 336.
26 LaForest in *Lavigne*, [1991] 2 S.C.R. 211 at 321.
27 Ibid.
28 *Reference re Secession of Quebec*, [1998] 2 S.C.R. 217 at para. 68.
29 Ibid., para. 80.
30 Ibid., para. 81.
31 In 1971, Canada adopted an official multiculturalism policy. In the
    decade between 1991 and 2001, Canada welcomed 2.2 million immi-
    grants and refugees. In 2001, 5.4 million people were born outside the
    country, or 18.4 per cent of the total population. For a discussion of the
    development of diversity in Canada and a critique of its effectiveness, see
    Richard Day, *Multiculturalism and the History of Canadian Diversity*
    (Toronto: University of Toronto Press, 2000).
32 Alan Cairns, ed., *Citizenship, Diversity and Pluralism: Canadian and Compar-
    ative Perspectives* (Montreal: McGill-Queen's University Press, 1999); Will
    Kmylicka and Wayne Norman, eds., *Citizenship in Diverse Societies*
    (Toronto: Oxford University Press, 2000).
33 Some believe that Canadians are weakened as a nation because of their
    vast differences. As noted, there have been times in Canada's history

when it has come perilously close to dissolving its national bonds because of these differences. If Canadians want to enjoy a stable future, this fear must be acknowledged and addressed. There is no doubt that Canada's cultural complexity can be a daunting challenge for unity. Difference can threaten the country's national integrity and identity. Nevertheless, a plurality of traditions need not weaken, threaten, or overwhelm Canada's historic and constitutional framework. Its history has shown that diversity can be reconciled with unity. Canada is best preserved and strengthened by extending this framework. The deal brokered at Confederation must include more than French and English political, cultural, religious, or legal traditions. Fortunately, such recognition is already a part of Canada's Constitution. Section 27 of the *Charter of Rights and Freedoms* guarantees individual rights will be interpreted in a manner consistent with the preservation and enhancement of the multicultural heritage of Canadians.

34 Francis Jennings, *The Invasion of America: Indians, Colonization and the Cant of Conquest* (New York: W.W. Norton, 1976), 111.

35 Royal Commission on Aboriginal Peoples, *Partners in Confederation: Aboriginal Peoples, Self-Government and the Constitution* (Ottawa: Supply and Services, 1993).

36 Yale Hart Richmond, Daniel K Richter, and James H Merrell, *Beyond the Covenant Chain: The Iroquois and Their Neighbors in Indian North America, 1600–1800* (University Park, PA: Penn State University Press, 2003).

37 William Cronon, *Changes in the Land: Indians, Colonists, and the Making of New England* (New York: Hill and Wang, 1983).

38 Antonia Mills, *Eagle Down Is Our Law: Witsuwit'en Feasts and Land Claims* (Vancouver: UBC Press, 1994).

39 Jeremy Webber, 'Relations of Force and Relations of Justice: The Emergence of Normative Community Between Colonists and Aboriginal Peoples' (1995) 33 *Osgoode Hall Law Journal* 623.

40 The Haudenosaunee are the Iroquois people of the Six Nations who live south, east, and west of Lake Ontario. The First Nations that make up the Haudenosaunee Confederacy are the Mohawks, Oneida, Onandaga, Cayuga, Tuscarora, and Seneca Nations. For further information about Haudenosaunee treaties, see Francis Jennings, William N. Fenton, Mary A. Druke, and David R. Miller, eds., *The History and Culture of Iroquois Diplomacy: An Interdisciplinary Guide to the Treaties of the Six Nations and Their League* (Syracuse, NY: Syracuse University Press, 1985).

41 The Anishinabek live to the north of Lake Ontario and surround Lake Michigan and Lake Superior. They are also sometimes known as the

Ojibway or Chippewa Indians. For a description of their treaties, see Larry Nesper, *The Walleye War: The Struggle for Ojibwe Spearfishing and Treaty Rights* (Lincoln: University of Nebraska Press, 2002); Cary Miller, 'Gifts as Treaties: The Political Use of Received Gifts in Anishinaabeg Communities' (2002) *The American Indian Quarterly* 221–45; Gilles Havard, *The Great Peace of Montreal of 1701: French Diplomacy in the Seventeenth Century,* trans. Phyllis Aronoff and Howard Scott (Montreal: McGill Queen's University Press, 2001); Peter Schmalz, *The Ojibwa of Southern Ontario* (Toronto: University of Toronto Press, 1991).

42 Victor Lytwyn, 'A Dish with One Spoon: The Shared Hunting Grounds Agreement in the Great Lakes and St Lawrence Valley Region,' in *Papers of the 28th Algonquian Conference,* ed. David H. Pentland (Winnipeg: University of Manitoba Press, 1997), 210–27.

43 Paul Williams, 'Oral Traditions on Trial,' in *Gin Das Winan Documenting Aboriginal History in Ontario,* ed. S. Dale Standen and David McNab, Occasional Papers of The Champlain Society, Number 2 (Toronto: The Champlain Society, 1996), 29–34.

44 Leo Waisberg, *The Ottawa: Traders of the Upper Great Lakes, 1715–1800* (MA thesis, McMaster University, 1977), 10, 20, 44, 47, 128–31.

45 See Laura Peers and Jennifer S.H. Brown, '"There is No End to Relationship among the Indians": Ojibwa Families and Kinship in Historical Perspective' (2000) 4 *The History of the Family: An International Quarterly* 529–55.

46 See generally Vernon Kinetz, *The Indians of the Western Great Lakes* (Ann Arbor: University of Michigan Press, 1940).

47 Harold Hickerson, 'The Feast of the Dead among the Seventeenth Century Algonkians of the Upper Great Lakes' (1960) 62 *American Anthropologist* 81–107.

48 The Wendat are sometimes known as the Huron. They are an Iroquoian-speaking people who formerly lived between Lake Simcoe and Georgian Bay in southern Ontario. The Wendat were a group of four tribes that were known as the Attignawantan, the Arendarhonon, the Attigneenongnahac, and the Tahontaenrat. These four groups originally lived in eighteen to twenty-five villages on the eastern shores of Georgian Bay off Lake Huron, numbering some 18,000 to 40,000 inhabitants.

49 Bruce G. Trigger, *The Children of Aataentsic: A History of the Huron People to 1600* (Kingston: McGill-Queen's University Press, 1976), 85–90.

50 For a general discussion of Ojibway warriors' duties, see Rebecca Kugel, *To Be the Main Leaders of Our People: A History of Minnesota Ojibway Politics, 1825–1898* (Lansing, MI: State University Press, 1998).

51 Robert Doherty, *Disputed Waters: Native Americans and the Great Lakes Fishery* (Lexington: University Press of Kentucky, 1990), 15–16.

52 Vernon Kinetz, *The Indians of the Western Great Lakes* (Ann Arbor: University of Michigan Press, 1940), 64–9.

53 In the following decades there were wars between the Anishinabek and Lakota/Dakota/Nakota beyond the western reaches of Lake Superior which pushed the Lakota/Dakota/Nakota further out onto the prairies.

54 Emerson W. Baker and John G. Reid, 'Amerindian Power in the Early Modern Northeast: A Reappraisal' (2004) 61, 3rd series *William and Mary Quarterly* 77–106; William B. Hart, 'Black "Go-Betweens" and the Mutability of "Race," Status, and Identity on New York's Pre-Revolutionary Frontier,' and Gregory Evans Dowd, '"Insidious Friends": Gift Giving and the Cherokee-British Alliance in the Seven Years War,' in *Contact Points: American Frontiers from the Mohawk Valley to the Mississippi, 1750–1830*, ed. Andrew R.L. Cayton and Fredrika J. Teute (Chapel Hill: University of North Carolina Press, 1998), 88–113 and 114–50, respectively; Richard L. Haan, 'Covenant and Consensus: Iroquois and English, 1676–1760,' and Mary A. Druke, 'Linking Arms: The Structure of Iroquois Intertribal Diplomacy,' in *Beyond the Covenant Chain: The Iroquois and Their Neighbors in Indian North America, 1600–1800*, ed. Daniel K. Richter and James H. Merrell (University Park, PA: Penn State University Press, 1987), 41–57 and 29–40, respectively; Lois M. Feister, 'Linguistic Communication between the Dutch and Indians in New Netherland' (1973) 20 *Ethnohistory* 25–38; William N. Fenton, 'Structure, Continuity, and Change in the Process of Iroquois Treaty Making,' and Michael K. Foster, 'Another Look at the Function of Wampum in Iroquois-White Councils,' in *The History and Culture of Iroquois Diplomacy: An Interdisciplinary Guide to the Treaties of the Six Nations and Their League*, ed. Francis Jennings, William N. Fenton, Mary A. Druke, and David R. Miller (Syracuse, NY: Syracuse University Press, 1995), 3–36 and 99–114, respectively; Nancy L. Hagedorn, '"Faithful, Knowing, and Prudent": Andrew Montour as Interpreter and Cultural Broker, 1740–1772,' in *Between Indian and White Worlds: The Cultural Broker*, ed. Margaret Connell Szasz (Norman: Oklahoma University Press, 1994), 44–60; Nancy L. Hagedorn, '"A Friend to Go Between Them": The Interpreter as Cultural Broker during Anglo-Iroquois Councils' (1988) 35 *Ethnohistory* 60–80; Eric Hinderaker, 'The "Four Indian Kings" and the Imaginative Construction of the First British Empire' (1996) 53, 3rd series *William and Mary Quarterly* 487–526; Francis Jennings, 'The Constitutional Evolution of the Covenant Chain' (1971) 115 *American Philosophical Society, Proceedings* 88–96; Peter Marshall,

'Colonial Protest and Imperial Retrenchment: Indian Policy, 1764–1768' (1971) 5 *Journal of American Studies* 1–17; Michael N. McConnell, 'Pisquetomen and Tamaqua: Mediating Peace in the Ohio Country,' in *Northeastern Indian Lives, 1632–1816*, ed. Robert S. Grumet (Amherst: University of Massachusetts Press, 1996), 273–94; James H. Merrell, '"The Cast of His Countenance": Reading Andrew Montour,' and Richard White, '"Although I am dead, I am not entirely dead. I have left a second of myself": Constructing Self and Persons on the Middle Ground of Early America,' in *Through a Glass Darkly: Reflections on Personal Identity in Early America*, ed. Ronald Hoffman, Michel Sobel, and Fredrika J. Teute (Chapel Hill: University of North Carolina Press, 1997), 13–39 and 404–18, respectively; Jon Parmenter, '*L'arbre De Paix*: Eighteenth-Century Franco-Iroquois Relations' (2003) 4 *French Colonial History* 63–80; Daniel K. Richter, 'Native Peoples of North America and the Eighteenth-Century British Empire,' in *The Oxford History of the British Empire*, vol. 2, *The Eighteenth Century*, ed. P.J. Marshall (Cambridge: Oxford University Press, 1998), 347–64; Daniel K. Richter, 'Cultural Brokers and Intercultural Politics: New York-Iroquois Relations, 1664–1701' 75 *Journal of American History* 40–67; Anthony F. C. Wallace, 'Origins of Iroquois Neutrality: The Grand Settlement of 1701' (1957) 24 *Pennsylvania History* 223–35; Cynthia J. VanZandt, 'Mapping and the European Search for Intercultural Alliances in the Colonial World' (2003) 1 *Early American Studies* 72–99.

55 Robert Williams Jr., *Linking Arms Together: American Indian Treaty Visions of Law and Peace, 1600–1800* (New York: Oxford University Press, 1997).

56 Richard White, *The Middle Ground: Indians, Empires, and Republics in the Great Lakes Region, 1650–1815* (New York: Cambridge University Press, 1991).

57 For a history, see generally William Wicken, *Mi'kmaq Treaties on Trial* (Toronto: University of Toronto Press, 2002); Thomas Issac, *Aboriginal and Treaty Rights in the Maritimes: The Marshall Decision and Beyond* (Saskatoon: Purich Publishing, 2001).

58 John Borrows, 'Wampum at Niagara: Canadian Legal History, Self-Government, and the Royal Proclamation,' in *Aboriginal and Treaty Rights in Canada*, ed. Michael Asch (Vancouver: UBC Press, 1998).

59 Arthur Ray, J.R. Miller, and Frank Tough, *Bounty and Benevolence: A History of Saskatchewan Treaties* (Montreal: McGill-Queen's University Press, 2000), 1–31.

60 JoEllen Vinyard, *Michigan: The World around Us* (New York: Macmillan/McGraw Hill, 1992), 101.

61 Francis Jennings, *Empire of Fortune: Crowns, Colonies and Tribes in the Seven*

Years War in America (New York: W.W. Norton, 1990); Seymour Schwartz, *The French and Indian War, 1754–1763: The Imperial Struggle for North America* (New York: Simon and Schuster, 1994).

62 J. Borrows, 'Constitutional Law from a First Nations Perspective: Self-Government and the Royal Proclamation' (1994) 28 *University of British Columbia Law Review* 1.

63 *Constitution Act, 1982*, Schedule B, to the *Canada Act, 1982*, (U.K.) 1982, c. 11.

64 John Richard Alden, *John Stuart and the Southern Colonial Frontier: A Study of Indian Relations, War, Trade, and Land Problems in the Southern Wilderness, 1754–1775* (New York: Gordon Press, 1966); Matthew Dennis, *Cultivating a Landscape of Peace: Iroquois-European Encounters in Seventeenth-Century America* (Ithaca, NY: Cornell University Press, 1993); Gregory Evans Dowd, *War under Heaven: Pontiac, the Indian Nations, and the British Empire* (Baltimore: Johns Hopkins University Press, 2002); Randolph C. Downes, *Council Fires on the Upper Ohio: A Narrative of Indian Affairs in the Upper Ohio Valley until 1795* (Pittsburgh, PA: University of Pittsburgh Press, 1940); Gilles Havard, *The Great Peace of Montreal of 1701: French-Native Diplomacy in the Seventeenth Century*, trans. Phyllis Aronoff and Howard Scott (Montreal: McGill-Queen's University Press, 2001); Eric Hinderaker, *Elusive Empires: Constructing Colonialism in the Ohio Valley, 1673–1800* (Cambridge: Cambridge University Press, 1997); Wilbur R. Jacobs, *Wilderness Politics and Indian Gifts: The Northern Colonial Frontier, 1748–1763* (1950; reprint, Lincoln, NE: University of Nebraska Press, 1966); Francis Jennings, *The Ambiguous Iroquois Empire: The Covenant Chain Confederation of Indian Tribes with English Colonies from Its Beginnings to the Lancaster Treaty of 1744* (New York: W.W. Norton, 1984); Francis Jennings, *Empire of Fortune: Crowns, Colonies and Tribes in the Seven Years War in America* (New York: W.W. Norton, 1988); Dorothy V. Jones, *License for Empire: Colonialism by Treaty in Early America* (Chicago: University of Chicago Press, 1982); James H. Merrell, *Into the American Woods: Negotiators on the Pennsylvania Frontier* (New York: W.W. Norton, 1999); D. Peter MacLeod, *The Canadian Iroquois and the Seven Years' War* (Toronto: Dundurn Press, 1996); Jane T. Merritt, *At the Crossroads: Indians and Empires on a Mid-Atlantic Frontier, 1700–1763* (Chapel Hill, NC: University of North Carolina Press, 2003); Larry L. Nelson, *A Man of Distinction among Them: Alexander McKee and British-Indian Affairs along the Ohio Country Frontier, 1754–1799* (Kent, OH: Kent State University Press, 1999); William R. Nester, *'Haughty Conquerors': Amherst and the Great Indian Uprising of 1763* (Westport, CT: Greenwood Publishing Group, 2000); Timothy J. Shannon, *Indians and*

Colonists at the Crossroads of Empire: The Albany Congress of 1754 (Ithaca, NY: Cornell University Press, 2000); J. Russell Snapp, *John Stuart and the Struggle for Empire on the Southern Frontier* (Baton Rouge, LA: Louisiana State University Press, 1996).

65 Dorothy V. Jones, 'British Colonial Indian Treaties,' in *Handbook of North American Indians*, vol. 4, *Indian-White Relations*, ed. Wilcomb Washburn (Washington, DC: Smithsonian Institute, 1988), 185.

66 Ibid.

67 David Murray, *Indian Giving: Economies of Power in Indian-White Exchanges* (Amherst: University of Massachusetts Press, 2000).

68 Richard White, *The Middle Ground: Indians, Empires and Republics in the Great Lakes Region, 1650-1815* (Cambridge: Cambridge University Press, 1991).

69 Lynda Gullason, '"No Less Than 7 Different Nations": Ethnicity and Culture Contact at Fort George-Buckingham House,' in *The Fur Trade Revisited: Selected Papers of The Sixth North American Fur Trade Conference, Mackinac Island, Michigan, 1991*, ed. Jennifer S.H. Brown, W.J. Eccles, and Donald P. Heldman (East Lansing/Mackinac Island: Michigan State University Press, 1994), 117–42; Jennifer S.H. Brown, *Strangers in Blood: Fur Trade Company Families in Indian Country* (Vancouver: UBC Press, 1980); Denys Delâge, *Le pays renversé: Amérindiens et européens en Amérique du nord-est, 1600–1664* (Montreal: Boréal Express, 1985). Published in English as *Bitter Feast: Amerindians and Europeans in Northeastern North America, 1600–64*, trans. Jane Brierley (Vancouver: UBC Press, 1993); Daniel Francis and Toby Morantz, *Partners in Furs: A History of the Fur Trade in Eastern James Bay, 1600–1870* (Montreal: McGill-Queen's University Press, 1983); George T. Hunt, *The Wars of the Iroquois: A Study in Intertribal Trade Relations* (Madison: University of Wisconsin Press, 1940); Harold A. Innis, *The Fur Trade in Canada: An Introduction to Canadian Economic History* (New Haven, CT: Yale University Press, 1930).

70 Arthur J. Ray and Donald B. Freeman, *'Give Us Good Measure': An Economic Analysis of Relations between the Indians and the Hudson's Bay Company before 1763* (Toronto: University of Toronto Press, 1978), 231–60, 285; Paul Thistle, *Indian-European Trade Relations in the Lower Saskatchewan River Region to 1840* (Winnipeg: University of Manitoba Press, 1986), 33–50; Victor P. Lytwyn, *Muskekowuck Athinuwick: Original People of the Great Swampy Land* (Winnipeg: University of Manitoba Press, 2002).

71 Bruce M. White, 'A Skilled Game of Exchange: Ojibway Fur Trade Protocol' (1987) *Minnesota History* 229.

72 For a description of the rigorous formalities involved in Ojibway diplo-

matic relationships, see Peter Jones (Kahkewaquonaby), *History of the Ojibway Indians with Special Reference to their Conversion to Christianity* (London: A.V. Bennett, 1861), 105–7, 111–28; and F.W. Major, *Manitoulin: The Isle of the Ottawas* (Gore Bay: Recorder Press, 1974), 11–15. For an example of the formalities of treaty making in Haudenosaunee culture, see *The History and Culture of Iroquois Diplomacy*, ed. Francis Jennings, William N. Fenton, Mary A. Druke, and David R. Miller (Syracuse, NY: Syracuse University Press, 1985), 18–21.

73 Wilbur R. Jacobs, *Wilderness Politics and Indian Gifts: The Northern Colonial Frontier, 1748–1763* (Lincoln: University of Nebraska Press, 1966).

74 Arthur Ray, J.R. Miller, and Frank Tough, *Bounty and Benevolence: A History of Saskatchewan Treaties* (Montreal: McGill-Queen's University Press, 2000).

75 Sylvia Van Kirk, *Many Tender Ties: Women in Fur-Trade Society, 1670–1870*, (Winnipeg: Watson and Dwyer, 1980).

76 Daniel Harmon's journal describes such a fur trade wedding in December 1801:

> Payet one of my Interpreters, has taken one of the Natives Daughters for a Wife, and to her Parents he gave in Rum & dry Goods &c. to the value of two hundred Dollars, and all the cerimonies attending such circumstances are that when it becomes time to retire, the Husband or rather Bridegroom (for as yet they are not joined by any bonds) shews his Bride where his Bed is, and then they, of course both go to rest together, and so they continue to do as long as they can agree among themselves, but when either is displeased with their choice, he or she will seek another Partner ... which is law here ...

Daniel Williams Harmon, *Sixteen Years in the Indian Country: The Journal of Daniel Williams Harmon, 1800–1816*, ed. W. Kaye Lamb (Toronto: Macmillan, 1957), 53.

77 *Connolly* v. *Woolrich* (1867) 17 R.J.R.Q. 75, 1 C.N.L.C. 70 (Que. S.C.), 79.

78 The continued existence of Aboriginal law as an important source of authority is illustrated in *Connolly v. Woolrich* (1867) 17 R.J.R.Q. 75, 1 C.N.L.C. 70 (Que. S.C.), aff'd. 1 C.N.L.C. 165, 17 R.J.R.Q. 266 (Que. Q.B.); *R v. Nan-e-quis-a Ka* (1889) 1 Terr. L.R. (C.A.); *R. v. Bear's Shin Bone* (1899) 3 C.C.C. 329 (N.W.T.S.C.); *Re Adoption of Katie* (1961) 32 D.L.R. (2d) 686 (N.W.T.T.C.); *Re Kitchooalik* [1972] 5 W.W.R. 203 (N.W.T.C.A.); *Mitchell v. Dennis* [1984] 2 C.N.L.R. 84 (B.C.S.C.); *Casimel v. Insurance Co. of British Columbia* [1992] 1 C.N.L.R. (B.C.C.A.); *Vielle v. Vielle* 1 C.N.L.R. 165 (Alta. Q.B.).

79 Richard White, *The Middle Ground: Indians, Empires and Republics in the Great Lakes Region, 1650–1815* (Cambridge: Cambridge University Press, 1991).
80 Vine Deloria Jr. and Raymond J. DeMallie, eds., *Documents of American Indian Diplomacy: Treaties, Agreements, and Conventions, 1775–1979* (Norman: University of Oklahoma Press, 1999).
81 *Haida Nation v. B.C. (Minister of Forests)*, [2004] 3 S.C.R. 511 at para. 25.
82 [2001] 1 S.C.R. 911 at para. 8.
83 See B. Slattery, 'Understanding Aboriginal Rights' (1987) 66 *Canadian Bar Review* 727.
84 See *Calder v. Attorney-General of British Columbia*, [1973] S.C.R. 313, and *Mabo v. Queensland* (1992), 175 C.L.R. 1, at 57 (per Brennan J.), 81–2 (per Deane and Gaudron JJ.), and 182–3 (per Toohey J.).
85 Gordon Christie, *Aboriginal Citizenship: Sections 35, 25 and 15 of Canada's Constitution Act, 1982* (2003) *Citizenship Studies* 481–95.
86 See *R. v. Van der Peet*, [1996], 2 S.C.R. 507 at para. 31.

> More specifically, what s. 35(1) does is provide the constitutional framework through which the fact that aboriginals lived on the land in distinctive societies, with their own practices, traditions and cultures, is acknowledged and reconciled with the sovereignty of the Crown. The substantive rights which fall within the provision must be defined in light of this purpose; the aboriginal rights recognized and affirmed by s. 35(1) must be directed towards the reconciliation of the pre-existence of aboriginal societies with the sovereignty of the Crown.

6 Challenges and Opportunities in Recognizing Indigenous Legal Traditions

1 Jeremy Webber, 'Legal Pluralism and Human Agency' (2006) 44 *Osgoode Hall Law Journal* 167.
2 All legal arguments commingle descriptive and prescriptive elements. Even judges, who may be regarded as the most authoritative legal commentators in the Canadian legal context, have descriptive and prescriptive aspects to their judgments. Sometimes these dual functions are explicit, as when readers can distinguish between the ratio of an arguments and obiter dicta. At most other times the distinction between what the law *is* and what it *should be* are hidden and implicit within their judgments. This is because of the cultural deference they are given: expectations about the result and force of their decisions often masquerade as

reality. Yet, despite all the ink spilled about judicial impartiality and lack of bias, the fact remains that claims about what the law *is* and *should be* are always contestable. Judges and all who support Canada's legal system hope that people regard their opinions as creating a perfect coincidence between *is* and *ought*. However, there is always the potential for dissent: on the bench, in Parliament, with the parties to the dispute, or more generally within the public's response to their opinions.

3 *Sunday Times v. United Kingdom* (1979), 2 E.H.R.R. 271.

4 In this vein I am reminded of some statutes and judicial opinions that have created rather than eliminated confusion.

5 Jan Vansina, *Oral Tradition as History* (Madison: University of Wisconsin Press, 1985), 124.

6 Ibid. For a general discussion of oral tradition as applied to Aboriginal peoples, see Julie Cruikshank, 'Oral Tradition and Oral History: Reviewing Some Issues' (1994) 75 *Canadian Historical Review* 410.

7 Ludwig Wittgenstein, *Philosophical Investigations,* trans. G.E.M. Anscombe, 3rd ed. (New York: Macmillan Publishing Co., 1958), 154, 155. He wrote that the meaning and understanding of a fact is to know 'how to go on.' If you do not have an understanding of 'how to go on' in a culture that is different from your own, you do not know the facts of that culture.

8 Martin Heidegger, *Being and Time,* trans. John Macquarrie and Edward Robinson (New York: Harper and Row, 1962), 157.

9 Richard Rorty, 'On Ethnocentrism: A Reply to Clifford Geertz' (1986) 25 *Michigan Quarterly Review* 115; Abdullahi Ahmed An-Na'im, 'Problems of Universal Cultural Legitimacy for Human Rights,' in *Human Rights in Africa,* ed. A. An-Na'im and Francis Deng (Washington: Brookings Institution, 1990), 331–67.

10 For example, in spatial terms, early Christians visualized the Garden of Eden as being in Mesopotamia and thus attempted to explain all human migration as somehow stemming from this point. Many Ojibway people trace their origin to Michilimackinac Island in the Great Lakes and reference their migrations from this place. Temporally speaking, Christianity, Islam, and Judaism have tended to view time as being linear, progressing, and marching on. Other cultures such as the Maya, Ainu, or Cree have thought of time as being cyclical and repetitive. Causality or change can also differ between groups. See Jan Vansina, *Oral Tradition as History* (Madison: University of Wisconsin Press, 1985), 125–33.

11 Vansina has written: 'Historical truth is also a notion that is culture specific.' Ibid., 129.

12 Charles Taylor, 'Understanding and Ethnocentricity,' in *Philosophy and the*

Human Science, Col. 2, Philosophical Papers (Cambridge: Cambridge University Press, 1985), 119, 121. Vansina states that since 'culture can be defined by what is common in the minds of a given group of people; ... people in a community share many ideas, values and images ... which are collective to them and differ from others.' Jan Vansina, *Oral Tradition as History* (Madison: University of Wisconsin Press, 1985), 124.

13 A leading enthnohistorian wrote: 'Historical records can be interpreted only when the cultural values of both the observer and the observed are understood by the historian. In the study of modern Western history, the experience of everyday life may suffice to supply such knowledge. Yet this implicit approach does not provide an adequate basis for understanding the behavior of people in earlier times or in cultures radically different from our own.' Bruce Trigger, *Natives and Newcomers: Canada's Heroic Age Reconsidered* (Montreal: McGill-Queen's University Press, 1985), 168.

14 Jan Vansina, *Oral Tradition as History* (Madison: University of Wisconsin Press, 1985), 124.

15 Ibid., 137.

16 Louise Mandell, 'Native Culture on Trial,' and Joan Ryan and Bernard Ominayak, 'The Cultural Effects of Judicial Bias,' in *Equality and Judicial Neutrality*, ed. Sheilah Martin and Kathleen Bias (Toronto: Carswell, 1987), 358 and 346, respectively; Robin Ridington, 'Cultures in Conflict: The Problem of Discourse,' in *Native Writers and Canadian Writing*, ed. W.H. New (Vancouver: UBC Press, 1990), 273.

17 Anthropologist Robin Ridington observed these problems in the factual underpinnings of the trial judge's decision in *Delgamuukw*. See Robin Ridington, 'Fieldwork in Courtroom 53: A Witness to Delgamuukw,' in *Aboriginal Title in British Columbia: Delgamuukw v. The Queen*, ed. Frank Cassidy (Lantzville, BC: Oolichan Books, 1992), 211–12. For further commentary on the historical and cultural assumptions of Chief Justice McEachern's decision in *Delgamuukw*, see Joel Fortune, 'Construing Delgamuukw: Legal Arguments, Historical Argumentation, and the Philosophy of History' (1993) 51 *University of Toronto Faculty of Law Review* 80; Michael Asch and Catherine Bell, 'Definition and Interpretation of Fact in Canadian Aboriginal Title Legislation: An Analysis of Delgamuukw' (1994) 10 *Queen's Law Journal* 503; Robin Fisher, 'Judging History: Reflections on the Reasons for Judgment on *Delgamuukw v. B.C*' (1992) 95 *B.C. Studies* 43; Geoff Sherrott, 'The Court's Treatment of the Evidence in *Delgamuukw v. B.C.*' (1992) 56 *Saskatchewan Law Review* 441.

18 Indigenous peoples might also argue that the phrase 'prescribed by law'

(to circumscribe individual action) does not apply under their legal traditions. The phrase 'prescribed by law' is primarily used in rights instruments and Indigenous peoples may feel they are not bound by the *Charter*, much like American Indians are not bound by the Bill of Rights.

19 (1979), 2 E.H.R.R. 271.

20 *Irwin Toy v. Quebec (A.G.)*, [1989] 1 S.C.R. 927, 44.

21 Ibid.

22 *R. v. Nova Scotia Pharmaceutical Society*, [1992] 2 S.C.R. 606 at 24.

23 Many Indigenous peoples have only a limited knowledge of only some of their traditions, while others may have lost that knowledge completely. Colonial processes and individual choice have been hard on Indigenous culture at certain levels. Therefore, while some members may find Indigenous traditions 'intelligible,' there may be a need to more broadly communicate them in different ways, with different cultural styles, if they are going to avoid being too vague for those expected to abide by them.

24 The Tlicho Land Claim Agreement creates a registry of laws (section 7.8), which includes the following terms:

> 7.8.1 The Tlicho Government shall maintain, at its principal administrative offices, a register on which it shall enter the text of all Tlicho laws, including any amendment to those laws.
> 7.8.2 Every person shall have reasonable access to the register during normal business hours.
> 7.8.3 The Tlicho Government upon request shall provide, at cost, copies of Tlicho laws.

25 For a publication outlining First Nations laws, see the *First Nations Gazette* (Saskatoon: Native Law Centre/Indian Taxation Advisory Board), published semi-annually.

26 Law Commission of Canada, *Justice Within: Indigenous Legal Traditions in Canada*, 2006, DVD.

27 Fourdirectionsteachings.com, and Nature's Laws at www.abheritage.ca/natureslaws/index2.html.

28 Recent examples being the *Reference re Secession of Quebec*, [1998] 2 S.C.R. 217; the *Manitoba Language Reference*, [1985] 1 S.C.R. 121; *Reference*, [1997] 3 S.C.R. 3.

29 *Nunavut Land Claims Agreement*, Article 23.

30 'Conciliator's Final Report: Nunavut Land Claims Agreement Implementation Planning Contract Negotiations for the Second Planning Period,'

by Thomas Berger, *Letter to Minister Prentice, March 1, 2006* retrieved 29
August 2009 from www.ainc-inac.gc.ca/pr/agr/nu/lca/lca1_e.html.

31 When students graduated from the Akitsiraq Law School, most secured
excellent articling experiences, including one student who clerked at the
Supreme Court of Canada. Though it is still early in their career, they
make a significant contribution to the profession as young lawyers in the
territory of Nunavut.

32 John Borrows, 'Listening for a Change: The Courts and Oral Tradition'
(2001) *Osgoode Hall Law Journal* 1.

33 *Logan v. Styres* (1959), 20 D.L.R. (2d) 416 (Ont. H.C.) (upholding forcible
eviction of traditional Haudenosaunee government).

34 For example, Joseph Trutch, in denying Aboriginal title in BC observed:
'The title of the Indians in the fee of the public lands, or any portion
thereof, has never been acknowledged by Government, but, on the contrary, is distinctly denied.' *British Columbia, Papers Connected with the
Indian Land Question, 1850–1875* (Victoria: Government Printer, 1875),
appendix B, 11.

35 John S. Milloy, *A National Crime: The Canadian Government and the Residential School System, 1879–1986* (Winnipeg: University of Manitoba Press,
1999).

36 Aborignal peoples are constantly charged with criminal offences for
hunting and fishing in traditional economic pursuits. Some high profile
cases are *R. v. Syliboy*, [1929] 1 D.L.R. 307 (N.S. Co. Ct.); *Simon v. The
Queen* (1985) 24 D.L.R. (4th) 390 (S.C.C.); *R. v. Horseman* (1990) 1 S.C.R.
901 (S.C.C.); *R. v. Cote* (1996) 138 D.L.R. (4th) 185 (S.C.C.); *R. v. Badger*
(1996) 133 D.L.R. (4th) 324 (S.C.C.); *R. v. Marshall*, [1999] 2 S.C.R. (S.C.C.).

37 *Thomas v. Norris*, [1992] 2 C.N.L.R. 139 (B.C.S.C.) (Aboriginal spirit
dancing not protected by the *Charter*); *Jack and Charlie v. The Queen* (1985)
21 D.L.R. (4th) 641 (S.C.C.) (taking fresh deer meat for an Aboriginal
death ceremony not protected by the Constitution).

38 Many bands were kept apart or relocated to prevent their association
because of a government fear they would organize to resist impingements of their rights.

39 A Crown fiduciary duty has recently been articulated in an attempt to
cure violations of Aboriginal rights stemming from differences in the way
Aboriginal peoples hold and access their rights. Significant cases in this
regard are *Guerin v. The Queen* (1984) 13 D.L.R. (4th) 321 (S.C.C.); *Kruger
v. The Queen*, (1985) 17 D.L.R. (4th) 591 (F.C.A.); *Blueberry River Indian
Band v. Canada* (1995) 130 D.L.R. (4th) 193 (S.C.C.). For a fuller discussion,
see Len Rotman, *Parallel Paths* (Toronto: University of Toronto Press, 1996).

40 *Canada (A.G.) v. Lavell*, [1974] S.C.R. 1349 (invidious distinctions in *Indian Act* on basis of sex upheld).

41 Barry Steven Mandelker, 'Indigenous People and Cultural Property Appropriation: Intellectual Property Problems and Solutions' (2000) 16 *Canadian Intellectual Property Review* 367.

42 See generally Titia Loenen and Peter Rodrigues, eds., *Non-Discrimination Law: Comparative Perspectives* (The Hague, Netherlands: Kluer International, 1999).

43 For an excellent discussion, see Erna Paris, *Long Shadows: Truth, Lies and History* (New York: Bloomsbury, 2000), 166–309.

44 Rainer Knopf, *Human Rights and Social Technology: The New War on Discrimination* (Ottawa: Carleton University Press, 1989).

45 Harold Cardinal, *The Unjust Society: The Tragedy of Canada's Indians* (1969; reprint, Douglas and McIntyre, 1999).

46 John L. Tobias, 'Protection, Civilization, Assimilation: An Outline History of Canada's Indian Policy,' in *Sweet Promises: A Reader on Indian-White Relations in Canada*, ed. J.R. Miller (Toronto: University of Toronto Press, 1991), 39–55.

47 See generally Ian Getty and Antoine S. Lussier, eds., *As Long as the Sun Shines and Water Flows: A Reader in Canadian Native Studies* (Vancouver: UBC Press, 1983).

48 *Andrews v. Law Society of BC*, [1989] 1 S.C.R. 143.

49 Ibid.

50 *Law v. Canada (Minister of Employment and Immigration)*, [1999] 1 S.C.R. 497.

51 Ibid., 25.

52 *Minority Schools in Albania* (1934), P.C.I.J. (Ser. A/B), 17.

53 *South West Africa Case*, [1966] I.C.J. Rep., 248.

54 Heather McRae, Garth Nettheim, Laura Beacroft, and Luke McNamara, *Indigenous Legal Issues: Commentary and Materials*, 3rd ed. (Sydney, Australia: Thomson Lawbook Co., 2003), 443–4.

55 For commentary, see Race Discrimination Commissioner, *Racial Discrimination Act 1975: A Review* (Canberra, Australia: AGPS, 1995), 63–4: 'Equality does not mean equal treatment. Recognition of the distinct cultural identity of minority groups is consistent with the notion of equality. Further, the mere use of race as a classifying criterion does not render a distinction discriminatory, but rather it lies in the invidious purpose or effects of that distinction.'

56 *R. v. Turpin*, [1989] 1 S.C.R. 1296.

57 Patrick Macklem, *Indigenous Difference and the Constitution of Canada* (Toronto: University of Toronto Press, 2001).

58 Mary Ellen Turpel, 'Reflections on Thinking About Criminal Justice
    Reform,' in *Continuing Poundmaker and Riel's Quest*, ed. R. Gosse, J. Hen-
    derson, and R. Carter (Saskatoon: Purich Publishing, 1994), 206–21. See
    also James (Sakej) Youngblood Henderson, 'Implementing Treaty Order,'
    in *Continuing Poundmaker and Riel's Quest*, ed. R. Gosse, J. Henderson, and
    R. Carter (Saskatoon: Purich Publishing, 1994), 52–62; Matthias Leonardy,
    First Nations Criminal Jurisdiction in Canada (Saskatoon: Native Law
    Centre, 1998); Bruce Wildsmith, 'Treaty Responsibilities: A Co-relational
    Model' (1992) *UBC Law Review: Special Edition, Aboriginal Justice* 324–37;
    Leonard Mandamin, Dennis Callihoo, Albert Angus, and Marion Buller,
    'The Criminal Code and Aboriginal People' (1992) *UBC Law Review:
    Special Edition, Aboriginal Justice* 5–40.
59 For an application of this concept in an Indigenous context, see James
    (Sakej) Youngblood Henderson, 'Empowering Treaty Federalism' (1994)
    58 *Saskatchewan Law Review* 241.
60 Geoff R. Hall, 'The Quest for Native Self-Government: The Challenge of
    Territorial Sovereignty' (1992) 50:1 *University of Toronto Faculty of Law
    Review* 39.
61 Ibid., 45–8.
62 *Libman v. R.*, [1985] 2 S.C.R. 179.
63 Geoff R. Hall, 'The Quest for Native Self-Government: The Challenge of
    Territorial Sovereignty' (1992) 50:1 *University of Toronto Faculty of Law
    Review* 39, 48–49.
64 Ibid., 55–60.
65 *Corbiere v. Canada (Minister of Indian and Northern Affairs)*, [1999] 2 S.C.R.
    203 (S.C.C.).
66 See the Windigo story, Jarris Papers, Metro Toronto Reference Library,
    Collection # S-125, Volume B-57.
67 There are some exceptions to using the *Indian Act* to define First Nations
    citizenship, though they are not very common. While the *Indian Act* cuts
    people off from federal recognized status, other communities might have
    membership codes which includes people that do not have status under
    the *Indian Act*. This is done by opting out of membership provisions of
    the *Indian Act* and adopting their own membership codes. In such
    instances, the federal government would not recognize people without
    Indian status for financial purposes.
68 I used the qualifier so-called in this sentence because of the insight that
    there is no such thing as race, biologically speaking. While race has a
    reality and impact in a sociological sense, we should reject racialized clas-
    sifications based on skin colour, hair texture, eye shape, and so on. For

more information, see Peter Li, *Race and Ethnic Relations in Canada* (Oxford: Oxford University Press, 1990), 316.

69 Royal Commission on Aboriginal Peoples, *The Final Report of the Royal Commission on Aboriginal Peoples*, vol. 2, *Restructuring the Relationship* (Ottawa: Supply and Services, 1996), 176–7.

70 Quoting Paul L.A.H. Chartrand, 'Aboriginal Self-Government: The Two Sides of Legitimacy,' in *How Ottawa Spends, 1993–1994: A More Democratic Canada ... ?* ed. Susan D. Phillips (Ottawa: Carleton University Press, 1993), 234, 236, in Royal Commission on Aboriginal Peoples, *Final Report of the Royal Commission on Aboriginal Peoples*, vol. 2, *Restructuring the Relationship* (Ottawa: Supply and Services, 1996), 173.

71 See the *Tlicho Land Claims Agreement*, retrieved 29 August 2009 from www.tlicho.com/agreement/tliagr_e.pdf, enacted *TliCho Land Claims and Self-Government Act*, 2005, c. 1.

72 See the Tlicho Constitution, retrieved 29 August 2009 from www.tlicho.com/constitution/tlicho_constitution.pdf.

73 For a discussion a better use of federal jurisdiction in relation to Indians and lands reserved for Indians under section 91(24), see generally Kent McNeil, 'Challenging Legislative Infringements of the Inherent Aboriginal Right of Self-Government' (2003) 22 *Windsor Yearbook of Access to Justice* 329–61; Dan Russell, *A People's Dream: Aboriginal Self-Government in Canada* (Vancouver: UBC Press, 2001), 72–4.

74 For more information on the duty to consult, see Kent McNeil, 'Aboriginal Rights, Resource Development, and the Source of the Provincial Duty to Consult in *Haida Nation* and *Taku River*' (2005) 29 *Supreme Court Law Review* (2nd series) 447–60; Richard Devlin and Ronalda Murphy, 'Recent Developments in the Duty to Consult: Clarification or Transformation' (2003) 14:2 *NJCL* 167–216; Debra Szatylo, 'Recognition and Reconciliation: An Alberta Fact of Fiction?' (2002) 1 *Indigenous Law Journal* 201–36.

75 For a discussion of this process in the United States, see Kevin Washburn, 'Testimony on Law Enforcement in Indian Country before the United States Senate Committee on Indian Affairs, 110th Congress, 1st Session (June 21, 2007),' retrieved 17 October 2008 from papers.ssrn.com/sol3/papers.cfm?abstract_id=1055621.

In most of the states that have federally-recognized Indian tribes, tribal governments have entered agreements with states and/or counties that facilitate cooperation. Many states and the federal government, of course, also provide mechanisms for state-wide recognition of tribal police as law enforcement officers. In other states, these agreements are struck at the local level. These agreements span a range of law enforcement activities, reflecting mutual aid efforts, cross-deputization or cross-commission agreements, extradition, and other cooperative action arrangements. They also sometimes address thorny issues such as liability and sovereign immunity. And in addition to normal law enforcement activity, the agreements also sometimes cover the sharing of information between agencies, such as prior arrests, traffic records, and other criminal history.

76 For further discussion in filling in jurisdictional gaps, see Carrie Garrow and Sarah Deer, eds., *Tribal Criminal Law and Procedure* (Lanham, MD: Altamira Press, 2004), 97–108; Robert Laurence, 'Service of Process and Execution of Judgment on Indian Reservations' (1982) 10 *American Indian Law Review* 257.

77 See Fred R. Ragsdale Jr., 'Problems in the Application of Full Faith and Credit for Indian Tribes' (1977) 7 *New Mexico Law Review* 133; Robert Laurence, 'The Enforcement of Judgments Across Indian Reservation Boundaries: Full Faith and Credit, Comity and the Indian Civil Rights Act' (1990) 69 *Oregon Law Review* 589.

78 This problem has developed in the United States. For an excellent article on this problem, see Kevin Washburn, 'American Indians, Crime and the Law' (2006) 104 *Michigan Law Review* 709.

79 For a discussion of section 88 of the *Indian Act*, see Kerry Wilkins, '"Still Crazy After All These Years": Section 88 of the *Indian Act* at Fifty' (2000) 38 *Alberta Law Review* 458–503.

80 Indian/government jurisdictional issues over non-members of the tribes are currently the most pressing issues before the United States Supreme Court, and tribal courts jurisdiction is being eroded in the process. For a critique, see Robert Williams Jr., *Like a Loaded Weapon: The Rehnquist Court, Indian Rights and the Legal History of Racism in America* (Minneapolis: University of Minnesota Press, 2005); David H. Getches, 'Conquering the Cultural Frontier: The New Subjectivism of the Supreme Court in Indian Law' (1996) 84 *California Law Review* 1573. Nevertheless, there is a doctrine of federal and state court deference to tribal court decisions that is still very significant. See *National Farmers Union Insurance Companies v. Crow Tribe of Indians* (1985) 471 U.S. 845 (U.S.S.C.); *Iowa Mutual Insurance Co. v. LaPlante* (1987) 480 U.S. 9 (U.S.S.C); *Strate v. A-1 Contractors* (1997) 520 U.S. 438 (U.S.S.C.); *Nevada v. Hicks* (2001) 533 U.S. 353 (U.S.S.C.).

81 Aboriginal and Treaty rights can impact on provincial matters. For the leading cases, see *Delgamuukw v. A.G.B.C.*, [1997] 3 S.C.R. 1010, paras.

172–83; and *R. v. Morris*, [2006] 2 S.C.R. 915, paras. 41–55. See also Kerry Wilkins, 'Of Provinces and Section 35 Rights' (1999) 22 *Dalhousie Law Journal* 185. For a discussion of the dominant tide of Canadian federalism which allows for substantial overlap between jurisdictions, see *Canadian Western Bank v. Alberta*, [2007] 2 S.C.R. 3, paras. 35–47.

82 Jennifer Nedelsky, 'Embodied Diversity and the Challenges to Law' (1997) 42 *McGill Law Journal* 91.

83 Antonio Domasio, *Descartes' Erro: Emotion, Reason and the Human Brain* (New York: Quill, 2000); Antonio Domasio, *The Feeling of What Happens: Body and Emotion in the Making of Consciousness* (New York: Harcourt, 1999); Antonia Domasio, *Looking for Spinoza: Joy, Sorrow and the Feeling Brain* (New York: Harcourt, 2003).

84 Martha Nussbaum, *Upheavals of Thought: The Intelligence of Emotions* (Cambridge: Cambridge University Press, 2001); Peter Goldie, *The Emotions: A Philosophical Exploration* (Oxford: Oxford University Press, 2000); Richard Wollheim, *On the Emotions* (New Haven, CT: Yale University Press, 2000).

85 For a description of troubling views towards Indigenous peoples in rural British Columbia, see Elizabeth Furniss, *The Burden of History: Colonialism and the Frontier Myth in Rural British Columbia* (Vancouver: UBC Press, 2000).

86 For a discussion of the high levels of interpersonal violence in Canadian Indigenous communities, see Anne McGillivray and Brenda Comaskey, *Black Eyes All of the Time: Intimate Violence, Aboriginal Women, and the Justice System* (Toronto: University of Toronto Press, 1999). For an American description, see Andrea Smith, *Conquest: Sexual Violence and American Indian Genocide* (Cambridge, MA: South End Press, 2005).

87 These kinds of concerns have led to innovative initiatives in the United States, relating to justice for victims of crime on Indian reservations. For more information, see Sarah Deer, Carrie A. Martell, Hallie Bongar White, and Maureen White Eagle, *A Victim Centered Approach to Violence against Native Women: Resource Guide for Drafting or Revising Tribal Laws against Domestic Violence* (Updated January 2008), retrieved 17 October 2008 from www.tribal-institute.org/download/DV_Code_Resource _Feb_08.pdf. The Tribal Law and Policy Institute has also developed resources to help children who are the victims of crime.

88 Alan Cairns, *Citizens Plus: Aboriginal Peoples and the Canadian State* (Vancouver: UBC Press, 2000), 201–3.

89 For a focused description of these concerns in an American context, see Robert Odawi Porter, *Sovereignty, Colonialism and the Indigenous Nations: A*

Reader (Durham, NC: University of North Carolina Press, 2005), 231–500.

90 Audre Lord, 'The Master's Tools,' in *Feminist Postcolonial Theory: A Reader*, ed. Reina Lewis and Sara Mills (New York: Routledge, 2003), 25.

91 See the work of Natividad Gutierrez Chong, *Mujeres y nacionalismo: de la Independencia a la nación del nuevo milenio* (México: Universidad Nacional Autónoma de México-Instituto de Investigaciones Sociales, 2004).

92 Ibid. For one example of an Indigenous group's experience with secession, see Grand Council of the Crees, *Never Without Consent: James Bay Crees' Stand Against Forcible Inclusion into an Independent Quebec* (Toronto: ECW Press, 1998).

93 While there are some notable exceptions of Indigenous peoples seeking political and legal existence separate from the state (for example, see 'Lakota Group Secedes from US,' *Rapid City Journal*, 20 December 2007), there are other Indigenous groups that see themselves as separate from the state. See, for example, Linda Pertusati, *Defense of Mohawk Land: Ethnopolitical Conflict in Native North America* (Albany: SUNY Press, 1997), 39–66. Indigenous peoples have not generally sought secession because they see such actions as being contrary to their treaties or inconsistent with their laws that see relationships as paramount in any political order. See Michael Asch, *Home and Native Land: Aboriginal Rights and the Canadian Constitution* (Toronto: Methuen, 1984).

94 There are rare instances where Indigenous peoples seek to use their traditions to disrupt Canadian unity. See S. Lambertus, *Wartime Images, Peacetime Wounds: The Media and the Gustafsen Lake Standoff* (Toronto: University of Toronto Press, 2004). For further discussion of Indigenous peoples conflict with the state, see John Borrows, 'Crown and Aboriginal Occupations of Land' (15 October 2005), retrieved 17 October 2008 from www.attorneygeneral.jus.gov.on.ca/inquiries/ipperwash/policy_part/research/pdf/History_of_Occupations_Borrows.pdf.

95 For a discussion of maladministration of Indigenous systems, see Tom Flanagan, *First Nations, Second Thoughts* (Montreal: McGill-Queen's University Press, 2000), 92.

96 *R. v. Williams*, [1998] 1 S.C.R. 1128; *R. v. Gladue*, [1999] 1 S.C.R. 688 (S.C.C.).

97 *Logan v. Styres* (1959), 20 D.L.R. (2d) 416 (Ont. H.C.) (upholding forcible eviction of traditional Haudenosaunee government).

98 For example, Joseph Trutch, in denying Aboriginal title in BC, observed: 'The title of the Indians in the fee of the public lands, or any portion thereof, has never been acknowledged by Government, but, on the

contrary, is distinctly denied.' *British Columbia, Papers Connected with the Indian Land Question, 1850–1875* (Victoria: Government Printer, 1875), appendix B, 11.

99 John S. Milloy, *A National Crime: The Canadian Government and the Residential School System, 1879–1986* (Winnipeg: University of Manitoba Press, 1999).

100 Aboriginal peoples are constantly charged with criminal offences for hunting and fishing in traditional economic pursuits. Some high profile cases are *R. v. Syliboy*, [1929] 1 D.L.R. 307 (N.S. Co. Ct.); *Simon v. The Queen* (1985) 24 D.L.R. (4th) 390 (S.C.C.); *R. v. Horseman* (1990) 1 S.C.R. 901 (S.C.C.); *R. v. Cote* (1996) 138 D.L.R. (4th) 185 (S.C.C.); *R. v. Badger* (1996) 133 D.L.R. (4th) 324 (S.C.C.); *R. v. Marshall*, [1999] 2 S.C.R. (S.C.C.).

101 *Thomas v. Norris*, [1992] 2 C.N.L.R. 139 (B.C.S.C.) (Aboriginal spirit dancing not protected by the *Charter*); *Jack and Charlie v. The Queen* (1985) 21 D.L.R. (4th) 641 (S.C.C.) (taking fresh deer meat for an Aboriginal death ceremony not protected by the *Charter*).

102 Many bands were kept apart or relocated to prevent their association because of a government fear they would organize to resist impingements of their rights.

103 A Crown fiduciary duty has recently been articulated in an attempt to cure violations of Aboriginal rights stemming from differences in the way Aboriginal peoples hold and access their rights. Significant cases in this regard are *Guerin v. The Queen* (1984) 13 D.L.R. (4th) 321 (S.C.C.); *Kruger v. The Queen*, (1985) 17 D.L.R. (4th) 591 (F.C.A.); *Blueberry River Indian Band v. Canada* (1995) 130 D.L.R. (4th) 193 (S.C.C.). For a fuller discussion, see Len Rotman, *Parallel Paths* (Toronto: University of Toronto Press, 1996).

104 *Canada (A.G.) v. Lavell*, [1974] S.C.R. 1349 (invidious distinctions in *Indian Act* on basis of sex upheld).

105 George Orwell, *Nineteen Eighty-Four* (1949; reprint, New York: Penguin, 2003), 30.

106 Judith Herman, *Trauma and Recovery* (New York: Basic Books, 1992), 7–8.

107 Erna Paris, *Long Shadows: Truth, Lies and History* (New York: Bloomsbury, 2000); Iris Chang, *The Rape of Nanking: The Forgotten Holocaust of World War II* (New York: Penguin, 1997); Samatha Power, *A Problem From Hell: America in the Age of Genocide* (New York: Basic Books, 2002); Anthony Hall, *The American Empire and the Fourth World* (Montreal: McGill-Queen's University Press, 2003).

108 These messages are examined in an influential series of books. See Henry Reynolds, *Why Weren't We Told: A Personal Search for the Truth*

About History (Toronto: Penguin Books, 2000); Henry Reynolds, *The Other Side of the Frontier: Aboriginal Resistance to the European Invasion of Australia* (Toronto: Penguin Books, 1995); Henry Reynolds, *The Law of the Land* (Toronto: Penguin Books, 2003).

109 This is British Columbia's defence to the Haida land title case.

110 *R. v. Bernard; R. v. Marshall*, [2005] S.C.C. 43.

111 For an early treatment of this issue, see Sidney Harring, *White Man's Law: Native People in Nineteenth-Century Canadian Jurisprudence* (Toronto: University of Toronto Press, 1998), 62–90.

112 *Mitchell v. M.N.R.*, [2001] 1 S.C.R. 911.

113 *Sawridge Band v. Canada*, [1995] 4 C.N.L.R. 121 (F.C.T.D.).

114 *Chippewas of the Sarnia Band v. Ontario* (A.G.), (2000), 51 O.R. (3d) 641; (2000), 195 D.L.R. (4th) 135; (2000), [2001] 1 C.N.L.R. 56 (Ont. C.A.).

115 Prime Minister Pierre Trudeau, quoted in Peter Cumming and Neil Mickenburg, *Native Rights in Canada*, 2nd ed. (Toronto: Indian-Eskimo Association, 1972), appendix 4.

116 John Borrows, 'Listening for a Change: The Courts and Oral Traditions' (2001) 39 *Osgoode Hall Law Journal* 1.

117 Wayne Warry, *Ending Denial: Understanding Aboriginal Issues* (Toronto: University of Toronto Press, 2008), 81.

118 While Dr Herman makes certain to indicate that these stages of recovery are not lockstep, but rather individual in nature, and can intermingle sequentially, it is important to note that failure to provide appropriate forums for these feelings can be a flashpoint for conflict.

7 The Role of Governments and Courts in Entrenching Indigenous Legal Traditions

1 Of course, this makes the point that the previous chapters were not solely concerned with how to implement Indigenous legal traditions but also dealt with the question of why this would be good for all peoples living in this land. Other themes in this work have also been highlighted, including a critique of colonialism, a discussion of the nature of law, a reminder of the differences between law and history, an examination of the role of agency in structuring our legal system, an evaluation of the psychology of law, and so on.

2 I am also aware that the line between governments and courts is unclear: governments interpret and enforce laws, and courts formulate, authorize, and administer laws.

3 All governments have obligations to their people and cannot be regarded

as legitimate if they do not act in their society's best interests. Of course, there is much room for debate in determining what is in a society's best interest and this sometimes provides a justification for not following a community's will.

4 In a news release from 21 June 2005, former minister of justice Irwin Cotler said:

> Today, Canadians across the country will celebrate the cultural richness and historical contributions that Aboriginal peoples – First Nation, Métis, and Inuit – have brought to Canadian society. I am personally proud to take part in this celebration, and to join with the Prime Minister and my cabinet colleagues to express our appreciation for the guidance and inspiration that Aboriginal peoples and groups provide to Canadians as we go about our daily lives.
>
> When I was asked by the Prime Minister to take on the role of Minister of Justice and Attorney General of Canada, his expectation of me and my colleagues was clear: we must each do everything possible within our portfolios to ensure that the quality of life for Aboriginal peoples in Canada improves. This is a legacy issue: reaching this goal will require personal and professional commitments at all levels. It will also require a principled approach, that we anchor our policies in fundamental principles. The seven 'R' principles that I am committed to following are:
> - Recognition – of the historical place of Aboriginal peoples in our society,
> - Respect – for the distinct constitutional status of Aboriginal peoples,
> - Redress – for historical wrongs, as exemplified by the recently concluded historical agreement on the residential school tragedy,
> - Responsiveness – with regard to our duty to consult Aboriginal groups,
> - Representation – to combat the over-representation of Aboriginal people in the criminal justice system as offenders and victims, while addressing the under-representation of Aboriginal people in the justice system,
> - Reconciliation – as the underlying dynamic of process and outcome,
> - Renewal – a healthier, healing relationship as the product of the previous six Rs. These principles already underpin our work at the Department of Justice where Aboriginal peoples are concerned. But there is still much more to be done.
>
> Today, as we continue toward our goal, it is my hope that a continued spirit of collaboration combined with this principled approach will

lead to this renewed relationship where all Aboriginal peoples enjoy healthy, vibrant communities, while participating fully in Canadian society.

Retrieved 30 August 2009 from www.justice.gc.ca/eng/news-nouv /nr-cp/2005/doc_31564.html.

5 Howard Adams, *Tortured People: The Politics of Colonization* (Penticton, BC: Theytus Books, 1999); Kent McNeil, *Emerging Justice? Essays on Indigenous Rights in Canada and Australia* (Saskatooon: University of Saskatchewan, Native Law Centre, 2001).

6 For a discussion of Indigenous peoples demographics in Canada, see Daniel J.K. Beavon, Jerry Patrick White, Dan Beavon, and Paul S. Maxim, *Aboriginal Conditions: Research as a Foundation for Public Policy* (Vancouver: UBC Press, 2003).

7 The failure to restrain state action was one of the main causes of family disruption in the residential schools era. For further discussion of this issue, see James Miller, *Shingwauk's Vision: A History of Native Residential Schools* (Toronto: University of Toronto Press, 1996); John Milloy, *A National Crime: National Crime: The Canadian Government and the Residential School System, 1879–1986* (Winnipeg: University of Manitoba Press, 1999); Brenda Child, *Boarding School Seasons: American Indian Families, 1900–1940* (Lincoln: University of Nebraska Press, 2000); Celia Haig-Brown, *Resistance and Renewal: Surviving the Indian Residential School* (Vancouver: Arsenal Pulp Press, 1998).

8 Vine Deloria Jr. and Clifford Lytle, *American Indians, American Justice* (Austin: University of Texas Press, 1983), 122.

9 For arguments that one can reconcile liberalism with cultural recognition, see Will Kymlicka, *Multicultural Citizenship* (Oxford: Clarendon Press, 1995); Joseph Caren, *Culture, Citizenship and Community: A Contextual Exploration of Justice as Even-Handedness* (Oxford: Oxford University Press, 2000); Ayelet Shachar, *Multicultural Jurisdictions* (Cambridge: Cambridge University Press, 2001); Alan Brudner, 'The Liberal Duty to Recognize Cultures' (2003) 8 *Review of Constitutional Studies* 129.

10 For a critical discussion of how the Canadian judiciary has mischaracterized concepts of culture, see Michael Asch, 'The Judicial Conceptualization of Culture after *Delgamuukw* and *Van der Peet*' (2000) 5 *Review of Constitutional Studies* 119; Michael Asch, 'Errors in *Delgamuukw*: An Anthropological Perspective,' in *Aboriginal Title in British Columbia: Delgamuukw v. The Queen*, ed. Frank Cassidy (Lantzville, BC: Oolichan Books, 1992), 221; Cathy Bell and Michael Asch, 'Challenging Assumptions: The

Impact of Precedent in Aboriginal Rights Litigation,' in *Aboriginal and Treaty Rights in Canada: Essays on Law, Equality and Respect for Difference*, ed. Michael Asch (Vancouver: University of British Columbia Press, 1997), 38.

11 For an argument recounting the importance of Indigenous peoples making their claims 'in context,' see Rosemary Coombe, 'The Properties of Culture and the Politics of Possessing Identity: Native Claims in the Cultural Appropriation Controversy' (1993) 6 *Canadian Journal of Law and Jurisprudence* 249.

12 Wesley Newcomb Hohfeld, *Fundamental Legal Conceptions*, ed. Walter Wheeler Cook (New Haven, CT: Yale University Press, 1919), 35–64.

13 *Lake Shore & M. S. R. Co. v. Kurtz*, (1894) 10 Ind. App., 60; 37 N.E., 303, 304.

14 When we acknowledge that Aboriginal rights have correlative legal consequences, as Hohfeld's theoretical framework suggests, section 35(1) could thus be seen as incorporating Crown obligations relative to Aboriginal peoples. If this were the case, section 35(1) could be read in the following light: 'The existing *Crown* and treaty *obligations* of the *Crown in right of Canada and the provinces* are hereby recognized and affirmed. The existing Aboriginal and treaty rights of the Aboriginal peoples of Canada are hereby recognized and affirmed.'

15 *R. v. Marshall*, [1999] 3 S.C.R. 456 at para. 48.

16 Ibid. at 1109. *R. v. Sparrow*, [1990] 1 S.C.R. 1075 at para. 1109.

17 See *Quebec Secession Reference*, [1998] 2 S.C.R. 217 at para. 63: 'The evolution of our democratic tradition can be traced back to the Magna Carta (1215) and before, through the long struggle for Parliamentary supremacy which culminated in the English *Bill of Rights* of 1689, the emergence of representative political institutions in the colonial era, the development of responsible government in the 19th century, and eventually, the achievement of Confederation itself in 1867 … [T]he Canadian tradition … is one of evolutionary democracy moving in uneven steps toward the goal of universal suffrage and more effective representation.'

18 See *R. v. Rahey*, [1987] 1 S.C.R. 588 at para. 98: 'The great defect of Magna Carta, however, lay in its failure to provide adequate mechanisms for the enforcement of the rights it purported to guarantee.'

19 See Kent McNeil, 'Aboriginal Title as a Constitutionally Protected Aboriginal Right,' *Beyond the Nass Valley: National Implications of the Supreme Court's Delgamuukw Decision* (Vancouver: Fraser Institute, 2000): '*Magna Carta* would have been received as part of the applicable statute law in

all the common law provinces. As a fundamental part of the British constitution, no doubt it applies in Quebec as well, despite the reintroduc-
tion of French civil law by the *Quebec Act*, 14 Geo. III (1774), c.83 (U.K.).
The Preamble to the *Constitution Act, 1867*, 30 & 31 Vict., c.3 (U.K.), provides that Canada shall have "a Constitution similar in Principle to that
of the United Kingdom."'

20 *An Act Declaring the Rights and Liberties of the Subject and Settling the Suc-*
cession of the Crown, 1689, 1 Will. & Mar. sess. 2, c. 2.
21 The *Charter* constrains the Crown relative to individual citizens and obli-
gates them to respect enumerated rights in the document.
22 *R. v. Sparrow*, 70 D.L.R. (4th) 385 at 412 (S.C.C.).
23 Governments must be guided by the Constitution's grant of authority
from the Imperial Parliament in England, as revised and adopted by
Canada's first ministers in 1982.
24 'The Government of Canada's Approach to Implementation of the Inherent Right and the Negotiation of Aboriginal Self-Government,' 1995.
Retrieved 18 October 2008 from www.ainc-inac.gc.ca/pr/pub/
sg/plcy_e.html.
25 Royal Commission on Aboriginal Peoples, *The Final Report of the Royal*
Commission on Aboriginal Peoples, vol. 2, *Restructuring the Relationship*
(Ottawa: Supply and Services, 1996), 320–1 and chap. 3. The Royal Commission also recommended that the *Recognition Act*:

> (a) establish the process whereby the government of Canada can recog-
> nize the accession of an Aboriginal group or groups to nation status
> and its assumption of authority as an Aboriginal government to exer-
> cise its inherent self-governing jurisdiction;
> (b) establish criteria for the re-recognition of Aboriginal nations,
> including
>> (i) evidence among the communities concerned of common ties of
>> language, history, culture and of willingness to associate, coupled
>> with sufficient size to support the exercise of a broad, self-governing
>> mandate;
>> (ii) evidence of a fair and open process for obtaining the agreement
>> of its citizens and member communities to embark on a nation
>> recognition process;
>> (iii) completion of a citizenship code that is consistent with interna-
>> tional norms of human rights and with the *Canadian Charter of Rights*
>> *and Freedoms*;
>> (iv) evidence that an impartial appeal process had been established

by the nation to hear disputes about individuals' eligibility for citizenship;

(v) evidence that a fundamental law or constitution has been drawn up through wide consultation with its citizens; and

(vi) evidence that all citizens of the nation were permitted, through a fair means of expressing their opinion, to ratify the proposed constitution;

(c) authorize the creation of recognition panels under the aegis of the proposed Aboriginal Lands and Treaties Tribunal to advise the government of Canada on whether a group meets recognition criteria (see vol. 5, *Renewal: A Twenty-Year Commitment*, Appendix A, Summary of Recommendations).

This book does not support the above recommendations in the form suggested by the Royal Commission because they could be used to remove recognition from Indigenous governments currently enjoying power within Canada. The burden of proof is on Aboriginal governments, and they have fewer resources and less support in the wider population than the federal government, which could lead to the termination of First Nations, Métis, and Inuit communities already recognized by the federal or provincial governments.

26 Royal Commission on Aboriginal Peoples, *The Final Report of the Royal Commission on Aboriginal Peoples,* vol. 2, *Restructuring the Relationship* (Ottawa: Supply and Services, 1996), 321–2. The Royal Commission also recommended the creation of a Canada-wide framework agreement to guide the development of subsequent treaties and self-government agreements between recognized Aboriginal nations and the federal and provincial governments. The Commission wrote: 'The framework discussions should have three primary purposes: to achieve agreement on the areas of Aboriginal self-governing jurisdiction; to provide a policy framework for fiscal arrangements to support the exercise of such jurisdiction; and to establish principles to govern negotiations on lands and resources and on agreements for interim relief with respect to lands subject to claims, to take effect before the negotiation of treaties.'

27 Cathy Bell, 'Métis Constitutional Rights in Section 35(1)' (1997) 36 *Alberta Law Review* 180, 189–92, 194–5.

28 Ibid., 183.

29 *R. v. Van der Peet*, [1996] 2 S.C.R. 507 at para. 44.

30 See Erica I.A. Diaz, 'Equality of Indigenous Peoples Under the Auspices of the United Nations: Draft Declaration on the Rights of Indigenous

Peoples' (1995) 7 *St. Thomas Law Review* 493; James Anaya, *Indigenous Peoples in International Law* (New York: Oxford University Press, 1996), 151–82; Sharon Venne, *Our Elders Understand Our Rights: Evolving International Law Regarding Indigenous Rights* (Princeton: Theytus Books, 1998), 107–71.

31 Economic and Social Council Commission 4/1995/2/1994/56 (1994), reprinted in 31 International Legal Materials (I.L.M.) 541 (1995).

32 Wilton Littlechild, 'Recognition of International Laws: An International Basis' (paper presented to the Joint Conference of the Canadian Bar Association and the Indigenous Bar Association, Ottawa, 4–5 March 2005), unpublished.

33 United Nations Declaration on the Rights of Indigenous Peoples, General Assembly Resolution 61/295 on 13 September 2007. Retrieved 31 August 2009 from www.un.org/esa/socdev/unpfii/en/drp.html, Articles 9, 19, 33.

34 Norway was the first country to ratify this convention, making its obligations applicable throughout the country. By virtue of the Storting's adoption of the *Human Rights Act* (1999) this ILO Convention 169 has been incorporated into Norwegian Law, and it takes precedence over Norwegian Law.

35 International Labour Convention. Convention 169 (1989) United Nations Treaty Series (U.N.T.S.) 383, entered into force 5 September 1991.

36 Ibid.

37 Proposed American Declaration on the Rights of Indigenous Peoples, approved by the Inter-American commission on Human rights on 26 February 1997 at its 133rd session, 95th regular session, published in the Annual Report of the Inter-American Commission on Human Rights, OAS DOC GEA/Ser. L/V/II.95.Doc 7 Rev.

38 Ibid.

39 Royal Commission on Aboriginal Peoples, *The Final Report of the Royal Commission on Aboriginal People,* vol. 2, *Restructuring the Relationship* (Ottawa: Supply and Services, 1996), 185.

40 *R. v. Sioui,* [1990] 1 S.C.R. 1025. Chief Justice Lamer observed:

> The mother countries did everything in their power to secure the alliance of each Indian nation and to encourage nations allied with the enemy to change sides. When these efforts met with success, they were incorporated in treaties of alliance or neutrality. This clearly indicates that the Indian nations were regarded in their relations with the European nations which occupied North America as independent nations.

41 *Calder v. A.G.B.C.*, [1973] 3 S.C.R. 313 at 328. Emphasis mine.
42 The reserved rights theory of Aboriginal governance is also consistent
    with the proposition articulated in *R. v. Van der Peet*, [1996] 2 S.C.R. 507 at
    para. 30: 'In my view, the doctrine of aboriginal rights exists, and is rec-
    ognized and affirmed by s. 35(1), because of one simple fact: when Euro-
    peans arrived in North America, aboriginal peoples were already here,
    living in communities on the land, and participating in distinctive cul-
    tures, as they had done for centuries.'
43 However, it has been that 'discovery' diminished Indian rights to land,
    Guerin v. R., [1984] 2 S.C.R. 325.
44 The Supreme Court of Canada accepted the idea in *R. v. Sioui*, [1990] 1
    S.C.R. 1025 that Aboriginal governance was multifaceted, even after the
    assertion of sovereignty. Chief Justice Lamer wrote:

> As the Chief Justice of the United States Supreme Court said in 1832 in
> *Worcester v. State of Georgia*, 31 U.S. (6 Pet.) 515 (1832), at pp. 548–9,
> about British policy towards the Indians in the mid-eighteenth century:
>   Such was the policy of Great Britain towards the Indian nations
>   inhabiting the territory from which she excluded all other Euro-
>   peans; such her claims, and such her practical exposition of the char-
>   ters she had granted: *she considered them as nations capable of maintain-
>   ing the relations of peace and war; of governing themselves, under her
>   protection; and she made treaties with them, the obligation of which she
>   acknowledged.* (Emphasis added by Justice Lamer)

> This 'generous' policy that the British chose to adopt also found expres-
> sion in other areas. The British Crown recognized that the Indians had
> certain ownership rights over their land; it sought to establish trade with
> them which would rise above the level of exploitation and give them a
> fair return. The Crown also allowed them autonomy in their internal
> affairs, intervening in this area as little as possible.

45 John Borrows, 'A Genealogy of Law: Inherent Sovereignty and First
    Nations Self-Government' (1990) 30 *Osgoode Hall Law Review* 291. The
    ability of Aboriginal peoples to exercise their powers of governance
    through the post-Confederation period was demonstrated every time a
    First Nations signed a treaty. Implied within the Aboriginal treaty-
    making power is that they had government authority which could be
    exercised by the group.
46 John Borrows, *Recovering Canada: The Resurgence of Indigenous Law*
    (Toronto: University of Toronto Press, 2002), 403.

47 R.S.C. 1985, c. I-5. For example, First Nations exercise pre-existing gover-
    nance powers through the Indian custom council system under the *Indian
    Act*. For a definition of band custom, see the *Indian Act*, section 2(i),
    'council of the band.' See *Bigstone v. Eagle* (1992), [1993] 1 CNLR 25
    (F.T.D).

48 [1990] 1 S.C.R. 1075 at 1097. See John Borrows, 'A Genealogy of Law:
    Inherent Sovereignty and First Nations Self-Government' (1990) 30
    Osgoode Hall Law Review 291, for an application of this principle in a spe-
    cific community context.

49 *R. v. Van der Peet*, [1996] 2 S.C.R. 507 at 286.

50 Ibid.

51 For the test to follow to prove Aboriginal rights, see ibid.

52 For cases involving the reception of First Nations law into Canadian law,
    see *Connolly v. Woolrich* (1867), 17 R.J.R.Q. 75 (Quebec Superior Court),
    affirmed as *Johnstone* v. *Connelly* (1869), 17 R.J.R.Q. 266 (Quebec Queen's
    Bench); *R. v. Nan-e-quis-a Ka* (1899), 1 Territories Law Reports 211
    (N.W.T.S.C.); *R. v. Bear's Shin Bone* (1899), 3 C.C.C. 329 (N.W.T.S.C.); *Re
    Noah Estate* (1961), 32 D.L.R. (2d) 686 (N.W.T.T.C.); *Re Deborah* (1972), 28
    D.L.R. (3rd) 483 (N.W.T.C.A.); *Michell v. Dennis*, [1984] 2 C.N.L.R. 91
    (B.C.S.C.); *Casimel v. I.C.B.C.*, [1992] 1 C.N.L.R. 84 (B.C.S.C.); *Vielle v.
    Vielle*, [1993] 1 C.N.L.R. 165 (Alta. Q.B.).

53 *R. v. Guerin*, [1984] 2 S.C.R. 335 at 378 (S.C.C.).

54 *Calder v. A.G.B.C.*, [1973] S.C.R. 313 at 328. See also *R. v. Van der Peet* at
    538. When Europeans arrived, Aboriginal peoples were 'already here,
    living in communities on the land, and participating in distinctive cul-
    tures, as they had done for centuries.'

55 Royal Commission on Aboriginal Peoples, *The Final Report of the Royal
    Commission on Aboriginal Peoples*, vol. 2, *Restructuring the Relationship*
    (Ottawa: Supply and Services, 1996), 189.

56 For most of Canada's history there has been very little recognition or pro-
    tection of Aboriginal peoples' fundamental human rights and personal
    freedoms. See *R. v. Sparrow*, [1990] 1 S.C.R. 1075 at 1103: 'For many years
    the rights of Indians to their aboriginal lands were virtually ignored.'

57 Even then, broader engagement does not always generate broad support.
    The referendum following the Charlottetown Accord is partial evidence
    of this. On the other hand, the referendum concerning treaties in British
    Columbia did not seem to hurt support for signing treaties in that
    province.

58 Similarly, section 25 is not powerful enough to shield Aboriginal collec-
    tivities from the assimilative pressures of the majority, and section 37 was

insufficient to bring about a political settlement between national Aboriginal organizations and first ministers.

59 Section 37 might have been, but the use of Aboriginal/first ministers conferences has been expanded.

60 Furthermore, section 35, in Part II of the *Constitution Act 1982*, is so influenced by the *Charter of Rights and Freedoms* in Part I of the same Act, that the jurisdictional concerns of Aboriginal peoples are lost. Section 1 lives within section 35, though in a somewhat modified form; it limits Aboriginal rights.

61 *Reference re Secession of Quebec*, [1998] 2 S.C.R. 217, at para. 55.

62 Ibid.

63 Ibid.

64 Ibid. at 58.

65 *A.G. Canada v. A.G. Ontario (Labour Conventions)*, [1936] 3 D.L.R. 673 (S.C.C.) at 721, per Cannon J.

66 See Bruce Ryder, 'The Demise and Rise of the Classical Paradigm in Canadian Federalism: Promoting Autonomy for the Provinces and First Nations' (1991) 36 *McGill Law Journal* 309.

67 *Reference re Secession of Quebec*, [1998] 2 S.C.R. 217 at para. 53.

68 *Canadian Western Bank v. Alberta*, [2007] 2 S.C.R. 3 at para. 42.

69 Laura Armand French, 'Adaptations of Aboriginal Justice in the United States' (1995) 6 *Critical Criminology* 72.

70 Val Napoleon, 'By Whom and By What Processes Is Restorative Justice Defined, and What Bias May This Introduce?' in *Critical Issues in Restorative Justice*, ed. Howard Zehr and Barb Toews (Mosney, NY: Criminal Justice Press, 2004), 33.

71 'A Word from the Commissioner,' Royal Commission on Aboriginal Peoples, *The Final Report of the Royal Commission on Aboriginal Peoples*, vol. 1 (Ottawa: Supply and Services, 1996), 1.

72 Ibid.

73 See Jay Sinha and Luc Gagné, Law and Government Division, 'BILL S-22: Federal Law–Civil Law Harmonization Act, No. 1: Legislative History of Bill S-22' (20 September 2000), retrieved 18 October 2008 from www2.parl.gc.ca/Sites/LOP/LegislativeSummaries/Bills_ls.asp?lang=E&ls=S22&Parl=36&Ses=2.

74 Federal Law–Civil Law Harmonization Act, No. 1, S.C. 2001, c. 4.

75 Lloyd Brown-John and Howard Pawley, *When Legal Systems Meet: Bijuralism in the Canadian Federal System* (Barcelona: Institut de Ciencies Politiques I Socials, 2004), 17. Available online at www.diba.es/icps/working_papers/docs/wp234.pdf.

76 The Preamble to the *Federal Law–Civil Law Harmonization Act* reads:

> WHEREAS all Canadians are entitled to access to federal legislation in
> keeping with the common law and civil law traditions;
> WHEREAS the civil law tradition of the Province of Québec, which
> finds its principal expression in the *Civil Code of Québec*, reflects the
> unique character of Québec society;
> WHEREAS the harmonious interaction of federal legislation and
> provincial legislation is essential and lies in an interpretation of federal
> legislation that is compatible with the common law or civil law tradi-
> tions, as the case may be;
> WHEREAS the full development of our two major legal traditions
> gives Canadians enhanced opportunities worldwide and facilitates
> exchanges with the vast majority of other countries;
> WHEREAS the provincial law, in relation to property and civil rights,
> is the law that completes federal legislation when applied in a
> province, unless otherwise provided by law;
> WHEREAS the objective of the Government of Canada is to facilitate
> access to federal legislation that takes into account the common law
> and civil law traditions, in its English and French versions;
> AND WHEREAS the Government of Canada has established a harmo-
> nization program of federal legislation with the civil law of the
> Province of Québec to ensure that each language version takes into
> account the common law and civil law traditions.

77 The Law Reform Commission (Australia), *The Recognition of Aboriginal
Customary Laws,* vols. 1 and 2, *Report No. 31* (Canberra: Australian Government Publishing Service, 1986).

78 Other countries have created Recognition Acts for pre-existing systems of
law. Some of the best examples of legislative recognition of Indigenous
legal traditions are found among the Pacific Island states. For example,
the *Cook Islands Act* 1915 (NZ), s. 422 states: 'Every title to and interest in
customary land shall be determined according to the ancient custom and
usage of the natives of the Cook Islands.' The *Constitution of Fiji* 1990, s.
100(3) (until 27 July 1998) states: 'Until such time as an Act of Parliament
otherwise provides, Fijian customary law shall have effect as part of the
laws of Fiji: Provided that this subsection shall not apply in respect of
any custom, tradition, usage or values that is, and to the extent that it is,
inconsistent with a provision of this constitution or a statute, or repug-
nant to the general principles of humanity.' Under the authority of the

preamble to the *Constitution of Kiribati* 1979, the *Laws of Kiribati Act* 1989, s. 4(2) states: 'In addition to the Constitution, the Laws of Kiribati comprise ... (b) customary law ...' The *Laws of Kiribati Act* 1989, sch. 1, para. 2 also states: ' ... customary law shall be recognised and enforced by, and may be pleaded in, all courts except so far as in a particular case or in a particular context its recognition or enforcement would result, in the opinion of the court, in injustice or would not be in the public interest.' The *Constitution of the Marshall Islands,* 1978, article X, ss. 1 and 2 states: 'Nothing in Article II shall be construed to invalidate the customary law or any traditional practice concerning land tenure or any related matter ...' and '... it shall be the responsibility of the Nitijela ... to declare, by Act, the customary law in the Marshall Islands.' The *Constitution of Nauru* 1968, s. 81 states: Custom and Adopted Laws Act 1971, s. 3: 'the institutions, customs and usages of the Nauruans ... shall be accorded recognition by every court, and have full force and effect of law' to regulate the matters specified in the Act. The *Niue Act* 1966, as amended by the *Niue Amendment Act* 1968 (No2), s. 23 states: 'Every title to and estate or interest in Niuean land shall be determined according to Niuean custom and any Ordinance or other enactment affecting Niuean custom.' The *Constitution of Samoa* 1962, article III(1) declares: 'Law... includes ... any custom or usage which has acquired the force of law in Samoa ... under the provisions of any Act or under a judgment of a court of competent jurisdiction.' The *Constitution of Solomon Islands* 1978, s. 76 and sch. 3, para. 3 enacts: 'Subject to this paragraph, customary law shall have effect as part of the law of Solomon Islands.' The *Tokelau Amendment Act* 1996 (NZ), preamble, para. 4 reads: 'Traditional authority in Tokelau is vested in its villages, and the needs of Tokelau at a local level are generally met through the administration of customary practices by elders.' The *Tokelau Amendment Act* 1967 (NZ), s. 20 states: 'The beneficial ownership of Tokelauan land shall be determined in accordance with the customs and usages of the Tokelauan inhabitants of Tokelau.' The preamble of the *Constitution of Tuvalu* 1986 and the *Laws of Tuvalu Act* 1987, s. 4(2) dictate: 'In addition to the Constitution, the Laws of Tuvalu comprise ... (b) customary law...' In addition, the *Laws of Tuvalu Act* 1987, sch. 1, para. 2 states: '... customary law shall be recognised and enforced by, and may be pleaded in, all courts except so far as in a particular case or in a particular context its recognition or enforcement would result, in the opinion of the court, in injustice or would not be in the public interest.' In the *Constitution of Vanuatu* 1980, article 47(1) states: ' If there is no rule of law applicable to a matter before it, a court shall determine the matter according to substantial justice and whenever possible in conformity with custom.' The Vanuatu Court of Appeal in *Joli v. Joli* (Court of Appeal decision 7 November 2003) found there was no inconsistency between the English legislation and custom. In Vanuatu under a clause in the Constitution, it is stated that laws which applied at the day of Independence continue to apply unless the Parliament of Vanuatu has passed legislation on the subject matter. Those pre-independence laws include the laws of general application of England and France provided, however, that the foreign laws pay sufficient regard to Vanuatu custom. An argument was raised that the English notions of dividing property and adjusting proprietary interests was inconsistent with the custom requirements for succession to land, and the court disagreed, thus upholding Indigenous law. The *Constitution of the Independent State of Papua New Guinea* dictates that '(1) An Act of Parliament shall, (2) Until such time as an Act of Parliament provides otherwise (a) the underlying law of Papua New Guinea shall be as prescribed …' In 2000, Papua New Guinea passed an *Underlying Law Act* that proclaims: 'The customary law shall apply unless: (*a*) it is inconsistent with a written law; or (*b*) its application and enforcement would be contrary to the National Goals and Directive Principles and the Basic Social Obligations established by the *Constitution*; or (*c*) its application and enforcement would be contrary to the basic rights guaranteed by *Division III.3 (Basic Rights) of the Constitution*.'

79 South Africa has laws that recognize Indigenous legal traditions. The *Constitution of the Republic of South Africa* affirms the continued applicability of traditional leadership and law and upholds the courts' and legislatures' authority to recognize and apply that law. Sections 211 and 212 of the *Constitution of the Republic of South Africa*, Act 108 of 1996 read:

> 211. (1) The institution, status and role of traditional leadership, according to customary law, are recognised, subject to the Constitution. (2) A traditional authority that observes a system of customary law may function subject to any applicable legislation and customs, which includes amendments to, or repeal of, that legislation or those customs. (3) The courts must apply customary law when that law is applicable, subject to the Constitution and any legislation that specifically deals with customary law.
> 212. (1) National legislation may provide for a role for traditional leadership as an institution at local level on matters affecting local communities. (2) To deal with matters relating to traditional leadership, the role of

traditional leaders, customary law and the customs of communities observing a system of customary law: national or provincial legislation may provide for the establishment of houses of traditional leaders; and national legislation may establish a council of traditional leaders.

Courts and legislatures have followed through with this recognition. Community Courts and Courts for Chiefs and Headmen have jurisdiction to hear certain matters on the level of magistrates' courts. They deal with customary disputes through an authorized African headman using indigenous law and custom, by an African against another African within a headman's area of jurisdiction. These courts are commonly known as chief's courts. A person with a claim has the right to choose whether to bring a claim in the chief's court or in a magistrate's court. The *Recognition of Customary Marriages Act,* 1998 (Act No. 120 of 1998) came into operation on 15 November 2000 and recognizes marriage negotiated, celebrated, or concluded according to any of the systems of Indigenous African customary law that exist in South Africa. See also Jill Zimmerman, 'The Constitution of Customary Law in South Africa: Method and Discourse' (2001) 17 *Harvard Black Letter Law Journal* 197; Hon. Yvonne Mokgoro, 'The Customary Law Question in the South African Constitution' (1997) 41 *St. Louis University Law Journal* 1279; Chuma Himonga, 'Transforming Customary Law of Marriage in South Africa and the Challenges to its Implementation with Specific Reference to Matrimonial Property' (2004) 32 *International Journal of Legal Information* 260; Lona N. Laymon, 'Valid-Where-Consummated: The Intersection of Customary Law Marriages and Formal Adjudication' (2001) 10 *South California Interdisciplinary Law Journal* 353; Andrew P. Kult, 'Intestate Succession in South Africa: The "Westernization" of Customary Law Practices within a Modern Constitutional Framework' (2001) 11 *Indiana International and Comparative Law Review* 697. (Thanks to Joanne St Lewis for these citations.)

80 Joanna Drzewieniecki, 'Las fuentes de la cultura legal en los Andes' (2003) 17:34 *Boletín de Antropología Universidad de Antioquia* (Colombia) 53–79.

81 Donna Lee Van Cott, 'A Political Analysis of Legal Pluralism in Bolivia and Colombia' (2000) 32 *Journal of Latin American Studies* 207–34.

82 Ibid.

83 G. Woodman, *Customary Land Law in the Ghanaian Courts* (Accra: Universities of Ghana Press, 1996).

84 K. Mason, 'The Inherent Jurisdiction of the Court' (1983) 57 *Queensland Law Journal* 449.

85 *Reference re Secession of Quebec,* [1998] 2 S.C.R. 217 at para. 242.

86 Ibid. at para. 67.
87 *Manitoba Language Rights Reference*, [1985] 1 S.C.R. 721 at 749.
88 Ibid., 753.
89 Ibid., 758.
90 Ibid., 768. The *Manitoba Language Rights Reference* applies this rule as follows:

> All rights, obligations and any other effects which have arisen under the Acts of the Manitoba legislature which are purportedly repealed, spent, or would currently be in force were it not for their constitutional defect, and which are not saved by the de facto doctrine, or doctrines such as res judicata and mistake of law, are deemed temporarily to have been, and to continue to be, enforceable and beyond challenge from the date of their creation to the expiry of the minimum period of time necessary for translation, re-enactment, printing and publishing these laws. At the termination of the minimum period these rights obligations and other effects will cease to have force and effect, unless the Acts under which they arose have been translated, re-enacted, printed and published in both languages ... para. 111.

91 These criteria come from the Supreme Court's test in *R. v. Van der Peet*, [1996] 2 S.C.R. 507.
92 *Reference re Secession of Quebec*, [1998] 2 S.C.R. 217, at para. 70.
93 Ibid., quoting from the *Manitoba Language Rights Reference*, [1985] 1 S.C.R. 721 at 749.
94 'Our law's claim to legitimacy also rests on an appeal to moral values, many of which are embedded in our constitutional structures. It would be a grave mistake to equate legitimacy with the "sovereign will" or majority rule alone, to the exclusion of other constitutional values.' Ibid., para. 67.
95 Ibid.
96 William Hagan, *Indian Police and Judges* (New Haven, CT: Yale University Press, 1966); Frank Pommersheim, *Braid of Feathers: American Indian Law and Contemporary Tribal Life* (Berkeley: University of California Press, 1995), 61–98.
97 Nell Jessup Newton, 'Tribal Court Praxis: One Year in the Life of Twenty Indian Tribal Courts' (1998) 22 *American Indian Law Review* 285.
98 Justin Richland and Sarah Deer, *Introduction to Tribal Legal Studies* (New York: Altamira Press, 2004), 361–419.
99 Barbara Atwood, 'Tribal Jurisprudence and Cultural Meanings of the Family' (2000) 79 *Nebraska Law Review* 577–656; Christine Zuni Cruz, 'Tribal Law as Indigenous Social Reality and Separate Consciousness'

(2001) 1 *Tribal Law Journal* 1; Matthew Fletcher, 'Rethinking the Role of Custom in Tribal Court Jurisprudence' (2007) 13 *Michigan Journal of Race and Law* 57–97.

100 Andrea Skari, 'The Tribal Judiciary: A Primer for Policy Development,' in *What Can Tribes Do? Strategies and Institutions in American Indian Economic Development*, ed. S. Cornell and S. Kalt (Los Angeles: UCLA, 1995).

101 Excerpt from Navajo Nation Bar Association Inc., 'Navajo Common Law,' retrieved 28 March 2008 from www.navajolaw.org/New2008/ncl.htm.

102 Ibid.

103 Stephen Cornell and Joseph Kalt, eds., *What Can Tribes Do? Strategies and Institutions in American Indian Economic Development* (Los Angeles: American Indian Studies Center, 1992).

104 John Borrows, *Recovering Canada: The Resurgence of Indigenous Law* (Toronto: University of Toronto Press, 2002), 21.

105 Albert Peeling and James Hopkins, 'Aboriginal Judicial Appointments to the Supreme Court of Canada' (unpublished paper prepared for the Indigenous Bar Association, April 2004), 21.

106 Ibid., 21.

107 *Supreme Court Act*, R.S.C. 1985, c. S-26, section 5.

108 Provincial unanimity is required for a constitutional amendment in accordance with section 41 for changes to the composition of the Supreme Court of Canada. Without an amendment stating that the Supreme Court must have at least one Aboriginal member, change could occur by constitutional convention.

8 Indigenous Legal Institution Development

1 Taiaiake Alfred, *Wasa'se: Indigenous Pathways of Action and Freedom* (New York: Broadview Press, 2005), 127.

2 Ibid.

3 Royal Commission on Aboriginal Peoples, *The Final Report of the Royal Commission on Aboriginal Peoples*, vol. 1, *Looking Forward, Looking Back* (Ottawa: Supply and Services, 1996), xxiv–xxv.

4 For a description of these duties, see the *Law Society Act*, R.S.O. 1990, c. L.8, s. 4.1 and s. 4.2.

5 For example, the Law Society of Upper Canada has an Aboriginal Issues Coordinator. Many law schools have programs in Indigenous legal issues to support Indigenous students and introduce Indigenous legal issues into the curriculum.

6 See Law Society of Upper Canada, *Final Report to Convocation: Task Force on the Rule of Law and the Independence of the Bar* (23 November 2006),

para. 3, retrieved 30 September 2008 from www.lsuc.on.ca/media /convnov2306_taskforce.pdf.

7 *Law Society Act*, R.S.O. 1990, c. L.8, s. 4.2.1.
8 Robert Gordon, 'The Independence of Lawyers' (1988) 68 *Boston University Law Review* 1 at 6–10, cited in Law Society of Upper Canada, *Final Report to Convocation: Task Force on the Rule of Law and the Independence of the Bar* (23 November 2006), para. 11, retrieved 30 September 2008 from www.lsuc.on.ca/media/convnov2306_taskforce.pdf.
9 The Navajo Nation Bar Association is a professional association of attorneys and tribal court advocates practising law on the Navajo Nation territories.
10 Navajo Nation Bar Association Inc., 'Purpose of Establishment,' retrieved 28 March 2008 from www.navajolaw.org/index.html/.
11 See the Indigenous Bar Association, 'IBA – Objectives,' retrieved 17 October 2008 from www.indigenousbar.ca/home/objectives.html.
12 Canadian Bar Association, *Touchstones for Change: Equality, Diversity and Accountability* (Ottawa: CBA Publications, 1993).
13 I have been a university student or professor in a law school setting for over two decades. During this time I have been heartened by the interest and enthusiasm of colleagues and students in searching for constructive solutions to remedying the injustice underlying Canadian–Indigenous relations. I do not think I could have developed the ideas explored in this book without the deep support for academic freedom offered by universities. While I treasure my Anishinabek citizenship, my life's experience with Indigenous legal issues, and my time for self-directed learning above my university affiliation, law schools have provided me with the resources and environment to bring ideas together in a way that would have been exceedingly difficult in most other settings. For example, I do not have clients or direct financial interests which would cause me to hold back or advance the issues discussed herein in any particular way. Furthermore I do not have any formal membership or affiliations with any political party, group, or Indigenous organization (beyond membership in my own First Nation) which might tempt me to champion, manipulate, or reject ideas through other people's pressure. While I have biases which I have attempted to identify, question, and sometimes overturn as I wrote this book, my university affiliation allows me to pursue more independent research than might be the case if I was a lawyer, civil servant, or member of a political group. As a result I have not felt compelled to shy away from any constructive proposal or respectful critique in the course of writing this work.

14 In fact, a variety of Indigenous legal processes might be followed in schools to explore different ways to vigorously yet respectfully disagree. For example, in a great-lakes context, where Anishinabek and Haudenosaunee legal traditions are present, this could lead to classroom discussions that seek 'peace, friendship, and respect' (*Gus Wen Tah* treaty values) in the midst of profound and deep-seated disagreement.

15 For example, Osgoode Hall Law School has an excellent clinical program that allows students to work with Aboriginal communities around the world. See www.osgoode.yorku.ca/legal_clinics/clinical_programs _aboriginal_intro.html. There have been many developments in the United States in a similar pattern; see Robert Laurence, 'Preparing American Indians for Law School: The American Indian Center's Pre-Law Summer Institute' (1992) 12 *Northern Illinois University Law Review* 278. There are now three graduate LL.M. programs in Indigenous legal studies in the United States (University of Arizona, Arizona State University, and University of Tulsa), with numerous JD programs specializing in Indian law (at universities in New Mexico, Arizona, Washington, Wisconsin, Kansas, Iowa, South Dakota, and Vermont) or Indian law clinics (in Colorado, Idaho, Montana). Other countries with Indigenous populations have also developed Indigenous-focused programs: the University of Waikato in New Zealand was created for the purpose of advancing Maori legal studies in a bicultural environment, though it has been slow in establishing itself. The University of New South Wales has an Indigenous Law Centre. The University of Tromso, in Norway, has led the way in teaching about Sami legal issues.

16 For comments on different Indigenous law programs in Canada, see Roger Carter, 'University of Saskatchewan Native Law Centre' (1980) 44 *Saskatchewan Law Review* 135; Donald Purich, 'Affirmative Action in Canadian Law Schools: The Native Student in Law School' (1986) 51 *Saskatchewan Law Review* 79; and Hugh MacAulay, 'Improving Access to Legal Education for Native People in Canada' (1991) 14 *Dalhousie Law Journal* 133. The Native Law Centre has both a research and a teaching mission. It offers a pre-law summer program for Indigenous students interested in gaining admission to law schools. It also publishes the *Canadian Native Law Reporter*, papers on theoretical and technical legal issues, and has an excellent resource library. The University of British Columbia's First Nations Legal Studies Program has operated since 1975. Originally an admissions program, it has evolved into a program that has assisted over 200 Indigenous law students graduate from its school. The University of British Columbia has a Centre for International Indigenous

Legal Studies to further its mission. Akitsiraq is a long-distance law program offered by the University of Victoria (UVic) to Inuit people in Canada's youngest territory, Nunavut. Fourteen Inuit students are studying at home in their own territory and will graduate with UVic law degrees in four years. UVic also offers a joint law degree and a master's of Indigenous governance at its main campus. Osgoode Hall Law School at York University has offered the Intensive Program in Lands, Resources, and First Nations Governments since 1994. This clinically based program immerses students in an Indigenous legal experience for all their credits over an entire semester. The June Callwood Program at the University of Toronto provides graduate scholarships for advanced Indigenous legal studies. It also facilitates internships with and gaining applied educational experiences from Indigenous communities. The Faculty of Law at the University of Alberta has an Indigenous Law Program that has support from both the director and the students.

17 There were approximately ten Indigenous law professors in Canada in 2009–10. For a discussion of the challenges an Indigenous law professor faced in his work, see Robert Williams Jr., 'Vampires Anonymous and Critical Race Practice' (1997) 95 *Michigan Law Review* 741.

18 John Borrows, 'Fourword/Foreword: Issues, Individuals, Institutions, Ideologies' (2002) 1 *Indigenous Law Journal* vii. For reflections from Indigenous law students about their experiences in law school, see Patricia Monture, 'Now That the Door Is Open: First Nations and the Law School Experience' (1990) 15 *Queen's Law Journal* 179; Tracy Lindberg, 'What Do You Call an Indian Woman with a Law Degree? Nine Aboriginal Women at the University of Saskatchewan College of Law Speak Out' (1996) 9 *Canadian Journal of Women and the Law* 301; Leah Whiu, 'A Maori Women's Experience of Feminist Legal Education in Aotearoa' (1994) 2 *Waikato Law Review* 161.

19 For example, the University of Victoria has extensive experience dealing with Indigenous legal education, including working with Indigenous communities in a law school context as evidenced through the law school's experience with the Akitsiraq Law School. Some of the initiatives at the school during the time the degree was being developed included:

1 An Endowed Chair in Aboriginal Economic Development cross-appointed to the law and business schools.
2 Law Foundation Endowed Professorship in Aboriginal Justice and Governance.
3 A graduate program focused on Indigenous legal issues.

4 An Indigenous student population that was approximately 9 per cent of the law school.

5 Three Indigenous teachers employed full time by the faculty (Heather Raven, Maxine Matilpi, and John Borrows).

6 A Summer Intensive Program in Indigenous Legal Studies held every third year.

7 A concurrent degree program for an LL.B. and a Master of Arts in Indigenous Governance.

8 Successful completion of the Akitsiraq Law School Program for Inuit students in Nunavut.

9 Six courses focused on Indigenous legal issues and many others that included components dealing with Indigenous legal issues.

10 An exchange program with the law school at Arizona State University to facilitate comparative Indigenous Legal Studies.

11 An annual Aboriginal Awareness Camp in which approximately one-quarter of the first-year class at UVic participated.

12 An excellent Academic and Cultural Support Program.

13 A large and active Indigenous Law Club.

14 Annual participation in the National Kawaskimhon Aboriginal Moot.

15 A Faculty Aboriginal Equity Plan.

16 A joint Aboriginal Restorative Justice Program with the Victoria Native Friendship Centre.

17 An Environmental Law Clinic with strong Aboriginal participation and content.

18 Frequent national and international visitors on Indigenous issues.

19 Active research support for Indigenous issues (Trudeau Fellows and Mentors, SSHRC MCRI, Virtual Scholar in Residence Award, BC Law Foundation grants, WED, etc.).

In my opinion, the depth of UVic's resources at the time, along with the critical mass of students and faculty, provided a strong enough base to take initial steps.

20 McGill describes their program as follows:

In 1999, the Faculty adopted a creative and challenging new approach to legal education that will prepare McGill graduates for careers that increasingly require knowledge of more than one legal system. From the very first year, students will be introduced to civil law and common law concepts and encouraged to compare and critically evaluate the two traditions. This dramatic and unique curriculum, which explores the common law and the civil law in an integrated fashion, is entirely different from the 'three-plus-one' programmes offered by other faculties. In such programs, students learn one legal system in three years, then receive additional exposure to the other tradition in a one-year add-on. McGill's trans-systemic method fosters not only outstanding analytical ability, but also critical reflection and openness to diverse approaches to legal problems.

21 Quote by Nicholas Kasirer on the cover of *To Leave No Stone Unturned*, ed. Vesna Antwan et al. (Montreal: McGill Faculty of Law, n.d.), retrieved 10 October 2008 from www.mcgill.ca/files/ViewBookBCL-LLB.pdf.

22 The Faculty of Law at the University of Victoria (UVic) has considered a program of study that could lead to an Indigenous Law degree. The University of Victoria Faculty of Law is a national leader in its relationships with Aboriginal peoples and organizations. This is reflected in the strong representation of Aboriginal people on its faculty and student body. The creation of a Chair in Aboriginal Justice and Governance and the successful delivery of the four-year Akitsiraq Law School program for Inuit students in Nunavut are two recent examples of the Faculty's expertise with and commitment to Aboriginal initiatives.

The Faculty of Law of the University of Victoria is committed to the following goals:
1 Broadening perspectives on Aboriginal/non-Aboriginal relationships,
2 Increasing knowledge and understanding of the Aboriginal issues in Canada,
3 Facilitating reconciliation and producing stronger partnerships and principles that result in more effective solutions to legal issues involving Indigenous peoples,
4 Promoting justice for Aboriginal peoples and greater social and economic stability for all,
5 Encouraging legal research and teaching skills that assist Aboriginal and all Canadian communities in setting new directions and generating new opportunities relative to Aboriginal legal issues.

23 This idea was shared with the law faculty, the University Provost, the executive body of the Law Society of British Columbia, the Indigenous Bar Association, law students, and leaders of some of the major Indigenous organizations and interested communities in British Columbia.

While the feedback about the initial concept was nearly universally positive, I decided that I would benefit from another year or two of immersion in Anishinabek law before a complete B.I.L./LL.B. program could be taught. While I have taught Anishinabek law over the last five years, and published a book and articles devoted to this subject, I wanted to ensure that I had the necessary base of knowledge to effectively teach in a four-year degree intensively focused on Indigenous law. I also hoped that delaying the formal approval and implementation of such a program would enable younger scholars who are in graduate school or their first years of teaching to further develop before it was launched. I realized that the offering of an Indigenous law degree (transsystemically or otherwise) would attract a great deal of scrutiny and, while perfection should never be the standard in legal education (or any other earthly endeavour), it is important that such a degree receive sufficient resources to develop credibility. It must also be rigorous enough to ensure its broader acceptance within Indigenous communities and provincial law societies. I wanted to get the ideas in this book in circulation for a few years before a decision was taken to launch a joint degree program.

24 Legal research and writing would be nested in the Constitutional Law Traditions course, and students would complete four legal research and writing assignments using materials from the Constitutional curriculum. It could be described as follows: *Law 1007 Legal Research and Writing:* This course will be taken within the Constitutional Law Traditions course, and students will complete four legal research and writing assignments using materials from the Constitutional curriculum. This course acquaints the first-year student with the variety of materials in the Law Library and provides knowledge of basic legal research techniques. The use of various research tools, including computers, is considered. Through a variety of written assignments, students become familiar with accepted principles pertaining to proper citation in legal writing and develop a degree of proficiency in legal writing and research.

25 Law 1000, Constitutional Law Traditions: Anishinabek law will form the Indigenous legal context of this course. Approximately one-third of the course will convey this tradition. Canada has a complex constitutional history, drawing upon written and unwritten laws and conventions. This course provides an introductory overview of constitutional relations of the Canadian political and legal system. The course is organized into three parts. The first part generally examines the manner in which Indigenous Nations historically formed relationships with other nations, and the ways in which they form relations with other Indigenous

Nations in the contemporary context. The second part of the course examines the nature of relations between Aboriginal, federal, and provincial levels of government. More specifically, the course looks at historical development, political judicial regulation of these relationships, as well as political reformulation of fundamental constitutional structures. Federalism is an element of this inquiry. The third part of the course focuses on the role Aboriginal rights and the *Canadian Charter of Rights and Freedoms* plays in the constitutional order. (Full-year course)

26 Law 1001, Criminal Law and Justice Traditions: Salish law will form the Indigenous legal context of this course. This course is an introduction to Canadian criminal law and Salish justice, both substantive and procedural, and focuses on the following topics:

- principles of Salish Justice
- the social, political, and constitutional context in which the Canadian criminal justice system operates
- significant aspects of Salish powers as they relates to the Canadian state in the Douglas treaties
- important elements of police and prosecutorial powers in the pretrial process and during trial
- the effect of the *Constitution Act, 1982* and the *Canadian Charter of Rights and Freedoms* on both criminal procedure and substantive criminal law
- substantive criminal law, including the theory and doctrine behind the concepts of restorative justice, mens rea, actus reus, and justifications and excuses. (Full-year course)

27 Law 1002, Comparative Indigenous Legal Traditions: The Indigenous peoples of Canada include, among others, the ancient and contemporary nations of the Innu, Mi'kmaq, Maliseet, Cree, Innu, Anishinabek, Haudenosaunee, Dakota, Lakota, Nakota, Dakota, Assinaboine, Saulteaux, Blackfoot, Secwepemec, Nlha7kapmx, Salish, Kwakwaka'wakw, Nuchah-nulth, Haida, Tsimshian, Gitksan, Wet'suwet'en, Tahltan, Gwichin, Dene, Inuit, and Métis. It is also estimated that there are over 800 million Indigenous peoples living throughout the world. Indigenous law and legal traditions are diverse. This course will expose students to the leading national and international academics and practitioners of Indigenous law. It considers the development, interpretation, and theories of Indigenous law from many perspectives. Guest lecturers will present their work and ideas to examine the frameworks in which a wide range of legal problems can be analysed and prescriptions evalu-

ated. This course is taught in the fall term only, with a final exam in December.

28 Law 1003, The Legal Process: This course provides a general perspective on the processes of decision-making throughout Canada's legal systems, by examining its major institutions and the function of substantive and procedural law within them. It provides first-year students with a transactional overview of their new discipline, and a background for courses in the second- and third-year program. It also introduces students to the institutional structure of the Canadian legal system and, at the same time, provides an analysis of the role of law in society. The course has a variety of components, namely, historical, institutional, cultural, procedural, and philosophical. The role of law in society, the function of the legal profession, the development of the legal system, the reception of English law in Canada, the contemporary legal system in British Columbia, the structure of the courts, problems of fact finding and evidence, stare decisis, sources of law, the legislative process, administrative tribunals, an introduction to jurisprudential concepts, future trends with respect to the role of law in society including law reform, legal services, the legal profession, and access to the law are all considered. (Full-year course)

29 Law 1004, Voluntary Obligations/Contracts: Métis law will form the Indigenous legal context of this course. The law of contracts is usually broadly classified either as part of the law of obligations or as part of the system of private law (which encompasses contracts, property, and torts). In general, the system of private law deals with the areas of law that concern primarily private interests and involve private disputes. The law of obligation deals with duties that a person owes to another person. The law of contracts deals with self-imposed duties, that is, binding agreements voluntarily concluded between parties. This course will interrogate why, how, and under what circumstances the common law and Métis law gave force to obligations voluntarily undertaken. This course will further examine the general principles of contract law in Canada as developed by the courts and the principles contained in the statutes regulating specific areas of contract law. Attention is given to the following issues: contract formation, interpretation, capacity to contract, excuse for performance, and remedies for breach. (Full-year course)

30 Law 1005, Involuntary and Hybrid Obligations/Torts: Inuit law will form the Indigenous legal context of this course. The law of torts, or civil wrongs, deals with disputes between individuals that arise when the acts or omissions of one person cause injury or property loss. Inuit law also

had substantive rules and procedures directed to loss or injury caused by acts or omissions of legal duties. The most important area in torts is negligence, which embraces unintentionally caused injury to the person, damage to property, and harm to economic interests. Other major areas of tort law are nuisance (unreasonable interference with the enjoyment of land), and intentional injuries whether to the person, property, or personal dignity and reputation. Analysis of tort law involves consideration of social values, deterrence, loss distribution and economic efficiency, as well as corporate and governmental responsibility. (Full-year course)

31 Law 1006, Property Law Traditions: Gitksan and Wet'suwet'en law will form the Indigenous context of this course. Property law explores how law regulates relationships among persons in which they acquire, use, and transfer resources. The course will introduce students to well-established doctrine as well as emerging fields of property law. The foundational topics the course addresses include the nature of property, the concept of possession, Aboriginal title, shared ownership and the doctrine of estates and conditional transfers. The course also cultivates an understanding of the intimate relation between law and social context and encourages students to approach their study of property law with critical sensibilities. (Full-year course)

32 Salish Nations and people are divided into coastal and interior groups. Coastal Salish people are found throughout southern Vancouver Island, Vancouver, the Fraser Valley, the Gulf Islands, and Puget Sound. Interior Salish people are traditionally from the Upper Fraser River and Pemberton Valley regions.

33 Law 2000, Salish Legal Traditions: This seminar will explore the pre-colonial foundations of Salish legal traditions in the Pacific North-west of North America. As the indigenous inhabitants of this region, the Salish developed legal systems grounded in the social, ecological, and spiritual realities of their environment. The core principles of these legal systems will be conceptualized by considering notions of identity (individual/collective), governance (autonomy/authority), entitlement (rights/responsibilities), and territoriality (geographical/spiritual) from both perspectives. To avoid privileging written texts (case law, legislation, alphabetic renderings of treaties), attention will be given to Salish oral tradition and its associated non-alphabetic semiotic systems such as carvings, clothing, petroglyphs, and other inscribed representations of material culture. (Full-year course)

34 Law 2001, Salish Language and Law: Language is a key to understanding legal relationships and obligations. This course will provide an introduc-

tion to the linguistic structures of the Salish family of languages, one of the major language families in British Columbia. The course will include discussion of oral and written literature and topics related to Salish obligations and law. Language revitalization as an element of legal development among Salish language communities will be discussed. The course provides theoretical as well as practical and hands-on experience in developing understandings about the importance of Indigenous language to understanding Indigenous laws. (Full-year course)

35 Law 2002, Salish Legal Writing and Advanced Legal Research: It is no exaggeration to observe that Indigenous writing is a well-established part of the Canadian landscape. This fact has significance for Indigenous law. The First Peoples of Canada have always had a *verbal* tradition: speeches, myths, legends, stories, songs, and poetry have been fashioned and transmitted from generation to generation since time immemorial. These expressions have always been a part of Indigenous life and continue to animate their interpretive understanding of the world. Of course, historically indigenous legal traditions were *oral* and, as such, contrasted sharply with the *written* cultures of the common law and civil law. Today, Indigenous written expression stands alongside oral traditions as important ways to convey meaning. This course will involve students in a study of Salish writing and expression. It builds on the research and writing skills learned in first-year law. Students explore a wide range of Salish and Canadian research sources, both legal and non-legal, including computer-assisted legal research. Students analyse various types of legal writing, Salish and non-Indigenous. The importance of context, organization, and audience in legal writing is stressed. Parts, sections, or clauses of written documents are analysed, evaluated, criticized, edited, and rewritten to improve and develop student analytical and writing skills. (Full-year course)

36 Incidentally, the joint-degree program is conceived as being an bachelor's degree, in recognition of the fact that the real 'masters' and 'doctors' of Indigenous law are mostly in Indigenous communities.

37 Law 301, The Administrative Law Process: This course investigates the nature and function of the administrative process with particular reference to the development of tribunals and agencies with a wide variety of disparate functions and interactions with private life. Similarly, the course investigates the way in which tribunals and courts interact, with specific reference to the judicial arsenal available for the control of administrative behaviour. Indigenous tribunals and tribunals that frequently deal with Indigenous issues and people will be one aspect of this course. (One-semester course)

38 Law 315, Business Associations: This course analyses and discusses the various legal forms for carrying on trade. The course recognizes that the corporation is of immense commercial and legal significance as an organizational form and hence will stress legislation and materials respecting the modern company. Students will, however, be exposed to sole proprietorship, partnership, and related agency principles. In addition, business development will also be examined in an Indigenous legal context. Across Canada, Indigenous communities and businesses hold tremendous potential to advance prosperity and well-being. This potential remains largely untapped as a result of substantive and administrative impediments to Aboriginal economic and business development. The course will address practical and meaningful strategies to dismantle these systemic barriers to bring significant benefits to Aboriginal peoples and communities, to the financial and business sectors, and to the economy and society of Canada as a whole. (One-semester course)

39 Law 322, Family Law: This course considers the institution of the family, both in its social and legal contexts. Specific reference is made to the law relating to adoption, reproduction, violence in intimate relationships, marriage, divorce, custody, matrimonial property, and support. Particular attention is paid to the manner in which family law both shapes and is shaped by social practices and ideologies. Furthermore, Indigenous legal traditions regarding family formation and dissolution will be examined. Finally, special family law rules in Canadian law relevant to Indigenous people will be addressed, including section 19 of the Federal Child Support Guidelines used to 'gross up' the income of Aboriginal persons whose income is free of tax and who are ordered to pay child support; section 89 of the *Indian Act* affecting the enforcement of child and spousal support orders; considerations of a child's Aboriginal heritage in determining custody, and so on. (One-semester course)

40 Law 3000, Nu-chah-nulth Legal Traditions: The Nuu-chah-nulth people are Indigenous peoples in the Pacific North-west on the West Coast of Vancouver Island. The Nuu-chah-nulth and other Pacific North-west cultures were famous for their Potlatch ceremonies, in which the host would generously bestow gifts on guests. The Potlatch contained many rules that helped to order society and bring respect to relationships. The Nu-chah-nulth also had principles related to traditional ecosystem management, called *ha huulhi*. The Potlatch, *ha huulhi*, and other Nu-chah-nulth legal principles and practices will be the focus of this course. (One-semester course)

41 Law 3001, Kwakwaka'wakw Legal Traditions: The Kwakwaka'wakw have many laws relative to relationships to land, animals, plants, family,

business partners, and other nations. One law, the Potlatch, takes the form of a ceremonial feast traditionally reinforced through the exchange of gifts and other ceremonies. This course will examine Potlatching and other laws within the Kwakwaka'wakw. It will also consider the Potlatch's relationship to Canadian law. Potlatching was made illegal in Canada in the late nineteenth century, largely at the urging of missionaries and government agents. Prosecutions and underground practices were a feature of Kwakwaka'wakw in this period. Today people continue to hold Potlatches and they are once again an important part of community life. The legal implications of this fact will be explored. (One-semester course)

42 Law 3002, Indigenous Moot: Indigenous Oral Advocacy Dispute Resolution: This course would allow students to participate in the resolution of a legal issue in a practice-oriented forum using a variety of Indigenous legal traditions. (One-semester course)

43 Law 307, Civil Procedure: This course is founded on an inquiry into the functions of a modern procedural system. Specific reference is made to the development of a process, which considers the extent to which the specific system under study aids in the achievement of just, speedy, and economic resolutions of justifiable conflicts on their merits. Students are introduced to the basic structure of a civil action and major items for consideration throughout the development of civil litigation. As a result, such matters as the expenses of litigation, jurisdiction, initial process, pleadings, amendment, joinder, discovery, disposition without trial, and alternatives to adjudication are discussed. (One-semester course)

44 Law 309, Evidence: This course examines the objective structure and content of the law governing proof of facts in both civil and criminal trials, as well as before administrative tribunals. Rules of evidence respecting burdens of proof and presumptions, competence and compellability of witnesses, corroboration, hearsay, character, opinion evidence, and a variety of other topics are critically examined in the light of the objectives of the legal process. The course will also focus on the rules of evidence relevant to Indigenous peoples presenting their knowledge in court. (One-semester course)

45 Law 316, Secured Transactions: This introductory course is about the law relating to commercial lending. When a business borrows money, lenders usually require some form of personal property as security for the loan. Although this area of the law arises from the common law, most Canadian provinces and territories have enacted comprehensive legislative schemes that govern commercial lending. In British Columbia, the *Personal Property Security Act* (*BCPPSA*) governs areas such as the different

kinds of security interests, creation, registration, priorities, and rights and remedies on default. Most of the class time will be spent on the *BCPPSA*. At the end of the course, there will be a very brief introduction to the law of negotiable instruments via the provisions of the *Bills of Exchange Act* that relate to commercial lending. At the end of the course, students should have a basic understanding of security devices provided for in the *BCPPSA* and an ability to apply the provisions of the *BCPPSA* to simple fact-situation based problems. More particularly, students should understand the common vehicles of commercial lending, the creation of commercial security interests, the priority structure for competing security interests, the basic rules relating to the realization of these securities, and some of the theory underlying their creation and use. Although the focus of this course is on commercial lending, students will gain some understanding of consumer transactions as set out in the *BCPPSA* and the *Bills of Exchange Act* in contrast to the commercial lending environment. Implications for Indigenous peoples will be considered throughout the course. (One-semester course)

46 Law 340, Indigenous Lands, Rights, and Governance: This is a course in modern Canadian Native law (or Aboriginal law) – the laws that relate to the special status and capacities of Aboriginal peoples and to their distinctive institutions – as part of the Canadian legal system. The emphasis is on current problems in the field of law as it is found and practised today. The course covers such topics as the core of federal jurisdiction under section 91(24); the extent to which provincial laws may extend to Indian reserves and Indian people; Aboriginal rights over Crown lands; the relationship between bands and neighbouring municipalities; exemptions and other similar issues of importance to Aboriginal people and non-Aboriginal people alike. (One-semester course)

47 Law 341, Historical Foundations of Aboriginal Title and Government: This course introduces students to Aboriginal title and self-government in their historical context. The focus is on common, constitutional, and statutory law in relation to Aboriginal title and rights, but reference is also made to the treaty process, reserve lands, and hunting and fishing. Although the course deals with all parts of Canada, the emphasis is on British Columbia. (One-semester course)

48 Law 343, Comparative Indigenous Rights: The U.S. Experience: The law relating to Indigenous peoples challenges many fundamental assumptions about legality and the rule of law. For example, in a leading case dealing with Indigenous rights, Chief Justice John Marshall observed, 'it is difficult to comprehend the proposition that the inhabitants of either

quarter of the globe could ... give the discoverer rights in the country discovered, which annulled the pre-existing rights of its ancient possessors.'
Yet, despite this problem with 'the doctrine of discovery,' the entrench-
ment of this principle is the foundational statement in the common law
of Aboriginal rights. This course will examine how the acceptance of 'discovery' has had serious ramifications on Indigenous peoples in the
United States to simultaneously preserve and dispossess them of their
rights. It will survey U.S. law governing the relationship between the
United States, the States, and Indian Nations, and will focus on the constitutional, statutory, and jurisprudential rules that make up the field of
federal Indian law. Topics to be addressed include the history of
federal–tribal relations; the origin and scope of federal power over Indian
affairs; the source and scope of tribal powers recognized under federal
law; the limits of state authority in Indian country (including taxation);
Indian law claims; and contemporary Indian policy. The course will be
comparative, but the readings will be almost exclusively drawn from U.S.
jurisprudence. (One-semester course)

49 Law 343, Aboriginal Politics and Self-Government: The course is an introduction to the study of Indigenous politics. The specific focus is on the
history and contemporary politics of First Nations in Canada and British
Columbia. However, this is situated in the broader context of the global
situation of Indigenous peoples, the historical contexts of European
imperial expansion and colonization over the last 500 years, the diverse
struggles and relationships that have developed among settler societies
and Indigenous peoples, with special reference to treaty relationships and
nation-to-nation relationships, the various attempts to transform these
unequal relationships today, the struggles of Indigenous peoples to gain
recognition in international law, and the development of Indigenous
peoples' global networks. The course studies the very different perspectives on these struggles and relationships in theory and practice. (One-
semester course)

50 Law 343, First Nations and Economic Development: This course examines the issues in both law and policy as they relate to the burgeoning
field of Indigenous development in Canada. The topic is both timely and
necessary as the state of Indigenous law in Canada raises serious issues
with respect to the law's capacity to accommodate Aboriginal self-determination and, more generally, recognize the constitutional status of Aboriginal peoples within the development paradigm. Examining this paradigm will include analysis of taxation, employment law, business
organizations and theory, and finance. Beyond the legal construct itself,

the social and economic consequences of particular business practices pose additional challenges to the cause of cultural preservation and a sense of community well-being. For example, we will examine whether or not particular business forums provide greater cultural integrity and whether there exists a relationship to the overall success of the project in question. These complex issues will form the basis of class lectures and discussions. As well, the use of case studies will further demonstrate the inherent and emerging tensions that intersect with indigenous develop-ment. (One-semester course)

51 Law 343, Self-Determination of Peoples: In this course students will read and discuss work by contemporary authors that bears on the historical development, current content, and normative justification of collective self-determination, more commonly known as the self-determination of peoples. Although the course includes a brief survey of the international legal and institutional context, the primary emphasis is on the conceptual underpinnings of the right to self-determination of peoples and on its plausibility and status as a norm in international ethics and international law. In particular, the readings will focus on the relationship between self-determination and respect for human rights and on the extent to which the right has internal as well as external dimensions (the extent to which the right generates duties for states vis-à-vis their own population and not just vis-à-vis the populations of other states). (One-semester course)

52 Law 362, Colonial Legal History: This course uses a website for both teaching and communications, linking students at UVic, UBC, and the Australian National University. It offers the study of legal history as a means of understanding the relationships between law, state, society, and culture in Canada in comparison and contrast with Australia. These two modern liberal democratic states that were previously clusters of British settler colonies, each one established at different times and for different purposes during the late eighteenth century and throughout the nine-teenth century, provide a rich setting for examining the growth of colo-nial legal culture, tensions between imperial governance and settler demand, and the competing pressures for centralization and pluralism in law and the administration of justice. The colonies of Upper Canada, Vancouver Island / British Columbia, New South Wales, and South Aus-tralia are the subjects of a detailed study. (Full-year course)

53 Law 368, Indigenous Women and the Law: This seminar examines the unique place of Indigenous women within the constructs of Canadian law and society. The seminar takes an interdisciplinary approach. Topics

canvassed are marital property, colonialism, government, membership, human rights, criminal justice, sexuality, employment, and children. The first objective of the seminar is to introduce the growing body of scholarship by and about Indigenous women. Secondly, by the end of the seminar, participants will be able to formulate a critical analysis of the political, economic, and social challenges faced by contemporary Indigenous women. This is not a course about developing solutions to the political, economic, and social challenges facing Indigenous women and their families in contemporary Canadian and Indigenous societies. (Half-term seminar)

54 Law 4000, Working with Elders and/or Lawkeepers in a Community Context: Students will work with an Elder, group of Elders, or lawkeepers to understand the transmission and meaning of oral traditions in Indigenous law. They will serve in a traditional capacity in learning the norms, principle, values, and application of the tradition under study. Students might live in a remote or rural setting, on the land, or in a crowded urban setting where Elders or lawkeepers are practising their legal traditions. (One-semester course)

55 Law 4001, Working with an Indigenous Political Community: Students will work with a political community to increase their understanding of the opportunities and challenges First Nations, Métis communities, and Inuit governments face in applying their laws in contemporary circumstances. Depending on the Indigenous Nation a student is working with, examples of placement might include Nisga'a Lisims Government, Haudensaunee Confederary, Mi'kmaq Grand Council, Inuit Circumpolar Conference, or an Indian band council. (One-semester course)

56 Law 4002, Working with an Indigenous Court or Dispute Resolution Body: Students will work in a tribal court or Indigenous dispute resolution body to better understand the application of Indigenous law to individuals within a community. Students learn the distinctiveness and diversity of a particular Indigenous judicial culture, to appreciate nuances of language and historical practices. Depending on the Indigenous Nation a student is working with, examples of placements might include the Cree Court in Saskatchewan, the Tsuu Tina and Peacemaker Court in Alberta, Aboriginal Legal Services of Toronto, the Tohono O'odham Court in Arizona, the Navajo Court in Arizona, the Colville Tribal Court in Washington State, and so on. (One-semester course)

57 Wider recognition and implementation of Indigenous legal traditions would also create a greater role for Indigenous legal education. The First Nations University of Canada or other Indigenous educational institu-

tions could work with Indigenous leaders to develop programs specific
to Indigenous groups and their laws. The First Nations Governance
Centre could provide valuable information and education.
58 John Borrows, *Recovering Canada: The Resurgence of Indigenous Law*
(Toronto: University of Toronto Press, 2002).

9 Living Law on a Living Earth: Religion, Law, and the Constitution

1 See chapter 2 in this volume for further discussion.
2 In approaching my work, I have adopted the methodology suggested by
Jim Tully:

> Firstly [I] start from and grant a certain primacy to practice. [I offer] a
> form of philosophical reflection on practices of governance in the
> present that are experienced as oppressive in some way... ·
> Secondly, [my] aim is not to develop a normative theory as the solution
> to the problems [we experience]. Rather [I] seek to disclose the histori-
> cally contingent conditions of possibility ... This approach is not a type
> of political theory ... but a species of 'practical philosophy' ... [I] seek
> to characterize the conditions of possibility of [our] problematic form
> of governance in a redescription ... that transforms [our] self-under-
> standing of those subject to and struggling within it, enabling [us] to
> see its contingent conditions and the possibilities of governing [our-
> selves] differently. Hence it is not only an interpretative political phi-
> losophy, but also a specific genre of critique or critical attitude towards
> ways of being governed in the present – an attitude of testing and pos-
> sible transformation.

See James Tully, *Public Philosophy in a New Key*, vol. 1, *Democracy and Civic
Freedom* (Cambridge: Cambridge University Press, 2008), 16.
3 See Helen Hornbeck Tanner, *Atlas of Great Lakes Indian History* (Norman:
University of Oklahoma Press, 1982), 58–9; George Quimby, *Indian Life in
the Upper Great Lakes Region: 11,000 B.C. to A.D. 1800* (Chicago: University
of Chicago Press, 1960), 2 and 38; and Thomas E. Lee, 'The Antiquity of
the Sheguiandah Site' (1957) 71 *Canadian Field-Naturalist* 117 at 123–6. Lee
speculates that the remains of an ancient quarry, workplace, and human
habitation may indicate that '30,000 years may be a conservative estimate
for the older components [of occupation] of the Sheguiandah site' on
Manitoulin Island in Lake Huron (123). See also J.V. Wright, *Ontario Pre-
history* (Toronto: National Museum of Man, 1972), 91–2.

4   William Warren, *History of the Ojibway Nation* (St Paul: Minnesota Histori-
    cal Society, 1885; reprint, Minneapolis: Ross and Haines, 1970), 41–53;
    Theresa Shenck, *The Voice of the Crane Echoes Afar* (New York: Garland
    Publishing, 1987).

5   The Odawa are also known as Otaouan or Ottawa. I refer to these people
    as the Odawa because that is what they prefer to be called. Historically,
    the Odawa had four known subdivisions: the Sinago, Kiskakon, Sable,
    and Nassauakueton. See Christian A. Feest, 'Ottawa,' in *Handbook of
    North American Indians*, vol. 15, ed. Bruce G. Trigger (Washington, DC:
    Smithsonian Institution, 1978), 772. See also Vernon Kinetz, *The Indians of
    the Western Great Lakes* (Ann Arbor: University of Michigan Press, 1940),
    246.

6   For a history of the Potawatomi, see R. David Edmunds, *The Potawatomis,
    Keepers of the Fire* (Norman: University of Oklahoma Press, 1978).

7   Harold Hickerson, *The Chippewa and Their Neighbors: A Study in Ethnohis-
    tory* (New York: Holt, Rinehart and Winston, 1970).

8   Ojibway is the common title applied to the Anishinabek people in
    Canada, and Chippewa is the name most frequently used in the United
    States. Throughout their history, the Ojibway have gone by different Euro-
    pean descriptions in various Great Lakes regions. Contemporary Western
    terminology still applies some divisions to the Ojibway. On the north
    shores of Lakes Ontario and Erie, the Ojibway are called Mississaugas, on
    the south shore of Lake Huron they are sometimes named Saugeens,
    while at the confluence of Lakes Huron and Superior around Sault Ste
    Marie they are often known as the Saulteaux. Ojibway are further classi-
    fied by their geographical location as Southeast Chippewas of Michigan's
    Lower Peninsula and adjacent Ontario, the Chippewas of Lake Superior,
    the Southwest Chippewas of interior Minnesota, the Northern Chippewa
    of the Laurentian uplands above the Great Lakes, and the Plains
    Chippewa or Bungees. See Edmund Jefferson Danziger Jr., *The Chippewa of
    Lake Superior* (Norman: University of Oklahoma Press, 1978), x and 8.

9   However, some people state that the Anishinabek came from east of the
    Great Lakes in the period before contact. See Andrew J. Blackbird, *History
    of the Ottawa and Chippewa Indians of Michigan* (Ypsilanti, MI: Ypsilanti Job
    Printing House, 1887), 79.

10 The other Indigenous legal culture to which I belong is the Canadian con-
    stitutional law community, which I am arguing should be fed by Anishin-
    abek law, along with the common law, civil law, and other Indigenous
    legal traditions, to make it truly Indigenous (home grown in its place of
    origin).

11 *Miche-makinock* means 'great turtle,' though others believed that this was a mistranslation and that Michilimackinac received its name as a memorial to an extinct group of people called the Mi-shi-ne-macki-naw-go, who used to occupy the island. See ibid., 19.

12 See Basil Johnston, *Ojibway Heritage* (Toronto: McClelland and Stewart, 1976), 14. For a description of Anishinabek cosmology, see Theresa S. Smith, *The Island of the Anishnaabeg: Thunderers and Water Monsters in the Traditional Ojibwe Life-World* (Moscow: University of Idaho Press, 1995).

13 Nicolas Perrot, 'Mémoire sur les moeurs, coustumes, et relligion des sauvages de l'Amérique septentrionale,' in *The Indian Tribes of the Upper Mississippi Valley and Region of the Great Lakes*, ed. Emma Blair (Cleveland: Arthur Clark, 1911), 4–5.

14 'The Great hare who had promised to form a broad and spacious land, took this grain of sand, and let it fall upon the rafts when it began to increase. Then he took a part of it and scattered this about, which caused the massive soil to grow larger and larger. When it had reached the size of a mountain, he started to walk around it and steadily increased in size to the extent of his path.' Ibid.

15 Such a tradition makes it easy to see why both the Anishinabek and Iroquois peoples referred to America as 'the Great Island.' See Frederick Baraga, *Chippewa Indians: As Recorded by Rev. Frederick Baraga in 1847* (New York: Studicia Slovenica, 1976), 8.

16 For example: 'After the creation of the earth all the other animals withdrew into the places which each kind found most suitable for obtaining therein their pasture or their prey. When the first ones died the Great Hare caused the birth of men from their corpses as also from those of the fishes that were found along the shores of the rivers which he had formed in creating the land. Accordingly, some of the people derive their origins from a bear, others from a moose and others, similarly, from various kinds of animals. And before they had intercourse with the Europeans they firmly believed this, persuaded that they had their being from those kinds of creatures whose origin was as above explained. Even today, the notion passes among them for undoubted truth.' Ibid., 6.

17 See Reuban Gold Thwaites, *The Jesuit Relations and Allied Documents, Travels, and Explorations of the Jesuit Missionaries in New France*, vol. 33, XXXIII, *Lower Canada, Algonkins, Hurons: 1648–49* (Cleveland: Burrows Brothers, 1898), 149 and 151: 'The great Lake of the Hurons ... The Eastern and Northern shores of this Lake are inhabited by various Algonquin Tribes, – Outaouakamigouek, Sakahiganiriouik, Aouasanik, Atchougue, Amikouek, Achirigouans, Nikikouet, Michisaguek,

Paoutagoung ... The last named are those whom we call the Nation of the
Sault. But let us return to our fresh water sea. On the South shore of this
fresh water, or Lake of the Hurons, dwell the following Algonquin tribes:
Ouachaskesouek, Nigouaoichirinik, Outaouasinagouek, Kichkagoneiak,
and Ontaanak, who are also allies of the Hurons.'

18 Heidi Bohaker, 'Nindoodemag: The Significance of Algonquian Kinship
Networks in the Eastern Great Lakes Region, 1600–1701' (2006) 63
William and Mary Quarterly 1 at para. 6.

19 Other groups also regard the Earth as living; see John Harding, *Animate
Earth* (Oxford: Oxford University Press, 2006).

20 Christopher Vescey, *Traditional Ojibwa Religion and Its Historical Changes*
(Philadelphia: American Philosophical Society, 1983).

21 See Basil Johnston, *Ojibway Heritage* (Toronto: McClelland and Stewart,
1976).

22 Michael Angel, *Preserving the Sacred: Historical Perspectives on the Ojibway
Midewiwin* (Winnipeg: University of Manitoba Press, 2002), 25.

23 Donald Smith, *Sacred Feathers: The Reverend Peter Jones (Kahkewaquonaby)
and the Mississauga Indians* (Toronto: University of Toronto Press, 1987), 11.

24 Selwyn Dewdney, *The Sacred Scrolls of the Southern Ojibway* (Toronto: University of Toronto Press, 1975).

25 Edward Benton-Banai, *The Mishomis Book: The Voice of the Ojibway*
(Hayward, WI: Indian Country Communications, 1988).

26 This is the position closest to mine as an Anishinabek and Christian; see
Hugh Nibley, 'Brigham Young and the Environment,' in *To the Glory of
God: Mormon Essays on Great Issues*, ed. T. Madsen and C. Tate (Salt Lake
City: Deseret Book, 1972), 3.

27 John Borrows, *Recovering Canada: The Resurgence of Indigenous Law*
(Toronto: University of Toronto Press, 2002), 29–55.

28 Ibid.

29 Basil Johnston, *Ojibway Ceremonies* (Toronto: McClelland and Stewart,
1982).

30 On my reserve, scientists are often sought to add to Anishinabek understandings of the Earth. The Cape Croker Indian Reserve has benefited
from scientists at the University of Guelph who have increased our
knowledge of the land. For examples of how science can be added to
Indigenous tradition in other contexts, see Fikret Berkes, *Sacred Ecology:
Traditional Ecological Knowledge and Resource Management* (New York:
Routledge, 1999).

31 For historic Anishinabek territorial locations, see Conrad Heidenreich,
'Mapping the Location of Native Groups, 1600–1760' (1981) 2:6 *Journal of*

the Historical Atlas of Canada 6; Conrad Heidenreich, 'Maps Relating to the First Half of the 17th Century and Their Use in Determining the Location of Jesuit Missions in Huronia' (1966) 3 *The Cartographer* 103; Conrad Heidenreich, 'Mapping the Great Lakes: The Period of Exploration, 1603–1700' (1980) 17 *Cartographica* 32; Conrad E. Heidenreich, 'Mapping the Great Lakes: The Period of Imperial Rivalries' (1981) 18 *Cartographica* 74; G. Malcolm Lewis, 'Changing National Perspectives and the Mapping of the Great Lakes between 1755 and 1795' (1980) 17 *Cartographica* 1; Conrad Heidenreich, 'An Analysis of the 17th Century Map "Nouvelle France"' (1988) 25 *Cartographica* 67; Helen Hornbeck Tanner, 'The Location of Indian Tribes in Southeastern Michigan and Northern Ohio, 1700–1817,' in *Indians of Northern Ohio and Southeastern Michigan*, ed. Erminie Wheeler-Voegelin (New York: Garland Publishing, 1974), 317; and Samuel de Champlain, *The Publications of Samuel de Champlain*, vol. 3 (Toronto: Champlain Society, 1971), 42–4 and 94–100.

32 My appreciation goes to Basil Johnston who shared this concept with me.

33 Again, thanks go to Basil Johnston for his insights about boundaries.

34 Jeremy Webber, 'Legal Pluralism and Human Agency' (2006) 44 *Osgoode Hall Law Journal* 167.

35 A similar principle applies to animals: *ojinee*. They are not to be disrespected or taken without their permission.

36 Basil Johnston, *Ojibway Ceremonies* (Toronto: McClelland and Stewart, 1982), 24–5.

37 Ibid., 25.

38 For criticism of the idea that Mother Earth is not an ancient Indigenous concept, see Sam Gill, *Mother Earth: An American Story* (Chicago: University of Chicago Press, 1987). For a response, see Jace Weaver, ed., *Defending Mother Earth: Native American Perspectives on Environmental Justice* (New York: Orbis Books, 1996). Whatever one's views on the antiquity of a belief in Mother Earth among the Anishinabek, the fact is that many current Anishinabek interpretations regard the Earth in this way, which is what makes the idea relevant as a legal concept. Law does not have to be ancient to be accorded respect.

39 Basil Johnston, *Ojibway Ceremonies* (Toronto: McClelland and Stewart, 1982), 25.

40 For example, the Earth is dependent on 'Grandfather' Sun and 'Grandmother' Moon for its life.

41 This is expressed by the word *meeyauwi-akeeyauh*, or 'every being must abide together in proper proportions.'

42 *R. v. Big M Drug Mart Ltd.*, [1985] 1 S.C.R. 295 at para. 118.

43 Ira Chaikin and Douglas Cole, *An Iron Hand upon Our People: The Law against the Potlatch on the North-West Coast* (Vancouver: Douglas and McIntyre, 1990).

44 C. Haig-Brown, *Resistance and Renewal: Surviving the Indian Residential Schools* (Vancouver: Tillacum Library, 1988); Elizabeth Mary-Furniss, *Victims of Benevolence: Discipline and Death at the Williams Lake Indian Residential School, 1891–1920* (Vancouver: Arsenal Pulp Press, 1994); J. Milloy, *A National Crime: The Canadian Government and the Residential School System, 1879–1986* (Winnipeg: University of Manitoba Press, 1999); Agnes Jack, *Behind Closed Doors: Stories from the Kamloops Indian Residential School* (Penticton: Theytus Books, 2001); J.R. Miller, *Shingwauk's Vision: A History of Native Residential Schools* (Toronto: University of Toronto Press, 1996).

45 Ben Berger, 'Law's Religion: Rendering Culture,' in *Law and Religious Pluralism in Canada*, ed. Richard Moon (Vancouver: UBC Press, 2008), 264–96.

46 *Thomas v. Norris*, [1992] 2 C.N.L.R. 139 (B.C.S.C.) (Aboriginal spirit dancing not protected by the *Charter*). For commentary, see Thomas Isaac, 'Individual versus Collective Rights: Aboriginal People and the Significance of *Thomas v. Norris*' (1992) 21 *Manitoba Law Journal* 618.

47 Bruce Ryder, 'State Neutrality and Freedom of Conscience and Religion' (2005) 29 *Supreme Court Law Review* (2nd series) 169.

48 *Syndicat Northcrest v. Amselem*, [2004] 2 S.C.R. 551 at para. 1. Of course, in the actual judgment, this statement is immediately qualified by the observation that 'respect for religious minorities is not a stand-alone absolute right; like other rights, freedom of religion exists in a matrix of other correspondingly important rights that attach to individuals. Respect for minority rights must also coexist alongside societal values that are central to the make-up and functioning of a free and democratic society.'

49 *Jack and Charlie v. The Queen*, [1985] 2 S.C.R. 332.

50 Ibid.

51 See John Borrows and Len Rotman, 'The Sui Generis Nature of Aboriginal Rights: Does It Make a Difference?' (1996) 36 *Alberta Law Review* 9 at 43–4: 'These understandings provide the "Aboriginal perspective on the meaning of the right at stake" and illustrate the reasons the Court must ... not ... [consider them] in the same way as one would individual rights ... [C]ourts must look to notions of collective physical and cultural survival, as well as specific Aboriginal laws, customs and practices ... as a more appropriate interpretive prism.'

52 The Court accepted the Crown's argument that the sale of liquor for sacraments was like the killing of deer for Coast Salish ceremonies in

terms of its religious significance. See *R. v. Jack and Charlie* (1982), 139 D.L.R. (3d) 25 at para. 37:

> The *Wildlife Act* does not in any way prohibit or regulate the burning ceremony, it regulates the killing of deer, meat from which may be used for such a ceremony.
>
> To draw the parallel analogy, the obtaining of wine for sacramental purposes is not part of the sacrament of Holy Communion, and regulation of the sale of wine does not, therefore, prohibit the exercise of that religious ceremony. Such regulation cannot, therefore, be said to affect religious freedom.
>
> No clergyman could raise a defence based on religious freedom, to a charge of obtaining wine illegally while liquor stores were closed, simply because it was intended to use the wine for the sacrament of Holy Communion. Similarly a defence based on 'freedom of religion' must fail the Appellants in this case, where the charge is killing a deer in the closed season. Since killing a deer is not, in itself, ceremonial, the *actus reus* of the offence cannot be regarded as a religious observance. If it is not such an observance, then logically, its prohibition by the *Wildlife Act* raises no question of religious freedom.

53 However, it should also be noted that the Court's jurisprudence surrounding freedom of religion has substantially developed since 1985. In the *Big M Drug Mart* case, the Supreme Court of Canada outlined the purpose that freedom of religion guarantees in section 2 of the *Charter*. Chief Justice Dickson observed that '[t]he values that underlie our political and philosophic traditions demand that every individual be free to hold and to manifest whatever beliefs and opinions his or her conscience dictates, provided *inter alia* only that such manifestations do not injure his or her neighbours or their parallel rights to hold and manifest beliefs and opinions of their own.' See *R. v. Big M Drug Mart Ltd.*, [1985] 1 S.C.R. 295 at para. 123.

54 Anishinabek people may also have equality rights arguments under section 15(1) of the *Charter* that might protect their religious beliefs and practices, if such receive less protection than other individual religious rights under the *Charter*. For an application of *Charter* equality rights to Aboriginal peoples, see *Corbiere v. Canada (Minister of Indian and Northern Affairs)*, [1999] 2 S.C.R. 203. Outside the Constitution, Aboriginal peoples might also attempt to use property, contract, tort law, or other common law doctrines to protect the Earth.

55 *Syndicat Northcrest v. Amselem*, [2004] 2 S.C.R. 551 at para. 39.

56 Ibid. at para. 135.

57 It does not require showing 'some sort of objective religious obligation, requirement or precept to invoke freedom of religion.' Ibid. at para. 48.

58 Ibid. at para. 65: '[T]he first step in successfully advancing a claim that an individual's freedom of religion has been infringed is for a claimant to demonstrate that he or she sincerely believes in a practice or belief that has a nexus with religion.'

59 *R. v. Jones*, [1986] 2 S.C.R. 284 at 314.

60 *Syndicat Northcrest v. Amselem*, [2004] 2 S.C.R. 551 at para. 65: '[The] second step is to then demonstrate that the impugned conduct of a third party interferes with the individual's ability to act in accordance with that practice or belief in a manner that is non-trivial.'

61 Ibid. at para. 61.

62 *Trinity Western University v. British Columbia College of Teachers*, [2001] 1 S.C.R. 772, 2001 SCC 31, at para. 29.

63 *Syndicat Northcrest v. Amselem*, [2004] 2 S.C.R. 551 at para. 62.

64 Ibid. at para 61.

65 Whether the Court restrains religious freedom's scope at this stage of the analysis depends on whether it finds 'an apparent infringement of more than one fundamental right.' *Multani v. Commission scolaire Marguerite-Bourgeoys*, [2006] 1 S.C.R. 256 at para. 28.

66 Ibid.

67 Jean McBean, 'The Implications of Entrenching Property Rights in Section 7 of the Charter of Rights' (1988) 26 *Alberta Law Review* 548 at 581.

68 *Ross v. New Brunswick School District No. 15*, [1996] 1 S.C.R. 825 at para. 72.

69 See Patrick J. Monahan, 'The Supreme Court of Canada in the 21st Century' (2001) 80 *Canadian Bar Review* 374; Errol P. Mendes, 'The Crucible of the Charter: Judicial Principles v. Judicial Deference in the Context of Section 1,' in *The Canadian Charter of Rights and Freedoms*, ed. Gérald-A. Beaudoin and Errol Mendes, 3rd ed. (Toronto: Carswell, 1996), 165.

70 John Borrows, 'Crown and Aboriginal Occupations of Land: A History and Comparison' (prepared for the Ipperwash Inquiry, 2005), available online at www.ipperwashinquiry.ca/policy_part/policing/pdf/History_of_Occupations_Borrows.pdf.

71 They might build roads over alvars and other places where the Earth's agency is infringed contrary to Anishinabek beliefs without knowing it.

72 In *RJR-MacDonald Inc. v. Canada (Attorney General)*, [1995] 3 S.C.R. 199 at para. 160.

73 J.E. Lovelock, *Gaia: A New Look at Life on Earth* (Oxford: Oxford University Press, 1979).

74 For a U.S. case that makes a similar point, see *Lying v. Northwest Cemetery Association* (1988) 484 U.S. 439 (U.S.S.C.).

75 A greater awareness of Anishinabek law may help judges to gain a deeper engagement with Anishinabek spirituality on its own terms and could help the courts take a more self-reflexive and self-conscious stance in their work.

76 John Borrows, *Recovering Canada: The Resurgence of Indigenous Law* (Toronto: University of Toronto Press, 2002).

77 Ibid.

78 *R. v. Marshall; R. v. Bernard*, [2005] 2 S.C.R. 220 at para. 48.

79 *R. v. Sparrow*, [1990] 1 S.C.R. 1075 at 1106.

80 *R. v. Sundown*, [1999] 1 S.C.R. 393 at para. 26; *R. v. Badger*, [1996] 1 S.C.R. 771 at paras. 88–92.

81 Harold Cardinal and Walter Hildebrandt, *Our Dream Is that One Day Our Rights Will Be Recognized* (Calgary: University of Calgary Press, 2001).

82 *R. v. Badger*, [1996] 1 S.C.R. 771 at para. 41.

83 John Borrows, 'Peace and Order: Indian Treaties in Saskatchewan' (paper prepared for the Office of the Treaty Commission, Saskatoon, 2003).

84 *Syndicat Northcrest v. Amselem*, [2004] 2 S.C.R. 551 at para. 53.

85 Ibid.

86 Ibid.

87 Ibid. at para. 80.

88 *Delgamuukw v. British Columbia*, [1997] 3 S.C.R. 1010 at para. 142.

89 Ibid. at para. 143.

90 While the Court has said that it will use Aboriginal law to prove occupation, this might not help Anishinabek people if certain of their laws characterized occupation as contrary to their legal relationships with land.

91 *R. v. Pamajewon*, [1996] 2 S.C.R. 821 at para. 25.

92 Ibid. See also *R. v. Van der Peet*, [1996] 2 S.C.R. 507 at para. 53.

93 *R. v. Marshall; R. v. Bernard*, [2005] 2 S.C.R. 220 at para. 39: 'Prior to constitutionalization of aboriginal rights in 1982, aboriginal title could be extinguished by clear legislative act.' See *R. v. Van der Peet*, [1996] 2 S.C.R. 507 at para. 125. 'Now that is not possible.' See also Kent McNeil, 'Extinguishment of Aboriginal Title in Canada: Treaties, Legislation, and Judicial Discretion' (2001–2) 33 *Ottawa Law Review* 301.

94 *R. v. Delgamuukw*, [1997] 3 S.C.R. 1010 at para. 180; *R. v. N.T.C. Smokehouse*,

[1996] 2 S.C.R. 672 at para. 75; *R. v. Van der Peet*, [1996] 2 S.C.R. 507 at para. 133.

95 For comments regarding the standards that the Crown must meet for extinguishment, see John Borrows, 'Not Extinguished: The Indian Act and Aboriginal Rights' (unpublished and in possession of the author).

96 *Thomas v. Norris*, [1992] 2 C.N.L.R. at para. 139; for commentary, see T. Isaac, 'Individual versus Collective Rights: Aboriginal People and the Significance of *Thomas v. Norris*' (1992) 21 *Manitoba Law Journal* 618.

97 *Thomas v. Norris*, [1992] 2 C.N.L.R. at 156. The Court wrote:

> Civil rights against such torts as assault and false imprisonment protect the freedoms and rights of Aboriginal and non-Aboriginal citizens of this country, from infringement, and punish offenders just as the criminal law does. They protect citizens from the wrongful conduct of others, including those who engage in such conduct while purporting to be exercising their religious practises or other freedoms or rights. In my opinion, conduct amounting to civil wrongs (rights from the point of view of the person wronged) should stand on the same footing as criminal conduct. If such conduct cannot be separated from the spirit dancing, and thus is an integral part of it, then in my opinion spirit dancing is not an Aboriginal right recognized or protected by the law.

98 Ibid.

99 Ibid.

100 For further commentary on issues related to extinguishment, see John Borrows, 'Physical Philosophy: Mobility and the Future of Indigenous Rights,' in *Indigenous Peoples and the Law: Comparative and Critical Perspectives*, ed. Benjamin Richardson, Shin Imai, and Kent McNeil (Oxford: Hart Publishing, 2009), 403–19.

101 *R. v. Van der Peet*, [1996] 2 S.C.R. 507 at para. 133, per Lamer.

102 [1996] 2 S.C.R. 672 at para. 78.

103 *R. v. Sparrow*, [1990] 1 S.C.R. 1075 at 1106.

104 *Delgamuukw v. British Columbia*, [1997] 3 S.C.R. 1010 at para. 165.

105 John Borrows, *'Let Obligations Be Done': The Calder Case* (Vancouver: UBC Press, 2006).

106 *Haida Nation v. British Columbia (Minister of Forests)*, [2004] 3 S.C.R. 511 at para. 48.

107 See *Mikisew Cree First Nation v. Canada (Minister of Canadian Heritage)*, 2005 SCC 69 at para. 1: 'The fundamental objective of the modern law of

aboriginal and treaty rights is the reconciliation of aboriginal peoples
and non-aboriginal peoples and their respective claims, interests and
ambitions.' The word *reconciliation* comes from Latin roots *re*, meaning
'again'; *con*, meaning 'with'; and *sella*, meaning 'seat.' *Reconciliation*,
therefore, literally means 'to sit again with.'

108 See *R. v. Côté*, [1996] 3 S.C.R. 139 at para. 59:

> [A] static and retrospective interpretation of s. 35(1) cannot be recon-
> ciled with the noble and prospective purpose of the constitutional
> entrenchment of aboriginal and treaty rights in the *Constitution Act,
> 1982*. Indeed, the respondent's proposed interpretation risks under-
> mining the very purpose of s. 35(1) by perpetuating the historical
> injustice suffered by aboriginal peoples at the hands of colonizers who
> failed to respect the distinctive cultures of pre-existing aboriginal soci-
> eties. To quote the words of Brennan J. in *Mabo v. Queensland* [No. 2]
> (1992), 175 C.L.R. 1 (H.C.), at p. 42: 'Whatever the justification
> advanced in earlier days for refusing to recognize the rights and inter-
> ests in land of the indigenous inhabitants of settled colonies, an unjust
> and discriminatory doctrine of that kind can no longer be accepted.'

109 *R. v. Sparrow*, [1990] 1 S.C.R. 1075 at 1112.
110 Ibid.
111 Ibid.
112 Ibid. See also, generally, *Osoyoos Indian Band v. Oliver (Town)*, [2001] 3
   S.C.R. 746.
113 *R. v. Adams*, [1996] 3 S.C.R. 101 at para. 54: 'In light of the Crown's
   unique fiduciary obligations towards aboriginal peoples, Parliament
   may not simply adopt an unstructured discretionary administrative
   regime which risks infringing aboriginal rights in a substantial number
   of applications in the absence of some explicit guidance.'
114 *R. v. Gladstone*, [1996] 2 S.C.R. 723 at paras. 59–80.
115 *Haida Nation v. British Columbia (Minister of Forests)*, [2004] 3 S.C.R. 511 at
   para. 16: 'The government's duty to consult with Aboriginal peoples
   and accommodate their interests is grounded in the honour of the
   Crown.'
116 Ibid. at paras. 49–50:

> The terms 'accommodate' and 'accommodation' have been defined as
> to 'adapt, harmonize, reconcile' ... 'an adjustment or adaptation to suit
> a special or different purpose ... a convenient arrangement; a settle-

ment or compromise': *Concise Oxford Dictionary of Current English* (9th ed. 1995), at p. 9 ... The Court's decisions confirm this vision of accommodation. The Court in *Sparrow* raised the concept of accommodation, stressing the need to balance competing societal interests with Aboriginal and treaty rights. In *R. v. Sioui*, [1990] 1 S.C.R. 1025, at p. 1072, the Court stated that the Crown bears the burden of proving that its occupancy of lands 'cannot be accommodated to reasonable exercise of the Hurons' rights.' In *R. v. Côté*, [1996] 3 S.C.R. 139, at para. 81, the Court spoke of whether restrictions on Aboriginal rights 'can be accommodated with the Crown's special fiduciary relationship with First Nations.' Balance and compromise are inherent in the notion of reconciliation.

117 *Paul v. British Columbia (Forest Appeals Commission)*, [2003] 2 S.C.R. 585; *Haida Nation v. British Columbia (Minister of Forests)*, [2004] 3 S.C.R. 511 at para. 44: 'The government may wish to adopt dispute resolution procedures like mediation or administrative regimes with impartial decision-makers in complex or difficult cases.'
118 *Taku River Tlingit First Nation v. British Columbia (Project Assessment Director)*, [2004] 3 S.C.R. 550 at para. 44.
119 *Delgamuukw v. British Columbia*, [1997] 3 S.C.R. 1010 at para. 169. See also *R. v. Sparrow*, [1990] 1 S.C.R. 1075 at para. 1119.
120 For further argument, see John Borrows, *Recovering Canada: The Resurgence of Indigenous Law* (Toronto: University of Toronto Press, 2002).

10 The Work Ahead: Cultivating Indigenous Legal Traditions

1 Eric Hobsbawm and Terence Ranger, eds., *The Invention of Tradition* (Cambridge: Cambridge University Press, 1983); Stephen Vlastos, ed., *Mirror of Modernity: Invented Traditions of Modern Japan* (Berkeley: University of California Press, 1998); Jane M. Jacobs, 'Tradition Is (Not) Modern: (Deterritorializing Globalization),' in *The End of Tradition?* ed. Nezer AlSayyad (New York: Routledge Press, 2004), 29.
2 K.M. Lysyk, QC, 'Reshaping Canadian Federalism' (1979) 13 *UBC Law Review* 1, 7; governments are endowed 'with both legislative jurisdiction and the wherewithal to exercise it is able to pioneer programs which, if their worth is demonstrated, may commend themselves for adoption elsewhere in the country.'
3 Ibid., 8–9. Professor Lysyk wrote: 'Another reason for guarding against undue centralization has to do with the desirability, in general, of

keeping democratic decision-making as close as possible to the citizenry.'

4 John Borrows, *Recovering Canada: The Resurgence of Indigenous Law* (Toronto: University of Toronto Press, 2002).

5 Heather McRae, Garth Nettheim, Laura Beacroft, and Luke McNamara, *Indigenous Legal Issues: Commentary and Materials* (Sydney: Thomson Lawbook, 2003), 380.

6 Terry Janke, *Our Culture/Our Future: Report on Australian Cultural and Intellectual Property Rights* (Surrey Hills, NSW: Michael Frankel, 1998), 77–8.

7 The wider context of this issue is discussed in a non-Indigenous context in G. Bruce Doern and Markus Sharaput, *Canadian Intellectual Property: The Politics of Innovating Institutions and Interests* (Toronto: University of Toronto Press, 2000).

8 See Linda Tuhiwai Smith, *Decolonizing Methodologies: Research and Indigenous Peoples* (Dunedin: University of Otaga Press, 1999), for an excellent discussion of how Indigenous peoples can reclaim their own research methodologies.

9 See John Borrows and Len Rotman, 'The Sui Generis Nature of Aboriginal Rights: Does It Make a Difference?' (1996) 36 *Alberta Law Review* 9

10 *R. v. Van der Peet*, [1996] 2 S.C.R. 507 at para. 41.

11 The story of Mandamin was kept alive in our family by Verna Patronella Johnston; see *Tales of Nokomis* (Toronto: Stoddart, 1975), 25–9. The version of the story retold in this article closely follows Basil Johnston, *Ojibway Heritage* (Toronto: McClelland and Stewart, 1976), 34–8. It was most recently retold by myself, and published as 'Challenge, Change and Development in Aboriginal Communities' (Sarah Morales, co-author) in Joseph Magnet and Dwight Dorey, eds., *Legal Aspects of Aboriginal Business Development* (Toronto: LexisNexis, 2005). I want to acknowledge my thanks for their permission to republish this excerpt.

12 For the use of Anishinabek stories as cases, see John Borrows, *Recovering Canada: The Resurgence of Indigenous Law* (Toronto: University of Toronto Press, 2002), 49–54.

13 There is a world of difference between being an Indian and being Anishinabe. An Indian is a creation of the European imagination and is legally inscribed on us by the federal government. There were no Indians in our territories prior to European arrival. In fact, there are only Indians in contemporary terms if the federal government is allowed to take control of Indigenous identities.

14 Ibid.

15 Ibid.
16 For the story of Verna Patronella Johnston's life, see R.M. Vanderburgh, *I Am Nokomis Too: The Biography of Verna Patronella Johnston* (Don Mills, ON: General Publishing, 1977).
17 As noted earlier, the version of the story retold in this article closely follows Basil Johnston, *Ojibway Heritage* (Toronto: McClelland and Stewart, 1976), 34–8.
18 Austin Sarat, ed., *Law, Violence and the Possibility of Law* (Princeton: Princeton University Press, 2001).
19 John Borrows (Kegedonce), *Drawing Out Law* (Toronto: University of Toronto Press, 2010).

Index

aadizookaanag (Anishinabek grandfathers), 242
*Aboriginal Customary Law Recogni-
tion Act*, 204
Act of Union of 1840, 110
adaawk (Gitksan verbal records), 33,
35, 97–8
adverse possession, 19, 123, 289n99.
See also prescription
Akitsiraq Law School, 145–7, 231–2,
363n31, 388n16, 389n19, 391n22
Alberta: courts in, 217, 402n56;
Métis in, 91, 163; University of,
388n16
alvar, 246–69
anishinabe (Anishinabek 'good
man'), 274, 330n92
Anishinabek: belief in living earth,
241–8, 261–3, 407n38; colonization
and, 268; Constitutional law and,
392n25; creation story, 79, 330n92;
culture, 79, 239, 280–1; history of,
404n8; intersocietal interaction of,
130–2, 156–7, 159–60, 260, 263,
293n37, 354n53; legal traditions,
77–84; religion of, 252–3, 269–70;
societal approbation, 80–1,

333n94; story of Mandamin,
274–9
anthropology, 9
Ariaga, Winona, 32
Aristotle, 29
assimilation: of civil law in
common law, 114–16; Hau-
denosaunee resistance to, 76;
history in Canada, 46, 127–8;
International Labour Organization and, 192; preventing legal
integration, 115–16, 221; as solution to cultural conflict, 127, 150;
as source of conflict, 127–9
Augustine, Stephen, 67–72, 321n33,
321n37
Aupilaarjuk, Mariano, 102
Austin, John, 12, 47
authority. *See* tribal authority
ayuukhl (Nisga'a legal code), 97–9,
339n178

bah'lats. *See* Potlatch
Barak, Aharon, 6
Bell, Catherine, 191
bijuridicalism: Canadian, 107, 124,
145; international, 300n2

bimeekumaugaewin (Anishinabek stewardship laws), 79–81, 333n94
Blackstone, William, 18, 71
Bohaker, Heidi, 242
British Columbia: discovery and, 112, 297n88; Indigenous relations with, 27, 99–100, 124, 266, 342n195, 379n57; University of, 388n16
British North America Act, 1867, 66, 127
Bureau of Indian Affairs, 209

Calder v. A.G.B.C., 16, 99, 196
Canada: creation through treaties, 21, 25–8; cultural diversity of, 122, 124, 127–9, 153, 206, 272; development of laws, 6–8, 19–20, 108, 153, 107–13; discovery and, 17–18; democracy in, 127; legal diversity of, 23–4, 44, 52–3, 107–9; legal hierarchy of, 12–20, 113; political failings of, 40, 46, 173, 179; reception of law in, 13–14, 21, 135; Upper/Lower, 110
Canadian Bar Association (CBA), 215, 227
Canadian Charter of Rights and Freedoms, 125, 141, 151–2, 155, 164, 187, 240, 248–69, 348n4, 380n60
Cape Croker, 4, 30, 247, 280, 406n30
Carrier people: clans, 337n140; customary law of, 52; dispute resolution in, 41–2; eagle down and, 95; legal tradition of, 91–6; name origins of, 338n143; Potlatch law and, 94
Cartier, Georges-Étienne, 126
Cayuga, 72, 74, 352n40

Christianity, 243; analogized to Indigenous religion, 252–3, 259, 321n37, 360n10; Indigenous interaction with, 26, 68, 243; as interpretive tool, 72
chus (Carrier law of eagle feather plumes), 96
Cicero, 29
circles: in Cree tradition, 85, 120; sacred nature of, 39, 245, 307n53
citizenship: assimilation and, 128; law enforcement and, 161; religious, 250, 259, 265; tribal, 77, 157–8, 175, 365n67, 375n25
Civil Code of Lower Canada, 110–11, 115
Civil Code of Quebec, 111, 114, 144, 185, 202, 214, 316n1
civil law: adaptability of, 21–2; application in Indian territory, 162; assimilation of, 114, 116; common law harmonization with, 202–3, 230–1; courts, 206–7; custom and, 24–5, 51, 109; history in Canada, 109–11; integrating with Indigenous law, 21, 119, 147, 152, 164, 183, 206, 231–2; legitimacy, 208; reception of, 21; Recognition Acts and, 182; supremacy over Indigenous law, 19, 266; survival of, 116–17; as time honoured, 108
Code Napoléon, 110
colonialism: alienating Indigenous groups, 9, 11, 143, 219; European law and, 13–15, 112; harmonization legislation and, 201; human rights and, 37, 191, 205; Indigenous law and, 36, 143, 153–4, 160, 179, 182, 413n108; legal societies

and, 223; secession and, 167;
scholarly research and, 9; Recognition Acts and, 182; religion and,
261–2; reserves and, 163
comity, 161
common law: adaptability of, 21–2,
106, 181, 185, 281; customary law
and, 51; denying Indigenous legal
tradition, 21, 170, 260; duties and
rights of, 79, 260; harmonization
with civil law, 202–3, 230–1;
history of, 14–15, 110–13, 135; in
Indian territory, 162; influence of
civil law, 114–15; integrating with
Indigenous law, 15–16, 118–22,
134, 147, 152–3, 163–4, 170, 183,
203–6, 231–2, 246–54; interpreting
history in, 71–2, 105, 108; legitimacy of, 208, 240; Recognition
Acts and, 182; supremacy of, 19,
113, 266; as time honoured, 108;
tradition of, 8–9, 56, 109, 218
comparative law, 115, 145–6, 229–31,
393n27, 399n48
conflict: assimilation engendered,
128; Canadian law and, 6, 202; in
Carrier tradition, 41–2, 95–6;
common law engendered, 14,
19–20, 170–4; in Cree tradition,
85; in Haudenosaunee tradition,
73; Indigenous legal resolution
of, 10–11, 25, 60, 104, 130–1,
135–6, 194; as inner struggle,
281; in Inuit tradition, 144; law
and, 3–4, 7, 38, 100, 131, 153–4,
240–1, 285, 292n36; Mandamin
and, 274 82; in Nisga'a tradition, 100; over natural resources,
31, 78, 133; in war, 129, 131–2,
293n37

conquest: doctrine of, 19–21, 122,
299n104; morality of, 20
conservation. See resource conservation
Constitution Acts, 13; amending, 160;
of 1867, 126, 144, 202; of 1982, 11,
21, 53, 117, 129, 133, 162, 164, 185,
188–91, 195, 198–201, 209, 216,
240, 248, 260, 266, 270
constitutions, tribal, 181–5
continuity, doctrine of, 135–6
Corbiere v. Canada, 156, 309n59
courts: bias in, 169, 250, 258–82,
359n2; Common Law, 111–12; in
harmonizing legal traditions,
206–18, 258; Indigenous, 39, 86,
99, 143, 207–14, 273; Indigenous
judges in non-Indigenous, 86,
215–18, 223; as liberal, 249–52,
259; Navajo Nation, 224–5;
section 35 of the Constitution Act,
1982 and, 198–201
creation stories: in Anishinabek tradition, 79–80, 241–2, 330n92,
332n93, 405n16; in Carrier tradition, 92; in Cree tradition, 85,
119–21; Indigenous law and,
24–5, 31, 63–5, 84; in Mi'kmaq tradition, 63–4, 319n19
Cree: circles, 307n53; court, 216; creation story, 119–21; legal tradition, 84–6, 134; treaties involving,
303
Crown: deference towards, 17,
254–6, 267–70; discovery and, 17,
122–4; extinguishment and,
265–7; fiduciary duties, 363n39;
interaction with Indigenous
peoples, 14, 18–20, 26–8, 132–6,
170–1, 182–3, 201, 378n44;

sovereignty of, 112, 136, 186–7,
196
culture: adaptability of, 59, 68, 130,
184–5, 219–20, 283; in
common/civil law, 109–13, 260,
262–5; defining, 11, 307n50,
360n12; devaluing, 19, 68–70, 140,
262, 350n17; diversity of, 128–9;
Indigenous law and, 10, 16, 86,
100–1, 108–9, 197, 210; integrating
different legal, 21, 38, 57, 117–19,
122, 130, 138, 164, 273; law and,
7–9, 24, 295n73; misappropriation
of, 148–9; obligations under, 79;
as pre-law, 12; protection of,
125–6, 188–9, 195
customary law, 12–13, 51–5;
accountability to, 80–1; in
common/civil law, 110–11, 343;
defining, 11, 16; devaluing, 12–13,
16, 66, 262; Indigenous law and,
24, 43, 52–5, 62–3, 87, 91, 144, 198,
315n110, 316n113; in legal hierarchy, 12–17, 56, 198; recognizing
Indigenous, 204, 215, 226, 381n78;
survival of, 136; protection of, 11,
125, 193–4

death, 4, 284; in Indigenous law,
63–4, 213, 246, 251–2; of Indigenous law, 148; of Mandamin, 277,
280; of Mayamaking, 81–2
Declaration on the Rights of Indigenous Peoples (UN), 191–2
Delgamuukw v. Attorney General
(British Columbia), 32–5, 69, 267,
321n37
democracy, 125–8, 155–6, 164–5;
Indigenous law and, 44–5, 88,
199, 208, 211, 281; Recognition

Acts and, 185–90; strengthening,
272; tribal citizenship and, 159–62
Dene, 25, 91
discovery: of Canada, 17; doctrine
of, 17, 20–1, 122, 297n86,
399n48
discrimination: in assimilation, 127;
in integrating legal traditions, 23,
122, 150–5, 167, 204; in international law, 151–2, 205; in legal
application, 157, 161, 262–5; in
legal interpretation, 20, 141; in
legal traditions, 18, 168–74, 227
dispute resolution: Indigenous law
societies and, 225, 231; Indigenous tradition of, 8, 121–2, 160–1,
181, 194, 206–9, 214, 270, 273;
legal training in Indigenous, 236,
398n42, 402n56
diversity: cultural, 126–9, 153–4,
167, 200, 351n31; legal, 60, 111,
124, 138, 177, 244
dodem, 77–9, 242, 244; nigig, 5

eagle down, 95
Earth: as living, 63–4, 239, 241–8,
254, 258, 261–2, 265–6; as recording legal principles, 35, 247; as
storyteller, 247; as trust responsibility, 246
education: in Canada, 126–7,
349n13, 390n20; of Indigenous
law, 143–8, 220–38, 240, 389n19;
in natural law, 29–32; legal
immersion and, 236; in Nisga'a
society, 101, 341n192
equality: in Canadian law, 53, 122,
178, 194, 202–4; in Indigenous
laws, 39, 92, 121, 150–5, 190,
315n110; in religion, 250, 259; in

treaties, 26; as unequal treatment, 151–2, 364n55

ethnocentrism, 9; law and, 12, 141, 148; occupation and, 18; reception and, 14–15

Eurocentrism, 14, 140

extinguishment, 20, 149, 196, 265–7

family: in Anishinabek society, 77–8; in Carrier society, 94, 98; in Cree society, 84; in Haudenosaunee society, 73; interracial, 134; law development and, 29–30, 82, 178–80; law societies and, 223; in Métis society, 86–7; in Mi'kmaq society, 61; religion and, 251–2; tradition development and, 271, 273

feasts, 40–2, 47, 129, 149; in Anishinabek tradition, 80; in Carrier tradition, 95–6; in Gitksan tradition, 311n61; in Mi'kmaq tradition, 319n19; in Nisga'a tradition, 97; of the Dead, 130; Potlatch law and, 346n45, 397n41

federalism: in Canada, 125, 201–6; Haudenosaunee resistance to, 76–7; Inuit law and, 147; legal integration and, 111, 125–6, 164, 188–91, 272; promoting experimentation, 272; tempering legal integration, 153–4, 199–201

Federal Law–Civil Law Harmonization Act, 202, 381n76

Federal Law–Indigenous Law Harmonization Act, 203–4

feedback effect, 68, 70

fight. *See* conflict

Foucault, Michel, 288n3, 290n20

Fuller, Lon, 16

fundamentalism: legal traditions and, 8–9, 238; preventing, 9, 36

Georgian Bay, 4, 31, 247, 261, 280, 353n48

Gitksan: organization of, 311n61; property law and, 233, 395n31; Seeley Lake and, 33–5; similarity to Carrier tradition, 96

Glorious Revolution, 186–7

Gosnell, Joseph, 98

governance, Indigenous, 52, 189, 196–201, 209, 273; cost of, 190; education in, 388n16; *Indian Act* and, 43; Inuit, 147, 184; international law and, 191–4; legitimacy of, 60, 117, 124; section 35 of the *Constitution Act, 1982* and, 191, 261

Great Law of Peace (*Kaianerekowa*), 42, 72–6

Gus Wen Tah (Two Row Wampum), 75–7

Haida, 40, 96

Hall, Geoff, 154

harmonization legislation, 201–6; in Australia, 204; internationally, 204–5

harmony: in Anishinabek tradition, 332n93; between legal traditions, 22, 36, 201–10, 221; in Cree tradition, 85; in Indigenous law, 11, 49, 167, 194, 211; in Mi'kmaq tradition, 319n19; in nature and family, 5, 30, 79–80, 85

Haudenosaunee: claimed independence from Canada, 27, 76; composition of, 352n40; diplomacy of, 130, 325n63; legal tradition of, 42,

72–7; at UN, 325n64; wars of,
131
Hayehwatha, 73–4
Henderson, Sakej, 61–2
Herman, Judith, 171–4
history: colonial, 160, 235, 249,
401n52; freezing law, 105; law as
distinguished from, 65–72, 170–2,
321n37; legal, 15, 113, 169;
records, 361n13
Hogg, Peter, 13, 15
Hohfeld, W.N., 79, 186, 374n14
hope, 174–6, 275–6, 330n92
Hudson's Bay Company, 132
human rights: disregard for, 264;
harmonizing legal traditions, 22,
151–2, 204–5; Recognition Acts
and, 185, 191–5
Huron (Lake), 31, 241, 247, 353n48,
404n8

Iacobucci, Frank, 151, 250
Indian, 415n13
Indian Act: assimilation and, 128,
150; citizenship and, 157–8;
extending Canadian law, 162;
hindering Indigenous law development, 42–6, 76–8, 99, 181, 197,
208; human rights and, 37–8
Indigenous Bar Association (IBA),
215, 226–7
Indigenous law: adaptability of, 35,
59–60, 70, 104, 116–17, 139, 147–8,
184, 205, 228–9, 280–2; applicability off reserve, 163–5; broader
normative value of, 10, 118–21,
217; characterized as pre-legal,
12; in court, 86, 173; devalued, 6,
69–70, 148, 169, 266; diplomacy
in, 75–6, 130–3; dissemination of,

142–4, 228–38; diversity of, 24, 60;
enforcement of, 161–2; history
and, 65–70; participation in creating, 36, 156–7, 178–80, 248, 281–2;
recognition of, 23, 117–23, 134–5,
137, 181–201, 227, 272–3; respect
for, 122, 208; responses to dispossession, 17–20; survival of, 11, 15,
135–6, 197, 280; weaknesses of,
10–11; in the United States,
209–13
Indigenous Peoples' Counsel (IPC),
226
International Labour Organization
(ILO), 192–3
Inuit: customary law, 144–5; government, 52–5; law school, 145–7,
388n16, 391n22; legal education,
232–3; legal tradition, 101–4; torts
and, 394n30
Inuit Qaujimajatuqangit (Inuit societal organization), 103
Iroquois Confederacy. See Haudenosaunee

Jack and Charlie v. The Queen, 250–2,
408n52
Jikonsahseh (Mother of Nations), 73
Johnson, Mary, 33, 35
Johnston, Basil, 31, 245–6, 274, 280
Johnston, Verna Patronella, 274, 280
Judicial Committee of the Privy
Council, 16, 18, 66, 114
jurisdiction, 206; tribal, 100, 159–60,
162, 179; with no tribal court, 163;
expanding, 163

Kaianerekowa. See Great Law of
Peace
Kant, Immanuel, 287n2

Kitchee Manitou, 242, 332n93
kungax (Carrier spirit power), 92–4
Kwakwaka'wakw, 40, 96, 235,
    301n6, 397n41
Kwayaskitotamowin (Cree just
    action/dealing), 84–6, 334n112

Labrador Inuit Land Claim Agreement,
    52–5, 144, 316n113
law: adaptability of, 59, 66–7, 70,
    285; Canadian hierarchy of,
    12–20, 61, 112–13, 121, 180; con-
    flict within, 60, 118; deliberative
    nature of, 35–6; diversity of,
    137–8; history and, 65–70, 105;
    reception of in Canada, 13–14,
    112, 122; as societal strength, 6–8;
    as social experience, 10; as
    trickster, 4
Law Commission of Canada, 10
law schools: Indigenous, 229–32;
    Indigenous law and, 144, 220,
    228–38; tribal Elders and, 236–7
law societies, 220–8; independence
    of, 222–3; Indigenous, 223–5
*Law v. Canada (Minister of Employ-
    ment and Immigration)*, 151
legal hierarchy: in Canada, 12–13,
    112–13; creation of, 13–14; impov-
    erishing Canadian law, 15;
    Indigenous law in, 19–20, 56, 121
legal pluralism, 8, 215, 239–41; in
    law school, 401n52
L'Heureux-Dubé, Claire, 115, 267
linguistics: in courts, 86; in culture,
    79, 129, 245; in human rights, 125;
    in law, 62, 84, 140, 145–6
Inapskuk (wampum readings), 64
L'nu'k. See Mi'kmaq
Locke, John, 18, 29

longhouse, 42, 73, 75–6, 325n63
Lyon, Noel, 28

Magna Carta, 186–7, 374n17
maligait (Inuit obligation to obey),
    102
mandamin, 80, 274–83
Mandamin, L.S. ('Tony'), 217
Manitoba Act, 88
Mayamaking, 81–2
McCallum, Margaret, 14
McCleod, Margaret, 274
McEachern, Allan, 32, 35
McGill Law School, 230–1, 390n20
McKay, Bert, 98, 339n177
McLachlin, Beverley, 15, 115, 135–6,
    169
Medewiwin Society, 243
media bias, 127, 173
Mediik (supernatural grizzly bear),
    34
Membertou, 63, 68, 321n37
Métis: citizenship of, 313n82; con-
    tract law and, 233, 394n29; fami-
    lies of, 336n129; language of,
    336n126; legal tradition, 86–91;
    Recognition Acts and, 184
Michabous, 241–2
Michee-Makinakong, 241
Mi'kmaq, land occupation of, 18
miyo-wicehtowin (Cree relationship
    law), 84–5, 334n112
mntu (Mi'kmaq spark of life), 63–4
Mohawk, 72–4, 352n40
Morin, Gerald, 86, 216
Mother Earth, 26, 39, 85, 121, 246,
    330n92; as recent development,
    262, 407n38
mothers: clan mothers, 42, 47, 50,
    73; as elders, 29–30; grandmoth-

ers, 103, 274–9, 319n19, 321n33, 330n92; tribe descent through, 92, 94–6, 212; virgin, 73

multi-juridical, 23; in Canada, 107, 160, 164, 177–80, 198, 268–70; developing in Canada, 142, 173–6, 181, 240, 263, 282; expertise in, 205–6; Haudenosaunee and, 76; Indigenous territory and, 166; in judicial analysis, 248, 258–60; law societies and, 222, 238; legal education and, 228–33, 235, 238; religious freedom and, 249, 252, 258–9, 266–7, 269; treaties and, 124

Nanabush, 4–5, 80, 284–5, 330n92
Napoleon, Val, 201
nation-building, 199
nature: contrasting conceptions of, 29; as legal personality, 64; offending, 30–1, 33–5, 85, 92–3, 98; punitive actions of, 34–5, 85, 93, 98; as source of law, 3–5, 28–33, 61–2. *See also* Mother Earth
Navajo Nation Bar Association, 210–13, 224–5
Nedelesky, Jennifer, 165
Nisga'a: feasts and, 40; governance, 100–1, 162, 341n188; legal traditions, 96–100, 339n177; similarity to Carrier tradition, 96
Nisga'a Final Agreement Act, 99–100, 341n193, 342n195
Nunatsiavut (Inuit central government), 53–4, 144
Nunavut, 102–4, 144–7, 184, 231–2
Nunavut Integrity Act, 103
Nunavut Land Claims Agreement, 144

occupation, doctrine of: based on treaties, 28; in Indigenous law, 131
Odaemin, 80–1
Odawa, 77, 241, 327n70, 327n73
Office of Treaty Commissioners, 25, 302n16
Ogijidah (Anishinabek peacekeepers), 131
Ohcinewin (Cree retributive suffering), 84–6
Ojibway, 77–80, 241, 327n72–n73, 328n79, 360n10
Oneida, 72, 74, 352n40
Onondaga, 72, 74–5, 324n62
Ontario: alvar and, 247; common law reception in, 112; Haudenosaunee in, 42–3, 325; legal education in, 233; Wendat in, 131
Ontario (Lake), 76, 352n40–n41, 404n8
Organization of American States, 191, 193–4
Orwell, George, 170
Osgoode Hall Law School, 13, 31; curriculum, 237, 388n15–n16

Parliament, in Canada, 13, 46, 60, 88, 111, 114, 116, 118, 127, 160, 170, 181, 187–203
pastahowin (Cree violations of natural law), 26, 84–6, 334n112
pdeek (Nisga'a clans), 96
peace and order, treaty provisions, 25; through wampum recitation, 65; Hayehwatha's teaching of, 74; in Canadian system, 108
pipe, 80, 129, 245, 257, 278, 307n53
piqujait (Inuit obligation to perform), 102

Potawatomi, 77, 241, 327n73
Potlatch: ceremony, 40–1, 129,
    312n76, 397n40; law, 94, 397n41;
    salmon and, 346n45
poverty, 36, 143, 262; law societies
    and, 225
'prescribed by law' standard, 141–2,
    361n18
prescription, 19–21, 122–3. *See also*
    adverse possession
*Proposed Declaration on the Rights of
    Indigenous Peoples* (OAS), 193–5

Quebec, 110; education in, 231,
    349n13; legal integration in, 111,
    114–17, 203, 214–16, 381n76;
    secession, 128
Quebec Act, 1774, 110

reception, doctrine of, 13–15, 112,
    122, 135, 294n59; education of,
    394n28; treaties and, 21, 177
Recognition Acts, 181–201, 202, 282;
    elements of, 190; human rights
    and, 191–8; Indigenous involve-
    ment in, 184–5; Royal Commis-
    sion proposed, 189
religion: court balancing with other
    rights, 255–7; court-determined
    triviality of, 253–4, 259; freedom
    of, 249, 254–6, 264, 269–70;
    Indigenous practice of, 130–1,
    242–3, 245, 247–8, 251; in law,
    24–5, 62, 97, 249–59; practitioner
    abuse of, 258; recognition of,
    261–4, 268–9; rights extinguish-
    ment and, 265–7
reserved rights doctrine, 123,
    378n42
reserves, 4, 271; jurisdiction over,

156–65, 399n46; limiting Indige-
    nous law, 219–21; violence on, 166
residential schools, 29, 36, 170,
    372n4
resource conservation: in Anishin-
    abek society, 77–9; in Carrier
    society, 92–3; in Inuit society, 103,
    147
restorative justice, 82–3, 86, 98
revisionism, legal, 59–60
*Ross v. New Brunswick School District
    No. 15*, 256
Rotman, Len, 251
Royal Commission on Aboriginal
    Peoples, 17, 63, 157, 189, 195–6,
    201, 219–20; critique of, 376n25
rule of law: extinguishment and,
    267; Indigenous law and, 37, 132,
    161, 169, 208–9, 272–3; law soci-
    eties and, 221–2, 227–8; legal inte-
    gration and, 6–7, 23, 122, 128, 229,
    231, 238, 282; limiting the Crown,
    186; Recognition Acts and, 181
R. v. Guerin, 17
R. v. Marshall; R. v. Bernard, 18, 67–8,
    71
R. v. Mitchell, 11, 135–6
R. v. N.T.C. Smokehouse Ltd., 267
R. v. Sparrow, 17, 186–7, 197–8
R. v. Van der Peet, 11, 15, 69, 197,
    273, 321n37, 359n86
Ryder, Bruce, 250, 259, 265

sakamowati (Mi'kmaq districts), 61
Salish, 40, 96, 395n32; legal educa-
    tion and, 233–4, 393n26,
    395n33–n34, 396n35; religious
    freedom of, 251–2, 266
science: as source of law, 32, 406n30;
    testing legal traditions, 9–10

Scott, Duncan Campbell, 127,
350n17
section 35(1), *Constitution Act, 1982,*
11; extinguishment of Indigenous
rights and, 265–7; freezing
Indigenous law, 67–9, 413n108;
Indigenous land and, 164, 264–5,
359n86, 378n42; justificatory
rights infringement, 267–8; protecting Indigenous traditions,
52–3, 117, 129; Recognition Acts
and, 185–7; religious freedom
and, 260–70
secularization, in Canadian law, 24
Seeley Lake, 33–5
self-determination, 192, 199, 235,
400n50, 401n51
Seneca, 72, 74, 352n40
shaming, 95, 98
sigidimnak' (highest ranking woman
in *wilp*), 96–7, 99
Silver Covenant Chain, 76–7
sim'oogit (highest ranking man in
wilp), 97, 99
South West Africa Case, 152
sovereignty: constraints on, 186–7
stare decisis, 112
storytelling: in court, 67; as source
of law, 30, 33–4, 63–4, 73–5, 79–81,
84, 92, 119–21, 139, 145; Mandamin and, 274–82
Sunday Times v. United Kingdom, 141
Supreme Court Act, 216
Supreme Court of Canada: recognition of Indigenous traditions,
11
Syndicate Northcrest v. Anselem, 250,
254

Tanaka, Noboru, 152

terra nullius, 17, 297n86
Thomas v. Norris, 265–7, 412n97
tirigusuusiit (Inuit consequences),
102–3
Tododaho, 74
tradition (cultural): adapting, 271;
as law, 7–10, 24; natural resources
and, 32; unifying, 23
tradition (legal, Canadian): adaptability of, 8–9, 238, 283; uniting
with Indigenous legal tradition,
149, 154, 206–9, 213–14, 218,
228–9
tradition (legal, Indigenous): adaptability of, 10, 244, 263, 279;
Anishinabek, 79; attacked, 135,
148–9; Canadian policy towards,
188–9; CBA and, 227–8; denial of,
168–74; devaluing, 15, 17–21;
dispute resolution in, 207; harmonization legislation and, 203–4;
Haudenosaunee, 75–7; IBA and,
226–7; Inuit, 102–4; law societies
promoting, 221–4; Nisga'a, 97,
99–100; protecting and promoting, 180, 193, 271; recognition
of/respect for, 11, 173–4, 178–80,
182, 218, 236, 272; rights derived
from, 193–4; self-determination
and, 192
tradition (oral), 140, 143–4; Haudenosaunee, 73; in Canadian law,
109
translation: in court, 86; of Indigenous law, 118, 139, 260; misunderstandings and, 148
trauma, of Indigenous past, 171–4
treaties: addressing Haudenosaunee
independence, 77; Anishinabek
and, 132; benefits of, 123–4; citi-

zenship and, 158; concerning
resources, 31, 133; Indigenous tradition and, 129, 134; in integrating
legal traditions, 20–1, 123, 147,
160; interpretation of, 27, 123, 136,
186; involving Nisga'a *ayuukhl*, 97,
99; Métis efforts in negotiating,
88; of Niagara, 133; reception and,
14, 21; sacred nature of, 25–6
tribal authority: derived from
respect, 94–5; derived from spiritual connection, 96
trickster, 4, 74, 98
Tsimshian, 40, 96
Tuscaroras, 72, 352n40

Ukaliannuk, Lucien, 146
United States v. Winans, 123

Vancouver, 4; reception of common
law, 112, 266; Salish and, 395n32

wahkohtowin (overarching Cree law),
84–6, 334n112
wampum, 65, 323n55; 'bowl with
one spoon,' 130; in Hau-
denosaunee tradition, 74–6, 130;
Indigenous law and, 57, 64–7; in
Mi'kmaq tradition, 68–70, 321n37;
readings, 47, 64; treaties and, 130,
132; 'two row,' 76
Webber, Jeremy, 137–8
Wendat, 73, 130–2, 353n48
Western legal tradition: cultural
base of, 108; of natural law,
29
Wetsuwet'en, 40, 94–5
wilp (Nisga'a house groups),
96–7
windigos (giant), 81, 84, 248
witnesses, in Carrier law, 96
Woolmington v. D.P.P., 71
Wright, Edmond, 100